Religion in America

ADVISORY EDITOR

Edwin S. Gaustad

THE GREAT SECOND ADVENT MOVEMENT

ITS RISE AND PROGRESS

By J. N. Loughborough

ARNO PRESS

A NEW YORK TIMES COMPANY

New York • 1972

Reprint Edition 1972 by Arno Press Inc.

Reprinted from a copy in
The Union Theological Seminary Library

RELIGION IN AMERICA - Series II
ISBN for complete set: 0-405-04050-4
See last pages of this volume for titles.

Manufactured in the United States of America

Library of Congress Cataloging in Publication Data

Loughborough, John Norton, 1832-1924.
    The great Second Advent movement.

    (Religion in America, series II)
    1. Adventists. 2. Seventh-Day Adventists.
I. Title.
BX6121.L6 1972   286'.7   71-38453
ISBN 0-405-04073-3

THE GREAT
SECOND ADVENT
MOVEMENT

J. N. LOUGHBOROUGH

THE GREAT SECOND ADVENT MOVEMENT

ITS RISE AND PROGRESS

BY J. N. LOUGHBOROUGH

"Though it tarry, wait for it; because it will surely come, it will not tarry." Habakkuk 2:3

REVIEW AND HERALD PUBLISHING ASSN.
WASHINGTON, D. C.
NEW YORK CITY   SOUTH BEND, IND.

PREFACE

THERE are already many useful books in the hands of the people, and my apology for adding another to the list, is that in these pages I state many things concerning Adventists, and especially Seventh-day Adventists, which have not heretofore been brought in this form before the people. Besides this, many who espoused the cause in later years, and who have not witnessed the things mentioned, have earnestly requested a narration of these facts and experiences from those earlier in the work. Having been familiar with the advent movement in 1843 and 1844, and having, since Jan. 2, 1849, proclaimed the doctrine, first as an Adventist, and since 1852 as a Seventh-day Adventist, I esteem it a pleasure to "speak the things I have seen and heard."

I have presented a statement concerning the advent movement, which from 1831 to 1844 spread to every civilized nation of the world.

Since 1845 there have been other bodies of Adventists which have proclaimed, and still are proclaiming, the near advent of Christ. Instead of tracing all of those bodies, it has been my purpose to give, at some length, the rise and progress of the Seventh-day Adventists, calling especial attention to those agencies which, in the providence of God, have aided in developing, from poverty and small beginnings, a people of whom, although they number only about one hundred thousand, some of their opponents have said, "From the energy and zeal with which they work one would judge that there were two million of them."

Even those who are only slightly conversant with Seventh-day Adventist history know that since 1845 Mrs. E. G. White has been prominently connected with the movement, both as a speaker and writer. They also know that connected with her work there have been peculiar exercises, or gifts. It has been my privilege to be present and witness the operation of this gift about fifty times. In these pages I have called attention to some twenty-six definite predictions made by Mrs. White which have been most accurately fulfilled.

In addition to my own observations, I have also presented the testimony of other eye-witnesses respecting their experiences. Such facts should have more weight with the candid reader than random statements made by those who have never been present on such occasions.

I commit the work to the readers, hoping that, with the blessing of God, the perusal of these pages may be a means of promoting the cause of Christ in many hearts, and trusting that all, as they read, will bear in mind the words of Paul to the Thessalonians, " Prove all things; hold fast that which is good."

J. N. LOUGHBOROUGH.

Mountain View, California, May 1, 1905.

CONTENTS

CHAPTER I

CHAPTER II

(v)

Europe — Application of the Parable — A World-wide Proclamation — How the Movement Started in Various Nations — Compared with the Reformation — Joseph Wolff's Labors — The Message in Germany and Russia — The Message in Great Britain — The Message in Holland — The Message in Tartary — The Message in America, India, and on the Continent — To Every Seaport on Earth — Three Thousand Proclaiming the Message — Hutchinson's *Voice of Elijah* Sent Broadcast — In the Sandwich Islands — The Message Compared with that of John the Baptist.

CHAPTER VI

A Definite Message — The Judgment at Christ's Coming — Reckoning of the 2300 Days — Admissions of Opponents — Professor Bush's Testimony — Wonders in the Heavens — The Fiery Aurora of 1837 — The Aurora of 1839 — Strange Appearances in the Sun — Wonders Fulfilling Scripture Predictions — The Messengers — William Miller — William Miller's Conversion — Joshua V. Himes — The United Labors of Miller and Himes — Other Prominent Adventist Preachers.

CHAPTER VII

An Angel a Symbol of Human Messengers — The Loud Cry of the First Message — The Time of the Loud Cry — The Fifth Trumpet — The Close of the Sixth Trumpet — Dr. Josiah Litch Predicts the Fall of the Ottoman Empire — The Turkish Sultan at War with the Pasha of Egypt — Intervention of the Allied Powers — The Prophecy Fulfilled — End of Turkish Independence — Public Interest in Prophecy Aroused — Hundreds Proclaiming the Message.

CHAPTER VIII

The Call to Supper — The Call to them that had been Bidden — Open Doors for the Message — A Mighty Wave of Revivals — An Experience in Richmond, Me. — Calls

CHAPTER IX

CHAPTER X

CHAPTER XI

CHAPTER XVII

CHAPTER XVIII

CHAPTER XIX

CHAPTER XX

CHAPTER XXI

CHAPTER XXII

CHAPTER XXV

CHAPTER XXVI

in Russia — Baptism in Hungary — Canvassing in Germany — The Scandinavian Mission — The First Book Published in Danish-Norwegian — Elder Matteson Becomes a Printer — The First Foreign Periodical — A Printing Office in Norway — Health Journals in Danish and Swedish — Elder Haskell in Scandinavia — Mrs. White Greatly Aids Scandinavia — New Office Building Erected in Norway — Twenty-five Churches in Scandinavia — School in Christiana — Forty Churches in Scandinavia in 1895 — Three Scandinavian Conferences — The British Mission — Tent-meeting in England — Laborers Increased in England — Ship Missionary Work — "History of the Sabbath" Placed in English Libraries — *Present Truth* Started — The Pacific Press in London — The Australasian Mission — The *Bible Echo* — First Church Organized in Australia — Australian Office Building — Tasmania Entered — Mrs. White in Australia — Elder Olsen in Australia — Australasian Union Conference — Elder Prescott in Australia — South African Mission — Elders Boyd and Robinson in South Africa — Elder Haskell in Africa — College Building in Africa — The South African Conference — Papers Published in South Africa — South African Union Conference — The Polynesian Field — Visit to Pitcairn — The *Pitcairn* Built — The *Pitcairn's* First Cruise — Death of Missionaries — The *Pitcairn's* Second Trip — The *Pitcairn's* Third Trip — The *Pitcairn's* Fourth Trip — The *Pitcairn* sold — The West Indies — Trinidad — Central America — Small Ship for Central America — Elder Hutchins' Death — South America — The Southern Missionary Society — Elder White's Missionary Steamer — Work of the Southern Missionary Society — Workers in the South — The Steamer *Morning Star* — How Money Came for the Southern Mission — In Many Lands — Mexico — Central Africa — The Gold Coast — India — Georgia Burrus in India — Hawaii, Sandwich Islands — Chinese Work in Hawaii — Summary of Missions. Jan. 1, 1903 — Strategic Points Established.

CHAPTER XXVII

The Tract and Missionary Society — Efficient Secretaries — Maria Huntley — The Effect on Local Churches — Tes-

CHAPTER XXVIII

ILLUSTRATIONS

GREAT SECOND ADVENT MOVEMENT

ITS RISE AND PROGRESS

CHAPTER I

INTRODUCTORY

HEN we speak of the second advent of Christ, we are touching a theme which in reality has been the hope of God's people since the expulsion of our first parents from the garden of Eden. In the words to the serpent, that the seed of the woman should bruise his head, was an assurance that finally a restorer would come, who should defeat the usurpations of Satan, and accomplish God's purpose in the earth. The supposition is that Adam and Eve thought this work would very soon be performed, and that an immediate descendant from them would be the victor. Yet in God's plan the promise of the Saviour from the apparent ruin embraced all that has since been developed in the carrying out of his "own purpose and grace, which was given us in Christ Jesus before the world began." [1]

Had Adam and Eve been given at once a view of the misery and woe which would fill the world during the long ages intervening between its ruin and its restoration, their grief would have been unbearable. The God of heaven, in his tender mercy and compassion, hid this view from them, leaving them to cherish the fond hope of soon being delivered into the glorious liberty of the children of God. Entertaining the

[1] 2 Tim. 1: 9.

thought that redemption was near would naturally incite them to greater earnestness in preparation to meet the event.

In like manner has it been with the people of God in all the generations since the days of Adam. They were certain that a great and important event was sometime in the future to occur — that Christ would finally come and establish his kingdom. They too, like Adam and Eve, believed the event was near at hand, and, like them, were unconscious of what would transpire between their own time and the event; otherwise, they might have become discouraged in pressing toward the mark of the prize.

This thought can be illustrated by the use of events that have occurred in the way of great discoveries. The men who originated them, although not aware of it, were actually fulfilling God's purpose; yet were they animated with ideas that did not prove to be in all respects in harmony with their own theories which moved them to action.

Far-reaching Effects of Columbus's Discoveries

Montgomery, in his " American History," edition of 1902, pages 8, 9, speaking of the theory that moved Columbus to start out on his voyage, and the carrying out of his plan of reaching the East Indies by sailing west, says:—

" Columbus thought that he could improve on the King of Portugal's project. He felt certain that there was a shorter and better way of reaching the Indies than the track Diaz had marked out. The plan of the Genoese sailor [Columbus] was as daring as it was original. Instead of sailing east, or south and east, he proposed to sail directly west. He had, as he believed, three good and solid reasons for such an undertaking: *First,* in common with the best geographies of his day, Columbus was convinced that the earth was not flat, as most men supposed, but a globe. *Secondly,* he supposed this globe to be much smaller than it is, and the greater part to be land instead of water. *Thirdly,* as he knew nothing, and surmised nothing, of the existence of the continent of America or of the Pacific Ocean, he imagined that the coast of Asia or the Indies was directly opposite Spain and the western coast of Europe. The entire distance across to Cipango, or Japan, he estimated would probably not exceed about four thousand miles.

"His plan was this: He would start from Europe; head his ship westward toward Japan, and follow the curve of the globe until it brought him to what he sought. To his mind it seemed as sure and simple as for a fly to walk around an apple.

"If successful in the expedition, he would have this immense advantage: He would enter the Indies directly by the front door, instead of reaching them in a roundabout way, and by a sort of side-entrance, as the Portuguese must.

"We see that this man, who understood practical mathematics, geography, and navigation as well as any one of his day, was right on the first point,— the shape of the earth,— but utterly wrong on the other two.

A Fortunate Mistake

"Yet, singularly enough, his errors were in one respect a help to him. The mistake that he made in regard to the distance was a most fortunate one. Had Columbus correctly reckoned the size of the globe, and the true length of such a voyage, he probably would not have sailed, since he would have seen at once that the proposed Portuguese route was both far shorter and cheaper. Again, could he have imagined or in any way foreseen that the American continent lay right across his path, that, in itself, might not then have induced him to start on a voyage of discovery, for his object was not to find a new country, but a new way to an old one."

The Great Hope of the Ages

So the people of God, coming down through the ages, have had the hope of Christ's coming before them "as an anchor of the soul, both sure and steadfast." [2] Though often mid sorrows and afflictions they in anguish cry out, " How long, O Lord, before deliverance will come? " yet have they pressed forward, and like Paul have said and still say, " What is our hope, or joy, or crown of rejoicing? Are not even ye in the presence of our Lord Jesus Christ at his coming? " [3]

Paul Sustained by the Hope

A few illustrations of the sustaining power of this hope, in this connection, must suffice. When Paul was arraigned before Felix, and permitted to speak for himself, he said, " After the way which they call heresy, so worship I the God of my fathers, believing all things which are written in the law and in the prophets ; and have hope toward God, which they themselves also allow, that there shall be a resurrection of the dead, both of the just and unjust." [4]

In his able plea when brought before Agrippa, Paul said, " Now I stand and am judged for the hope of the promise made of God unto our fathers ; unto which promise our twelve tribes, instantly serving God day and night, hope to come. For which hope's sake, King Agrippa, I am accused of the Jews. Why should it be thought a thing incredible with you, that God should raise the dead? " [5] When at last he was in Rome to appear before Cæsar, he said to the Jews, " For the hope of Israel I am bound with this chain." [6]

Paul spoke freely of that hope in his letter to Titus: " For the grace of God that bringeth salvation hath appeared to all men, teaching us that, denying ungodliness and worldly lusts, we should live soberly, righteously, and godly, in this present world, looking for that blessed hope, and the glorious appearing of the great God and our Saviour Jesus Christ." [7]

Peter Rejoicing in the Hope

Peter speaks of the same hope as follows: " Blessed be the God and Father of our Lord Jesus Christ, which according

---

[2] Heb. 6: 19.   [3] 1 Thess. 2: 19.   [4] Acts 24: 14, 15.
[5] Acts 26: 6 - 8.   [6] Acts 28: 20.   [7] Titus 2: 11 - 13.

to his abundant mercy hath begotten us again unto a lively hope by the resurrection of Jesus Christ from the dead, to an inheritance incorruptible, and undefiled, and that fadeth not away, reserved in heaven for you, who are kept by the power of God through faith unto salvation ready to be revealed in the last time. Wherein ye greatly rejoice, though now for a season, if need be, ye are in heaviness through manifold temptations: that the trial of your faith, being much more precious than of gold that perisheth, though it be tried with fire, might be found unto praise and honor and glory at the appearing of Jesus Christ." [8]

God's Purpose in Creation

The Scriptures reveal the purpose of God in creating the world; and from the word of prophecy we also learn his plan concerning the future: " Thus saith the Lord that created the heavens, God himself that formed the earth and made it; he hath established it, he created it not in vain, he formed it to be inhabited." [9] When he had formed it, he gave it to man. The psalmist says, " The heaven, even the heavens, are the Lord's; but the earth hath he given to the children of men." [10] But when he gave it to man, man was upright, as expressed by the wise man, " This only have I found, that God hath made man upright; but they have sought out many inventions." [11]

We read of the Lord's dealing with the race, that " when he separated the sons of Adam, he set the bounds of the people according to the number of the children of Israel," [12] that is, according to the number of the true Israel that shall at last be gathered on the earth as subjects of his future kingdom. It is expressed by Paul in these words: " God . . . hath made of one blood all nations of men for to dwell on all the face of the earth, and hath determined the times before appointed, and the bounds of their habitation; that they should seek the Lord, if haply they might feel after him, and find him, though he be not far from every one of us; for in him we live, and

[8] 1 Peter 1: 3 - 7.   [9] Isaiah 45: 18.   [10] Ps. 115: 16.
[11] Eccl. 7: 29.   [12] Deut. 32: 8.   [13] Acts 17: 26 - 28.

move, and have our being." [13]   When this original purpose
respecting the earth is carried out, " thy people also shall be
all righteous." [14]   Again it is said of them in that state,
" The inhabitant shall not say, I am sick: the people that
dwell therein shall be forgiven their iniquity." [15]   That will
be the time when " the *meek* shall inherit the earth; and shall
delight themselves in the abundance of peace." [16]

Christ's Second Coming not a Fable

It is stated in the second epistle of Peter that " we have
not followed cunningly devised fables, when we made known
unto you the power and coming of our Lord Jesus Christ, but
were eye-witnesses of his majesty. For he received from
God the Father honor and glory, when there came such a voice
to him from the excellent glory, This is my beloved Son, in
whom I am well pleased. And this voice which came from
heaven we heard, when we were with him in the holy mount.
We have also a more sure word of prophecy, whereunto ye
do well that ye take heed, as unto a light that shineth in a
dark place, until the day dawn, and the day-star arise in your
hearts." [17]

In this scripture the apostle refers to the transfiguration
on the mount as a proof of the second coming of Christ.
Previous to this scene our Saviour had said to his apostles,
" There be some standing here, which shall not taste of death,
till they see the Son of man coming in his kingdom " [18] — as
recorded by Luke, " There be some standing here, which shall
not taste of death, till they see the kingdom of God." [19]

This promise was literally fulfilled in the transfiguration
itself. In this " vision " on the mount they saw Jesus glorified, as he will appear when he comes in his kingdom. They
saw Elias (Elijah), who was taken to heaven without tasting
death, representing those who will be translated — changed
from mortal to immortal — " in a moment, in the twinkling of
an eye," when the Lord comes. [20]   There was also Moses,

[14] Isa. 60: 21.   [15] Isa. 33: 24.   [16] Ps. 37: 11.   [17] 2 Peter 1: 16 - 19.
[18] Matt. 16: 28.   [19] Luke 9: 27.   [20] 1 Cor. 15: 51, 52.

one who had died, representing those who will be raised from the dead to meet the Lord. So in this "vision" they had a view of Christ coming in his kingdom, as he had promised them.

Prophecy a More Sure Word

Though the apostles had seen this glorious sight on the mount of transfiguration, and had heard the voice of God's approval, the apostle Peter affirms: "We have a *more sure* word of prophecy." By this statement he is not discounting what they saw and heard on that memorable occasion. They then heard the voice of God once, but in the great lines of prophecy, extending down to Christ's second coming, we have the voice of God oft repeated. In fact, every definite prophetic prediction fulfilled or recorded in history is the voice of God to us. It must be in this sense that the word of prophecy is "*more sure.*" The Revised Version translates it, "*made sure.*" The prophecy is made sure by each and every specification fulfilled. Each and every event predicted, when fulfilled, is an assurance that the remaining events predicted will surely come to pass.

The Nature of Prophecy

The following testimonials from eminent Bible students on the nature of prophecy are forcible: —

Thomas Newton makes the assertion that "prophecy is history anticipated and contracted; history is prophecy accomplished and dilated. Lying oracles have been in the world; but all the wit and malice of men and devils cannot produce any such prophecies as are recorded in the Scriptures."

Sir Isaac Newton testifies that "the giving ear to the prophets is a fundamental character of the true church."

Dr. A. Keith says that "prophecy is equivalent to any miracle, and is of itself miraculous. . . . The voice of Omnipotence alone could call the dead from the tomb,— the voice of Omniscience alone could tell all that lay hid in dark futurity, which to man is as impenetrable as the mansions of the dead,—and both are alike the voice of God."

Matthew Henry said that "in God's time, which is the best time, and in God's way, which is the best way, prophecy shall certainly be fulfilled. Every word of Christ is very pure, and therefore very sure."

The Object of Prophecy

We may learn from the words of Christ to his apostles one object of the Lord in giving prophecy. Speaking prophetically of the things that would take place in the career of Judas, he said, "I tell you before it come, that, when it is come to pass, ye may believe that I am he." [21]

The Lord says also by the prophet Isaiah, "I am God, and there is none like me, declaring the end from the beginning, and from ancient times the things that are not yet done, saying, My counsel shall stand, and I will do all my pleasure." [22]

Again, "I have declared the former things from the beginning, and they went forth out of my mouth, and I showed them; I did them suddenly, and they came to pass. . . . I have even from the beginning declared it to thee; before it came to pass I showed it thee; lest thou shouldest say, Mine idol hath done them, and my graven image, and my molten image, hath commanded them. Thou hast heard, see all this; and will not ye declare it? I have showed thee new things from this time, even hidden things, and thou didst not know them. They are created now, and not from the beginning; even before the day when thou heardest them not, lest thou shouldest say, Behold, I knew them." [23]

From this language the force of prophetic fulfilments as a proof of the divine origin of prophecy is seen, as well as its being a demonstration of the power of the Lord above all the gods of the heathen. It is also observed from these words that prophecy occupies a very important place in the Scriptures

[21] John 13: 19.   [22] Isa. 46: 9, 10.   [23] Isa. 48: 3 - 7.

of truth. These facts being true, it is surprisingly strange that
so many people give little or no attention to the study of the
prophetic portions of the Sacred Scriptures.

Prophecy not Sealed

The uninformed say they are unlearned, and therefore cannot understand the prophecies. On the other hand, many of
the educated, and some of them among the ministry, say:
" The prophecies are sealed, and cannot be understood. We
all know that the book of Revelation is a sealed book."

In the Revelation, the beloved John was given a special
command not to seal the book. [24]   Also in this book a blessing
is pronounced upon those that " hear the words of this
prophecy, and keep those things which are written therein." [25]
How could the things contained in a *sealed* book be kept if
they were not, and could not be, understood? The Lord said
by Moses, " The secret things belong unto the Lord our God;
but those things which are revealed belong unto us and to our
children forever, that we may do all the words of this law." [26]

That the Lord designed the prophecies of Daniel to be
understood is evident from his words to his disciples respecting them. We read: " When ye therefore shall see the
abomination of desolation, spoken of by Daniel the prophet,
stand in the holy place (whoso readeth, let him understand),' [27] that virtually says, Understand Daniel the prophet.

The Lord exposes the fallacy of the claim that prophecy
cannot be understood, in these words: " The vision of all
is become unto you as the words of a book that is sealed, which
men deliver to one that is learned, saying, Read this, I pray
thee: and he saith, I cannot, for it is sealed: and the book is
delivered to him that is not learned, saying, Read this, I pray
thee: and he saith, I am not learned. Wherefore the Lord said,
Forasmuch as this people draw near me with their mouth, and
with their lips do honor me, but have removed their heart far
from me, and their fear toward me is taught by the precept
of men: therefore, behold, I will proceed to do a marvelous

[24] Rev. 22: 10.   [25] Rev. 1: 3.   [26] Deut. 29: 29.   [27] Matt. 24: 15.

work among this people, even a marvelous work and a wonder: for the wisdom of their wise men shall perish, and the understanding of their prudent men shall be hid." [28] Had the people to whom the prophet here refers followed the sure word of prophecy, they need not have drifted away from God's law, and substituted for his precepts the commandments of men.

Prophecy not of Private Interpretation

It is not that prophecy has some deep, hidden, mysterious meaning that so many fail to understand it. The apostle Peter has said of it, " Knowing this first, that no prophecy of the scripture is of any private interpretation. For the prophecy came not in old time by the will of man; but holy men of God spake as they were moved by the Holy Ghost." [29] It is plainly implied from this language that what is essential to an understanding of prophecy is the reception of that spirit which spake through the prophets. Of that spirit, promised to all who seek it, it is written, " He will guide you into all truth." [30]

Prophecy Fulfilled

In the study of prophecy there are certain facts that should ever be kept in mind: God, who is infallible, is the author of prophecy, and when the time comes for the fulfilment of a prediction, the very event predicted will occur. Again, as the Lord, who has power to foresee just what men will do, specifies a time when a thing will transpire, when that time comes, a true fulfilment of the prophecy is met. In other words, a false fulfilment of prophecy in the specified time for the true, is an impossibility. In harmony with this axiom, we may say, when the Lord's time comes for his message of truth to be given to the world, the message makes its appearance every time.

At one time, when the writer had given a discourse on the fulfilment of prophecy, an infidel who was present came

[28] Isa. 29: 11 - 14.   [29] 2 Peter 1: 20, 21.   [30] John 16: 13.

forward and said, " I must congratulate you interpreters of prophecy as being very fortunate. In your study of history, you seem so readily to find that which exactly fits the prophecy." " Yes," was our reply, " it fits because it was made to fit. If you should go to a glove store to buy a pair of gloves, would you not expect to find those that would fit your hand? " He replied, " Of course I would, because they were made to fit." " So," said the writer, " that God who knew just what men would do, made the predictions concerning them, and when those men come upon the stage of action, and do the very things he predicted, the true historian makes a record of their actions, which, compared with the prediction, are an exact fit."

Prophecy a Light in the Darkness

The apostle Peter says we should give heed to prophecy as unto a light shining in a dark place. Without the lamp of prophecy the future would be total darkness. The purpose of light is to dispel darkness — when traveling in a dark place, to show the pathway, and to show the pathway clearly, that the traveler may be enabled, step by step, to see and choose the way. " Thy word," the psalmist says, " is a lamp unto my feet, and a light unto my path." [31] The wise man says, " The path of the just is as the shining light, that shineth more and more unto the perfect day." [32] Thus it is seen, as we pass down the stream of time, that the word of God, especially in its prophetic fulfilments, will open more and yet more, making it clearer and still clearer to the Bible student that he is surely in the pathway leading to everlasting light and eternal day.

Three Prominent Events from Eden to the End

In considering the pathway of the Lord's people from Eden down to the end, in the light of the Scriptures, there are three events that stand out in special prominence. The first is the first advent of Christ, the incarnation, the coming of Emmanuel, God manifest in the flesh; the second, the great

[31] Ps. 119: 105. [32] Prov. 4: 18.

Reformation after the Dark Ages — the 1260 years of oppression, in which the word of the Lord was almost wholly kept from the common people — a coming of the church out of her wilderness state, and the placing of the Scriptures where all might read and know his will; the third, the second coming of our Lord to bring in the times of restitution of all things spoken of by the mouth of all his holy prophets since the world began; this, to close up "the conflict of ages," the conflict between sin and righteousness, to bring in the age of glory, toward which all the ages have been tending.

Prophecy Gives Way-Marks to the End

In giving heed to the sure word of prophecy as unto a light that is to guide our steps, discovering to us the correct path through the darkness, it cannot be otherwise than that we shall find the pathway clearly marked out in the prophetic word all the way down the stream of time to the second advent of Christ. This being the case, those who follow closely the light of prophecy will not only recognize the signs and tokens that the great day is near, but will also recognize the work of the Lord as it steadily moves on in messages of truth which are to prepare a people to meet him in peace at his coming.

While the Scriptures declare that the day of the Lord will come upon the masses as "a thief in the night," [33] it also says of those standing in the counsel of the Lord, "Ye, brethren, are not in darkness, that that day should overtake you as a thief. Ye are all the children of light, and the children of the day." [34]

Remember the Lord's Leadings

In calling to remembrance the Lord's leadings in the advent movement, it is well to note that it has ever been the design of God that his people should remember the manifestations of his providence and power in their behalf. In giving the reasons for the backsliding of Israel from God, the psalmist says, "They forgot God their Saviour, which had

[33] 1 Thess. 5: 2; 2 Peter 3: 10.   [34] 1 Thess. 5: 4, 5.

done great things in Egypt; wondrous works in the land of Ham, and terrible things by the Red Sea." [35] If it was good for Israel to call to remembrance the leadings of the Lord with them, is it not good also for us? In ecstasy the psalmist again says, " Bless the Lord, O my soul, and forget not all his benefits." [36]

In all ages the Lord has had important truths, calculated, by his grace, to lead out a people from the bondage of sin, and fit them for an entrance into the heavenly Canaan; and it is profitable to consider the dealings of the Lord with those who have proclaimed these truths.

Great Results from Smallest Means — D'Aubigne's Testimony

D'Aubigne, in his " History of the Reformation," says, " God, who prepares his work through ages, accomplishes it by the weakest instruments, when his time has come. To effect great results by the smallest means, such is the law of God. This law, which prevails everywhere in nature, is also found in history." [37]

When God, in ancient time, began choosing a special people in order to establish them as a peculiar nation for himself, it was by calling one man — Abraham — who dwelt among the heathen, in Ur of the Chaldees. From him sprang a numerous progeny; but of them, when exalted to the dignity of a nation, the God of heaven said: " The Lord did not set his love upon you, nor choose you, because ye were more in number than any people; for ye were the fewest of all people." [38]

Then again, when he would deliver his people from their bondage in Egypt, he chose as their leader one who, in his infancy, was hidden for three months in his mother's house, and afterward placed in a simple, rude ark composed of bulrushes and daubed with pitch, and committed to the keeping of the River Nile. This same Moses, however, was one who, when he came to years of understanding, chose the humble path of suffering with the people of God rather than the enjoyment to be found in the " pleasures of sin for a season." [39]

Gideon's Victory

Afterward, when the Lord would deliver Israel from the Midianites and the Amalekites, who came upon their land " as grasshoppers for multitude," and destroyed the increase of the earth, leaving " no sustenance for Israel, neither sheep, nor ox, nor ass," the Lord sent an angel to Gideon. This son of Joash was reduced to the extremity of threshing out a little wheat and hiding it from his enemies. When the angel notified him that he should deliver Israel, Gideon with astonishment inquired, " Wherewith shall I save Israel? behold, my family is poor in Manasseh, and I am the least in my father's house." [40] This same humble, poor man went out with his three hundred men, with their simple lamps and pitchers (an action which would seem like foolishness to finite judgment), and making God their strength, they gained a mighty victory. Previous to the deliverance, Gideon might have uttered a lamentation like that of the prophet Amos when he inquired, " By whom shall Jacob arise? for he is small." [41]

The Babe in the Manger

In the Lord's appointed time the Saviour of mankind was born, and the shepherds found him lying in a manger. His earthly relatives followed the humble though honorable pursuits of life. Concerning his earthly poverty the Saviour said, " The foxes have holes, and the birds of the air have nests; but the Son of man hath not where to lay his head." [42] He chose his apostles " from among that lower rank, which, although not the meanest, does not reach the level of the middle classes. Everything was thus intended to manifest to the world that the work was not of man, but of God."

39 Heb. 11: 25.   40 Judges 6: 4, 5, 15.   41 Amos 7: 2.   42 Matt. 8: 20.

Not Many Wise Called

Paul said of the work in the days of the primitive church:
" The foolishness of God is wiser than men; and the weakness
of God is stronger than men. For ye see your calling, brethren, how that not many wise men after the flesh, not many
mighty, not many noble, are called; but God hath chosen the
foolish things of the world to confound the wise; and God
hath chosen the weak things of the world to confound the
things which are mighty; and base things of the world, and
things which are despised, hath God chosen, yea, and things
which are not, to bring to naught things that are; that no
flesh should glory in his presence." [43]

Humble Men in the Reformation

We find the same principle exemplified in the lives of the
great Reformers of the sixteenth century. The historian says:
" The Reformer Zwingle emerged from an Alpine shepherd's
hut; Melanchthon, the theologian of the Reformation, from an
armorer's shop; and Luther from the cottage of a poor miner."
Of himself, Luther said: " My parents were very poor. My
father was a poor wood-cutter (afterwards he became a miner),
and my mother has often carried wood upon her back, that
she might procure the means of bringing up her children.
They endured the severest labor for our sakes."

The apostle James, speaking of the calling of the people
to the Lord's service, says, " Hearken, my beloved brethren,
nath not God chosen the poor of this world, rich in faith, and
heirs of the kingdom which he hath promised to them that
love him? " [44]

Early Methodists

In looking down on the advancing line of reformers to
the early days of Methodism, when the doctrine of free
grace was assiduously proclaimed, we find it accompanied by
the power of God. As it was faithfully set before the people,

[43] 1 Cor. 1: 25 - 29.   [44] James 2: 5.

with the tender love of Christ, and was grasped by living faith, the believers not only found remission of past sins, but a sanctifying power to enable them to lead a life of holiness. Methodism had a humble beginning, and was blessed according to the faith and simple trust of the ministry and laity.

In tracing the incidents and experiences connected with the advent movement, we find that, as in every work of the Lord in the accomplishment of which man is an agent, its origin was among the poor and obscure; but let none decide against it on this account before carefully examining the evidence upon which this great work is based, lest they be found in the position of those of whom the Lord inquired, " Who hath despised the day of small things? " [45]

Eck's Retort to Luther

For the benefit of those who may be inclined to decide whether a doctrinal point is right or wrong by the few or many who accept it, we quote, in part, the controversy between Luther and Eck. As Luther took his position upon the Scriptures, and presumed to dispute the right of men to place their opinions above the word of God, Eck retorted in these ironical words: " I am surprised at the humility and modesty with which the reverend Doctor undertakes to oppose, alone, so many illustrious fathers, and pretends to know more than the sovereign pontiffs, the councils, the doctors, and the universities! . . . It would be surprising, no doubt, if God had hidden the truth from so many saints and martyrs until the advent of the reverend Father."

This retort might well be met with that of Zwingle to John Faber, at Zurich, when the latter expressed his " amazement at the pass to which things had come, when the ancient usages which had lasted for twelve centuries were forsaken, and it was clearly concluded that Christendom had been in error fourteen hundred years." Zwingle quickly replied that " error was not less error because the belief of it had lasted fourteen hundred years, and that in the

[45] Zech. 4: 10.

worship of God antiquity of usage was nothing unless ground or warrant for it could be found in the sacred Scriptures." [46]

The Word of the Lord vs. Human Wisdom

The danger of leaning to the opinions of men, instead of settling the question, " What is truth? " by the word of the Lord, is sharply defined by the prophet Hosea when he says, " Ye have plowed wickedness, ye have reaped iniquity; ye have eaten the fruit of lies; because thou didst trust in thy way, in the multitude of thy mighty men." [47] The tendency of the human heart has always been to trust in man ; but as we approach the time when the Lord is to " arise and shake terribly the earth," the prophet Isaiah exhorts, " Cease ye from man, whose breath is in his nostrils; for wherein is he to be accounted of? "[48]

Being thus cautioned in the Scriptures respecting our danger in this direction, let none hastily pass condemnation on the advent movement, as though unworthy of consideration because of its humble beginning, or because those called great in the eyes of the world have not espoused the cause. Rather let all weigh carefully its claims. Truth is of inestimable value, compared with which mere opinions of men are but worthless chaff.

[46] Wyne's "History of Protestantism," Cap. XII, par. 16, 17.   Cassel Edition, p. 458.
[47] Hos. 10: 13.   [48] Isa. 2: 22.

CHAPTER II

THE PLAN OF SALVATION UNFOLDED

OPE deferred maketh the heart sick: but when the *desire* cometh, it is a tree of life."[1] "For thus saith the Lord of hosts: Yet once, it is a little while, and I will shake the heavens, and the earth, and the sea, and the dry land: and I will shake all nations, and the *Desire* of all nations shall come: and I will fill this house with glory, saith the Lord of hosts."[2]

From the time that Adam was driven from the garden of Eden and the tree of life, the words addressed to Satan respecting the seed of the woman — "It shall bruise thy head," — has given hope of the final defeat of the devil, the overthrow of his wily schemes, and a restoration to the tree of life. The expected One — the promised Seed — thus became the "*Desire* of all nations."

In the above quotation from Haggai it appears that the coming of this *Desired* One is connected with the time when the Lord shall shake both the heavens and the earth. Paul, in writing to the Hebrews, placed that shaking in the future, saying, "Yet once more I shake not the earth only, but also heaven. And this word, Yet once more, signifieth the removing of those things that are shaken, as of things that are made, that those things which cannot be shaken may remain. Wherefore we receiving a kingdom which cannot be moved, let us have grace, whereby we may serve God acceptably with reverence and godly fear."[3] This language concerning the *one* shaking, yet to come, seems to place it

---

[1] Prov. 13: 12.   [2] Haggai 2: 6, 7.   [3] Heb. 12: 26 - 28.

(38)

in close connection with the final setting up of God's kingdom, under Christ, the promised Seed, "the Desire of all
nations."

The restoration to be accomplished through Christ can
be clearly viewed in these last days by all who have the
whole Bible open before them. It was not so with the an-
cients. The word of the Lord came to them, "precept upon
precept, precept upon precept: line upon line, line upon line;
here a little, and there a little." [4] So in the revelation to
them of the plan of salvation, it was like the path of the
just, "as the shining light, that shineth more and more unto
the perfect day." [5] Thus it becomes a matter of much interest
to trace briefly the gradual unfolding of that plan to his ancient people.

Delay not Revealed at First

The Lord did not at once defer their hope, making their
heart sick by revealing to them the fact that it would be
hundreds of years before they should reach the consummation
of their hopes in the promised Seed. From facts recorded
we infer that they were allowed to think that the first child
born would be that Seed: and that very soon, in some way,
Eden would be restored, and they again have access to the
tree of life. When Cain was born, Eve exclaimed, "I have
gotten a man from the Lord." [6] Some Hebrew scholars testify that literally and fully rendered the text reads, "I have
gotten a man, *the* Lord." That is, Here is the Seed that
is to do this lordly work of defeating Satan. There is
no record of any such expression on the part of Eve when
Abel was born. She could, and naturally would, suppose
the first-born was the one to fulfil the promise. How her
hopes must have fallen, and even died, as the character of
Cain developed, and she witnessed his evil course that finally
led to the killing of his brother. Before Abel was slain they
must have received some light and knowledge concerning
the future sacrifice to be made in their behalf; for Abel, as

[4] Isa. 28: 13.   [5] Prov. 4: 18.   [6] Gen. 4: 1.

divinely instructed, brought his lamb for an offering, while
Cain, who had been taught the same as his brother, brought
an offering of the fruits of the ground, and this even mingled
with the spirit of wrath and jealousy. Abel's offering was
more acceptable than Cain's, for it was made " by faith,"
and of it Paul writes, " He being dead yet speaketh." [7]

Is Seth the Seed ?

After the death of Abel, Seth was born, when hope revived; " for God," said Eve, " hath appointed me another
seed instead of Abel, whom Cain slew." [8] Afterward Seth
was counted in the line of descent from Adam. (See Gen.
5: 3.) Cain, the real first-born, is not counted in the pedi-
gree. Quite probably Eve supposed that Seth was now the
promised Seed. It appears from the record that after the
birth of Seth, men began to call themselves by the name
of the Lord. (See margin of Gen. 4: 26.) Perhaps they
did this on the supposition that Seth was the one who was
to be the final ruler, the Lord, and overthrow Satan's usurped
dominion.

Hope Centered on Noah

In the brief record of events from the time of Adam to
the birth of Noah, but little more than the genealogy of the
race is given. In the birth of Noah (" the upright," *margin)* hope sprang up again, and the people said, " This same
shall comfort us concerning our work and toil of our hands
because of the ground which the Lord hath cursed." [9] The
divine word is silent as to how, or the way, they expected
comfort; but the hope was entertained that the curse upon
the earth was in some way to be mitigated. A knowledge
of the wickedness that existed in Noah's day, when men were
to so fill the world with sin and violence that the race would
be swept from the earth by a flood, and only Noah and his
family escape the destruction; and the fact that he was for

[7] Heb. 11: 4.   [8] Gen. 4: 25.   [9] Gen. 5: 29.

one hundred and twenty years to warn the world of the impending destruction, were all withheld from them.

Babel Built

Following the flood, the people were instructed, through Noah, to replenish the earth; but as they began to multiply, they rejected the Lord's plan of ruling them. Nimrod established the kingdom of Babel (afterward called Babylon, the first of earthly governments).[10] A little later the people began the building of the tower of Babel, to make unto themselves a name, and to prevent their being scattered abroad, just contrary to what the Lord, through Noah, had taught them. Instead of patiently waiting for the Lord to accomplish his purposes, they took the matter into their own hands, when God confounded their language, and thus they were scattered.

Abraham to be Heir of the World

Tracing the brief record down to the tenth in descent from Noah, we have the call of Abraham, to whom the Lord said, " All the land which thou seest, to thee will I give it, and to thy seed forever. And I will make thy seed as the dust of the earth: so that if a man can number the dust of the earth, then shall thy seed also be numbered. Arise, walk through the land in the length of it and in the breadth of it; for I will give it unto thee." [11] Notwithstanding this promise to Abraham that he should possess the land, the Lord assured him that he would die. Paul says he went out into " a place which he should *after* receive for an inheritance." [12] This question of the fulfilment of the promise was undoubtedly made plain to Abraham in a vision from God, for he " looked for a city which hath foundations, whose builder and maker is God." [13] In Rom. 4: 13 it is stated that the promise was " that he should be the heir of the world; " not in its present state, but sooner or later, after he should live again.

[10] Gen. 9: 1; 10: 9, 10.   [11] Gen. 13: 15 - 17.   [12] Heb. 11: 8.   [13] Heb. 11: 10.

From a human standpoint Abraham failed to see how the seed promised could be his own offspring. He therefore suggested the calling of Eliezer, his steward, the seed. The Lord said, Not so; but it will be one that " shall come forth out of thine own bowels." Now the Lord begins to reveal to him that the final work of his seed is not to have an immediate accomplishment. He said to Abraham, " Thy seed shall be a stranger in a land that is not theirs, and shall serve them; and they shall afflict them four hundred years. . . . And thou shalt go to thy fathers in peace; thou shalt be buried in a good old age." [14]

Abraham's wife proposed an unwise plan for hastening the fulfilment of the promise; but after Isaac was born, a real son of Abraham and Sarah, his lawful wife, the Lord said of Ishmael and his mother Hagar, " Cast out this bond-woman and her son."

In the test of Abraham's faith in the offering of Isaac upon the altar, he learned a lesson upon the subject of the resurrection of the dead. It is said of him, " Accounting that God was able to raise him [Isaac] up, even from the dead; from whence also he received him in a figure." [15]

The Real Seed

Abraham was at one time instructed that the real Seed, through whom all the nations were to be blessed, though of his posterity after the flesh, would in reality be the Christ of God for the Lord said not to him, " Seeds, as of many; but as of one, And to thy Seed, which is Christ " [16] The apostle Paul said of this, " The Scripture, foreseeing that God would justify the heathen through faith, preached before the gospel unto Abraham, saying, In thee shall all nations be blessed." [17] The promise to Abraham was renewed to Isaac and his seed, [18] and also to Jacob. [19]

As Jacob had twelve sons, the question would now naturally arise, Through which is the lineage of the true Seed

[14] Gen. 15: 13 - 15.   [15] Heb. 11: 19.   [16] Gal. 3: 16.
[17] Gal. 3: 8.   [18] Gen. 26: 3 - 5.   [19] Gen. 28: 13.

to be traced? In the inspired testimony borne by Jacob respecting his sons, the case was settled: " The scepter shall not depart from Judah, nor a lawgiver from between his feet, until Shiloh come; and unto him shall the gathering of the people be." [20] In fulfilment of this it is well to note here that the Israelites, although subject to the various nations, were permitted to have their Sanhedrin. Thus Judah — the tribe of the Jews so named from Judah — had some voice in their government until Shiloh (Christ) did actually come.

The Time Hidden

The patriarchs were in possession of some knowledge concerning the restoration and the promised Seed; but when or how long before he should come was still hidden from them. As the posterity of Jacob multiplied in Egypt, and the Assyrian — Pharaoh (Isa. 52 : 4) — who " knew not Joseph," [21] oppressed them, their minds naturally reverted to the 400 (actually 430) years mentioned to Abraham as the period covering their afflictions and their sojourn as strangers, hoping that deliverance from these would usher in the promised inheritance.

When Moses was born, his parents saw that " he was a proper child." [22] Light must have been given them that he was to be, under God, Israel's deliverer from their cruel bondage. Undoubtedly this knowledge was imparted to Moses; for when, at the age of forty years, he decided fully to go with the oppressed Israelites, and suffer affliction with them rather than to be called the son of Pharaoh's daughter and heir to the Egyptian throne, * and when he began to plead the cause of his people, and in their defense slew an Egyptian, he marveled greatly that they failed to recognize his work; " for he supposed his brethren would have understood how that God by his hand would deliver them." [23]

---

* See Josephus's "Antiquities of the Jews," Book II, chap. ix, par. vii; " Spiritual Gifts," vol. i, pp. 165, 166.

[20] Gen. 49: 10. [21] Ex. 1: 8; Acts 7: 18. [22] Heb. 11: 23. [23] Acts 7: 25.

When the Lord's time came for the Israelites to leave Egypt, they departed, and on the predicted time to a day. Ex. 12:40, 41. They could not have considered Moses as their final ruler and the seed to whom the promise was made, for he was of the tribe of Levi, and had not Jacob in his inspired prediction declared that Judah should be their ruler until the Shiloh should come?

"I Shall See Him, but not Now."

When the Israelites were on their way to Canaan, Balak, the king of Moab (a descendant of Lot), called Balaam to curse Israel. The Lord turned his curse into a blessing, through which they received additional light, calculated to dispel the thought that the final deliverance from Satan's usurpation would be immediate on their entrance into Canaan. The Scripture account of it reads, Balaam, in a vision from God, said, " I shall see him, but not now; I shall behold him, but not nigh: there shall come a Star out of Jacob, and a Scepter shall rise out of Israel, and shall smite the corners of Moab, and destroy all the children of Sheth." [24]

This multitudinous seed that sprang from Abraham is spoken of by Paul on this wise: " Therefore sprang there even of one, and him as good as dead, so many as the stars of the sky in multitude, and as the sand which is by the sea-shore innumerable. These all died in faith, not having received the promises, but having seen them afar off, and were persuaded of them, and embraced them, and confessed that they were strangers and pilgrims on the earth." [25]

The heart of Israel need not have fainted or been discouraged by the prediction of Balaam that the consummation of their hope is " not now," nor " near;" for the Lord, not long before this prophecy, had pledged his own life that the glorious state should finally come. Through Moses he said, " But as truly as I live, all the earth shall be filled with the glory of the Lord." [26] In the days of the prophet Habakkuk, 863 years later, the same truth was reiterated,

[24] Num. 24: 17.   [25] Heb. 11: 12, 13.   [26] Num. 14: 21.

but spoken of as an event yet future: " for the earth shall be filled with the knowledge of the glory of the Lord, as the waters cover the sea." [27]

The Sanctuary Service a Type of the True

When the Lord brought Israel out of Egypt, he proclaimed in the audience of all the camp his law of moral precepts, and gave them a copy of the same on stone, graven by his own finger, that they might continually be pointed forward to that Saviour who would finally make a sacrifice of himself for them; and that by virtue of his precious blood their sins might be cleansed away, he had a sanctuary erected in the wilderness. This tabernacle, or sanctuary, in all its construction, Moses was admonished to make exactly like the pattern which the Lord showed to him in the mount. [28] The service in this sanctuary was a shadow of the real service of Christ in the heavenly sanctuary. [29] While the purpose of God in the offerings and sacrifices of the sanctuary was to keep before men a shadow of " good things to come," [30] Satan's effort was to lead the people to regard the offering itself, instead of Christ and his actual service, of which this was only an example. Thus he sought to lead them to trust in their own works for salvation.

It was the Lord's purpose to be the ruler of his people, — the Israelites,— to fight their battles and subdue the nations. He had his method of ruling, as is shown by the following text: " When he had destroyed seven nations in the land of Canaan, he divided their land to them by lot. And after that he gave unto them judges about the space of four hundred and fifty years, until Samuel the prophet." [31]

Israel Calls for a King

The Israelites evidently disliked the Lord's manner of ruling them. It was, however, his purpose and his will that

[27] Hab. 2: 14. [28] Ex. 25: 40; 26: 30; 27: 8; Acts 7: 44.
[29] Heb. 8: 3 - 5; 9: 8 - 12. [30] Heb. 10: 1. [31] Acts 13: 19, 20.

they should be a peculiar people, distinct from all others around them. Had they strictly followed his instructions, the nations even would say of them, " Surely this great nation is a wise and understanding people. For what nation is there so great, who hath God so nigh unto them, as the Lord our God is in all things that we call upon him for? " [32]

In their dissatisfaction they requested of Samuel that he appoint a king over them, and the Lord said to Samuel, " They have rejected me, that I should not reign over them." [33] Again they said to Samuel, and a little more imperatively, " Now make us a king to judge us like all the nations." [34] Carefully did Samuel lay before them the oppression that would come upon them in case they had a king, but ".nevertheless the people refused to obey the voice of Samuel; and they said, Nay; but we will have a king over us; that we also may be like all the nations; and that our king may judge us, and go out before us, and fight our battles." [35]

So they had kings to rule them for about five hundred years, first, as one kingdom under Saul, David, and Solomon; then as divided into the two kingdoms, Israel and Judah. A very few of their kings were good and just, but most of them were wicked, leading the people into idolatry and gross iniquities. So the people were not only like the nations around them in having a king, but like them in wickedness, in forsaking the God of their fathers, and in worshiping idols and the hosts of heaven.

The Lord said of this kingly rule, by the mouth of the prophet Hosea, " O Israel, thou hast destroyed thyself; but in me is thine help. I will be thy king; where is any other that may save thee in all thy cities? and thy judges of whom thou saidst, Give me a king and princes? I gave thee a king in mine anger, and took him away in my wrath." [36]

[32] Deut. 4: 6, 7.   [33] 1 Sam. 8: 7.   [34] 1 Sam. 8: 5.
[35] 1 Sam. 8: 19, 20.   [36] Hosea 13: 9 - 11.

The Kingdom Overturned

This kingly rule continued until the Chaldeans burned Jerusalem, took the vessels of the temple, and carried Judah captive to Babylon, where they remained for seventy years, as predicted against them. At the cessation of this monarchical ruling, the Lord said by the prophet Ezekiel, to Zedekiah, their last king, " Thou profane wicked prince of Israel, whose day is come, when iniquity shall have an end, thus saith the Lord God: Remove the diadem, and take off the crown: this shall not be the same: exalt him that is low [the ruler of Babylon], and abase him that is high [this highly self-exalted ruler of the tribe of Judah]. I will overturn, overturn, overturn it: and it shall be no more, until he come whose right it is; and I will give it him." [37]

This rightful ruler, the true Seed, is Christ. Of him the prophet Micah wrote, " Thou, O tower of the flock, the strong hold of the daughter of Zion, unto thee shall it come, even the first dominion [dominion over the earth, restored in Christ] : the kingdom shall come to the daughter of Jerusalem." [38]

When Israel lost the scepter, it passed into the hands of the king of Babylon. As they were successively under the rule of Medo-Persia, Greece, and Rome, the kingdom was three times overturned. In the reign of Cæsar Augustus, emperor of Rome, Christ, the rightful heir to the throne of David,— the true Seed of the woman, of Abraham, and of David,— was born, and in the manner predicted.

That the people might know that the rightful Ruler, the true Seed, was more than an ordinary mortal man with a short-lived kingdom, the Lord moved the psalmist thus to write: " I will make him my first-born, higher than the kings of the earth. My mercy will I keep for him forevermore, and my covenant shall stand fast with him. His seed also will I make to endure forever, and his throne as the days of heaven." " His seed shall endure forever, and his throne

[37] Eze. 21: 25 - 27.   [38] Micah 4: 8.

as the sun before me. It shall be established forever as the moon, and as a faithful witness in heaven." [39]

In the prophecy of Isaiah we read further of this Ruler as follows: " Unto us a child is born, unto us a son is given: and the government shall be upon his shoulder; and his name shall be called Wonderful, Counsellor, The mighty God, The everlasting Father, the Prince of Peace. Of the increase of his government and peace there shall be no end, upon the throne of David, and upon his kingdom, to order it, and to establish it with judgment and with justice from henceforth even forever. The zeal of the Lord of hosts will perform this." [40]

Translation of Enoch and Elijah

Instances are recorded of persons in ancient times being translated to heaven without tasting death. Of Enoch, the seventh from Adam, it is said, he " walked with God: and he was not; for God took him." [41] " By faith Enoch was translated that he should not see death; and was not found, because God had translated him: for before his translation he had this testimony, that he pleased God." [42]

Again, as Elijah and Elisha were walking together, " it came to pass, as they still went on, and talked, that, behold, there appeared a chariot of fire, and horses of fire, and parted them both asunder; and Elijah went up by a whirlwind into heaven. And Elisha saw it, and he cried, My father, my father, the chariot of Israel, and the horsemen thereof. And he saw him no more." [43]

Enoch prophesied of Christ's coming as the judge of all the earth, in these words: " Behold, the Lord cometh with ten thousands of his saints, to execute judgment upon all, and to convince all that are ungodly among them of all their ungodly deeds which they have ungodly committed, and of all their hard speeches which ungodly sinners have spoken against him." [44]

[39] Ps. 89: 27 - 29, 36, 37.   [40] Isa. 9: 6, 7.   [41] Gen. 5: 24.
[42] Heb. 11: 5.   [43] 2 Kings 2: 11, 12.   [44] Jude 14, 15.

Job Taught the Lord's Coming

Job, who is supposed to have lived in Moses' time, had some knowledge concerning the coming of Christ and the resurrection; for he said, " O that my words were now written! O that they were printed in a book! that they were graven with an iron pen and lead in the rock forever! For I know that my Redeemer liveth, and that he shall stand at the latter day upon the earth; and though after my skin worms destroy this body, yet in my flesh shall I see God: whom I shall see for myself, and mine eyes shall behold, and not another." [45]

The Throne of David the Lord's Throne

The throne of David was called the throne of the Lord. " Solomon sat on the throne of the Lord as king instead of David his father." [46]   The Lord had " sworn with an oath to him [David], that of the fruit of his loins, according to the flesh, he would raise up Christ to sit on his throne: he seeing this before spake of the resurrection of Christ, that his soul was not left in hell, neither his flesh did see corruption." [47]   And it is further said of Christ's future reign, He shall sit upon the throne of David. (See Isa. 9:7.) Again, " The kings of the earth set themselves, and the rulers take counsel together, against the Lord, and against his Anointed. . . . Yet have I set my king upon my holy hill of Zion. I will declare the decree: the Lord hath said unto me, Thou art my Son; this day have I begotten thee." [48]   Again, " The Lord said unto my Lord, Sit thou at my right hand, until I make thine enemies thy footstool." [49]

The Jews Perplexed

These texts perplexed the Jews. Here was a problem they could not solve: if David called him Lord, how was he then his son? How could he be a child born of the seed

[45] Job 19: 23 - 27.   [46] 1 Chron. 29: 23.   [47] Acts 2: 30, 31.
[48] Ps. 2: 2 - 7.   [49] Ps. 110: 1.

4

of David, and yet be Immanuel — God with us? Yet Isaiah, their own prophet, declared, "A virgin shall conceive, and bear a son, and shall call his name Immanuel." [50]

Christ well knew the question that would put to silence the caviling Pharisees, hence he asked them, " What think ye of Christ? whose son is he? They say unto him, The son of David. He saith unto them, How then doth David in spirit call him Lord, saying, The Lord said unto my Lord, Sit thou on my right hand, till I make thine enemies thy footstool? If David then call him Lord, how is he his son? " [51]

This subject is again alluded to in Ps. 45: 6, 7: " Thy throne, O God, is forever and ever: the scepter of thy kingdom is a right scepter. Thou lovest righteousness, and hatest wickedness: therefore God, thy God, hath anointed thee with the oil of gladness above thy fellows." [52] With these Scriptures before the mind, the Jewish people must have had exalted conceptions of the character of the future Ruler and Restorer. It could not have been otherwise.

The Seed of Divine Origin

Minute instruction was given concerning Christ and his birth, for the Lord by Micah the prophet designated his divine origin, and even the little village where he was to be born: " But thou, Bethlehem Ephratah, though thou be little among the thousands of Judah, yet out of thee shall he come forth unto me that is to be ruler in Israel; whose goings forth have been from of old, from everlasting " (margin, Heb., from " the days of eternity ") [53]

God's Presence Manifest in the Shekinah and the Cloud

Later in the history of the Israelites, when Solomon had finished the erection of the temple, which he said must be exceedingly " magnifical," the shekinah of God's glory took its position between the cherubim over the mercy-seat. The record says that at the dedication of the temple, as the priests

[50] Isa. 7: 14.   [51] Matt. 22: 42 - 45; Ps. 110: 1.   [52] Heb. 1: 8, 9.   [53] Micah 5: 2.

came out of the holy place, "the cloud filled the house of the Lord, so that the priests could not stand to minister because of the cloud: for the glory of the Lord had filled the house of the Lord." [54] The presence of the Lord in this temple was manifest to the eyes of the people in the cloud of glory. The Lord responded to the prayer of Solomon on this occasion, and said unto him, "I have heard thy prayer, and have chosen this place to myself for an house of sacrifice." [55]

The people sinned,— went into idolatry,— and consequently their city and sanctuary were in ruins for seventy years. After the captivity, the temple was rebuilt under the hand of Zerubbabel. Although inferior in splendor to the one built by Solomon, yet the Lord said of it by his prophet, "The glory of this latter house shall be greater than of the former." [56] This house was beautified by Herod, and in its courts the Saviour taught. The former house had a cloud of glory representing the Lord, but into the second came the Saviour himself, the Maker of all things.

Glorious Reign of the Stem of Jesse

To the expectant, waiting ones in Isaiah's day, the representations through his prophecy of the glorious things connected with the final redemption must have been a source of strength and encouragement. These prophecies again delineate most clearly the line whence this expected Deliverer should come, as follows: "And there shall come forth a rod out of the stem of Jesse, and a Branch shall grow out of his roots: and the spirit of the Lord shall rest upon him, the spirit of wisdom and understanding, the spirit of counsel and might, the spirit of knowledge and of the fear of the Lord; and shall make him of quick understanding in the fear of the Lord; and he shall not judge after the sight of his eyes, neither reprove after the hearing of his ears: but with righteousness shall he judge the poor, and reprove with equity

[54] I Kings 8: 10, 11.   [55] 2 Chron. 7: 12.   [56] Haggai 2: 9.

for the meek of the earth: and he shall smite the earth with the rod of his mouth, and with the breath of his lips shall he slay the wicked." [57]

The Resurrection Taught by the Prophets

The prophet Isaiah also taught the doctrine of the resurrection of the dead, in these comforting words: " In this mountain shall the Lord of hosts make unto all people a feast of fat things, a feast of wines on the lees, of fat things full of marrow, of wines on the lees well refined. And he will destroy in this mountain the face of the covering cast over all people, and the vail that is spread over all nations. He will swallow up death in victory; and the Lord God will wipe away tears from off all faces; and the rebuke of his people shall he take away from off all the earth; for the Lord hath spoken it. And it shall be said in that day, Lo, this is our God; we have waited for him, and he will save us: this is the Lord; we have waited for him, we will be glad and rejoice in his salvation." [58]

The Renewed-Earth Kingdom

The same prophet says that it is to be a renewed earth in which the final reign shall be established: " For, behold, I create new heavens [atmospheric heavens] and a new earth; and the former shall not be remembered, nor come into mind [margin, Heb., " come upon the heart," that is, to be de sired again]. But be ye glad and rejoice forever in that which I create: for, behold, I create Jerusalem a rejoicing, and her people a joy. And I will rejoice in Jerusalem, and joy in my people: and the voice of weeping shall be no more heard in her, nor the voice of crying. There shall be no more thence [from the time the new earth is created] an infant of days [a short-lived child], nor an old man that hath not filled his days [premature old age]: for the child shall die an hundred years old [in days when men attained to lives of nine hundred years children might be one hundred

[57] Isa. 11: 1 - 4.   [58] Isa. 25: 6 - 9.

years old]; but the sinner being an hundred years old [in later years of an hundred-year life-time] shall be accursed. [Those dying at the time the new earth is brought in are those who perish in the "perdition of ungodly men." 2 Peter 3.7.] And they shall build houses, and inhabit them; and they shall plant vineyards, and eat the fruit of them. They shall not build, and another inhabit; they shall not plant, and another eat: for as the days of a tree [the tree of life, Septuagint] are the days of my people, and mine elect shall long enjoy the work of their hands." [59]

Ezekiel looks down through the long vista of time to the resurrection of the dead. Through him the Lord says, " Behold, O my people, I will open your graves, and cause you to come up out of your graves, and bring you into the land of Israel." [60]

"He Hath Borne Our Sorrows"

To Isaiah, the gospel prophet, was revealed more fully the trial, sufferings, and death of the Saviour in behalf of men. " Who," says the prophet, " hath believed our report? and to whom is the arm of the Lord revealed? For he shall grow up before him as a tender plant, and as a root out of a dry ground: he hath no form nor comeliness; and when we shall see him, there is no beauty that we should desire him. He is despised and rejected of men; a man of sorrows, and acquainted with grief: and we hid as it were our faces from him; he was despised, and we esteemed him not. Surely he hath borne our griefs, and carried our sorrows: yet we did esteem him stricken, smitten of God, and afflicted. But he was wounded for our transgressions, he was bruised for our iniquities: the chastisement of our peace was upon him; and with his stripes we are healed." [61]

Are these events so wonderful to transpire in my day? the people, as well as the prophet, might have asked. The answer would have been, Not now will they happen; the

[59] Isa. 65: 17 - 22.   [60] Eze. 37: 12.   [61] Isa. 53: 1 - 5.

time has not yet arrived for the coming of this great Deliverer; but says the prophet, " Thine eyes shall see the King
in his beauty; they shall behold the land that is *very
far off."* [62]

Daniel's Prophecies Reveal the Future

It was, however, through the prophet Daniel that the
Lord began to instruct his people concerning consecutive kingdoms that should arise and bear rule down to the setting
up of his everlasting kingdom; and to reveal a special period
of time, from an event then yet to occur, to the actual appearing and the cutting off of the Messiah. The interpretation of
Nebuchadnezzar's dream revealed that the four kingdoms
which were to rule the world would diminish in power and
grandeur in the ratio of the diminishing value of gold,
silver, brass, and iron; and that finally the broken, disunited
state of the kingdoms would be comparable to the brittleness
of iron mixed with miry clay. Then was to come the kingdom of heaven that should follow the reduction of those kingdoms that were to become like the chaff of the summer's
threshing floor, so that no place should be found for them,
while God's kingdom would fill the whole earth.

Then, in the vision of the seventh chapter, under symbols
of the four great beasts, the same ground is again covered,
and other features of these kingdoms presented. In this
chapter is traced the career and work of the " little-horn "
power that should arise, after the division of the fourth
kingdom into ten parts, overthrowing or subduing three of
them to establish itself as a spiritual ruler over them all.
This papal power is to continue in the divided and brittle
state of the fourth kingdom, even for 1260 years. Thus
were revealed events reaching to the time when Christ receives
the kingdom from his Father, and gives it to the saints of
the Most High; a kingdom which shall finally bear rule over
all the earth, and shall stand forever.

[62] Isa. 33: 17.

The Twenty-three Hundred Days

In the eighth chapter of Daniel, under the vision of the ram, the goat, and the " little horn that waxed exceeding great," the prophet is again carried down to the end of time. In verses 13 and 14 his attention is called to a period of time — 2300 days — extending to the judgment. A long stretch of time was this, and so the prophet understood it; for the angel informed him that the vision was yet for many days. As yet no date had been given for the beginning of the days, and so he closes the chapter by saying, " I was astonished at the vision; but none understood it."

The Seventy Weeks to Messiah

'The ninth chapter tells of the angel coming to Daniel, in response to his petition, to give him skill and understanding. He informed him of a period of seventy weeks. Sixty-nine of these weeks of years [that, we are told, is the meaning of the word *shevooim,* rendered " weeks "] would extend to the Messiah. The point from which the period was to begin, " the commandment to restore and build Jerusalem," had not as yet been given. The question arises, How could Daniel know where the sixty-nine weeks would end? In the twelfth chapter the time question is again considered, and to his inquiry, " What shall be the end of these things? " he is told to go his way, for the words are " closed up and sealed to the time of the end," when the " wise shall understand."

Undoubtedly this time question is one of the instances the apostle Paul alludes to when he says, " Of which salvation the prophets have inquired and searched diligently, who prophesied of the grace that should come unto you: searching what, or what manner of time the Spirit of Christ which was in them did signify, when it testified beforehand the sufferings of Christ, and the glory that should follow." [63]

[63] 1 Peter 1: 10, 11.

Fate of the Ungodly

Malachi, the last of the Old Testament prophets, leaves a thrilling description of the final destruction of the wicked: " Behold, the day cometh, that shall burn as an oven; and all the proud, yea, and all that do wickedly, shall be stubble: and the day that cometh shall burn them up, saith the Lord of hosts, that it shall leave them neither root nor branch. But unto you that fear my name shall the Sun of righteousness arise with healing in his wings: and ye shall go forth, and grow up as calves of the stall. And ye shall tread down the wicked; for they shall be ashes under the soles of your feet in the day that I shall do this, saith the Lord of hosts." [64]

With all these facts recorded in the Old Testament in the possession of the Israelites, unfolding to them so many features of the plan of salvation, how great must have been the interest of the diligent students of the word as they saw and realized that they were nearing the time when this promised Seed would come. While the masses, and even those who read the Scriptures in the synagogues every Sabbath, failed to understand the word (Acts 13: 27), the devout, studious ones, who faithfully searched the Scriptures under the guidance of the Spirit, undoubtedly prayed earnestly, as did the apostle John in this dispensation, " Come, Lord Jesus, *and come quickly.*"

[64] Mal. 4: 1 - 3.

CHAPTER III

THE COMING OF THE PROMISED SEED

HEN the fulness of the time was come, God sent forth his Son, . . . made under the law, to redeem them that were under the law, that we might receive the adoption of sons." [1]

"Now to him that is of power to stablish you according to my gospel, and the preaching of Jesus Christ, according to the revelation of the mystery, which was kept secret since the world began, but now is made manifest, and by the scriptures of the prophets, according to the commandment of the everlasting God, made known to all nations for the obedience of faith: to God only wise, be glory through Jesus Christ forever." [2]

"By revelation he made known unto me the mystery; as I wrote afore in few words, . . . which in other ages was not made known unto the sons of men, as it is now revealed unto his holy apostles and prophets by the Spirit. . . . Unto me, who am less than the least of all saints, is this grace given, that I should preach among the Gentiles the unsearchable riches of Christ; and to make all men see what is the fellowship of the mystery, which from the beginning of the world hath been hid in God, who created all things by Jesus Christ." [3]

It has been said that in the Old Testament the gospel lies concealed; in the New Testament it is revealed. As expressed by another, "As they departed from God, the Jews in a great degree lost sight of the teachings of the ritual service. That service had been instituted by Christ himself. In every part it was a symbol of him; and it had been full

---

[1] Gal. 4: 4, 5.   [2] Rom. 16: 25 - 27.   [3] Eph. 3: 3 - 9.

of vitality and spiritual beauty. But the Jews lost the spiritual life from their ceremonies, and clung to the dead forms. They trusted to the sacrifices and ordinances themselves, instead of resting upon him to whom they pointed.

Looking for Temporal Rule

" While the Jews desired the advent of the Messiah, they had no conception of his mission. They did not seek redemption from sin, but deliverance from the Romans. They looked for the Messiah to come as a conqueror, to break the oppressor's power, and exalt Israel to universal dominion. Thus the way was prepared for them to reject the Saviour.

" The people, in their darkness and oppression, and the rulers, thirsting for power, longed for the coming of one who would vanquish their enemies and restore the kingdom to Israel. They had studied the prophecies, but without spiritual insight. Thus they overlooked the scriptures that point to the humiliation of Christ's first advent, and misapplied those that speak of the glory of his second coming. Pride obscured their vision; they interpreted prophecy in accordance with their selfish desires.

" For more than a thousand years the Jewish people had waited the Saviour's coming. Upon this event they had rested their brightest hopes. In song and prophecy, in temple rite and household prayer, they had enshrined his name. And yet at his coming they knew him not. The Beloved of heaven was to them ' as a root out of a dry ground;' he had ' no form nor comeliness;' and they saw in him no beauty that they should desire him. ' He came unto his own, and his own received him not.' " [4]

Of the Lineage of David

As the time predicted by Daniel drew near, when " Messiah the Prince "— the anointed One — was to appear, the Jewish people could have reasoned, and undoubtedly did so, on this wise: The Messiah after the flesh is to be of the house and

[4] " Desire of Ages," pp. 29, 30 - 34.

lineage of David, therefore his birth must be in that line; and according to the regulations of the Jewish law and customs, he must be anointed for public service at the age of thirty years; and if he is to appear as the anointed at that age, then his birth must be thirty years before the termination of the sixty-nine weeks of years, which are to extend to the coming of the Messiah.

Predictions of Simeon and Anna

About this time all Israel was in expectation. The earnest, devoted students of the Scriptures were looking for the birth of him who was to be their Ruler and Governor. To the aged and pious Simeon it was revealed " by the Holy Ghost that he should not see death before he had seen the Lord's Christ." [5]

When the infant Saviour was brought to the temple, Simeon knew that this child was the one referred to — the Christ. " Then took he him up in his arms, and blessed God, and said, Lord. now lettest thou thy servant depart in peace, according to thy word; for mine eyes have seen thy salvation, which thou hast prepared before the face of all people: a light to lighten the Gentiles, and the glory of thy people Israel. . . .

" And Simeon blessed them [Joseph and Mary], and said unto Mary his mother, Behold, this child is set for the fall and rising again of many in Israel; and for a sign which shall be spoken against (yea, a sword shall pierce through thy own soul also), that the thoughts of many. hearts may be revealed.

" And there was one Anna, a prophetess, the daughter of Phanuel, of the tribe of Aser. . . . And she coming in that instant gave thanks likewise unto the Lord, and spake of him to all them that looked for redemption in Jerusalem." [6]

Angels Visit the Shepherds

Previous to this the glad news of the Saviour's birth had been heralded by angels to the shepherds on the plains

[5] Luke 2: 26.   [6] Luke 2: 28 - 38.

of Bethlehem.   Into the listening ear of the shepherds, angels
chanted these melodious strains:—

> " Glory to God in the highest:
> On earth peace, good will to men."

The Wise Men Visit Bethlehem

Then came the wise men of the East who had seen " the
star arise," as predicted by Balaam.   Following its guidance
they reached Jerusalem, where it became necessary to inquire for the new-born King.   On being instructed that
Bethlehem was to be the birthplace of the Desired One, they
journeyed on; and guided thither by the star which again
appeared, they were led to the humble place where the Saviour
lay.   Here they worshiped the holy Child, presenting him
with gifts of gold, frankincense, and myrrh, and then took
their long journey homeward.

The Saviour at Twelve Years of Age

From childhood to twelve years of age little is recorded
of Christ the Saviour, except his increase in wisdom and
stature, and his dutiful submission to his parents.   But at
the age of twelve, having accompanied Joseph and Mary up
to Jerusalem to attend the annual feast, he there astonished
the priests with the knowledge shown in his questions, and
in the answers given to their knotty problems.   From this
time until he entered upon his public labors, the humble
occupation of a carpenter was honored by him as he worked
with Joseph, the husband of Mary.

The Mission of John the Baptist

For six months previous to his public ministry, Christ's
mission was heralded by John the Baptist.   The people came
in vast crowds to hear John, and to be baptized of him.   As
they " were in expectation [expecting the Messiah to come]
and all men mused [" reasoned or debated," margin] in their
hearts of John, whether he were the Christ or not; John an-

swered, saying unto them all, I indeed baptize you with water; but one mightier than I cometh, the latchet of whose shoes I am not worthy to unloose: he shall baptize you with the Holy Ghost and with fire: whose fan is in his hand, and he will thoroughly purge his floor, and will gather the wheat into his garner; but the chaff he will burn with fire unquenchable." [7]

Jesus Baptized

As John was administering the rite of baptism, he saw Jesus coming to him to be baptized, and said, " Behold the Lamb of God, which taketh away the sin of the world. . . . And John bare record, saying, I saw the Spirit descending from heaven like a dove, and it abode upon him. And I knew him not: but he that sent me to baptize with water, the same said unto me, Upon whom thou shalt see the Spirit descending, and remaining on him, the same is he which baptizeth with the Holy Ghost. And I saw, and bare record that this is the Son of God." [8]

The Voice from Heaven

Not only was Christ's Messiahship attested by the visible descent of the Holy Spirit in a bodily shape like a dove, but also by a voice from heaven. In Matthew's Gospel we read, " Jesus, when he was baptized, went up straightway out of the water: and, lo, the heavens were opened unto him, and he saw the Spirit of God descending like a dove, and lighting upon him: and lo a voice from heaven, saying, This is my beloved Son, in whom I am well pleased." [9]

Although " John did no miracle," the people, when they saw the mighty power that attended Christ's ministry, were constrained to say, " All things that John spake of this man were true." [10]

Christ Anointed According to Law

In connection with Luke's record of the baptism and the same anointing by the Holy Spirit in the form of a dove,

[7] Luke 3: 15 - 17.   [8] John 1: 29 - 34.   [9] Matt. 3: 16, 17.   [10] John 10: 41.

we read, " Jesus himself began to be about thirty years of age." [11]

After our Lord's long fast of forty days, and the fierce temptations of the devil in the wilderness, which immediately followed his baptism, he " came to Nazareth, where he had been brought up; and as his custom was, he went into the synagogue on the Sabbath day, and stood up for to read. . . . The Spirit of the Lord is upon me, because he hath anointed me to preach the gospel to the poor. . . . And he began to say unto them, This day is this scripture fulfilled in your ears." [12]

The Time is Fulfilled

Mark, in recording the same occurrence, says, " The *time* is fulfilled, and the kingdom of God is at hand: repent ye, and believe the gospel." [13] The time predicted for the Anointed to appear had come. The anointing by the Holy Ghost had taken place at his baptism, and he was now entering upon his ministry, just in the time and manner predicted by the holy prophets of old.

Visible Proof of Christ's Messiahship

The ministry of Christ was accompanied with a constant performing of miracles, which, to the people, even if they failed fully to comprehend his parables and words, were a visible proof that he was the Immanuel, or that " God was with him." [14] In these miracles Christ was giving to the world not only an evidence of the power of God in himself, but also a practical demonstration of the character of God and of his loving kindness. When Philip, after three years of con-tinuous association with Christ, witnessing his mighty mira-cles, said, " Lord, show us the Father, and it sufficeth us," Jesus said unto him, " Have I been so long time with you, and yet hast thou not known me, Philip? He that hath seen me hath seen the Father: and how sayest thou then, Show

---

[11] Luke 3: 23. [12] Luke 4: 16 - 21.
[13] Mark 1: 15. [14] Acts 10: 38; John 3: 2.

us the Father? . . . Believe me that I am in the Father, and the Father in me; or else believe me for the very works' sake." [15]

John Perplexed

Although at the baptism of Christ, John had witnessed the visible descent of the Holy Spirit, and had heard the voice from heaven proclaiming him to be the Son of God, and had himself declared that he was "the Lamb of God that taketh away the sin of the world," events were shaping so differently from his anticipations that he, in his gloomy prison, was troubled and confused.

"Like the Saviour's disciples, John the Baptist did not understand the nature of Christ's kingdom. He expected Jesus to take the throne of David; and as time passed, and the Saviour made no claim to kingly authority, John became perplexed and troubled." [16] "Calling unto him two of his disciples, [he] sent them to Jesus, saying, Art thou he that should come? or look we for another?" "In that same hour he [Jesus] cured many of their infirmities and plagues, and of evil spirits; and unto many that were blind he gave sight. Then Jesus answering said unto them, Go your way, and tell John what things ye have seen and heard." [17]

It was with difficulty that the Jews or even the disciples could see clearly many truths which the Saviour uttered, because they were so established in the belief that when the Messiah should come he would break off the Roman yoke, which was to them so galling, and immediately restore the kingdom of David, and reign as a temporal king.

Jesus began his preaching by saying, "Repent, for the kingdom of heaven is at hand." [18] When his twelve apostles were sent forth, they bore the same message, "The kingdom of heaven is at hand." [19] Still later in his ministry, when the seventy were sent out, it was with the words, "The kingdom of God is come nigh unto you." [20]

[15] John 14: 8 - 11.   [16] "Desire of Ages," p. 244.   [17] Luke 7: 19 - 22; Matt. 11: 4.
[18] Matt. 4: 17.   [19] Matt. 10: 7.   [20] Luke 10: 9.

People Amazed at Christ's Work

The wonderful words and teachings of Christ led the people to say, " Never man spake like this man." [21]   And when he healed the blind and dumb man, "All the people were amazed, and said, Is not this the son of David?" [22] or in other words, Is not this the seed of David, the promised Saviour? "When he was come into his own country, he taught them in their synagogue, insomuch that they were astonished, and said, Whence hath this man this wisdom, and these mighty works? Is not this the carpenter's son? is not his mother called Mary? and his brethren, James, and Joses, and Simon, and Judas?" [23]

About the third year of Christ's ministry, when he was in the temple attending the feast of dedication, the Jews came about him, and said unto him, "How long dost thou make us to doubt? If thou be the Christ, tell us plainly." [24]   In the previous year, when he had wrought the mighty miracle of feeding the five thousand with the " five barley loaves and two small fishes," he "perceived that they would come and take him by force, to make him a king, [hence] he departed again into a mountain." [25]

Christ Teaching the Disciples of His Death

In teaching his disciples, Christ made it an important point to dispel the idea of a temporal reign to begin immediately, and to show them that he must die and rise again, go away and come again. So he inquired of them, "What and if ye shall see the Son of man ascend up where he was before?" [26]   After charging them "that they should tell no man that he was Jesus the Christ," we read: "From that time forth began Jesus to show unto his disciples, how that he must go unto Jerusalem, and suffer many things of the elders and chief priests and scribes, and be killed, and be raised again the third day. Then Peter took him, and began to

[21] John 7: 46.   [22] Matt. 12: 23.   [23] Matt. 13: 54, 55.
[24] John 10: 24.   [25] John 6: 15.   [26] John 6: 62.

rebuke him, saying, Be it far from thee, Lord; this shall not be unto thee." [27]

At the same time he told them there were some standing there who would not die until they had seen the Son of man coming in his kingdom. [28] About eight days after, this prophecy was fulfilled; and.the aposle Peter refers to that "vision" of Christ coming in his kingdom as proof of the actual second coming of Christ yet in the future. [29]

At one time when Christ and his disciples were in Galilee, Jesus said to them, "The Son of man shall be betrayed into the hands of men; and they shall kill him, and the third day he shall be raised again. And they were exceeding sorry." [30] And still they failed to understand, to comprehend, his meaning, for even while he was seeking to impress their minds with the solemn truth of his death and resurrection, they were debating the question among themselves as to who should be the greatest in the kingdom of heaven. [31]

On another occasion Peter said to Jesus, "We have forsaken all, and followed thee; what shall we have therefore? And Jesus said unto them, Verily I say unto you, That ye which have followed me, in the regeneration when the Son of man shall sit in the throne of his glory, ye also shall sit upon twelve thrones, judging the twelve tribes of Israel." [32] Still the thought of a kingdom soon to be established was uppermost in their minds, and they, human like, began to look for the highest place in the kingdom.

Then comes the ambitious mother of James and John, sons of Zebedee, asking Christ that her sons be favored with high positions — one on the right hand and the other on the left of his throne; or, perhaps, one to be Premier of the government, and the other Secretary of State. But Christ said plainly, "Ye know not what ye ask." [33]

[27] Matt. 16: 20 - 22; Mark 9: 31.   [28] Matt. 16: 28; Luke 9: 27.
[29] 2 Peter 1: 16 - 19.   [30] Matt. 17: 22, 23.   [31] Matt. 18: 1; Mark 9: 33, 34.
[32] Matt. 19: 27, 28; Luke 22: 28 - 30.   [33] Matt. 20: 20 - 24.

5

Triumphal Entry into Jerusalem

Not far from this time a great and startling event occurred. It was the raising of Lazarus from the tomb, he who had been dead four days. Such a mighty miracle so aroused and amazed the people that the Pharisees were alarmed, who, with the priests, at once called a council; and in their deliberations they asked, "What do we? for this man doeth many miracles. If we let him thus alone, all men will believe on him; and the Romans shall come and take away both our place and nation." [34] While a Satanic power from beneath was thus taking hold of those who were seeking to destroy Christ, a power from on high was moving the masses to glorify him, and fulfil what had been predicted concerning him.

Upon the occasion referred to above, the people turned out *en masse,* not only to see Jesus, but to see Lazarus also, whom he had raised from the dead. Now to them it seemed certain that Jesus was their long-expected king, and as they met him coming toward Jerusalem, seated on a colt, the words of Scripture came forcibly to their minds, " Fear not, daughter of Sion: behold, thy king cometh, sitting on an ass's colt." [35] A mighty shout of triumph went up from that vast throng, which greatly disturbed the cold-hearted, calculating Pharisees. Among themselves they said, " Perceive ye how ye prevail nothing? Behold, the world is gone after him." [36] To their request that Christ should stop the shouting, he replied, " I tell you that, if these should hold their peace, the stones would immediately cry out." [37] The Lord had said of this occasion, " Shout," and if the people did not fulfil his word, he would put a voice into the stones of the street, and they would shout; for his word must be fulfilled.

Christ to Go Away and Return Again

Not only did our Saviour seek to direct the minds of the disciples to the fact that he was to die and rise again, but

[34] John 11: 47, 48.   [35] John 12: 15.   [36] John 12: 19.   [37] Luke 19: 40.

he desired also to teach them that the kingdom was not to come until he should go away and return again. Referring to his crucifixion he said, " I, if I be lifted up from the earth, will draw all men unto me. This he said, signifying what death he should die. The people answered him, We have heard out of the law that Christ abideth forever; and how sayest thou, The Son of man must be lifted up? Who is this Son of man? " [38]

To impress the minds of the disciples more fully with the fact that he was to go away, and return again, before his kingdom would be established on earth, he said, " Little children, yet a little while I am with you. Ye shall seek me; and as I said unto the Jews, Whither I go, ye cannot come; so now I say to you. . . . Simon Peter said unto him, Lord, whither goest thou? Jesus answered him, Whither I go, thou canst not follow me now; but thou shalt follow me afterwards." [39] He then encouraged their anxious and sorrowing hearts with these words: " Let not your heart be troubled: ye believe in God, believe also in me. In my Father's house are many mansions: if it were not so, I would have told you. I go to prepare a place for you. And if I go and prepare a place for you, I will come again, and receive you unto myself; that where I am, there ye may be also." [40]

Parable of the Nobleman

Again the Saviour sought to correct the erroneous idea that the kingdom was immediately to appear, by the use of the following parable as he and the disciples were going up to Jerusalem: " A certain nobleman went into a far country to receive for himself a kingdom, and to return. And he called his ten servants, and delivered them ten pounds, and said unto them, Occupy till I come. . . . And it came to pass, that when he was returned, having received the kingdom, then he commanded these servants to be called unto him, to whom he had given the money, that he might know how much every man had gained by trading." [41] In this parable

[38] John 12: 32 - 34.   [39] John 13: 33 - 36.   [40] John 14: 1 - 3.   [41] Luke 19: 11 - 15.

the Lord represents himself by the nobleman. He was to go to a far country — to his Father — and there receive the kingdom, before returning to reign.

In response to the question of the disciples, " What shall be the sign of thy coming, and of the end of the world? " [42] the Saviour gave them a list of the events that were to transpire down through the great tribulation that should come upon the church, and the definite signs that would occur. When these appeared, they might know that his coming was near, even at the doors, and that the generation that saw them would not pass off the stage of action until he came. [43]

Forsaken by All the Disciples

But with all the instruction given the apostles by Christ concerning his death and humiliation, they utterly failed to grasp the truth he had taught them respecting his trial and crucifixion. So faint a conception had they of the truth that when the trial came, their hope died, and they all " forsook him and fled." [44]   Even Peter, the ever zealous Peter, who so confidently affirmed that if all men forsook him, he never would, was, a few hours later, denying his Lord, and with an oath declaring that he knew not the man.   So dull were they in comprehension of the Lord's statement that on the third day after his crucifixion he would rise from the dead, they questioned and reasoned among themselves " what the rising from the dead should mean." [45]   Indeed, so void of faith were they that after he died, and his body had been placed in Joseph's new tomb, they made preparations for embalming him. With hope gone — buried with Christ in the tomb — what a Sabbath day to the disciples! With hearts burdened with grief and disappointment, and no pitying, compassionate Saviour, whose life had been filled with acts of tenderness and mercy, near to comfort and strengthen, how desolate was their condition!

[42] Matt. 24: 3.   [43] Matt. 24; Luke 21; Mark 13.   [44] Mark 14: 50.
[45] Mark 9: 10.

Stirring Events of the Resurrection Morning

The morning of the first day of the week dawns! What a stir in heaven and on earth! A mighty angel comes down from the realms of glory to Joseph's tomb, with a message commanding the Son of God to arise. "And, behold, there was a great earthquake: for the angel of the Lord descended from heaven, and came and rolled back the stone from the door, and sat upon it. His countenance was like lightning, and his raiment white as snow: and for fear of him the keepers did shake, and became as dead men." [46] " Many bodies of the saints which slept arose, and came out of the graves after his resurrection, and went into the holy city, and appeared unto many." [47] Think of such callers as these in Jerusalem, at the doors of their friends, with the message that the crucified Christ was risen from the dead, and that they too had been brought to life by his power, to bear witness concerning his resurrection. What activity among the disciples and the holy women — running hither and thither to tell the glad news, " He is risen from the dead, for we have seen and talked with him! "

Jesus Walks into the Country

"And, behold, two of them went that same day to a little village called Emmaus, which was from Jerusalem about threescore furlongs [seven and one-half miles]. And they talked together of all these things which had happened. And it came to pass, that, while they communed together and reasoned, Jesus himself drew near, and went with them. But their eyes were holden that they should not know him. And he said unto them, What manner of communications are these that ye have one to another, as ye walk, and are sad? And one of them, whose name was Cleopas, answering said unto him, Art thou only a stranger in Jerusalem, and hast not known the things which are come to pass there in these days? And he said unto them, What things? And they said unto

[46] Matt. 28: 2 - 4.   [47] Matt. 27: 52, 53.

him, Concerning Jesus of Nazareth, which was a prophet mighty in deed and word before God and all the people: and how the chief priests and our rulers have delivered him to be condemned to death, and have crucified him. But we trusted that it had been he which should have redeemed Israel: and beside all this, to-day is the third day since these things were done. Yea, and certain women also of our company made us astonished, which were early at the sepulcher: and when they found not his body, they came, saying, that they had also seen a vision of angels, which said that he was alive. And certain of them which were with us went to the sepulcher, and found it even so as the women had said: but him they saw not.

"Then he said unto them, O fools, and slow of heart to believe all that the prophets have spoken: ought not Christ to have suffered these things, and to enter into his glory? And beginning at Moses and all the prophets, he expounded unto them in all the Scriptures the things concerning himself." [48]   As he was about to partake of a meal with them, he brake the bread and gave thanks, " and their eyes were opened, and they knew him. . . . And they said one to another, Did not our heart burn within us, while he talked with us by the way, and while he opened to us the Scriptures?" [49]

Now, at last, the disciples can see, after the problem is fully demonstrated to them, that there was a death and a resurrection connected with the Saviour's mission. But how will they regard the question of his kingdom? ' He showed himself alive after his passion by many infallible proofs, being seen of them forty days, and speaking of the things pertaining to the kingdom of God; and, being assembled together with them, commanded that they should not depart from Jerusalem, but wait for the promise of the Father, which, saith he, ye have heard of me. For John truly baptized with water; but ye shall be baptized with the Holy Ghost not many days hence.

[48] Luke 24: 13 - 27.   [49] Verses 31, 32.

Wilt Thou Now Restore the Kingdom?

"When they therefore were come together, they asked of him, saying, Lord, wilt thou at this time restore again the kingdom to Israel? [as much as to say, We have learned that it was necessary that you must be crucified, and rise from the dead, according to the Scriptures, but are you not going to restore the kingdom now?] And he said unto them, It is not for you to know the times or the seasons, which the Father hath put in his own power. But ye shall receive power, after that the Holy Ghost is come upon you: and ye shall be witnesses unto me both in Jerusalem, and in all Judea, and in Samaria, and unto the uttermost part of the earth. And when he had spoken these things, while they beheld, he was taken up; and a cloud received him out of their sight. And while they looked steadfastly toward heaven as he went up, behold, two men stood by them in white apparel; which also said, Ye men of Galilee, why stand ye gazing up into heaven? This same Jesus, which is taken up from you into heaven, shall so come in like manner as ye have seen him go into heaven." [50]

Jesus to Remain in Heaven until the Restitution

Now that the Saviour had left them, and they had indeed seen him "ascend up where he was before," they had the assurance that the Holy Spirit would teach them concerning the time when the kingdom will come. So, Peter in his instructions to the people, after the reception of the Spirit, said, " He shall send Jesus Christ, which before was preached unto you: whom the heaven must receive until the times of restitution of all things, which God hath spoken by the mouth of all his holy prophets since the world began." [51]

To the apostle Peter were given also by the Holy Spirit the facts concerning the three worlds: First, the one before the flood, which was destroyed by water; second, the present world reserved unto fire,— fire with which the earth is stored,

[50] Acts 1: 6 - 11.   [51] Acts 3: 20, 21.

as the Revised Version reads,— that fire which shall prove
the perdition, ruin, and destruction of ungodly men; third
the new earth, " wherein dwelleth righteousness;" or, as some
translate, " wherein the righteous shall dwell." [52]

The apostle Paul set forth the resurrection of God's
people, and the change of all his saints from mortal to immortal, " in the twinkling of an eye, at the last trump."
He stated to the Corinthians that Christ is now upon his
Father's throne, and will there remain till all his enemies
are subjected to him. That is, till he shall have the kingdom — his kingdom — given into his hands by the Father,
as prophesied in Dan. 7 : 13, 14 ; Ps. 2 : 8, 9. To the church
in Thessalonica he presented the coming of Christ and the
resurrection as their only hope, and as containing the true
consolation when their loved ones were separated from them
by the hand of death. [53]

The Master's Return Indefinite

As yet the church had no definite knowledge as to the
time when the Master would return. When the apostle in
his first letter to the Thessalonians, said, " We which are alive
and remain shall be caught up," the brethren understood
him to mean that Christ was coming while some of them
were still alive. In his second epistle he corrects their wrong
conception of his letter, and tells them that " that day shall
not come, except there come a falling away first, and that
man of sin be revealed, the son of perdition; who opposeth
and exalteth himself above all that is called God, or that
is worshiped." [54]

The Apostasy

And still the church is left to grope its way in the dark
as to the *time* of Christ's second coming. The brethren have
learned that there is to be an apostasy; but of how long duration, was the question. An answer was afterward given to
John while in vision on the isle of Patmos, in the symbols

[52] 2 Peter 3: 5 - 13.   [53] 1 Thess. 4: 13 - 18.   [54] 2 Thess. 2: 3, 4.

found in chapters twelve and thirteen of the Revelation —
the "time, times, and a half," the "forty and two months,"
the "twelve hundred and sixty days" (years) ; but as yet the
event marking the opening of that long period had not occurred. So the church was still hoping and waiting for
Christ's coming without positively knowing the exact time
of his appearing; for when that time of tribulation should
be passed, a little season of conflict and triumph would still
remain for the "remnant" church. [55]

With the closing up of the New Testament records we
have the theme of Christ's second coming clearly set before
us. About one verse out of every thirty mentions in some way
the second coming of our Lord Jesus Christ. Of this, and the
position of the church with reference to that hope through
the ages intervening to modern times, Robert Patterson, D. D.,
speaks in a paper called the *Interior,* under the caption
"The Blessed Hope." on this wise :—

The Temporal Millennium — Patterson

"When our Lord left his church on earth to go to
the Father, he left her in a sorrowful condition. His five
hundred disciples were surrounded by the whole world of
his enemies, organized into anti-Christian religions and governments by one of the highest intelligences, animated by the
most venomous malice, and educated by the experience of
ages in the most effectual modes of destruction. The Lord
was not ignorant of our danger ; nor in his last discourses did
he extenuate it, nor promise any abatement of the world's en-
mity and the church's tribulation. But he did promise that
he himself would return to overthrow his enemies, and that
he would support us till that blessed day. 'The world hateth
you. In the world ye shall have tribulation. Ye shall weep
and lament, but the world shall rejoice. Ye shall be sorrowful, but your sorrow shall be turned into joy. . . . Ye now
therefore have sorrow, but I will see you again, and your
heart shall rejoice, and your joy no man taketh from you.

[55] Rev. 12: 17.

If I go away, I will come again, and receive you unto myself, that where I am, there ye may be also.'

" Such was the blessed hope of his personal return with which he comforted his church on his personal departure. During all the period of his absence, he said we must suffer tribulation; and so it has come to pass. If we are to enjoy any period of outward peace during his absence, if his church is to be delivered from the assaults of the world, if there is to be any age of purity when the tares shall not grow among the wheat, or if, at his coming, he shall be welcomed by the population of an earth filled with the glory of the Lord, or indeed even be able to find faith in the earth, it will be to him a most unexpected surprise. Jesus did not know of this millennium. We say he did not know of it, because he did not tell us of it; and he says, ' I have called you friends, for all things which I have heard of my Father I have made known unto you.' But in all his discourses and parables there is not the least hint that we are to hope for any period of peace or glory before his coming. The apostles are equally ignorant of a Christless millennium. For three hundred years after our Lord's departure the blessed hope of the church was the hope of his return.

" But when, in the progress of her predicted apostasy, the bride of Christ began to solace herself in his absence with the friendship of the kings of earth, very naturally she averted her eye from the eastern sky, and from the return of her Lord, which would put an end to her worldly grandeur. When the Reformers put the gospel trumpet to their mouths . . . the dreams of a Christless millennium were instantly swept away, . . . and the church again began looking for the coming of the Lord to destroy antichrist. . . . In their letters, sermons, and confessions of faith, the Reformers proclaimed their premillennial hopes.

" The Westminster Assembly conclude their confession with a declaration of their faith in the second coming of the Lord in words which fully express the faith of premillennarians. They proclaim in these weighty words: 'As Christ would have us certainly persuaded that there shall be a day of judgment, both to deter all men from sin, and for the greater consolation of the godly in their adversity, so will he have that day unknown to men, that they may shake off all carnal security, and be always watchful, because they know not at what hour the Lord will come: and may ever be prepared to say, Come, Lord Jesus: and come quickly!' [56]

" Our reforming ancestors strengthened their hearts by looking for the coming of the Lord, and encouraged each other by the cry, Hold the field! for he is coming with legions of help,' a sentiment embodied recently in a popular revival hymn, but familiar to the old Scottish Covenanters.

" But ere long a second apostasy from the faith set in among the reformed churches. It was known in Scotland as Moderatism; in England, as Arianism, and more recently, as Broad Churchism; and in America it called itself Unitarianism; and in Germany, Rationalism. Setting up human reason as the judge, and our very limited modern observation as the evidence, and denying that any event could occur but according to the course of observed laws of nature, it reduced Jesus to the rank of a Jewish rabbi, rather in advance of his day, but totally unacquainted with modern science. Of course the notion of such a person returning from the invisible world to reign upon the earth was remanded to the Hebrew mythology.

Daniel Whitby on the Millennium

" The promises of his second coming and reign on earth were interpreted to mean simply the spread of his gospel, and the submission of a great part of the world to Christianity for a period of a thousand, or, as some thought, 360,000 years; during which mankind was to advance in the arts of civilization, and enjoy unexampled peace and prosperity. And at the close of that extended cycle, too vast for the common mind to see across, possibly some great convulsion of nature

56 "Confession of Faith," Chap. 33, sec. 3.

would occur, and it might be said the Lord would come and destroy the world, and call the human race to judgment This theory was elaborated and popularized by an English commentator named Whitby [Daniel Whitby died in 1726}, who, by his published correspondence, is proved to be an Arian, but whose commentaries were popular with his own class, and whose mythical millennium was received with favor by many of the orthodox pensioners and friends of the state churches of Europe, to whom it promised a long lease of tithes and honors. Through their influence it was imported into America, where it was immediately utilized as material for platform platitudes and perorations."

Such were the theories in various portions of the earth as we approach the time when the Lord sent forth the solemn warning of his coming, even " at the doors."

CHAPTER IV

THE TIME OF THE END

T HEN said I, O my Lord, what shall be the end of these things? And he said, Go thy way, Daniel: for the words are closed up and sealed till the *time of the end*. . . . The wicked shall do wickedly: and none of the wicked shall understand; but the wise shall understand." [1]

" He said unto me, Understand, O son of man: for at the *time of the end* shall be the vision." [2]

" But thou, O Daniel, shut up the words, and seal the book, even to the *time of the end;* many shall run to and fro, and knowledge shall be increased." [3]

What is here meant by the " time of the end "? It cannot be the actual end itself, for in that case the part of Daniel's prophecy which was " sealed up " would be of no avail to humanity. As " things which are revealed belong to us," [4] this portion must be of use at some time. So the expression, " time of the end," must refer to a period just before the end itself, in which the things spoken of to Daniel will be understood.

The Day of His Preparation

It undoubtedly refers to that time called by the prophet Nahum " the day of his preparation." Here the prophet was speaking of the destruction of Nineveh with " the noise of a whip, and the noise of the rattling of the wheels, and of the prancing horses, and of the jumping chariots." [5] The prophet's attention is first called to a greater calamity which

[1] Dan. 12: 8 - 10.   [2] Dan. 8: 17.   [3] Dan. 12: 4.
     [4] Deut. 29: 29.   [5] Nahum 3: 2.

is to come upon all the world, when "the mountains quake at him, and the hills melt, and the earth is burned at his presence, yea, the world, and all that dwell therein. Who can stand before his indignation? and who can abide in the fierceness of his anger? His fury is poured out like fire, and the rocks are thrown down by him. . . . He will make an utter end; affliction shall not rise up the second time." [6]

Chariots with Flaming Torches

Still further does the prophet speak of this day of preparation: "The chariots shall be with flaming torches in the day of his preparation, and the fir trees shall be terribly shaken. The chariots shall rage in the streets, they shall jostle one against another in the broad ways: they shall seem like torches, they shall run like the lightnings. He shall recount his worthies: they shall stumble in their walk; they shall make haste to the wall thereof, and the defense shall be prepared." [7]

What an accurate description of the modern lightning train, with the conductor constantly counting and recounting his passengers, from station to station, and they stumbling as they walk when the train is in motion. Then there is the mighty consumption of fir trees for railway ties, trestle work, snow sheds, etc. It is said that one road over the Sierra Nevada Mountains has forty-seven miles of fir-tree snow sheds. And this the prophet said would be in the "day of his preparation."

This time of the end is also spoken of by the prophet Joel when the command is given to the Lord's servants, "Blow ye the trumpet in Zion, and sound an alarm in my holy mountain: let all the inhabitants of the land tremble; for the day of the Lord cometh, for it is nigh at hand." [8]

And again by the prophet Zephaniah it is said, "Gather yourselves together, yea, gather together, O nation not desired; before the decree bring forth, before the day pass as the chaff, before the fierce anger of the Lord come upon you,

[6] Nahum 1: 5 - 9.   [7] Nahum 2: 3 - 5.   [8] Joel 2: 1.

before the day of the Lord's anger come upon you. Seek
ye the Lord, all ye meek of the earth, which have wrought
his judgment; seek righteousness, seek meekness: it may
be ye shall be hid in the day of the Lord's anger." [9]

To ascertain more fully what is meant by the expression
" time of the end," and when it begins, we will notice another
instance where the same term is used. In the eleventh chapter
of Daniel a persecuting power is introduced which was to hold
its dominion until the time of the end. The Lord said of
that persecuting power, " Some of them of understanding shall
fall, to try them, and to purge, and to make them white, even
to the time of the end: because it [the time of the end]
is yet for a time appointed." [10]

The Work of the Little Horn

Protestant commentators generally are agreed in applying this power and the " little horn " of Daniel seven, to the
Roman church which had the civil power in its hands for the
" appointed " time. That appointed time was the " time,
times, and a half." [11] This was the 1260 prophetic days —
1260 years — of the civil rule of the little horn, extending from
538 to 1798 A. D. At the latter date the civil power of the
little horn was taken away, at the " time appointed." So
at that time the people had ceased to " fall " by the hand
of that power as they had previously been falling. This
year, then,— 1798,— marks the beginning of that period of
time in this prophecy called " the time of the end."

The year 1798 closed the " thousand two hundred and
threescore days " —1260 years — in which the Lord's " Two
Witnesses " (the Old and New Testaments) were to
" prophesy . . . clothed in sackcloth." [12] During the Dark
Ages of persecution the Scriptures were kept in the Greek
and Latin languages, and these languages the common people
did not understand. This holding back the Scriptures is
compared to clothing them " in sackcloth."

[9] Zeph. 2: 1 - 3.   [10] Dan. 11: 35.   [11] Dan. 12: 7.   [12] Rev. 11: 3.

The Two Witnesses Slain

"When they shall have finished their testimony [in the sackcloth state], the *beast* that ascendeth out of the bottomless pit shall make war against them [Satan stirring up and working through worldly men], and shall overcome them and kill them. And their dead bodies shall lie in the street of the great city, which spiritually is called Sodom and Egypt, where also our Lord was crucified ["is crucified," Danish and Revised Version]. And they of the people and kindreds and tongues and nations shall see their dead bodies *three days and a half,* and shall not suffer their dead bodies to be put in graves." [13]

The Reign of Terror

The slaying of these Witnesses was accomplished during the "reign of terror" in France, from 1792 to 1795 — three and one-half years. Although the French Revolution continued some six or seven years, it was during the first three and one-half years that they made their great effort to destroy the Bible, religion, and all who dared to speak in favor of either. While the French Revolution professed to be warring against monarchy and priestcraft, it actually became a war for the extermination of God and the Bible. Of the times just preceding the Revolution we read, "Never let it be forgotten that before the Revolution of 1792, the promoters of infidelity in France are stated to have raised among themselves and spent £900,000 [$4,500,000] in one year, nay, again and again, in purchasing, printing, and dispersing books to corrupt the minds of the people and prepare them for desperate measures." [14]

Infidel Writers

"The way for such a Revolution was prepared by the writings of Voltaire, Mirabeau, Diderot, Helvetius, D'Alembert, Condorcet, Rousseau, and others of the same stamp, in

[13] Rev. 11: 7 - 9.   [14] Anderson's "Annals of the English Bible," p. 494.

which they endeavored to disseminate principles subversive of both natural and revealed religion. Revelation was not only impugned, but entirely set aside; the Deity was banished from the universe, and an imaginary phantom under the name of the Goddess of Reason, was substituted in its place." [15]

In the year 1793 the views of the people were such that theatrical performers were loudly cheered for their blasphemous railery against God and the Bible. As a sample we quote: " The commedian Monert, in the Church of St. Roche [Paris], carried impiety to its height. ' God, if you exist,' said he, ' avenge your injured name! I bid you defiance. You remain silent. You dare not launch your thunders. Who after this will believe in your existence?' " [16]

Blasphemous Work in Lyons, France

As to how those who killed the Witnesses, " *crucified* the Son of God afresh, and put him to an open shame " (Heb. 6:6), will appear in the proceedings of a féte held by Fouche, in Lyons, in honor of Chalier, the Governor of Lyons, who had been put to death. Before his arrival at Lyons, Fouche ordered that " all religious emblems should be destroyed; and that over the gates of the churchyards should be written; *Death is an eternal sleep.* . . . The bust of Chalier was carried through the streets, followed by an immense crowd of assassins and prostitutes. After them came an ass bearing the gospel, the cross, and the communion vases, which were soon consigned to the flames, while the ass was compelled to drink out of the communion cup the consecrated wine." [17]

A Festival of Reason held in Paris is thus described: " They went in procession to the convention, and the rabble . . . caricatured in the most ludicrous manner the ceremonies of religion. . . . Men, wearing surplices and copes, came singing hallelujahs, and dancing barmagnole, to the bar of the convention. There they deposited the host, the boxes in which it was kept, and the statues of gold and silver.

[15] " Thomas Dick on the Improvement of Society," page 154.
[a] Thier's " French Revolution," vol. ii, page 371.   [17] *Ibid.*, p. 338.

6

They made burlesque speeches. . . . ' O you,' exclaimed a deputation from St. Denis, ' O you, instruments of fanaticism, blessed saints of all kinds, be at last patriots, rise *en masse,* and serve the country by going to the mint to be melted.' " [18]

God's Word Emerges from Obscuirty

"After three days and a half the Spirit of life from God entered unto them " (the Witnesses), and they " ascended up to heaven in a cloud." [19]   God's time had come for his word to come out from obscurity and be replaced before the world. The time had come (1798) for missionary work to be done in the whole world.   In 1804 the British Bible Society was organized.   This was followed by scores of other Bible societies, and now the Bible is translated into all the leading languages of the world.   Thus the Scriptures, the Two Witnesses, coming into prominence where all can see and read them, is compared to their ascending to heaven in a cloud.

In the time of the French Revolution, Voltaire stated that in one hundred years the Bible would be obsolete.   In the one hundredth year from that date more Bibles were circulated in France alone than were known to be in existence when Voltaire made this vain boast.   And the house even in which he made the statement is said to be used now as a Bible house.

Rosetta Stone Discovered

There are two points connected with the year 1798 and the French people, that we must notice: First, in that year the French army, under General Berthier, overthrew the papal government in Rome, accomplishing (unknown to themselves) the fulfilment of the prophecy concerning this event, contained in the very book against which they had made war; second, in the same year, at Fort St. Julien, on the Rosetta branch of the Nile, the *French* army, while making an excavation, discovered the famous *Rosetta stone,* which is now deposited in the British Museum.   On this stone is an inscription in three

[18] *Ibid.,* p. 365.   [19] Rev. 11: 11, 12.

forms: Hieroglyphics, the writing used by the priests; the demotic, the form of writing used by the common people; and Greek. This is the key that unlocked the hitherto mysterious demotic and hieroglyphic writings. Now, as expressed by another, " the pick and shovel, unearthing these writings in demotic characters, is furnishing more proof of the correctness of ancient Bible records than comes from any other source outside the Scriptures themselves." So the very people who thought to exterminate the Bible were, all unconsciously to themselves, used to bring about a fulfilment of prophecy in taking away the dominion of the papacy at the end of the 1260 years, and also discovered the key to the very writings which confirm the truthfulness of the Scriptures they tried so hard to destroy.

"Thou Shalt Stand in Thy Lot"

What was it that the angel stated to Daniel should occur at the time of the end? From the time he heard the saint say, " Unto two thousand and three hundred days, then shall the sanctuary be cleansed," [20] his mind was filled with anxiety as to what should be " the end of these things," and " how long " it should be.[21] Finally he is given to understand that a knowledge of the time is not for his day. It is said to him, " Go thou thy way till the end be: for thou shalt rest, and stand in thy lot at the end of the days." [22]

Some have supposed this language referred to the final end of the world, and that at that time Daniel, with the rest of the Lord's people, would receive his reward, and stand in his lot of inheritance. The Hebrew word for lot of inheritance, region of country, etc., is, we are told, *gheh-vel*. That is not the word that is translated *lot* in this scripture; the word here is *goh rahl*. Hebrew scholars tell us that this word, *goh rahl*, occurs seventy-six times in the Old Testament, and that it is the same word that is used in speaking of the typical cleansing of the sanctuary, where lots were cast to determine which of the two goats was to be slain. As the high priest

[20] Dan. 8: 14. [21] Dan. 12: 6 - 8. [22] Dan. 12: 13.

took the blood of the Lord's goat and went into the sanctuary to perform the work of cleansing, all Israel stood without, afflicting their souls and confessing their sins, that they might stand clear, and receive the blessing of the high priest as he should come out of the sanctuary. Thus, on that day, Israel stood in their lot.

When the final cleansing of the sanctuary should come, at the close of the twenty-three hundred days, Daniel's case, with the cases of all the righteous dead, was to come in review before God. So Daniel stands in his lot.

The Words Sealed until 1798

In response to Daniel's inquiry, " O my Lord, what shall be the end of these things?" [23] he is told, " The words are closed up and sealed till the time of the end." [24]   What so exercised the mind of Daniel was the *" when? "* the *" how long? "* and *" what shall be the end? "* These were the points that perplexed and troubled the prophet, and these things only were to be closed up and sealed till the " time of the end," and not the whole book of Daniel, as some have thought. Previous to this period of 1798, students of prophecy had light concerning the seventy weeks, and understood that they commenced B. C. 457, Christ's public ministry, his death, etc., occurring in exact harmony with the reckoning of the sixty-nine and seventy weeks from that date. This exact fulfilment of the Saviour's mission in harmony with this reckoning had given them a mighty proof that he was indeed the true Messiah, and that the date of the commencement of the seventy weeks was thus unalterably fixed. Their failing to discover that the seventy weeks was the first part of the twenty-three hundred days, left the matter sealed up until after 1798, as predicted.

Key to the 2300 Days

Now let us look at the facts in the case. Until the year 1798 the exponents of prophecy had no light as to when

[23] Dan. 12: 8.   [24] Dan. 12: 9.

the twenty-three hundred days would end. They could understand the symbols, the image and the beasts of the book of Daniel, but could not tell where the twenty-three hundred days would end, for as yet they had no understanding as to when the days began. As proof on this point we read in the *Midnight Cry,* an Adventist paper then published in New York City, under date of June 15, 1842, " It is truly interesting to find the various independent writers who *since 1798* have seen what was *entirely unperceived before* — that the seventy weeks was a key to the twenty-three hundred days."

Many Discovering the Light

As this knowledge was " sealed up " until the Lord's appointed time came for its opening up to the understanding of his people, so just as truly when the " time of the end " came, many were to " run to and fro " through the Scriptures, searching out these things. By comparing a few translations of the text, this idea will be made very plain.

Dr. Adam Clarke says: " Many shall endeavor to search out the sense; and knowledge shall be increased — by this means."

In the German Bible of Luther, revised, we read: " So shall many come over it, and find great understanding."

The German Parallel Bible reads: " Many shall run it through, and so the knowledge will be increased."

The German Bible of L. Van Ess, admitted also by the pope to Catholic readers, translates it: " Many will search it through, and the knowledge will be great."

The Swedish Bible reads: " Many shall search in it, and knowledge shall become great."

The Danish-Norwegian, revised, reads: " Many shall eagerly search, and knowledge shall become much."

We read in the *Midnight Cry* of June 15, 1842, of this searching for and obtaining knowledge on that which previous to 1798 was sealed up: " Is it not a wonderful coincidence that so many writers, without any knowledge of one another, came to the same conclusion about the same time?"

We herewith present a list of twenty different parties who discovered the truth concerning the close of the twenty-three hundred days, not by communication with each other, but as the result of diligent searching of the Scriptures, led by the influence of the Spirit of God. Heading this list we place William Miller of the State of New York; then follow A. J. Krupp, of Philadelphia, Pa.; David McGregor, of Falmouth, Maine; Edward Irving, of England; Archibald Mason, of Scotland; W. E. Davis, of South Carolina; Joseph Wolff, who labored in various parts of Asia; Alexander Campbell, in his debate with Robert Dale Owen, in 1829; Captain A. Landers, of Liverpool, England; Leonard Heinrich Kelber, of Stuttgart, Germany; Laucunza, of Spain; Hentzepeter, of The Hague, Holland; Dr. Capadose, of Amsterdam, Holland; Rau, of Bavaria; priests of Tartary, in 1821; Bible students of Yemen, in their book called " Seera;" Hengstenberg, in another part of Germany; Russians on the Caspian Sea; Molokaners on the shores of the Baltic, etc.

As to how this subject opened from time to time to the students of prophecy, and that too without a knowledge of one another, the following will show:—

In the *Midnight Cry* of June 15, 1842, are these words: " Just received, a *book,* with the following title, ' Two Essays on Daniel's Prophetic Numbers of 2300 Days, and a Christian's Duty to Inquire into the Church's Deliverance, by Archibald Mason, minister of the gospel, Wishawtown, Scotland, Newberg. Printed from the Glasgow edition. by Ward M. Gazeley, 1820.' In this book Mason says, ' I have lately seen a small pamphlet, which was first published in America, by the Rev. Wm. E. Davis, of South Carolina, and republished in 1818 at Warkington, in the south of England. This author asserts that the twenty-three hundred days commenced with the seventy weeks (chap. 9: 29). In this opinion I am constrained to concur.' "

Davis, of South Carolina

In the same number of the *Midnight Cry,* the editor said, " Davis's book must have been written about 1810." Speaking of the reasoning set forth in the book, he states, " The reader might really fancy himself reading the productions of Miller, Litch, Stores, or Hale, but we believe that no one of the present second advent writers knew of the existence of this book till last week. The editor of this paper [the *Cry*] never heard of it before. Davis's position on *time,* endorsed by Mason. was that the twenty-three hundred days would end with the Jewish year 1843 — our year 1844."

Joseph Wolff and Twenty Others

In the *Midnight Cry* of Aug. 31, 1843, we read that " in 1822 Joseph Wolff (of England) published a book entitled ' He Will Come Again, the Son of Man in the Clouds of Heaven.'" And further, that " in 1826 twenty persons, of all orthodox persuasions, met in London, with Mr. Wolff, to study the Bible. They came unanimously to the same conclusion. They added 45 years to the 1260." Adding 45 years to the 1260 years which terminated in 1798, would bring us to the end of 1843, Jewish year, which is really our 1844.

Alexander Campbell's Position

In the same number of the paper it is stated of Alexander Campbell that, " in 1829 he had his celebrated debate with Robert Owen, the infidel, in which he contended that Daniel's visions extend to the end of time, that the twenty-three hundred days are years, and will end about 1847 years from the birth of Christ, which, according 'to his own showing. was four years before the common account." So his reckoning would actually end the twenty-three hundred days at the close of 1843 full Jewish years from the A. D. period — really 1844.

In the *Midnight Cry* of Sept. 21, 1843, is a statement
concerning a book received with this title, "A Voice to Britain and America, in a Scriptural statement of the second
advent of our Lord and Saviour, which we daily pray for,
saying, ' Thy kingdom come, thy will be done in earth as it
is in heaven,' [25] by Captain A. Landers, of Liverpool, published by S. Kent and Co., 1839."

" He, like the others, gives a calculation of the time,
giving the end of the twenty-three hundred days as 1847 years
from the actual birth of Christ." That would be our 1844,
as he was born four years before the common account. [26]

Leonard Heinrich Kelber

In the *Review and Herald* of May 17, 1892, is an article
from Pastor L. R. Conradi, of Hamburg, Germany, in which
he says : —

" The most of our readers have perhaps heard of the
noted Lutheran prelate Bengel, who in the last century [ac-
cording to Schaff, Bengel died in 1751], fixed the time of our
Lord's appearing in the year 1836, his calculations being
based on the number 666 in the Revelation. But long ere
this time expired, another man began to write, a chief school-
master, named Leonard Heinrich Kelber. His first pamphlet
appeared in 1824, called ' The End Near,' containing an exposition of Matthew 24 and 25. It was printed in Bavaria.
But in 1835 a larger pamphlet, with the same title, appeared
in Stuttgart, containing 126 pages. This will be of special
interest, and to give our readers a better idea, I add a translation of the title page : ' The End Comes, proven in a thorough and convincing manner from the word of God and the
latest events; invalidating totally all prejudice against waiting
for the coming of our Lord, or reckoning of the time; showing
plainly how prelate Bengel erred seven years in reference
to the great decisive year; for not 1836, but the year 1843,
is the terminus, at which the great struggle between light and

[25] Matt. 6: 10.   [26] Marginal date of Matt. 2: 1.

darkness will be finished, and the long-expected reign of peace of our Lord Jesus will commence on earth.'

"A second edition appeared in 1841, also in Stuttgart, and as far as I know another in Saxony. As the title page indicates, the pamphlet, after meeting the common prejudices, shows in a clear and explicit manner the existing connection between the twenty-three hundred days of Daniel 8 and the seventy weeks of Daniel 9, and brings them to the year 1843 (Jewish 1843 — ours 1844). Then in the remainder of the book he shows by the signs of the times that this event must be near.

" The fact that several editions appeared would alone testify to the interest it created. Brother Schäche, now living in Australia, saw an advertisement of it, even in the distant province of Silicia, and after ordering it, read it with great interest, behind locked doors. In the book no trace can be found that the author had any knowledge of any similar movement in the world, and yet by the Spirit of God he came to the same conclusions.

" In 1842 he wrote a still larger pamphlet of 286 pages, also at Stuttgart, on ' Cardinal and Scriptural Thoughts Concerning the Creation and Duration of the World; or a thorough answer to the question: Why God has created the world in six successive days — the nearness of our Lord to judge antichrist — the great and joyful events of the year 1843.' "

"Ben Ezra" (Laucunza)

About the year 1812, Laucunza, in Spain, published a book entitled, " The Coming of Messiah in Majesty and Glory." The writer assumed the anonymous title of " Ben Ezra," and is supposed to have been a converted Jew. Edward Irving, of England, after his work on the second advent was started, translated the above book into English. So it told its story in at least two languages.

It is truly interesting, after the lapse of years, to bring together the conclusions of the various students who, from the beginning of the last century down to 1840, reckoned out the period of twenty-three hundred days, and located the seventy weeks as the first part of that period, and then to find them all agree as to the termination of the period in 1844.

1844 the True Terminus of the 2300 Days

The question may arise, Can we rest assured that 1844 is the true date for the close of the twenty-three hundred days? Yes! For as surely as a false fulfilment of a prophecy cannot come in the right time for the true fulfilment, so surely must we come to the conclusion that the year 1844 is the correct terminus for the twenty-three hundred days. God, who sealed up that knowledge till 1798, and promised that *then* the light would shine out, by his unerring Spirit guided those who earnestly sought him for a correct understanding of the time. His time had come for "knowledge" on that subject to "be increased," and *he gave the true light.*

Having found the terminus of the time that was brought to the understanding of the people in the "time of the end," it is well to inquire as to the significance of that discovery. We find in that period, in the closing up of the gospel work, definite time is to be proclaimed for the session of the judgment. "And I saw," says John, "another angel fly in the midst of heaven, having the everlasting gospel to preach unto them that dwell on the earth, and to every nation, and kindred, and tongue, and people, saying with a loud voice, Fear God, and give glory to him; for the hour of his judgment is come: and worship him that made heaven, and earth, and the sea, and the fountains of waters." [27] Literal angels do not preach the gospel to men. Man is the agent chosen by the Lord himself to preach his gospel to the end of the world. [28] This angel, then, is a symbol of a gospel message which announces the time come for the judgment to "begin at the house of God." [29] Such a message could not be given from the Scriptures until the time that leads to the judgment was discovered in the Scriptures. The twenty-three-hundred-day

[27] Rev. 14: 6, 7.   [28] Matt. 28: 19, 20.   [29] 1 Peter 4: 17.

period, as already intimated, reaches to the investigative judgment of God's people.

The Day of Atonement a Time of Judgment

The day of atonement, the cleansing of the earthly sanctuary, was and is still understood by the Jews to be a day of judgment. And even now, in their scattered condition, though they cannot have all the service of the ancient time that was connected with that solemn day, it is observed as a day of judgment. In proof of this we will first quote from a Jewish paper published in San Francisco, California, called *The Jewish Exponent,* the organ of the orthodox Jews west of the Rocky Mountains. In the issue for September, 1892, was the announcement that before the issuing of the next number, the seventh month and day of atonement would come. Their name for the seventh month is *Tishree,* and that of the sixth is *Ellul;* so the paper stated, " The month of Ellul is here, and the monitory sounds of the *Shofar* [the trumpet that was to be blown from the first to the tenth day of the seventh month, Ps. 81 : 3, 4] are to be heard every morning in the orthodox synagogues, advising preparation for the day of memorial, and the *final judgment* of *Yom Kippur."* As they were in the close of *Ellul,* the sixth month, and *Tishree,* the seventh month, was about to open, they would, every morning for ten days, hear the trumpet announcing the *final judgment* of the year in that typical system.

Testimony of a Jewish Rabbi

Again, in the year 1902, Rabbi Isidore Myer, of a large congregation of Jews in San Francisco, Cal., in announcing the day of atonement, said: " While crossing the threshold of time from one year to another, the Israelite is forcibly reminded of the creation and of the universal sovereignty of the Creator, and is called upon to celebrate, with blast of trumpet, the anniversary, so to speak, of the birth of time and of the coronation of the great King. He is also sum-

moned by the voice of the same trumpet, or *Shofar,* to scruti-
nize retrospectively his actions of the past year while he
stands tremblingly before the all-seeing eye of Eternal Justice *sitting on the throne of judgment."*

As in the Jewish temple service the sanctuary was cleansed
once every year, it must have been apparent to Daniel that
this cleansing of the sanctuary at the end of the twenty-
three hundred days must relate to something besides the
yearly typical service. The Lord had already instructed his
people that, when using symbols in prophecy, the time given
should be counted "each day for a year." [30] So this period
of twenty-three hundred days, as we have seen, comes down
to the close of Christ's work as high priest in the heavenly
sanctuary — to the investigative judgment of those whose
cases, through confession, have been brought into the heavenly
sanctuary.

The Judgment Message Due in 1844

The period of time having been discovered when the
judgment of the saints would commence, the way was opened
so that, in the Lord's order of events, as marked in prophecy,
the message could be given, "The hour of his judgment is
come." Mark, it does not say that immediately on the discovery of that period of time the message would be proclaimed,
but that the light previously "sealed up" should be made
plain. We see clearly that this was accomplished. In succeeding chapters it will appear that the Lord just as definitely
marked the time when the advent message would be proclaimed, and just as literally was the proclamation given
to the world.

[30] Num. 14: 34; Eze. 4: 6.

CHAPTER V

THE SECOND ADVENT MESSAGE

OW learn a parable of the fig-tree: When his branch is yet tender, and putteth forth leaves, ye know that summer is nigh; so likewise ye, when ye shall see all these things, know that it [margin, he] is near, even at the doors. Verily I say unto you, This generation shall not pass, till all these things be fulfilled. Heaven and earth shall pass away, but my words shall not pass away." [1]

In this scripture our attention is directed to the *time* when it is possible to learn that the coming of Christ is " at the doors " with the same assurance that we *know* that summer is near when we see the first tender young leaves putting forth. It may also be known that we have come to the generation which shall not pass off the stage of action until Christ himself shall come. When the time comes to *learn* the parable, it is emphatically true that it is the Lord's time to raise up teachers to teach the parable. The inquiry of the apostle on another occasion is equally applicable here, " How shall they hear without a preacher? and how shall they preach, except they be sent? " [2]

The Time for the Signs

In the previous chapter we saw how knowledge was obtained concerning the termination of the twenty-three-hundred-day period, and that it extended to the " hour of his judgment." In the parable here introduced we are brought to the Lord's time for this parable and the " judgment "

[1] Matt. 24: 32 - 35.   [2] Rom. 10: 14, 15.

message to be proclaimed to the world. After speaking of the great " tribulation " which was to come upon his people which should be " shortened," the Saviour said, " Immediately after the tribulation of those days shall the sun be darkened, and the moon shall not give her light, and the stars shall fall from heaven, and the powers of the heavens shall be shaken: and then shall appear the sign of the Son of man in heaven." [3]

Mark, it does not say of the last sign mentioned that it is a sign of his coming; but a sign that the Son of man is there, is *seen* coming. The events given in this text as signs on which to base faith in his near coming, are the signs in the sun, moon, and stars. The other events which follow take place in connection with his actual coming in the clouds of heaven. So immediately after the third of these signs — the one in the stars — comes the Lord's time to raise up his teachers to teach that Christ's coming is at the doors.

Now as to the time of the appearance of these signs: It was to be *immediately* after the tribulation that the sun was to be darkened. [4] As Mark records, it was to be " in those days, *after* that tribulation." [5] Our Saviour had said that the days should be shortened. By the decree of Maria Theresa, and the Acts of Toleration from 1773 to 1776, the rage of persecution against the church was shortened. Although the persecuting power retained control of the civil arm until 1798, its persecutions were closed about 1773. Comparing the statements of the Saviour would place the first of these signs between 1773 and 1798.

The Dark Day and Night

On the 19th of May, 1780, the sun was supernaturally darkened. It was no eclipse, as the moon had fulled the day before. Notwithstanding this there was a darkness over all the northeastern portion of the United States from eleven o'clock in the morning until eleven o'clock at night. On that occasion not only was the sun darkened, but the moon refused

[3] Matt. 24: 29, 30.　　　[4] Matt. 24: 29.　　　[5] Mark 13: 24.

to reflect the light of the sun. It was a darkness that prevented the sun from shining on the disc of the moon. And as expressed by Noah Webster, many years after, "No satisfactory reason has ever been assigned for this darkness."

Of this dark day Herschel, the astronomer, said: "The Dark Day in North America was one of those wonderful phenomena of nature which will always be read of with interest, but which philosophy is at a loss to explain."

Those describing the darkness of the night of May 19, 1780, said, notwithstanding there was a full moon, that "if every luminous body in the universe had been struck out of existence, the darkness could not have been more complete."

The Falling Stars

The third of these signs, the falling of the stars, was fulfilled on the 13th of November, 1833. On that night, or rather from five hours previous to the day dawn, there was a meteoric shower compared by some to streams of fire coming down from heaven; by others, to sparks of fire flying off of some great piece of fire-works. This phenomenon covered all North America, from the Gulf of Mexico on the south to Hudson's Bay on the north, and from the Sandwich Islands on the west to within a few hundred miles of Liverpool on the east. Wherever observed, it was the same continuous shower of stars, falling as thick as snowflakes in a snow-storm.

Concerning this star shower in 1833, we further quote from the Connecticut *Observer* of Nov. 25, 1833: —

"The editor of the *Old Countryman* makes a very serious matter of the 'falling stars.' He says, 'We pronounce the rain of fire, which we saw on Wednesday morning last, an awful type, a sure forerunner, a merciful sign, of that great and dreadful day which the inhabitants of the earth will witness when the sixth seal shall be opened. The time is just at hand, described not only in the New Testament, but in the Old Testament; and a more correct picture of a fig-tree casting its fruit when blown by a mighty wind, it was not possible to behold."

Thomas Burnett's Prediction

The people had been taught by those of former times to look for a literal fulfilment of this sign. Thomas Burnett, in his "Theory of the Earth," printed in London, A. D. 1697, said of Matt. 24: 29:—

"No doubt there will be all sorts of fiery meteors at that time; and amongst others those called *falling stars,* which, though they are not considerable, singly, yet if they were multiplied in great numbers, falling, as the prophet says, as leaves from the vine or figs from the fig-tree, they would make an astonishing sight. . . . We need not look upon these things as hyperbolical and poetic strains, but as barefaced prophecies, and things that will *literally* come to pass."

Olmstead's Testimony Professor

Professor Olmstead, of Yale College, Mass., who has been called "America's greatest meteorologist," said of the falling stars of Nov. 13, 1833:—

"The extent of the shower of 1833 was such as to cover no inconsiderable part of the earth's surface, from the middle of the Atlantic on the east to the Pacific on the west; and from the northern coast of South America to undefined regions among the British possessions on the north. The exhibition of shooting stars was not only visible, but everywhere presented the same appearance."

Of this display, which began about 11 P. M., Nov. 12, and continued until about 4 A. M. of the 13th, the professor says:—

"Those who were so fortunate as to witness the exhibition of shooting stars on the morning of Nov. 13, 1833, probably saw the greatest display of celestial fire-works that has ever been seen since the creation of the world, or at least within the annals covered by the pages of history."

Star Shower Seen Also in Europe

In a book published by Leonard Heinrich Kelber, in Stuttgart, Germany, in the year 1835, we learn that this sign was repeated on that side of the Atlantic, in the same month, but a few days later. He says:—

"On November 25, 1833, there was a fine display of falling stars on the continent of Europe," and "in Minsterburg, Silesia, stars fell like a rain of fire. With them fell balls of fire, making the night so light that the people thought that the houses near them must be on fire.

"At the same time in Prin, Austria, there was a falling of stars that covered a space of over five hundred square miles. It was described by some as like streams of fire coming down from heaven. Some called it a rain of fire. Horses were frightened by it, and fell to the ground. Many people were made sick through fear."

Application of the Parable

Coming down in this line of prophecy past the fulfilment of the third sign,—the falling of the stars,—our Saviour says, "*Now* learn a parable of the fig-tree." This language does not apply to the generation that was living when our Lord gave this discourse, but to the generation that was to see these things *fulfilled*—not fulfilling, but *fulfilled!* The things to be fulfilled as tokens that Christ is at the door do not include the shaking of the heavens when he will be seen actually coming. These signs of his near coming include this third sign, the one in the stars. The Lord's appointed time for the people to learn a parable of the fig-tree dates this side of 1833. Here is the Lord's time for the world to be aroused to the great truth that his coming is at the doors, and that his coming will be before the generation who hear that parable shall pass away. So we see how the time is marked out in this prophecy when the great advent proclamation should be given to the world.

7

A World-wide Proclamation

In fulfilment of this prediction we find that right then and there in 1833, the Lord was raising up his messengers or ministers in various parts of the world, who from 1833 to 1844 sounded the cry of Christ's coming near, "even at the doors;" and these taught the parable of the fig-tree, pointing to these signs of his coming, even as he had instructed them to do. This message, either by the living teacher or through the agency of the printed page, went to every missionary station in the world, and to every seaport on the earth.

The extent of the message has been plainly set forth by the editor of the *Voice of Truth,* of Rochester, N. Y., in an issue of January, 1845:—

"The everlasting gospel, as described in Rev. 14:6, 7, has been preached to every nation, kindred, tongue, and people; saying with a loud voice, 'Fear God, and give glory to him; for the hour of his judgment is come: and worship him that made heaven, and earth, and the sea, and the fountains of waters.' No case can be more clearly substantiated with facts than that this message has been borne to every nation and tongue under heaven, within a very few years past, in the preaching of the coming of Christ in 1843 [1843, Jewish time — our time, 1844], or near at hand. Through the medium of lectures and publications, the sound has gone into all the earth, and the words to the end of the world."

Some people, unacquainted with the facts, have looked upon the second advent movement as limited to a certain locality, supposing it a work connected with William Miller and a few hundred ministers associated with him in the northern portion of the United States. To such it may be a surprise to learn that the movement in America, in which Elders Miller and Himes were prominent leaders, was but a small part of a great movement that, as stated above, went "to the ends of the earth."

HOW THE MOVEMENT STARTED IN VARIOUS NATIONS

The Lord's time came for this proclamation to go forth to the world, and in a score or more of different parts of the earth, at about the same time, men were raised up, who, without a knowledge of one another's work, went forth to sound this message to all parts of the earth. Those mentioned in chapter IV, who received the light respecting the close of the twenty-three hundred days, with one exception,— A. Campbell,— were moved upon to engage in the proclamation of the first angel's message of Revelation 14; this also by direct agency of the Spirit of God, and not by communicating the light to one another.

Compared with the Reformation

If we apply the same rule to this movement that D'Aubigne applied to the rise of the great Reformation of the sixteenth century, it must surely be counted as the Lord's message and in the Lord's time. Of that Reformation as a whole the historian said:—

"Germany did not communicate the truth to Switzerland, nor Switzerland to France, nor France to England. All these countries received it from God, just as one part of the world does not transmit the light to another part; but the same shining globe communicates it directly to all the earth. Christ, *the day spring from on high,* infinitely exalted above all mankind, was, at the period of the Reformation, as at the establishment of Christianity, the divine fire which gave life to the world. In the sixteenth century, one and the same doctrine was at once established in the homes and churches of the most distant and diversified nations. The reason is, that the same Spirit was everywhere at work producing the same faith.

"The Reformation of Germany and that of Switzerland demonstrate this truth. Zwingle had no intercourse with Luther. There was, no doubt, a link between these two men; but we must search for it above the earth. He who from heaven gave the truth to Luther, gave it to Zwingle. God was the medium of communication between them. ' I began to preach the gospel,' says Zwingle. ' in the year of grace 1516, in other words, at a time when the name of Luther had never been heard of in our country. I did not learn the doctrine of Christ from Luther, but from the word of God. If Luther preaches Christ, he does what I do; that is all.' " [6]

Speaking of the work of Farel and Lefevre in France, the historian says —

" The Reformation in France, therefore, was not a foreign importation. It had its birth on the French soil; it germinated in Paris; it had its first roots in the university itself, which formed the second power in Roman Christendom. God placed the principles of the work in the honest hearts of men of Picardy and Dauphiny before its commencement in any other country.

" We have seen that the Swiss Reformation was independent of the German Reformation. The French Reformation was in its turn independent of both. The work began at once in these different countries, without any communication with each other; as, in a battle, all the different forces comprising the army move at the same instant, though the one does not tell the other to march, because one and the same command, proceeding from the same Commander-in-Chief, is heard by all. The time was accomplished, the people were prepared, and God began the Reformation of his church in all countries at once. Such facts demonstrate that the great Reformation of the sixteenth century was a divine work." [7]

Of the Reformation in England, under Thos. Bilney, Fryth, Tyndale, and others, D'Aubigne further says:—

" The Reformation of England commenced, therefore, independently of Luther and Zwingle, holding solely from

[6] " History of the Reformation," Book viii, chap. 1, pars. 2, 3.
[7] *Ibid.*, Book xii, chap. 3, par. 10.

God. There was in all these countries of Christendom a simultaneous action of the divine word. The origin of the Reformation at Oxford, Cambridge, London, was the Greek New Testament published by Erasmus. [Tyndale and Thomas Bilney quitted Cambridge in the year 1519.] There came a day when England was proud of this high origin of the Reformation." [8]

The advent proclamation arose in a similar manner to that above traced in the Reformation. Men were moved out simultaneously in more than four times as many parts of the world, with no knowledge of, or any communication of sentiment with, one another, and began the proclamation of the same Scripture truths, not simply in *four* nations of the earth, but to the whole civilized world.

Joseph Wolff's Labors

It may be well at this point to call attention to facts respecting the extent of the advent proclamation:—

"In 1831 Joseph Wolff, D. D., was sent as a missionary from Great Britain to labor among the Jews of Palestine. He, according to his journals, down to the year 1845, proclaimed the Lord's speedy advent in Palestine, Egypt, on the shores of the Red Sea, Mesopotamia, the Crimea, Persia, Georgia, throughout the Ottoman Empire, in Greece, Arabia, Turkey, Bokhara, Afghanistan, Cashmere, Hindostan, Thibet, in Holland, Scotland, Ireland, at Constantinople, Jerusalem, St. Helena, also on shipboard in the Mediterranean, and in New York City, to all denominations. He declares that he has preached among Jews, Turks, Mohammedans, Parsees, Hindoos, Chaldeans, Yesedes, Syrians, Sabeans, to pashas sheiks, shahs, the kings of Organtsh and Bokhara, the queen of Greece, etc." [9]

In Yemen, the region inhabited by the descendants of Hobab, Moses' father-in-law, Joseph Wolff saw a book of which he thus speaks: "The Arabs of this place have a book

[8] "History of the Reformation," Book xviii, chap. 2, par. 12.
[9] "Voice of the Church," p. 343.

called ' Seera,' which treats of ' The Second Coming of Christ, and His Reign in Glory!' " [10]

In Yemen he spent six days with the Rechabites, of whom he says: " They drink no wine, plant no vineyards, sow no seed, live in tents, and remember the words of Jonadab the son of Rechab. With them were children of Israel, of the tribe of Dan, who reside near Terim in Hatramawt, who expect, in common with the children of Rechab, the speedy arrival of the Messiah in the clouds of heaven."

We see, from the above, that in those fourteen years, Wolff himself had proclaimed the news of Christ's coming at the doors, in more than twenty different nations. During the same time the doctrine was extensively agitated in Germany, particularly in the South among the Moravians.

The Message in Germany- and Russia

An English writer, Mourant Brock, informs us that " in Wurtemberg. there was a Christian colony numbering hundreds, who looked for the speedy advent of Christ." The doctrine was proclaimed in other parts of Germany by Hengstenberg, at that time said to be the most talented theologian in Germany.

In the *Review and Herald* of Dec. 13, 1892, Pastor L. R. Conradi of Germany says:—

" Bengel, in Germany, kindled the love for the appearing of our Lord in many a heart, which led thousands to study the prophetic word as never before. . . . The light shone in Germany, and publications showing the application of the twenty-three hundred days were circulated there. A religious awakening followed, especially in Wurtemburg, and as persecution arose, hundreds of families went to Southern Russia, and there spread it among their own countrymen who had moved there many years before. As the pastors closed their churches, with very few exceptions they would hold their ' stunden,' or ' hour ' of meetings, in private houses, and hundreds were converted. Even at that time the Sabbath was

[10] Wolff's " Mission to Bokhara."

discussed among them, but no one making a start, it was smothered. A Russian farmer was converted in the 'stunden,' and then began the same work among the Russians. This finally led to the great ' Stundist' movement of the present day, whose influence extends to the most distant corner of Siberia and the Trans-Caucassus."

In the *Review and Herald* of July 31, 1891, is a statement from Pastor Conradi respecting Brother Schäche of Australia, who, at the time of which he speaks, was a resident of Silesia, and labored a part of the time in the interest of the home mission of Father Gosner, a noted German evangelist divine. From Brother Schäche he gives the following respecting Kelber's book: —

" After 1836, or when Bengel's Computation had expired, there appeared in the Schweidnitz county paper a notice from the bookstore of Mr. Sommerfeldt there, concerning a book from L. Henry Kelber, concerning the great and glad events which were to take place in the years 1843 and 1844. The exact title of the book I do not remember. We procured the said book, and read it with a number of interested persons, with locked doors, in the year 1839 - 40. The book showed from Daniel, and the Revelation, and Matthew 24, that the end was at hand, and had also a table of computation, showing how the above date was reached."

The Message in Great Britain

In an English publication entitled " The Millennium," it is stated that " seven hundred ministers of the Church of England were raising the cry of the return of the Redeemer." Among some of the most talented ministers of the time were those who proclaimed the advent doctrine in England from 1840 to 1844. Of these we will mention the names of Bickersteth, Birks, Brooks, Brock, Habershon, Plyn, Fremantle, Nathan Lord, McNeil, Winters, Cummings, J. A. McCaul. D. D.. Dr. Nisbett, Rev. A. Dallas, M. A. [in his book, " Look to Jerusalem," page 114, he applies the parable of

Matthew 24 to this generation], Burgess, Routon, Gunner, Barker, Bonham, Dealtry, etc.

The Message in Holland

The doctrine of the second advent was proclaimed in Holland by Hentzepeter, said to have been, at that time, the ablest minister in that country. He was keeper of the Royal Museum at The Hague, under the appointment of the king. He says of himself, in a letter written to the editor of the *Midnight Cry,* in June, 1844, that his attention was first called to the subject by a very impressive dream. He investigated the Scriptures on the subject, and in the year 1830 published a pamphlet setting forth the doctrine. In 1841 he published another pamphlet on the end of the world. In the same letter he says the first information he received in regard to William Miller and others who were proclaiming publicly the doctrine of the near approach of Christ, was in 1842, by conversing with a man who came to Holland from America.

The Message in Tartary

As early as 1821 the doctrine of the Lord's coming was believed and taught in Tartary. About this time an Irish missionary was sent to that country, and a Tartar priest put the question to him, " When will Christ come the second time? " He made answer that he knew nothing at all about it, whereupon the priest expressed great surprise at such an answer from a missionary who had come to teach them the doctrines of the Bible, and remarked that he thought " everybody might know that who had a Bible." The priest then gave his views, stating that he thought Christ would come about A. D. 1844. This fact is found in the *Irish Magazine,* 1821.

The Message in America, India, and on the Continent

In " Advent Tracts," Vol. II, page 135, 1844, Mourant Brock of England says: —

"It is not merely in Great Britain that the expectation of the near return of the Redeemer is entertained, and the voice of warning raised, but also in America, India, and on the continent of Europe. In America, about three hundred ministers of the word are thus preaching 'this gospel of the kingdom;' whilst in this country, about seven hundred of the Church of England are raising the same cry."

To Every Seaport on Earth

E. R. Pinney, of Seneca Falls, N. Y., a devoted Baptist minister who gave his life to the proclamation of the advent doctrine, in his "Exposition of Matthew 24," pages 8, 9, said: —

"As early as 1842. second advent publications had been sent to every missionary station in Europe, Asia, Africa, and America, both sides of the Rocky Mountains. . . . The commanders of our vessels and the sailors tell us that they touch at no port where they find this proclamation has not preceded them, and frequent inquiries respecting it are made of them."

Three Thousand Proclaiming the Message

Pastor G. W. Mitchel, of Zanesville, Ohio, another minister who himself proclaimed the doctrine, said to the writer in a conversation at Newark, Ohio, Aug. 8, 1894, that Elder William Miller told him, in a conversation at McConnellsville, Ohio, in September, 1844, that he had the " names and addresses of three thousand ministers in various parts of the globe who were proclaiming, 'Fear God, and give glory to him; for the hour of his judgment is come,' the greater portion of these being in North America and Great Britain."

William Miller, in speaking of the extensive spread of this " cry," said: —

"One or two in every quarter of the globe have proclaimed the news, and *all agree* in the *time*,— Wolff of Asia; Irving, late of England; Mason of Scotland; Davis of South

Carolina; and quite a number in this region, are, or have been, giving the cry." [11]

Hutchinson's "Voice of Elijah" Sent Broadcast

Elder R. Hutchinson, in 1837, was sent from England as a Wesleyan missionary to Canada. He finally settled in Montreal. He had a very extensive acquaintance in foreign countries. In the years 1843 and 1844 he published a paper called the *Voice of Elijah*, in which he treated of the advent doctrine. Having ready access to vessels for foreign countries, and being privileged to send large parcels of his papers with no expense for postage, he sent them in great quantities to all parts of the earth. He said of his own work, that he sent them freely to Nova Scotia, New Brunswick, New Foundland, England, Ireland, Scotland, Wales, France, Germany, Constantinople, Rome, and all parts of the British kingdom and its colonies.

In the Sandwich Islands

In the *Midnight Cry* of Oct. 12, 1843, was a letter from a Mrs. O. S. Burnham, of Kaloa, Isle of Kaui, Sandwich Islands. She, with her husband, were school teachers at that place. They accepted, and were proclaiming, the advent doctrine there, and a company of believers was worshiping with them on the islands.

The Message Compared with that of John the Baptist

Thus we see that the advent doctrine was proclaimed to an extent quite sufficient to fulfil the scripture predictions concerning it.

The message which was to herald the first advent of Christ was stated by the prophet Isaiah in these words: "The voice of him that crieth in the wilderness, Prepare ye the way of the Lord, make straight in the desert a highway for our God. Every valley shall be exalted, and every mountain and hill shall be made low: and the crooked shall be

[11] " William Miller's Lectures," p. 238, 1843.

made straight, and the rough places plain: and the glory
of the Lord shall be revealed, and all flesh shall see it together :
for the mouth of the Lord hath spoken it." [12]   This prophecy
was accomplished in the labors of " John the Baptist, preaching in the wilderness of Judea, and saying, Repent ye: for the
kingdom of heaven is at hand." [13]

This man, alone, during six months of labor in the one
country of Judea, fulfilled this wonderful prediction.   While
this prophecy limited John's work as to time and place, it
is not so with those prophecies which relate to the heralding
of the second advent, ·for the work was to be with a " *loud
cry,*" world wide in its extent.

Thus it is seen, in the light of the facts presented, how
accurately prophecy concerning the advent message was fulfilled.   God's time came for the parable of the fig-tree to be
taught, for the first announcement of the first angel's message
to be given, and he raised up his messengers to herald the cry
to all nations, peoples, and tongues.

[12] Isa. 40: 3 - 5.   [13] Matt. 3: 1, 2.

CHAPTER VI

THE MESSAGE AND THE MESSENGERS

"RITE the vision, and make it plain upon tables, that he may run that readeth it. For the vision is yet for an appointed time, but at the end it shall speak, and not lie: though it tarry, wait for it; because it will surely come, it will not tarry." [1]

"And I saw another angel fly in the midst of heaven, having the everlasting gospel to preach unto them that dwell on the earth, and to every nation, and kindred, and tongue, and people, saying with a loud voice, Fear God, and give glory to him; for the hour of his judgment is come: and worship him that made heaven, and earth, and the sea, and the fountains of waters." [2]

Those who gave the advent proclamation claimed that this "vision" with its "appointed" time, mentioned by the prophet Habakkuk, included the visions of the prophecies of Daniel and the Revelator. These they made so plain in their delineations of them upon their prophetic charts, that he who read the interpretation could indeed "run" and impart the information to others.

A Definite Message

The proclamation by the Adventist people was not simply the announcement made by Paul before Felix, "Righteousness, temperance, and judgment *to come;*" nor was it the statement made by Martin Luther, after having completed the translation of the Bible, when, a short time before his death,

[1] Hab. 2: 2, 3.　　　[2] Rev. 14: 6, 7.

he is reported to have said, " I am persuaded that the judgment is not far off; yea, that the Lord himself will not be
absent above *three hundred years* longer." Neither was it
the statement made by John Wesley, when he said he
" thought the millennium might commence in about *one hundred years.*" The Adventists claimed to be giving the message
symbolized in Rev. 14:6, 7, " The *hour* of his judgment is
come," and the cry of Rev. 10:6, " Time shall be no longer."
Such a prophecy could not be accomplished by an announcement of an event that was " *to come,*" coming " in *three hundred years,*" or " in *one hundred years,*" but in definite time,
" *is come.*" Just such a message, with just such definiteness as
that demanded by the above prophecies, was heralded by the
Adventist people to the whole world.

The Judgment at Christ's Coming

At the time this message was first announced, every Christian denomination held that the judgment would take place
at the second coming of Christ. So a people under those
circumstances, giving the message of the hour of judgment
come, while holding that view, would necessarily proclaim the
second coming of Christ. In fact, that which gave force to
the message, and most mightily moved the people, was the
proclamation of definite time. First they claimed that the
end of the world would come some time during the " Jewish
year " 1843, and that this was embraced in the time between
March 21, 1843, and March 21, 1844. After this time passed
by, we learn in the *Midnight Cry* of the year 1844 that the
definite day was fixed upon for the termination of the prophetic times. This was the tenth day of the seventh Jewish
month, corresponding to Oct. 22, 1844.

Reckoning of the 2300 Days

The basis of the time — 1843 — was the twenty-three
hundred days of Daniel 8. It was claimed that as these
" days " were connected with prophecies where beasts were

chosen to represent kingdoms, "days" must be used sym-
bolically to represent years, according to the Lord's interpretation of symbolic time, as given in Num. 14:34 and Eze.
4:5, 6; that the seventy weeks — 490 days — of Daniel 9 were
to be the first part of the twenty-three hundred days, and that
the two periods began together. The event given in Daniel
9, which marked the beginning of the seventy weeks, was the
" going forth of the commandment to restore and build Jerusalem." That commandment went forth in the seventh year
of Artaxerxes Longimanus, 457 B. C., as recorded in Ezra 7.

That this was the true date for the beginning of the
seventy weeks was demonstrated by the fact that in just
sixty-nine weeks — 483 years — from 457 B. C., or in A. D.
27, Christ was baptized by John and entered upon his ministry, saying, " The time is fulfilled," [3] etc. The opening of
the ministry of Christ, A. D. 27, his crucifixion three and one-
half years from that date, " in the midst [middle] of the
[seventieth] week," the close of the special work among the
Jews, A. D. 34, and the speedy conversion of Saul, the apostle
to the Gentiles, proved that the seventy weeks did terminate at
that date, and therefore that they began B. C. 457. They figured
the matter out thus: From 2300 take 457, and there remains
1843. And as the 457 years were before Christ, we are
brought for the close of the 2300 days to the close of 1843.

Admissions of Opponents

It has been truthfully said that " admissions in favor of
truth from the ranks of its opponents furnish the highest
kind of evidence." None of the opponents of the advent message ever intimated that the investigative judgment of the
Lord's people was an event to take place before Christ's
coming; but reasoned on this point in harmony with the Adventists. As proof of this statement we quote from two
prominent opponents.

Mr. N. Colver, preaching in Marlboro Street Chapel,
Boston, in 1842, in opposition to Adventists, said: —

[3] Mark 1: 14, 15.

"If these days are years, the world will end in 1843; any school boy can see it; for if 490 terminated at the death of Christ, the 2300 days would terminate in 1843; and the world must end, unless it can be shown that some other event is to take place, and I do not see how that can be done."

Professor Stuart, about the same time, said: "It is a singular fact that the great mass of interpreters in the English and American world have, for many years, been wont to understand the *days* designated in Daniel and the Apocalypse as the representation, or symbols, of *years*. I have found it difficult to trace the origin of this general, I might say almost universal, custom."

Professor Bush's Testimony

Professor Bush said: "Whoever attacks Mr. Miller on his point of *time,* attacks him on his strongest point. His time is right; but he is mistaken in the event to occur." Bush was a believer in the conversion of the whole world before the coming of Christ. His theory was that the millennium would begin in 1844.

The ministers of the advent faith taught in their public discourses that the world's history showed the various nations to be in just the condition symbolized by the image of Daniel 2, when the stone was to smite the image on the feet, and the God of heaven set up his kingdom; and in chapter 7, when "the kingdom and dominion and greatness of the kingdom under the whole heaven shall be given to the saints of the Most High." They also called attention to the fact that the signs — physical, political, and moral — were just what the Scriptures foretold would be seen when the Lord was about to appear.

Wonders in the Heavens

The Lord through the prophet Joel says: "I will show wonders in the heavens and in the earth, blood, and fire, and

pillars of smoke. The sun shall be turned into darkness, and
the moon into blood, before the great and terrible day of the
Lord come." [4] The Adventists believed and taught that
the aurora borealis of the last centuries (commonly called
northern lights) was the "fire and pillars of smoke" that
meets the specification of the prophet; and from the best information to be obtained from history (we refer to the Edinburg
Encyclopedia as testimony), it had rarely been seen previous
to this period.

So, while the message of the Lord's speedy coming was
going to the remotest parts of the earth, signs were hung out
in the heavens which gave edge to the truth, and arrested the
attention of the people.

On Jan. 25, 1837, there was a most magnificent display
of the fiery aurora borealis, which seemed to lead the
minds of many directly to the prophet Joel's prediction
of what was to precede the great day of the Lord. The
following description of the scene is from the New York
Commercial Advertiser of Oct. 22, 1839. It agrees exactly
with the scene as the writer witnessed it in Victor, Ontario
County, N. Y.

The Fiery Aurora of 1837

"On the evening of Jan. 25, 1837, there was a remarkable exhibition of the same phenomena [meaning the aurora
borealis] in various parts of the country, as our readers will
doubtless recollect. Where the ground was covered with
snow, the sight was grand and 'fearful' in a most unpre-
cedented manner. In one place, situated near a mountain,
the people who witnessed the scene, informed us that it
resembled 'waves of fire rolling down the mountain,' and
generally, so far as learned, the snow covering the ground
appeared like fire mingled with blood, while above (as the
apostle says), 'the heavens being on fire,' resembled so much
the prophetic description of the last day that many were
amazed; the children beholding it were affrighted, and in-

[4] Joel 2: 30, 31.

quired if it were the coming of the judgment; and even the animals trembled with much manifest alarm."

It was not alone in America that this sign of the prophet Joel was displayed, but as the doctrine of the Lord's coming was gaining publicity in Great Britain, the same sign was hung out in the heavens in that country. The New York *Commercial Advertiser* of Oct. 22, 1839, quotes the following from London papers concerning a remarkable phenomenon witnessed in that country on the night of September 3: —

The Aurora of 1839

"LONDON, SEPT. 5 [1839].— Between the hours of ten on Thursday night and three yesterday morning, in the heavens was observed one of the most magnificent specimens of these extraordinary phenomena, the falling stars and northern lights, witnessed for many years past. The first indication of this singular phenomenon was ten minutes before ten, when a light crimson, apparently vapor, rose from the northern portion of the hemisphere, and gradually extended to the center of the heavens, and by ten o'clock or a quarter past, the whole, from east to west, was one vast sheet of light. It had a most alarming appearance, and was exactly like that occasioned by a terrific fire. The light varied considerable; at one time it seemed to fall, and directly after rose with intense brightness. There were to be seen mingled with it volumes of smoke, which rolled over and over, and every beholder seemed convinced that it was 'a tremendous conflagration.'

"The consternation of the metropolis was very great; thousands of persons were running in the direction of the supposed awful catastrophe. The engines belonging to the fire brigade stations in Baker Street, Farringdon Street, Watling Street, Waterloo Road, and likewise those belonging to the west of London stations — in fact, every fire engine in London, was horsed and galloped after the supposed 'scene of destruction' with more than ordinary energy, followed by carriages, horsemen, and vast mobs. Some of the engines proceeded as far as High Gate and Halloway [about four miles] before the error was discovered. These appearances lasted for upwards of two hours, and toward morning the spectacle became one of grandeur.

"At two o'clock in the morning the phenomenon presented a most gorgeous scene, and one very difficult to describe. The whole of London was illuminated as light as noon-day, and the atmosphere was remarkably clear. The southern hemisphere, at the time mentioned, though unclouded, was very dark; but the stars, which were innumerable, shone beautifully. The opposite side of the heavens presented a singular but magnificent contrast; it was clear to extreme, and the light was very vivid; there was a continual succession of meteors, which varied in splendor — they appeared formed in the center of the heavens, and spread till they seemed to burst. The effect was electrical. Myriads of small stars shot out over the horizon, and darted with such swiftness toward the earth that the eye could scarcely follow the track; they seemed to burst also, and throw a dark crimson vapor over the entire hemisphere. The colors were most magnificent.

"At half past two o'clock the spectacle changed to darkness, which, on dispersing, displayed a luminous rainbow in the zenith of the heavens, and round the ridge of darkness that overhung the southern portion of the country. Soon afterward columns of silvery light radiated from it. They increased wonderfully, intermingled among crimson vapor which formed at the same time, and when at full height the spectacle was beyond all imagination. Stars were darting about in all directions, and continued until four o'clock, when all died away."

Strange Appearances in the Sun

While the living preachers were setting forth the truth of the Lord's coming, many and varied wonders in the heavens were seen in various parts of the world. Of these our space

will permit only the representation of the appearance
of the sun in Norwich, England, in December, 1843. A
similar one occurred in New Haven, Conn., Sept. 9, 1844, for
two hours before and after noon, and was witnessed by
thousands of people.

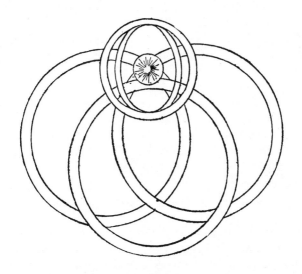

STRANGE APPEARANCE OF THE SUN.

The small inner circle represents the sun. It was of a light orange hue. The outer part of
the two circles at unequal distances from and surrounding the sun, appeared of the same hue ; but
the inner part of these circles was a deep yellow, the sky within those circles appearing of a dusky
brown color, and the three large circles passing through and below the sun, appeared as of distinct
bright light.

Of the occurrence in England we read, in a letter from
E. Lloyd, London, Jan. 3, 1844, as follows:—

"There has been a remarkable ' sign in the sun,' seen by
the principal citizens of Norwich and the surrounding country, such as has never been seen in England before. It was
seen in December last, about 12 o'clock at noon, and continued
for two hours. It very much alarmed the inhabitants. It
occurred just before Brethren Winter, Burgess, and Routon

opened their mission in that city. It seemed to prepare the way for the truth, so that they met with good success there."

The account of the phenomenon as it occurred in New Haven, Conn., is given in the *Midnight Cry* of Oct. 10, 1844, and was taken from the New Haven *Palladium* of Sept. 10, 1844. In the account in the *Cry* the editor says, "No philosopher has been able to give an explanation of the cause of this phenomenon which satisfies himself."

An account of this sight which appeared in connection with the sun in New Haven, Conn., Sept. 9, 1844, was also published in the Hartford *Courant* of Sept. 12, 1844, and reads as follows: —

"The rings around the sun on Monday, Sept. 9, 1844, for two hours before and after midday, appear to have been generally observed by our citizens with much interest, and have awakened an intelligent curiosity to learn more respecting appearances of the same kind and their cause.

"The present halo was remarkable for its duration, and afforded favorable opportunities for observation. About midday it consisted chiefly of two complete rings, one about forty-five degrees in breadth, encircling the sun at its center, and the other about seventy-two degrees broad, having its center in the zenith, while its circumference passed through the sun. The smaller circle was accompanied by an ellipse of the major axis, and of small eccentricity. Directly opposite the sun, and thirty-six degrees north of the zenith, the large circle was intersected by two other circles of nearly or quite the same diameter, forming at the point of intersection a bright spot, such as would naturally result from the combined light of three luminous rings. The ring that encircled the sun exhibited the colors of the rainbow, frequently with much vividness and beauty. The other rings were white and fainter, as they were more distant from the sun. Small portions of circles, however, with prismatic [rainbow] hues, appeared at different times, both in the east and west. . . . Such uniformity of structure must depend on *some law* which regulates the formation of halos; but the nature of the law is not fully developed. . . . Not much difficulty has been experienced in accounting for the production of the ring that encircles the sun, since the cause is somewhat similar to that which produces the rainbow, but to explain the origin of the ring which has its circumference in the sun's center, has been found more difficult."

Wonders Fulfilling Scripture Predictions

Of the use that was made, both in England and America, of these wonders seen in the heavens, we may learn by reading from the " Exposition of the Twenty-fourth of Matthew " by Sylvester Bliss, published in Boston in 1843. After quoting some of the above accounts, he says: —

" Thus the ' great signs ' and ' fearful sights ' that are predicted in the Scriptures of truth, seem to be all fulfilled, as well as those which the Saviour declared should precede his coming.

" As sure as the leaving out of the trees is an indication of summer, just so sure, on the fulfilment of these signs, are Christians to know that the coming of Christ is near, even at the doors. It is not a mere permission to know it, but our Saviour commands them to know it." [5]

THE MESSENGERS

Having called attention to some of the leading features of the second advent message, as first proclaimed, it may be of interest to notice a few of those who acted a prominent part in the great proclamation. We have already given the names of many who were among the most talented ministers of that time in foreign lands who gave the cry. As we call attention to some of those who led out in America, upon whom the Lord laid the burden of the work, it will serve to illustrate still further that the Lord's hand was indeed in the movement.

[5] " Exposition of the Twenty-Fourth of Matthew," pp. 49 - 60. S. Bliss, Boston, Mass., 1843.

William Miller

First we will note ,the case of William Miller, who was so prominent in the advent movement in the United States that with many the movement is only known as " *Millerism.*"

William Miller was born in Pittsfield, Mass., in February, 1782. In his early childhood, marks of more than ordinary intellectual strength and activity were manifested. A few years made these marks more and more noticeable to all who were in his society. He possessed a strong physical constitution, an active and naturally well-developed intellect, an irreproachable moral character. He had enjoyed the limited advantages of the district school but a few years before it was generally admitted that his attainments exceeded those of the teachers usually employed.

Mr. Miller married in 1802, and settled in Poultney, Vt. The men with whom he associated from the time of his removal to Poultney, and to whom he was considerably indebted for his worldly favors, were deeply affected with skeptical principles and deistic theories. They were not immoral men. but as a class were good citizens, and generally of serious deportment, humane, and benevolent. However, they rejected the Bible as the standard of religious truth, and endeavored to make its rejection plausible with such aid as could be obtained from the writings of Voltaire. Hume, Volney, Paine, Ethan Allen, and others. Mr. Miller studied these works closely, and at length avowed himself a deist. He has stated himself that his deistical life covered a period of twelve years, beginning about 1804.

Receiving a captain's commission, he entered the army in 1810. On his return from the army, he moved his family to Low Hampton, N. Y., to begin there the occupation of farming in 1812. As a farmer, he had more leisure for reading. He found that his deistical views gave him no assurance of happiness beyond the present life. Beyond the grave all was dark and gloomy. To use his own words: " Annihilation was a cold and chilling thought, and accountability was sure destruction to all. The heavens were as brass over my head, and the earth as iron under my feet. *Eternity! — what was it? And death! — why was it?* The more I reasoned, the further I was from demonstration. The more I thought, the more scattered were my conclusions. I tried to stop thinking, but my thoughts would not be controlled. I was truly wretched, but did not understand *the cause.* . . . Soon after, suddenly the character of the Saviour was vividly impressed upon my mind. It seemed there might be a being so good and compassionate as to himself atone for our transgressions, and thereby save us from suffering the penalty of sin. I immediately felt how lovely such a being must be; and imagined that I could cast myself into the arms of, and trust in the mercy of, such an one."

William Miller's Conversion

He further said: "I saw that the Bible did bring to view just such a Saviour as I needed; and I was perplexed to find how an uninspired book should develop principles so perfectly adapted to the wants of a fallen world. I was constrained to admit that the Scriptures must be a revelation from God. They became my delight; and in Jesus I found a friend. . . . The Bible now became my chief study, and I can truly say, I searched it with great delight. I found the half was never told me. I wondered why I had not seen its beauty and glory before, and marveled that I could have ever rejected it."

William Miller's manner of studying the Bible is thus described by himself: "I determined to lay aside all my prepossessions, to thoroughly compare scripture with scripture, and to pursue its study in a regular, methodical manner. . . . Whenever I found anything obscure, my practice was to compare it with all collateral passages; and, by the help of Cruden, I examined all the texts of scripture in which were found any of the prominent words contained in any obscure portion. . . . In this way I pursued the study of the Bible, in my first perusal of it, for about two years, and was fully satisfied that it is its own interpreter.

"While thus studying, I became satisfied if the prophecies which have been fulfilled in the past are any criterion by which to judge of the manner of the fulfilment of those which are yet future, that the popular views of the spiritual reign of Christ — a temporal millennium before the end of the world, and the Jews' return — are not sustained by the word of God. . . . I found it plainly taught in the Scriptures that Jesus Christ will again descend to this earth, coming in the clouds of heaven, in all the glory of his Father.

"I felt a delight in studying the Scriptures which I had not before supposed could be derived from its teachings. I commenced their study with no expectation of finding the time of the Saviour's coming, and I could at first hardly believe the result to which I had arrived; but the evidence struck me with such force that I could not resist my convictions. I became nearly settled in my conclusions, and began to wait, and watch, and pray for the Saviour's coming."

Again he says: "I believed; and immediately the duty to publish this doctrine, that the world might believe and get ready to meet the Judge and Bridegroom at his coming, was impressed upon my mind. I need not here go into a detailed account of my long and sore trials. Suffice it to say, that after a number of years I was compelled by the Spirit of God, the power of truth, and the love of souls, to take up my cross and proclaim these things to a dying and perishing world."

Mr. Miller, like those moved out by this message in other countries, first thought to fulfil his commission by writing and publishing in the public journals and in pamphlets. He first published his views in the *Vermont Telegraph*, a Baptist paper, printed in Brandon, Vt. This was in the year 1831. He first spoke in public on the subject in the year 1832. He said of this meeting, "The Lord poured his grace on the congregation, and many believed to the salvation of their souls."

In 1836 his lectures were printed in some of the public journals of the day. In the winter of 1837 - 38 his lectures were issued in a pamphlet. In 1838 a second pamphlet of 204 pages was printed, and in this pamphlet Mr. Miller stated that the Ottoman power *might* fall in the year 1839 or 1840. His first lectures in any of the large cities were in the year 1836. He then spoke in the cities of Randolph, Lowell, Gratton, and Lynn, Mass.

Down to 1840 Mr. Miller stood almost alone as a public speaker on the theme of the near advent of Christ. In that year, suddenly, hundreds joined him in proclaiming the message. What produced this great change will be noted in the following chapter. In the winter of 1839 - 40 Mr. Miller gave a series of lectures in Exeter, N. H. He there first met Elder J. V. Himes, who at that time accepted the faith, and from that date stood side by side with Elder Miller as publisher and ardent preacher of the great second advent message.

Joshua V. Himes

Concerning this earnest worker in this great movement we cannot do better than to quote from his biographer, who says :—

" Joshua V. Himes was born at Wickford, R. I., May 19, 1805. His father was well known as a West India trader, and was prominent as a member of St. Paul's Episcopal church in Wickford. His mother possessed an amiable disposition, and a love for the Saviour, which she poured into the willing ears of her son.

" It had been the intention of the father to educate his son, Joshua, to the ministry of the church to which he belonged himself, but circumstances prevented it. God had another work for that son to do, and he was ordering things in that way which should bring about the desired result.

In 1817 the father sent out a valuable cargo in charge of Captain Carter, with Alexander Stewart as supercargo. These men proved unfaithful, and having reached a West Indian port, sold both vessel and cargo, and fled. This event changed all the plans which had been made for the future of young Joshua, who was to have been sent to Brown University, in Providence, R. I. Instead, in April, 1821, he was taken to New Bedford, Mass., and bound to William Knights to learn the cabinet-maker's trade.

"Reaching his new home, he entered earnestly upon the work assigned him, determined to become a master at his trade. He soon found, however, that his religious surroundings were not altogether to his taste. He says, ' My master was a Unitarian, and he took me to his church. The Rev. Orville Dewey was the pastor. He was a late convert from orthodoxy. My training under Bishop Griswold and Rev. William Burge, rector of St. Paul's, Wickford, and often hearing the eloquent Dr. Crocker of St. John's, in Providence, R. I., quite unfitted me for accepting Mr. Dewey's eloquent negations of the teachings of Christ and his apostles.'

"There being at that time no Episcopal church in New Bedford, he decided to attend the First Christian church [not Disciple], and subsequently united with that body. 'Here,' he says, 'I found the open Bible and liberty of thought, and made good use of both.' This church was under the pastoral care of Rev. Moses Howe. Rev. Mr. Clough baptized Joshua V. Himes on Feb. 2, 1823. With a heart burning with zeal for his Master, he began at once, at the age of eighteen years, to tell the story of the cross and to urge men to repent. He says of himself:—

"'I soon became an exhorter, and license was given me to improve my gift. . . . I served out my apprenticeship with satisfaction, and received commendation. But for five or six years I was in the habit of doing overwork and thus obtained one or two days in the week for study and missionary work in destitute neighborhoods, the fruits of which I gave to my pastor.'

"In 1825 he was commissioned as missionary of the conference of Christian churches in southern Massachusetts. There was no plan or means for the support of missionaries,' says Elder Himes, ' and I resolved to enter into business for my support, and preach what I could.'

"In 1828 he left New Bedford, not with misgivings or lack of energy, but with a determination that was bound to win, going to Plymouth, where he preached God's word in school-houses, in improvised rooms, and wherever he could get a hearing. In 1829 he prosecuted the same character of work at Fall River until 1830, when he moved to Boston as pastor of the First and Second Christian churches; and here he remained for thirty-three years. In 1839 he became a convert to the Advent cause, as expounded by the famous Elder William Miller. He entered the new cause with all the enthusiasm he possessed, and his ministrations were full of fire and power. In 1840, he began the publication of the *Signs of the Times,* advocating the cause into which he had thrown his whole heart. All his money, all his labor, all his energy were thrown into the lap of this cause, and thousands of converts were won."

The United Labors of Miller and Himes

From 1840 to the autumn of 1844 the labors of Elders Miller and Himes were largely united as they went from city to city, in the summer with their mammoth tent, in the winter in churches and public halls. The great physical force of Elder Himes preserved him till he entered his ninety-second year. His faculties of mind were vigorous to the last. In the year 1894, Sept. 28, he gave a most stirring discourse to a congregation of over three thousand Seventh-day Adventists on the camp-ground in Lansing, Michigan. He seemed to speak with much of the earnestness and vigor of olden days. This was truly marvelous for a man who was three months into his ninety-first year, and who was suffering with an incurable malady from which he died the following year.

Elders Miller and Himes, stood, as it were, in the "fore front of the battle" in the second advent movement in America, and were only two among scores who labored with them in proclaiming the doctrine of the advent of Christ, whose leading characteristics were firmness of purpose and sterling integrity. These men were largely of that class called by the world "self-made men," — men who had developed by contact with the stern realities of life, who had learned to decide upon the merits of a cause from principle and not from policy. They were of the character of those who Elder Miller said usually accepted the message from the churches, "the most pious, devoted, and living members." This fact was confirmed by the ministers of the various churches, who said, after the final separation of the Adventists from them, "It [the doctrine] has taken the *cream* of our flock."

Other Prominent Adventist Preachers

It may be of interest to mention by name some of the men who acted a prominent part with Elders Miller and Himes in the movement of those early times. First to head the list is Charles Fitch, of Cleveland, Ohio, who in 1842 suggested the idea of having charts to illustrate the visions of Daniel and the Revelation. The origin of the thought was based upon Habakkuk 2:2, 3. The death of Charles Fitch occurred Oct. 10, 1844.

Dr. Josiah Litch, of Philadelphia, who, as we shall see in the following chapter, was moved upon by the Lord to proclaim a truth that in its fulfilment caused the sudden and rapid development of interest in the advent message.

Elon Galusha, of Lockport, N. Y., a noted Baptist minister, whose writings and ministrations on the subject of the Lord's near coming made a great stir in that denomination.

E. R. Pinney, of Seneca Falls, N. Y., another devoted minister of the Baptist church whose ministry and writings were a power in the work. He could well be called " The salt of the earth."

Geo. Storrs, of New York City, who previous to his conversion to the advent doctrine was a prominent revivalist. His writings exerted a mighty influence in moving the people to a greater consecration of self and substance to the work; especially was this the case in the closing weeks of the twenty-three hundred days. It was he, who, after the disappointment, brought to the consideration of the Adventist people and the world, his six sermons on the nature of man, the state of the dead, and future punishment.

Elder Stockman, of Portland, Maine, was another earnest worker in William Miller's revivals in that city. His death occurred a few weeks before the close of the Jewish year 1843, while the Adventist people were hoping and expecting the Lord would come at that time. [6]

There were other men of prominence that for lack of space we will merely mention, such as N. N. Whiting, who made a translation of the New Testament into English, known as " Whiting's Translation " ; S. S. Snow, F. G. Brown, Appollos Hale, L. D. Mansfield, Geo. Needham, O. R. Fassett; George, Wesley, and Edwin Burnham (three brothers), all efficient workers in the message.

---

[6] It can readily be seen, as represented in " Early Writings," page 13, why Elders Fitch and Stockman were anxious to know what had happened since they fell asleep.

CHAPTER VII

THE RAPID ADVANCEMENT OF THE MESSAGE

AND I saw another mighty angel come down from heaven, clothed with a cloud: and a rainbow was upon his head, and his face was as it were the sun, and his feet as pillars of fire; and he had in his hand a little book open: and he set his right foot upon the sea, and his left foot upon the earth, and cried with a loud voice, as when a lion roareth: and when he had cried, seven thunders uttered their voices. . . . And the angel which I saw stand upon the sea and upon the earth lifted up his hand to heaven, and sware by him that liveth forever and ever, who created heaven, and the things that therein are, and the earth, and the things that therein are, and the sea, and the things which are therein, that there should be time no longer: but in the days of the voice of the seventh angel, when he shall begin to sound, the mystery of God should be finished, as he hath declared to his servants the prophets." [1]

An Angel a Symbol of Human Messengers

As already shown, the work of preaching the gospel has been committed to man, and the Lord has promised his blessing on that instrumentality till the " end of the world." [2] So the angel bearing this message must be a symbol of a message concerning *time* which is to be preached to earth's inhabitants. The message is proclaimed from a book that is " *open*," clearly implying that it had once been *closed*. These messengers are esteemed of God; for the " bow," a

---

[1] Rev. 10: 1 - 7.   [2] Matt. 28: 19, 20.

token of God's covenant, is over them, and they stand clothed with the light of God's glory, and declare the message on the authority of the Creator of all things. That which is here declared is a *time* message, once " sealed," but now proclaimed from an " open " book.

In previous chapters it has been proved that the Lord marked the time when the light should be given relative to the close of the great prophetic period — twenty-three hundred days — leading to the investigative judgment; that the prediction that knowledge should be increased was accurately fulfilled by the raising up of many to whom he revealed that light; and that he also marked the time when the " parable of the fig-tree " should be *learned,* by raising up his teachers then and there to go forth and herald that parable to the world. Just so accurately has he marked the point when the time message should swell to its *loud cry,* and just so accurately was that fulfilled.

The Loud Cry of the First Message

The point of time when the loud cry of this proclamation was to be made is a question of interest. It is here placed between the sounding of the sixth and seventh trumpets, which may be seen not only by its position in the Scripture record, but by the message itself, which says: " In the days of the voice of the seventh angel, when he shall begin to sound, the mystery of God should be finished, as he hath declared to his servants the prophets." This is conclusive evidence that the time proclaimed in this message extends to the sounding of the seventh trumpet.

The Time of the Loud Cry

When the seventh angel sounds, we read that " the temple of God was opened in heaven, and there was seen in his temple the ark of his testament." [3] In the service of the earthly sanctuary, the apartment containing the ark — the most holy place — was opened only once a year; that was on the day

[3] Rev. 11: 19.

of atonement, and for the purpose of blotting out sins — the cleansing of the sanctuary. The time spoken of by the prophets, when this cleansing work, as accomplished by Christ, should take place, is at the close of the twenty-three hundred days. [4] It is also stated that when the seventh angel sounds, voices in heaven say that the time is come for the dead to be judged. [5]

This prophetic symbol of Revelation 10 presents the time when this message is to go forth " with a loud voice," and finally, " as when a lion roareth." The *time* when, according to this prophecy, the message was to increase to its " loud cry " is from the close of the sixth trumpet to the end of that prophetic period leading to the cleansing of the sanctuary, in other words, to the end of the twenty-three hundred days. The first four trumpets met their fulfilment in the wars of the Goths, Vandals, Huns, etc., which divided Western Rome into ten parts or kingdoms.

The Fifth Trumpet

The fifth trumpet presents the rise of Mohammedanism with its cloud of errors, but especially the period of " five months," or one hundred and fifty literal years from the time they " had a king over them." July 27, 1299, Othman, the founder of the Ottoman empire, invaded the territory of Nicomedia. From that time the Ottomans harassed and " tormented " the Eastern empire of Rome till July 27, 1449, the one hundred and fifty years of the sounding of the fifth trumpet. At that time the Turks came with their forces against the city of Constantinople itself, using gunpowder in their warfare; and from a ponderous cannon, which the historian Gibbon says required sixty oxen to draw, they fired great rocks against the walls of Constantinople.

The Close of the Sixth Trumpet

About this time John Palleologus, who is set down by historians as the last Greek emperor, died. Constantine

[4] Dan. 8: 14.   [5] Rev. 11: 18.

Decozes was the rightful heir to the throne, but it is said that his fears of Amurath, the Turkish sultan, who was waging this warfare against him, led him to ask permission of Amurath to ascend the throne. Such an act would almost seem a resignation of the throne to the Turks. In fact, very shortly the Ottomans had possession of the city of Constantinople and the Eastern empire of Rome. Thus they (politically) " killed " that empire which they had before " tormented." They were to " slay " it for " an hour, and a day, and a month, and a year."

Taking this as prophetic time, a day for a year, how long a time would it be? The problem is a simple one: a year, 360 days, or years; a month, 30 days, or years; and one day, one year,— in all, 391 days, or, literally, 391 years. An hour being the twenty-fourth part of a day, as a symbol, would be half a month, or fifteen days. The whole time of Mohammedan independent rule of Eastern Roman territory would therefore be 391 years and 15 days. This added to July 27, 1449, brings us to August 11, 1840, for the termination of the period of Turkish independence, as set forth under the sixth trumpet.

Dr. Josiah Litch Predicts the Fall of the Ottoman Empire

In 1838 Dr. Josiah Litch, of Philadelphia, Pa., having embraced the truth set forth by William Miller, united in the work of giving greater publicity to the message. He prepared articles for the public print on the subject of the seven trumpets of the Revelation. He took the unqualified position that the sixth trumpet would cease to sound and the Ottoman power fall on the 11th day of August, 1840, and that that would demonstrate to the world that a *day* in symbolic prophecy represents a *year* of literal time.

Some of the brethren, even those who believed with him on this point, trembled with fear for the result " if it should not come to pass " as he said. This did not, however, daunt him, but he went forward to do all in his power to give publicity to his views on the Turkish question.   Public journals spread abroad the claim he had made on the subject.   Infidel clubs discussed the question in their meetings, and said, " Here is a man that ventures something, and if this matter comes out as he says, it will establish his claim without a doubt that a day in prophecy symbolizes a year, and that twenty-three hundred days is so many years, and that they will terminate in 1844."

The publication of Dr. Litch's lecture made a general stir, and many thousands were thus called to watch for the termination of the difficulties that had sprung up between Mehemet Ali, the pasha of Egypt, and the Turkish sultan. Hundreds said, " If this affair terminates as the doctor has asserted, it will establish the ' year-day ' principle of interpreting symbolic time, and we will be Adventists."

The Turkish Sultan at War with the Pasha of Egypt

For several years previous to 1840, the sultan had been embroiled in a war with Mehemet Ali, pasha of Egypt.   In 1838 the trouble between the sultan and his Egyptian vassal was for the time being restrained by the influence of the foreign embassadors.   In 1839, however, hostilities were again begun, and were prosecuted until, in a general battle between the armies of the sultan and Mehemet, the sultan's army was entirely cut up and destroyed, and his fleet taken by Mehemet and carried into Egypt.   So completely had the sultan been reduced, that, when the war again began in August, he had only two first-rates and three frigates as the sad remains of the once powerful Turkish fleet.   This fleet Mehemet positively refused to give up and return to the sultan, and declared that if the powers attempted to take it from him, he would burn it.   In this posture affairs stood, when, in 1840, England, Russia, Austria, and Prussia interposed, and determined on a settlement of the difficulty ; for it was evident that, if let alone, Mehemet would soon become master of the sultan's throne.

Intervention of the Allied Powers

" The sultan accepted this intervention of the allied powers, and thus made a voluntary surrender of the question into their hands. A conference of these powers was held in London, the sheik, Effendi Bey Likgis, being present as Ottoman plenipotentiary. An ultimatum was drawn up, to be presented to the pasha of Egypt, whereby the sultan was to offer him the hereditary government of Egypt, and all that part of Syria extending from the Gulf of Suez to the Lake of Tiberias, together with the province of Acre, for life; he, on his part, to evacuate all other parts of the sultan's dominions then occupied by him, and to return the Ottoman fleet. In case he refused this offer from the sultan, the four powers were to take the matter into their own hands, and use such other means to bring him to terms as they should see fit.

" It was apparent that just as soon as this ultimatum should be put into the hands of Mehemet Ali, the matter would forever be beyond the control of the former [the sultan], and the disposal of his affairs would, from that moment, be in the hands of the foreign powers.

The Prophecy Fulfilled — End of Turkish Independence

" The sultan dispatched Rifat Bey on a government steamer to Alexandria, to communicate the ultimatum to the pasha. It was put into his hands, and by him taken in charge, on the eleventh day of August, 1840! On the same day a note was addressed by the sultan to the embassadors of the four powers, inquiring what plan was to be adopted in case the pasha should refuse to comply with the terms of the ultimatum; to which they made answer that provision had been made, and there was no necessity of his alarming himself about any contingency that might arise. This day the period of three hundred ninety-one years and fifteen days allotted to the continuance of the Ottoman power ended; and where was the sultan's independence? — Gone! " [6]

[6] See " Thoughts on Daniel and the Revelation," pp., 497, 498.

From that day to this the sultan has had to move under the dictation of the powers, and watch the dismemberment of his kingdom, as slice by slice it has been appropriated to their own use.

Public Interest in Prophecy Aroused

This striking fulfilment of the prophecy had a tremendous effect upon the public mind. It intensified the interest of the people to hear upon the subject of fulfilled and fulfilling prophecy. Dr. Litch said that within a few months after August 11, 1840, he had received letters from more than one thousand prominent infidels, some of them leaders of infidel clubs, in which they stated that they had given up the battle against the Bible, and had accepted it as God's revelation to man. Some of these were fully converted to God, and a number of them became able speakers in the great second advent movement. Some expressed themselves to Dr. Litch on this wise: " We have said that expositors of prophecy quote from the musty pages of history to substantiate their claims of prophetic fulfilments ; but in this case we have the living facts right before our eyes."

To illustrate how, just at the close of the sixth trumpet, the advent message began to go " with a loud voice," I will note a case as related to me by one of the actors in this message.

In the year 1840, E. C. Williams, an extensive tent and sail maker, of Rochester, N. Y., accepted the message, and invited Elders Miller and Himes to come to Rochester and speak to the thousands of that city. They replied that they lacked the money necessary to secure a hall of sufficient size to accommodate the people. He replied, " I have a circular tent 120 feet in diameter. I will pitch it, seat it, and care for it, *free.* Come on and proclaim the message." " They came," he said to me, " and the tent did not half hold those who came to hear, so I put in a forty-foot splice, making a tent 160 x 120 feet in size. This tent was filled with people daily, and hundreds crowded near on the outside, all eager to hear the word."

Hundreds Proclaiming the Message

To meet the growing interest, large tents were used, and grove meetings were held in the summer season. Some of the largest church buildings and public halls were used in the winter, and all were packed to their utmost capacity with interested listeners. Instead of Elder Miller now standing, as he had previous to 1840, " almost alone " in declaring the message, about three hundred joined him in publicly proclaiming the termination of the twenty-three-hundred-day period, and in giving the cry, " There shall be time no longer," and, " The hour of his judgment is come." Thus we see how, when the Lord's time came for the message to make its world-wide advancement, his word was fulfilled, and the millions were moved with a desire to hear the call.

What was true of the movement in America was true in other countries. From the year 1840, instead of a few individuals scattering their publications, scores sprang, as it were, to the front to proclaim the cry. In England there were seven hundred ministers of the Church of England alone proclaiming the message, to say nought of the scores of others engaged in the same work. In more than a score of the different leading nations of the earth a message was going with that zeal which led the looker-on to say, " This people are terribly in earnest."

CHAPTER VIII

THE MARRIAGE SUPPER OF THE LAMB

CERTAIN man made a great supper, and bade many; and sent his servant at supper time to say to them that were bidden, Come; for all things are now ready." [1]

" Blessed are they which are called unto the marriage supper of the Lamb." [2]

The supper is the last meal of the day. In this parable there are three calls to supper. This parable must not be confounded with the calls to *" dinner"* spoken of in Matthew 22 : 1 - 7. The *" dinner"* is the mid-day meal. In the parable respecting the calls to dinner, we learn that those who made the call were " spitefully entreated " and slain, and that even the son of the king was killed. The king who had sent forth the call " destroyed those murderers, and burned up their city."

This parable of tne calls to " dinner," showing the fate of those who first rejected that call, fittingly represented what actually came upon those who rejected the gospel of Christ, and slew him and his apostles. The Lord sent armies against that nation, who " destroyed those murderers, and burned up their city " — Jerusalem.

The Call to Supper

This call to *supper* in the parable undoubtedly has reference to the " marriage supper of the Lamb." A blessing is pronounced on those who are called to that " marriage supper." A marriage supper follows the marriage. The marriage of the Lamb occurs before he comes; for, as we have already seen, when Christ finally comes, he will " return from the wedding." [3]

This call to the marriage supper, then, must be the same as the first angel's message of Revelation 14, and the time proclamation of the tenth chapter, already noticed. As re· corded by Luke, this first call to supper goes to " them that were bidden." Who were those that had been bidden? — Those who had heard and accepted the gospel of Christ. They profess to love Christ, and to love his second appearing as the full fruition of their hope. Why should not the call go first to them? As it was necessary that the gospel should first be spoken to the Jews who had the Scriptures, and claimed to be looking for the coming of the Messiah, [4] so the message of Christ's second coming was first presented to those who claimed to be his followers, and to love his appearing.

The Call to Them that Had Been Bidden

The first call to the supper, being to those who had been bidden, must go to the churches. Now, as a matter of fact, the proclamation of the near coming of Christ, from the year 1833 to the spring of 1844, was made *in the churches*, and to quite a large extent was seconded by the ministers of those churches. William Miller's first publication of his views on the near coming of Christ was in a Baptist paper of Brandon, Vt. The labors of himself and his associates up to April, 1844, were largely in church buildings or halls secured by the churches of the day.

Elder Himes thus speaks of the labors of Elder Miller down to the spring of 1844: " He labored among all parties and sects, without interfering with their organizations or dis-cipline, believing that the members of the different com-munions could retain their standing, and at the same time prepare for the advent of their King."

Elder Himes, in speaking of his own and Elder Miller's united labors, further states: " Most of the ministers and

[3] Luke 12: 36.   [4] Acts 13: 45.

churches that opened their doors to us and our brethren who were proclaiming the advent doctrine, co-operated with us until the last year " — the year 1844.

Open Doors for the Message

Concerning his work and the nature of it, Wm. Miller said: " Doors have opened to me to proclaim this doctrine of the second coming of Christ among almost all denominations, so that I have been able to comply with but a small portion of the calls. . . . in every place where I have been, the most pious, devoted, and living members of the churches do most readily embrace the views thus proclaimed; while the worldly professor, the Pharisee, the bigot, the proud, haughty, and selfish, scoff at and ridicule the doctrine of the second coming of Christ."

Respecting the nature of the advent message, the same can be said of it that D'Aubigne said of the Reformation, — It " was accomplished in the name of a spiritual principle. It had proclaimed for its teacher, the word of God; for salvation, faith; for arms, the Holy Ghost; and had by these very means rejected all worldly elements."

A Mighty Wave of Revivals

The nature of the revivals that followed the proclamation of the advent message are thus described by L. D. Fleming, pastor of the Casco street Christian church, of Portland, Maine :—

" The interest awakened by his [Wm. Miller's] lectures is of the most deliberate and dispassionate kind, and though it is the greatest revival I ever saw, yet there is the least passionate excitement. It seems to take the greatest hold on the male part of the community. What produces the effect is this: Brother Miller simply takes the sword of the Spirit, unsheathed and naked, and lays its sharp edge on the naked heart, and it cuts! that is all. Before the edge of this mighty weapon, infidelity falls, and universalism withers.

False foundations vanish, and Babel's merchants wonder. It seems to me that this must be a little the nearest like apostolic revivals of anything modern times have witnessed."

An Experience in Richmond, Me.

As an illustration of the revival work that went with the preaching of the advent doctrine, we will quote from the report of one who was actively engaged in that movement. In speaking of a quarterly meeting held at Richmond, Me., representing thirty Freewill Baptist churches, he says:—

"As I entered the place of worship, Elder Rollins, who was seated by the side of the pulpit at the farther end of the house, arose and said, 'Brother White, you will find a seat here by me.' After the sermon, liberty was given for remarks, and I spoke with freedom upon the Christian life, and the triumphs of the just at the second advent of Christ. Many voices cried, 'Amen! amen!' and most in that large congregation were in tears. . . . Near the close of that meeting, after getting my consent, Elder Rollins arose and said: 'Brother White, who sits at my right side, will speak at the Reed meeting-house this evening, upon the second coming of our Lord Jesus Christ. Come up, brethren, and hear for yourselves. We have sufficient room to entertain you all. Come up, brethren, it will not harm any of you to hear upon this subject. . . . He very well knew that most of his brethren would leave their meeting in the village, and go three miles to hear me, and that their appointed business session would be broken up. And so it was. Three fourths of the ministers and nearly every delegate left, and the Reed meeting-house was crowded at an early hour. My subject was Matthew 24. The Spirit of God gave me great freedom. The interest was wonderful.

"As I closed with an exhortation to Christians to fully consecrate themselves and be ready, and to sinners to seek Christ and get ready for the coming of the Son of man, the power of God came upon me to that degree that I had to support myself with both hands hold of the pulpit. It was a solemn hour. As I viewed the condition of sinners, lost without Christ, I called on them with weeping, repeating several times, ' Come to Christ, sinner, and be saved when he shall appear in his glory. Come, poor sinner, before it shall be too late. Come, sinner, poor sinner, come.'

" The place was awfully solemn. Ministers and people wept, some aloud. At the close of every call to the sinner, a general groan was heard throughout the entire assembly. I had stood upon my feet explaining the chapter and exhorting for more than two hours, and was getting hoarse. I ceased speaking, and wept aloud over that dear people with depth of feeling such as he only knows whom God has called to preach his truth to sinners. It was nine o'clock, and to give liberty to others to speak would be to continue the meeting till midnight. It was best to close with the deep feeling of the present, but not till all had had a chance to vote on the Lord's side. I then called on all in the congregation who would join me in prayer, and those that wished to be presented to the throne of mercy, that they might be ready to meet the Saviour with joy at his second coming, to rise up. Every soul in that large house, as I was afterwards informed by persons in different parts of it, stood up. After a brief season of prayer, the meeting closed.

" The next morning I returned to the village, accompanied by at least seven eighths of that Freewill Baptist quarterly meeting. Every one was telling what a glorious meeting they attended the evening before.

Calls for the Message in Other Places

" At intermission, delegates and ministers invited me to join them in making arrangements as to time when I could lecture to the several congregations in that quarterly meeting who had commodious houses of worship. It was then in the middle of February, and it was decided that there remained not more than six weeks of firm sleighing, giving the people a good chance to attend meetings. Twelve of the most important places were selected for my labors in six weeks. I was to give ten lectures, which would require me to speak twenty times a week. This gave me only half a day each week, which I generally found very necessary to travel fifteen or twenty miles to the next place of meeting." [3]

Hundreds Converted

Revivals and the conversion of hundreds everywhere followed the preaching of the advent doctrine, and especially was this the case as they approached the termination of the Jewish year 1843 (March 21, 1844). It was during that winter that the writer in his native village —Victor, N. Y. — first heard upon the subject, and though only twelve years of age, accepted, so far as understood, the second advent faith. Solemn indeed was the impression upon the people, not only in meetings, but everywhere. Victor was at that time only a village of some two hundred inhabitants, but the country round about was thickly settled. As the result of that series of meetings held in that small village, there were five hundred converts reported.

Testimony of the Methodist Year Book

As to the mighty wave of revivals that followed in the track of the advent proclamation, we find in the Methodist Year Book that " during the four years from 1840 to 1844, 256,000 conversions took place in America." What was true in America was equally true in the other countries where the call was made. " A mighty power went with the preaching, and souls were converted everywhere." As the first call to the marriage supper went to the churches,— " them that were bidden," — it was through them extended to all who would come and share in the salvation awaiting the people of God. Whether the message was preached, prayed, or sung in " advent melodies," the mighty moving of the Spirit of God accompanied the work.

Children Preaching in Sweden

In this connection we will notice how the Lord wrought to introduce the proclamation in those countries where the law forbade the preaching of anything contrary to the " established church." Sweden was one of those countries. There the Lord used little children to introduce the work. The first of this manifestation was in the summer of 1843, in Eksjo, southern Sweden. A little girl, only five years of age, who had never learned to read or sing, one day, in a most solemn manner, sang correctly a long Lutheran hymn, and then with great power proclaimed " the hour of his judgment is come," and exhorted the family to get ready to meet the Lord; for he was soon coming. The unconverted in the family called upon God for mercy, and found pardon. This movement spread from town to town, other children proclaiming the message. The same movement among children was manifest to some extent in Norway and Germany.

"Yes! I Had to Preach"

In 1896, while holding meetings in seventeen different parts of Sweden, I passed through several places where the children had preached in 1843, and had opportunity to converse with those who had heard the preaching, and with men who had preached when they were children. I said to one of them, " You preached the advent message when you was a boy?" He replied, *"Preached!* Yes, I had to preach. I had no devising in the matter. A power came upon me, and I uttered what I was compelled by that power to utter."

Boquist and Walbom in Orebro, Sweden

In Orebro Laen (county) this work spread until older persons were moved to proclaim the message. Then the civil authorities, instigated by the priests of the " established church," arrested two young boys, Walbom, eighteen years of age, and Ole Boquist, fifteen years of age, saying they would

make a public example of them. They whipped their bare
backs with birch rods, and placed them, with their bleeding
wounds, in Orebro prison. When these wounds healed, they
took them out of the prison, demanding of them, " Will you
cease preaching this doctrine? " Though they beat them with
rods the second time, opening their wounds afresh, all the
answer they could obtain was, " We will preach the preaching
that the Lord bids us." Through the intercession of a prominent lady parishioner in Orebro, King Oscar I. told the authorities to let those boys out of the prison, and to let that people
alone. So the victory for the truth was gained in Sweden.

Boquist's Testimony

In the *Review and Herald* of Oct. 7, 1890, is a very interesting narrative in regard to the children's preaching, written
by O. Boquist himself. He says : —

" In the year 1843 a religious movement occurred among
the people in Karlskoga Parish, in Orebro Laen. The leaders
in this movement were children and young men, who were
called ' *rapare.*' These preached with divine power, and proclaimed before the people, with great decision, that the hour
of God's judgment had come.

" In the fall of the same year, I, O. Boquist, then fifteen
years of age, with another young man, Erik Walbom, eighteen
years of age, became so influenced by this unseen power that
we could in nowise resist it. As soon as we were seized by
this heavenly power, we began to speak to the people, and to
proclaim with a loud voice that the judgment hour had come,
referring them to Joel 2 : 28 - 32 and Rev. 14 : 6, 7.

Children in Vision

The people informed me that those who were thus influenced by this heavenly power were lost to everything around
them. They were actually in vision from God, and spoke
with a power that carried a mighty convicting influence. They
said that these little children, while under that influence,

would speak with the force and dignity of full-grown men and women. So those who saw it were led to conclude that it was the Lord using them prophetically to utter these solemn truths. The writer continues: —

"The people congregated in large numbers to listen to us, and our meetings continued both day and night, and a great religious awakening was the result. Young and old were touched by the Spirit of God, and cried to the Lord for mercy, confessing their sins before God and man.

"But when the priest in the church was apprised of this, many efforts were put forth to silence us, and thus to stop the prevailing religious excitement; but all efforts were unavailing. The sheriff was then requested to cause our arrest, and during six weeks a fruitless search was made to find us in the forest, whither we had fled for refuge.

"Finally, however, we were summoned to appear before the pastor of the church. Our number had increased so that forty young men and women presented themselves at the parsonage, where we were submitted to a long trial. All but myself and Walbom were permitted to return to their homes; but we were arrested, and on the following day were placed in custody in the Orebro prison, where we were associated with thieves in cell 14, as though we had committed some great crime."

Boquist's Sister's Testimony

On Sept. 22, 1896, the sister of Boquist, seventy-two years of age, attended our meeting at Orebro, and told us about the experience of her brother; for she witnessed his whipping, imprisonment, and liberation. She sang for us the hymn that Boquist and Walbom sang as they walked out of the prison on to the bridge over the moat surrounding that sixteenth century castle, used in 1843 as a prison. The power of the 1843 movement accompanied the testimony and the singing of the hymn. Translated into English, the hymn is as follows: —

Hymn Sung by Boquist and Walbom

" No one can ever reach the eternal rest,
  Who hath not forward with strong vigor pressed;
  No one can ever reach that shining goal,
  Unless he forward press with heart and soul.
  His urgent strife must last until the end;
  On this alone our hopes must all depend.
  Narrow the gate is called, the way named Small,
  But grace and choice are free for one and all;
  But all depends on pressing, pressing on;
  By that alone the haven can be won.

" Make strong, yea, strong resistance, O my soul!
  To all that comes between thee and thy goal.
  Gainst every hindrance fight. Stand firm! stand steady!
  For those who forward press the crown is ready.
  If you the joys of heaven would ever taste,
  Press forward past each hindrance. Be in haste;
  Leave, leave, O leave the wiles of all the world,
  Thy banner of resistance still unfurled!

" When the world calls thee, ' Come and with us go,'
  Do not obey; that pathway leads to woe.
  What the world asks, refuse at any cost,
  If you comply, dear soul, you will be lost.
  For love of Christ I offer this advice:
  Strive in God's strength; this is the crown's own price
  To every hindrance make resistance strong;
  The crown is worth the strife, however long.

" The heaven of glory is worth all thy life,
  Worth all thy praying, longing, all thy strife.
  No disappointment in that realm can live,
  The crown is worth all longing thou canst give.
  Therefore wake up, and sharply look around,
  Make ready for the judgment's trumpet sound;
  For wedding garment, pure and white and whole,
  Will be required of every suppliant soul
  Who seeks an entrance to that city fair;
  Therefore awaken, and thyself prepare.

"You cannot anchor on that heavenly shore,
   Nor enter in that land 'prepared before,'
   Unless you have the offered life of faith;
   For this the Scripture very plainly saith.
   'Tis faith alone that can the sinner save,
   And ransom you from out the cruel grave.

"Then listen, dear, and rise from thy sad fall;
   God's grace abundant is, and free for all.
   Believe, repent, and hear the Saviour say,
   In words of beauty, 'This, this is the way.'
   The world is all invited, let all come,
   And take by force a crown within that home.

"The Lord is willing. anxious to bestow
   This gift on all who in his way will go.
   Spare not thyself the struggle, but press on.
   And soon, full soon, the victory will be won.
   God's hand doth seek thy soul; he'll give thee rest;
   Jesus is knocking, seeking for thy best.
   Wake! 'tis God's Spirit that disturbs thy sleep;
   They only will be saved who vigils keep."

The Boy Preacher at Karlskoga

A gentlemen at Orebro related to me an occurrence at Karlskoga, where he resided in 1843. He said: —

"A little boy eight years of age, who had never learned to read his letters, began to preach the message, quoting many scriptures. The people said, 'That boy is just filled with Bible.' This circumstance occurred after King Oscar had spoken in favor of the persecuted ones, so the priest of that place could not get the boy before the court to stop the work; but he told the people to bring the boy before him, and he would expose him, and show them his ignorance of the Bible.

"Before a crowd of people the priest opened his hymn book, and asked the boy to read for him. The boy replied, 'I cannot read;' but turning his back to the priest, he sang

the hymn through correctly from first to last, the priest meanwhile looking on the book in astonishment. The priest said
to the lad, 'You seem to know everything.' The boy replied, 'No. We are not always permitted to tell all we
do know.'

"The priest then opened the New Testament and said to
the boy, 'Read for me in this.' The boy replied, 'I cannot
read.' The priest inquired. 'What do you know about the
Bible anyway?' His reply was, 'I know where there is a
text that has the word *and* in it fourteen times.' The priest
said, 'No! there is no such text in the Bible.' The lad said,
Will you please read for me Rev. 18:13?' 'Yes,' said the
priest. As he read the people counted, and sure enough the
word *and* was there just fourteen times, and among the fourteen times was the 'binding of the souls of men.' The people
shouted, 'There! *there!* the boy knows more about the
Bible than the priest!' Much chagrined, the priest dropped
the subject, and left the people unmolested after that."

So, out of the mouth of children the Lord confirmeth
his word, and in this wonderful manner brought his truth
to the ears of the people whose laws forbade the preaching
of any doctrine but that of the "established religion."

Gifts of the Spirit Connected with the Message

It was not in Sweden alone that the Lord, in connection
with the advent movement, spoke to his people through the
gifts of his Spirit. In Scotland, in England, and also in
America the Lord has instructed his people by special revelations.

William Foy's Visions

In the year 1842 there was living in Boston, Mass., a
well-educated man by the name of William Foy, who was an
eloquent speaker. He was a Baptist, but was preparing to
take holy orders as an Episcopal minister. The Lord
graciously gave him two visions in the year 1842, one on the

10

18th of January, the other on February 4. These visions bore clear evidence of being the genuine manifestations of the Spirit of God. He was invited from place to place to speak in the pulpits, not by the Episcopalians only, but by the Baptists and other denominations. When he spoke, he always wore the clergyman's robe, such as the ministers of that church wear in their services.

Mr. Foy's visions related to the near advent of Christ, the travels of the people of God to the heavenly city, the new earth, and the glories of the redeemed state. Having a good command of language, with fine descriptive powers, he created a sensation wherever he went. By invitation he went from city to city to tell of the wonderful things he had seen; and in order to accommodate the vast crowds who assembled to hear him, large halls were secured, where he related to thousands what had been shown him of the heavenly world, the loveliness of the New Jerusalem, and of the angelic hosts. When dwelling on the tender, compassionate love of Christ for poor sinners, he exhorted the unconverted to seek God, and scores responded to his tender entreaties.

Vision of the Three Steps

His work continued until the year 1844, near the close of the twenty-three hundred days. Then he was favored with another manifestation of the Holy Spirit,— a third vision, one which he did not understand. In this he was shown the pathway of the people of God through to the heavenly city. He saw a great platform, or step, on which multitudes of people gathered. Occasionally one would drop through this platform out of sight, and of such a one it was said to him, "Apostatized." Then he saw the people rise to a second step, or platform, and some there also dropped through the platform out of sight. Finally a third platform appeared, which extended to the gates of the holy city. A great company gathered with those who had advanced to this platform. As he expected the Lord Jesus to come in a very short time, he failed to recognize the fact that a third message was to follow the first and second messages of Revelation 14. Consequently the vision was to him inexplainable, and he ceased public speaking. After the close of the prophetic period, in the year 1845, he heard another relate the same vision, with the explanation that "the first and second messages had been given, and that a third was to follow." Soon after this Mr. Foy sickened and died.

With such manifestations of the power of God in connection with the preaching of his coming "at the doors," and with the rejoicing of thousands who were turning from sin to serve the Lord and to wait for his coming, the people were doubly assured that this was indeed the Lord's message to the world.

But March 21, 1844, came, and passed, and the Lord did not come. The conviction of the devoted and thoughtful, however, was that they had moved in harmony with the mind of the Lord, and that in due time all would be made plain.

CHAPTER IX

THE TARRYING TIME

HEN shall the kingdom of heaven be likened unto ten virgins, which took their lamps, and went forth to meet the bridegroom. And five of them were wise, and five were foolish. They that were foolish took their lamps, and took no oil with them: but the wise took oil in their vessels with their lamps. While the bridegroom tarried, they all slumbered and slept." [1]

Christ is the bridegroom of the parable. [2] The going forth to meet the bridegroom must therefore represent a movement on the part of the Lord's people to meet Christ at his coming, for the subject of the discourse of Matthew twenty-four and twenty-five is the coming of the Lord. The word of the Lord is the lamp. [3] All the virgins took their lamps. The foolishness of a part of the virgins consisted in their taking simply the theory of the truth, without that earnest consecration to the Lord which would develop the graces of the Spirit in the heart of the believer. This work is represented in the parable by "oil in their vessels." The tarrying of the bridegroom must represent some disappointment on the part of those going forth expecting to meet their Lord.

The Time when the Parable Applies

The word "then," with which the parable opens, gives us a clue to the time of its application. It follows close upon what had been stated in the previous chapter, not after

---

[1] Matt. 25: 1 - 5.   [2] Mark 2: 18 - 20.   [3] Ps. 119: 105.

(148)

the Lord's second coming, but after the parable of the fig-tree had been proclaimed, announcing that Christ's coming is " at the doors," and that the generation has come which will not pass until Christ himself appears in the clouds of heaven. It also applies at a time when some of the servants who have been giving the message say in their hearts, " My Lord delayeth his coming; and begin to smite their fellow-servants, and to eat and drink with the drunken."

Smiting their Fellow-Servants

These have been " fellow-servants," harmoniously pro-claiming the same message; but now a part of them turn from that which they have taught, and " smite " their fellow-servants who are giving the " meat in due season " — de-claring the needful preparation to meet the soon-coming Lord. They " smite " in the same manner that it was proposed to smite Jeremiah. The people said, " Come, and let us smite him with the tongue, and let us not give heed to any of his words." [4] So did these servants begin to teach in a manner to hinder the work of the " faithful " servants. This same class are thus addressed, " Remember therefore how thou hast received and heard, and hold fast, and repent. If there-fore thou shalt not watch, I will come on thee as a thief, and thou shalt not know what hour I will come upon thee." [5]

The parable of the virgins applies at a time when " fel-low-servants " are turning from the message of the near coming of the Lord, and " begin to smite." They also begin to do something else — to " eat and drink with the drunken." They join in feasting with those who wish to gratify their appetites. Solomon said of such, " Be not among winebibbers; among riotous eaters of flesh; for the drunkard and the glutton shall come to poverty." [6]

The First Disappointment

The inquiry will now arise, " What was there in the advent experience that answers to these statements? " There

[4] Jer. 18: 18.　　[5] Rev. 3: 3.　　[6] Prov. 23: 20, 21.

were movements which accord fully with the prophecy. Those
giving the message down to April, 1844, labored among the
churches, and the ministers of the various churches united
with their efforts. Thus they were " fellow-servants."

Those giving the message taught that the twenty-three
hundred days of Dan. 8 : 14 would terminate with the Jewish
year 1843, which would be in our year 1844. They proclaimed
the hour of God's judgment to come at the close of that
period. Every denomination in the land at that time held
that the judgment day would be introduced by the second
coming of our Lord. Thus it will readily be seen that the
Adventists supposed the Lord would come at the close of
that prophetic period. They said, " This period may terminate with the month, March 21, 1844, the last of the natural
Jewish year 1843." So they looked to the last of March or
the first of April, 1844, as a time when the Saviour might
come.

Evil Servants Developed

When the last of March came, and passed by, and the
Lord did not come, those who had previously labored with
the Lord's messengers, but had not from the heart fully
consecrated their lives to the message, turned against it, began to oppose the work, and to do all in their power to
hedge up the way of those who still continued teaching the
doctrine of the Lord's near coming and the judgment hour
message. " In their hearts " they said, " My Lord delayeth
his coming." With their lips they now taught that all the
world must be converted before the Lord would come; that
the Jews must all return to Palestine, and establish their
temple service in Jerusalem, before Messiah would come.
Some even taught that Christ's coming was a " spiritual coming," that it took place at conversion, and also at the death
of his people.

Giving "Meat in due Season"

While these thus turned against their fellow-servants,
.those who still held fast the faith were calling the believers
together in halls and groves, giving them the "meat in due
season" — showing them that the signs of the times and
fulfilled prophecy declared, the same as before their disappointment, that Christ's coming was "near, even at the doors."

Church Feasting

While they were doing this there began what was before
unknown in Protestant churches — the calling of the people
together in the church for feasting and "making of sport."
All who would come were invited to partake with them of
their dainties.

The first we ever heard of anything of this kind in
America was in the month of May, 1844, just after the disappointment. It was on this wise: While William Miller,
in a hall in Rochester, N. Y., was instructing and exhorting
several hundred Adventists, telling them, "We are in the
tarrying time of Matthew twenty-five; hold fast your faith;
we shall soon have more light on this matter," there was
appointed in the basement of one of the largest meeting-
houses in Rochester, "a festival." A crowd of people came
together, both church members and unbelievers, and while
the president of a theological college made fun for the crowd
by ridiculing William Miller, they sold to them oysters, ice-
cream, sweetmeats, and for twenty-five cents a small pamphlet
which this man had prepared. The book was called "An
Exposé of Millerism."

In less than a fortnight from that time another denomination in the same city appointed "a festival" in a public
hall, charging twenty-five cents admission, and inviting all
who would to come and partake with them of their oysters,
ice-cream, cake, and sweets. Then and there began this modern feasting in churches, which has developed into "crazy

socials," "grab bags," "fish ponds," "kissing bees," and so
on. This feature of feasting in churches has grown to that
extent that now a modern church building is not up to the
standard unless it has its kitchen, pantry, and dining-room.
This state of things is that which began in the " tarrying
time," just as designated in the parable.

Wm. Miller himself speaks of the incident that occurred
in Rochester in the following words: " One of the D. D.'s
in Rochester, Mr. ———, of the ——— church, wrote a
pamphlet against Millerism, called his lords and ladies into
the house of the Lord, made a great feast of oysters and
other ' picnics,' Belshazzar-like, drank their coffee and tea,
ate their costly delicacies, and sold their ice-cream and sweetmeats, and his pamphlet against the second advent of the
dear Saviour.

" The night before I left, another of the reverend gentlemen had a picnic feast at a public house, or hall, and sold
as above, his tickets, ice-cream, and sweetmeats. I was
happy to hear that some of the churches of the different
sects did not approve of such Babylonian feasts; and I do
hope, in my soul, that not all of these sectarian churches will
be found ' eating and drinking with the drunken ' when Christ
shall come. I am astonished that these reverend gentlemen
do not see themselves in the glass of God's word; and I
would recommend them to read Luke 14: 12 - 14; Matt.
24: 48 - 51; Luke 13: 25 - 28; 2 Peter 2: 13; Jude 10 - 21.
These are the last times surely."

If Elder Miller had obtained a view of what the churches
have since entered into, in their donation parties, with " ring
guess-cakes, ten-cent kissing bees, donkey shows, crazy
socials, holy lotteries," and other chance game arrangements,
etc., he would have recoiled with holy horror.

The Tarrying Time

The Adventists found consolation in the scriptural fact
that when the announcement was made of the near coming of

the Lord there would be connected with it a "*tarrying time.*"
This they saw in our Saviour's words in Matt. 25 : 5, 6, and
in Hab. 2 : 1 - 3.

As to their attitude in the spring of 1844, we quote from
the *Midnight Cry* of May 9, 1844 : —

" Having passed the point of the apparent termination of
the prophetic periods, we are placed in a position which God
foresaw his children would be placed in at the end of the
vision ; and for which he made provision, by the prophet
Habakkuk, when he says, ' I will stand upon my watch, and
set me upon the tower, and will watch to see what he will
say unto me, and what I shall answer when I am reproved,'
or as it reads in the margin, ' argued with.' ' And the Lord
answered me, and said, Write the vision, and make it plain
upon tables, that he may run that readeth it. For the vision
is yet for an appointed time, but at the end [of the prophetic
periods] it shall speak and not lie : though it tarry [beyond
their apparent termination], wait for it ; because it will surely
come, [in the fulness of the prophetic times, beyond which]
it will not tarry.' [7]

" That this admonition has reference to the present time,
is evident from Paul's quotation of it in Heb. 10 : 36 - 39 :
' For ye have need of patience, that after ye have done the
will of God, ye might receive the promise. For yet a little
while, and he that shall come will come, and will not tarry.
Now the just shall live by faith ; but if any man draw back,
my soul shall have no pleasure in him. But we are not of
them who draw back unto perdition ; but of them that believe
to the saving of the soul.'

" We believe that we are occupying that period spoken
of by the Saviour, when the bridegroom tarries (Matt. 25 : 5)
— to which the kingdom of heaven should be likened, — when
' that evil servant [there having been an apparent failure in
the time] shall say in his heart, My Lord delayeth his coming,
and shall begin to smite his fellow-servants, and to eat and

[7] Hab. 2: 1 - 3.

drink with the drunken,' and the Lord should ' come in a day when he looketh not for him.'

"We believe that we are now occupying that period of time spoken of by Peter, when their ' judgment now of a long time lingereth not, and their damnation slumbereth not; ' where they were to ' privily bring in damnable heresies.' [8] These, Peter says, were to be, even as there were false prophets when the Scriptures were indited. As therefore they of the house of Israel said, ' The days are prolonged, and every vision faileth,' [9] so must there have been a time when there would be an apparent passing of the time, that the scoffers of 2 Peter 3:4 might inquire, ' Where is the promise of his coming? ' and flatter themselves that ' all things continue as they were from the beginning of the creation.'

"We believe it was in view of such a tarrying of the vision that the apostle James said, ' Be patient, therefore, brethren, unto the coming of the Lord; ' ' be ye also patient; stablish your hearts: for the coming of the Lord draweth nigh.' And, ' Behold, the Judge standeth before the door.'

"And we believe in anticipation of the passing by of the expected time that our Saviour admonished us, in the twelfth chapter of Luke, ' Let your loins be girded about, and your lights burning; and ye yourselves like unto men that wait for their Lord, when he will return from the wedding; that when he cometh and knocketh, they may open unto him immediately.' [10] To *wait* implies a passing of the time, for till that time we do not *wait*. Therefore our Lord adds, ' Blessed are those servants whom the Lord *when he cometh* shall find watching.'

"We shall continue, God willing, to proclaim, ' Behold, the Bridegroom cometh; go ye out to meet him; ' and, ' The hour of his judgment is come.' And we trust we shall not fail to continue to cry aloud to the world and church, to arouse themselves from their songs of ' peace,' and to listen

[8] 2 Peter 2: 1, 3.   [9] Eze. 12: 22.   [10] Luke 12: 35, 36.

to God's overtures of mercy. We intend to continue waiting and watching for the coming of the Lord, believing that it is just upon us."

A Vindication of Their Work

A good idea as to how the Adventists viewed their work previous to March 21, 1844, and just after that date, can be obtained by reading the following quotation, taken from an article under the caption, " Vindication," in the *Advent Herald* of Nov. 13, 1844, published by J. V. Himes, S. Bliss, and A. Hale : —

" We were not hasty in embracing our opinions. We believe that we were honest and sincere inquirers after truth. We obeyed our Saviour's command to search the Scriptures. We relied not upon our own wisdom ; but we looked to God for guidance and direction, and endeavored to lay ourselves upon his altar, trusting that he would direct our footsteps aright. We examined all the arguments which were advanced against us with a sincere desire to know the truth and be kept from error ; but we must confess that the varied and multiform positions of our opponents only confirmed us in our views. We saw that whether we were right or wrong, our opponents *could not be right;* and they had no agreement among themselves. The arguments of each were so weak and puerile that they were under the necessity of continually undoing what they had themselves done ; and by their opposite and contradictory views they demonstrated that however they might regard *our* opinions, they had no confidence in the opinions of each other. And, moreover, there was not a cardinal point in our whole position in which we were not sustained by one or more of those who labored to disprove the immediate coming of the Lord. While we had the literal rendering of the Scriptures to sustain us, our opponents endeavored in vain to prove that the Scriptures are not to be understood literally, although every prophecy which has been fulfilled has been so in its most literally minute particulars.

The Disappointment Explained

" But the time — the year 1843, the Jewish year — passed, and we were disappointed in not beholding the King in his beauty. And all who opposed us honestly supposed that every distinctive characteristic of our belief had been demonstrated to be false; and that we should, as honest men, abandon our whole position. And therefore it was with surprise that they saw us still clinging to our hope, and still expecting our King.

" We, however, in our disappointment, saw no reason for discouragement. We saw that the Scriptures indicated that there must be a tarrying time, and that while the vision tarried we must wait for it. We saw also that with the end of the year the period could not be fully terminated, even upon the supposition that our chronology was correct; and that they could only be fulfilled some time in the present year; and yet we frankly and fully admitted to the world that we were mistaken in the definite point to which we had looked with so much confidence; but while we were thus mistaken, we can see the hand of God in that matter. We can see that he has made use of that proclamation as an alarm to the world, and a *test* to the church. It placed his people in an attitude of expectation. It called out those who were willing to suffer for his name's sake. It demonstrated to whom the cry of the Lord's coming was tidings of great joy, and to whom it was an unwelcome sound in their ears. It has shown the universe who would welcome the Lord's return, and who would reject him at his second, as the Jews did at his first advent. And we regard it as a step in the accomplishment of God's purpose, in this ' day of his preparation,' that he might lead forth a people who should only seek the will of the Lord, that they might be prepared for his coming."

HISTORY OF THE MOVEMENT AFTER MARCH, 1844

A brief history of the advent movement after March 21, 1844, is set forth in the following, taken from the *Signs of the Times* of Oct. 31, 1844: —

"After the passing away of 1843,— the Jewish Year,— the great body of the Adventists settled down in the belief that we could henceforth reckon on particular times with no degree of positiveness. They believed that we were where our chronology points, at the end of all the prophetic periods, at the termination of which the advent is expected; and that while we should have to wait only the little while that our chronology might vary from God's time, yet they believed that we could have no more clue to the definite time. They had all taken their lamps and gone forth to meet the Bridegroom; but the Bridegroom had tarried beyond the time (1843) in which he was expected. During this tarrying of the vision, it seemed to be the determination of all to *wait* for it, believing it could not be delayed, and that it might be momentarily expected. It was, however, soon very evident that multitudes were forming plans for the future, which they would not form if they believed the Lord would come this year; and that they had fallen asleep with regard to a realizing sense of the Lord's immediate appearing. In other words, they thought he might come any day, or that it might be delayed some little while, during which they might enjoy a refreshing repose. Well, this was as our Saviour said it would be, ' While the Bridegroom tarried, they all slumbered and slept.'

Attention Called to the Autumn of 1844

"As early as May, 1843, Brother Miller had called our attention to the seventh month of the Jewish sacred year, as the time of the observance of those types which point to the second advent; and the last autumn we looked to that point of time with much interest. After it had passed away,

Brother S. S. Snow fully embraced the opinion that, according to the types, the advent of the Lord, when it does occur, must occur on the tenth day of the seventh month; but he was not positive as to the year. He afterward saw that the prophetic periods do not actually expire until the present year, 1844; he then planted himself on the ground that about the 22nd of October — the tenth day of the seventh month of this present year — we should witness the advent of the Lord of glory. This he preached in New York, Philadelphia, and other places during the past spring and summer; and while many embraced his views, yet no particular manifestation of its effects was seen until about July.

Crops Left in the Fields

" In the early part of the season some of our brethren in the north of New Hampshire had been so impressed with the belief that the Lord would come before another winter, that they did not cultivate their fields. About the middle of July,— which was the evening of the midnight of the Jewish day-year (evening-morning, reckoning from the new moon of April, the commencement of this Jewish year), others who had sown and planted their fields were so impressed with a sense of the Lord's immediate appearing, that they could not, consistently with their faith, harvest their crops. Some, on going into their fields to cut their grass, found themselves entirely unable to proceed, and, conforming to their sense of duty, left their crops standing in the field, to show their faith by their works, and thus to condemn the world. This rapidly extended through the north of New England.

The Judgment to Precede the Advent

" During the same time our brethren in Maine had embraced the view that the judgment must precede the advent; that it synchronized with the harvest, and was not only at the end of the world, but occupied a period immediately preceding the end. In accordance with this view, they thought that we were in the judgment, that the dividing line was being drawn, and that the servants of God were being sealed in their foreheads, the accomplishment of which would be the signal for the four angels holding the four winds of the earth (Rev. 7:1), to loose their hold.

A Midnight Awakening

"About the middle of July the blessing of God in reclaiming backsliders began to attend the proclamation of the *time,* and those who embraced either of the views referred to, manifested a marked change in their deportment, and a sudden waking out of sleep, as was predicted. 'At midnight there was a cry made, Behold, the Bridegroom cometh; go ye out to meet him. Then all those virgins arose and trimmed their lamps.' From July these movements were in different parts of New England, and distinct from one another; but they were all attended by the blessing of God in reclaiming many whose lamps had well-nigh gone out, and in the sanctification of his saints. At the Exeter camp-meeting, all these influences met, mingled into one great movement, and rapidly spread through all the advent bands in the land."

CHAPTER X

THE MIDNIGHT CRY

A T midnight there was a cry made, Behold, the bridegroom cometh; go ye out to meet him. Then all those virgins arose, and trimmed their lamps." [1]

We have already spoken of the *tarrying time* brought to view in this parable of the " ten virgins," and will now give special attention to that part of it introduced in the above text, designated by the Adventist people as the " midnight cry." A prominent writer upon this subject, in a periodical called the *Midnight Cry,* Oct. 3, 1844, says:—

" But how came we into this tarrying night? Because we commenced the vision [the vision of the twenty-three hundred days] in the *spring,* instead of the fall, 457 B. C. We fell short of reaching the destined port six months and a few days over. It threw us into the tarrying night, six months."

Another writer, S. S. Snow, in the *Cry* of Aug. 22, 1844, speaking of the twenty-three hundred days, said: —

" They began at the going forth of the decree to restore and build Jerusalem. The decree was made at the first by Cyrus, renewed by Darius, and completed by Artaxerxes Longimanus in the seventh year of his reign. It was promulgated and went into effect in the autumn of the year B. C. 457, when Ezra, having arrived at Jerusalem by the good hand of the Lord, restored the Jewish commonwealth, appointed magistrates and judges, and commenced the building of the wall." [2]

As the time of the vision was twenty-three hundred full years, it would require all of 457 and all of 1843 to make twenty-three hundred, and if the decree did not go forth

[1] Matt. 25: 6, 7.   [2] See Dan. 9: 25; Ezra 7: 21 - 26; 9: 9; Neh. 1: 3; 2: 12 - 17.

until the seventh month of 457 B. C., it was taught that the period would not end until the seventh month of 1844. As the observance of the tenth day of the seventh month seemed to be the event which marked the beginning of the period, so it was shown conclusively that on the tenth day of the seventh month (Jewish time), Oct. 22, 1844, the twenty-three hundred days would end, and the time come for the sanctuary to be cleansed. All the evidence used for the close of the period in 1843 applied with equal force to the reckoning for 1844, and with it an assurance that they had discovered what seemed a certain solution of the cause of their disappointment. The manner in which the Adventists proclaimed the "true midnight cry," as it was then denominated, cannot be better illustrated than by quoting from the writings of those who were prominently engaged in the work at that time.

"Go Ye Out to Meet Him"

In the *Cry* for Oct. 3, 1844, was an article written by George Storrs, under the heading, "Go Ye Out to Meet Him," in which he said : —

"I take up my pen with feelings such as I never before experienced. *Beyond a doubt,* in my mind, the *tenth day of the seventh month* will witness the revelation of our Lord Jesus Christ in the clouds of heaven. We are within a *few days* of that event — awful moment to those unprepared, but glorious to those who are ready.

"'Behold, the Bridegroom cometh' this year; 'go ye out to meet him.' We have done with the nominal churches and all the wicked, except so far as this cry may affect them. Our work is now to wake up the 'virgins who took their lamps and went forth to meet the bridegroom.' Where are we now? 'If the vision *tarry,* wait for it.' Is not that our answer since last March or April? — Yes. What happened while the Bridegroom *tarried?* — The virgins all slumbered and slept, did they not? Christ's words have not failed; and 'the Scriptures cannot be broken.' It is of no use for us to pre-

11

tend that we have been awake; we have been slumbering,
not on the *fact* of Christ's coming, but on the time. We came
into the *tarrying time;* we did not know ' how *long* ' it would
tarry, and on that point we have slumbered. Some of us have
said in our sleep, ' Don't fix *another* time! ' so we slept. Now
the trouble is to wake us up. Lord, help, for vain is the help
of man. Speak *thyself,* Lord. O that the ' Father ' may
now ' make known ' *the time.*

The Midnight of the Message

"How long is the tarrying time? — Half a year. How
do you know? — Because our Lord says, at *midnight,'* while
the Bridegroom tarried. The vision was for twenty-three
hundred evening-mornings, or days. An ' evening, or *night,*
is half of one of those prophetic days and is, therefore, *six
months.* That is the whole length of the tarrying time. The
present strong cry of *time* commenced about the middle of
July, and has spread with great rapidity and power, and is
attended with a demonstration of the Spirit, such as I never
witnessed when the cry was ' 1843.' It is now literally, ' *Go
ye out to meet him.*' There is a leaving *all* that I never
dreamed could be seen. When this cry gets hold of the heart,
farmers leave their farms, with their crops. There is a strong
crying with tears, and a consecration of all to God, such as
I never witnessed. There is a confidence in this truth such
as was never felt in the previous cry, in the same degree, and
a weeping or melting glory in it that passes all understanding
except to those who have felt it.

"On this present truth, I, through grace, dare venture
all, and feel that to indulge in doubt about it would be to
offend God and bring upon myself ' swift destruction.' I
am satisfied that now ' whosoever shall seek to save his life.'
where this cry has been fairly made, by indulging in an ' *if it*
don't come,' or by a fear to venture out on this truth, shall
lose his life.' It requires the same faith that led Abraham
to offer up Isaac, or Noah to build the ark, or Lot to leave

Sodom or the children of Israel to stand all night waiting for their departure out of Egypt, or for Daniel to go into the lions' den, or the three Hebrews into the fiery furnace. We have fancied that we were going into the kingdom without such a test of faith, but I am satisfied we are not. This last truth brings such a test, and none will venture upon it but such as dare to be accounted fools, madmen, or anything else that antediluvian Sodomites, a lukewarm church, or sleeping virgins are disposed to heap upon them. Once more would I cry, ' Escape for thy life; ' ' Look not behind you; ' ' Remember Lot's wife.' "

Storrs's Flat Rock

In the *Midnight Cry* of Oct. 10, 1844, there appeared, from the pen of George Storrs, the following, under the heading, " The Finale," but called by the Adventists, " Storrs's Flat Rock " : —

" How shall we be ready for that day? — Believe God's truth, and venture out upon it, by strong faith that gives glory to God. We must have the same state of mind that we would have if we knew we were to die upon that day, the same entire consecration to God and deadness to the world.

" I cannot better illustrate what I mean than to suppose a large flat rock in the midst of the ocean. A promise is made by a glorious and mighty prince that at a given time he will send a splendid steamer to carry all persons whom he shall find there with the evidence that they fully credited his word, to a glorious country. Many venture out to the rock. Some, when they are safe on the rock, cut the rope, and their craft with which they came there drifts away from them, and they look after it no more, but are watching for the arrival of the steamship. They have no doubt of the truth of the promise, and risk all upon it. Others who come there think it is enough that they are on the rock. But they would be ' wise and not run too great a risk.

"According to *thy faith* be it unto thee" had been sounded before the time the steamer was expected. The day arrives. The prudent ones, it may be, intend to cut their boats loose, and let them float off, if they *see* the steamer coming. It appears in sight; but now it is too late to let go their boats without being discovered; and besides, the same prudence would dictate now that they do not let their boats float away till they are *certain* that they are not mistaken in the approaching vessel. Now it comes so near that they cannot possibly cut loose without being discovered.

"The steamer arrives at the rock. 'What is the evidence that you had implicit confidence in the promise of the arrival of the steamer?'—'Our boats are cut loose, and have floated away from us, so that we could not possibly get to land, and must have perished if the steamer had not arrived, for it is a rock where no other vessel ever passes.' 'That is enough,' cries the commander of the steam vessel; '*come on board;* such confidence shall not be disappointed.'

"Those who had kept their boats made fast to the rock now crowd around and strive to get on board the steamer. The commander asks, 'What mean those boats I see made fast to the rocks, yonder, or whose ropes have only been cut since I arrived in sight?' They answer, 'We thought we would be *prudent,* so that *if* the steamer did not arrive, we might have something with which to get back to land.' 'You made provision for the flesh, then,' cries the commander, 'did you, and so doubted my words? *According to thy faith be it unto thee.* The evidence is against you. You made provision to return, and now you must reap the fruit of your unbelief.' 'So they could not enter in because of unbelief.' O, awful state of despair!

"Cut your ropes now, brethren; let your boats float out of sight; yea, make haste before the 'sign of the Son of man appear.' Then it will be too late. Venture *now,* and venture *all.* O, my heart is pained for you; don't dally; push off that boat, or you are lost; for 'whosoever shall seek to save his life shall lose it,' so saith Jesus Christ, our Lord and Judge. Make haste, then, once more I entreat you, O make haste! Let go every boat by which you are now calculating to escape to land ' *if* it don't come.' That ' if ' will ruin you. It is now the last trial and temptation. Do as our Lord did with the last temptation of the devil — ' Get thee hence, Satan,' said he. Then the devil leaveth him, and ' behold, angels came and ministered unto him.' So will it be with you when you have gained this triumph."

Rapid Work of the Midnight Cry

As to the rapidity, power, and effect of the message of the " midnight cry," we gain a correct idea from the words of N. Southard, editor of the paper from which we have previously quoted — the *Midnight Cry*. In the copy dated Oct. 31, 1844, he says : —

"At first the definite time was generally opposed; but there seemed to be an irresistible power attending its proclamation, which prostrated all before it. It swept over the land with the velocity of a tornado, and it reached hearts in different and distant places almost simultaneously, and in a manner which can be accounted for only on the supposition that God was in it. It produced everywhere the most deep searching of heart and humiliation of soul before High Heaven. It caused a weaning of affections from the things of this world, a healing of controversies and animosities, a confession of wrongs, a breaking down before God, and penitent, broken-hearted supplications to him for pardon and acceptance. It caused self-abasement and prostration of soul, such as we never before witnessed. As God, by Joel, commanded, when the great day of God should be at hand, it produced a rending of hearts and not of garments, and a turning unto the Lord with fasting and weeping and mourning. As God said by Zechariah, a spirit of grace and supplication was poured out upon his children ; they looked to him whom they had pierced, and there was a great mourning in the land, every family apart, and their wives apart: and those who were looking for the Lord afflicted their souls before him."

The People Moved by a Supernatural Power

Again, of this stirring proclamation he says:—

" It seemed to us to have been so independent of human agency that we could but regard it as a fulfilment of the ' midnight cry,' after the tarrying of the Bridegroom, and the slumbering and sleeping of the virgins, when they were all to arise and trim their lamps. And the last work seems to have been done; for there has never been a time before when the respective advent bands were in so good a state of preparation for the Lord's coming."

Worldly Possessions Disposed of

Under the stirring proclamation of the advent doctrine, many disposed of their worldly possessions, using their substance in sustaining the public speakers in their labor, or scattering the printed papers and tracts, or supplying the wants of the needy, thus giving to the world the best evidence of their sincerity and earnestness; while those who clung to their earthly possessions, and made no special sacrifice for the work, were marked by the worldling as not really believing what they professed. By way of illustration I will give two instances, one on each side of the question.

A Potato Field

The first is that of a believer who lived in New Ipswich, N. H., by the name of Hastings, who had a large field of splendid potatoes which he left undug. His neighbors were anxious about them, and came to him offering to dig them and put them in the cellar for him *free,* if he would let them, " for," said they, " you may want them." " No! " said Mr. Hastings, " I am going to let that field of potatoes preach my faith in the Lord's soon appearing."

That fall, as may be learned from the Claremont (N. H.) *Eagle,* the New York *True Sun,* and various other public journals, the potato crop was almost a total loss from the " potato rot." As expressed in the *Sun,* " How painful it is to learn that whole crops of this valuable esculent have been destroyed by the rot. A correspondent of a Philadelphia paper says the potato crop in that State is ruined. The only section from which little complaint is heard, is Maine, but even there the crop has not escaped the disease."

As the fall was mild, and Mr. Hastings's potatoes were left in the ground until November, none of them rotted. Consequently he had an abundant supply for himself and his unfortunate neighbors who had been so solicitous for his welfare the previous October, and who, in the spring, were obliged to buy seed potatoes of him, and were glad to pay a good price for them. What they supposed was going to be such a calamity to Mr. Hastings, God turned to a temporal blessing, and not only to him but to his neighbors also.

Denied His Faith

The second instance occurred in my own place of residence. It was that of a church-member who had much to say in meeting about the Lord's coming in the fall of 1844. He was a man of considerable property, and among other things, had a lot of hogs at just the right age for keeping over for the spring market. An uncle of mine, who made no religious pretensions, and whose business was the buying and selling of stock, went to this professed Adventist to buy his hogs, but learned from him that he did not wish to sell them, as he was going to keep them over till next spring for " store hogs." Uncle came to my grandfather, who was an Adventist believer, and said, " That man doesn't believe what he professes." " Why? " asked grandfather. " Because," said uncle, " he says the Lord is coming, and the world is coming to an end this fall, but he wants to keep his hogs till next spring.   He need not talk to me; he doesn't believe a word of it."

Means Offered too Late

There were men who held on to their means, struggling all the while under the conviction that they should use it to advance the work, until it was too late to invest it.   Such came to those engaged in printing the message, urging them with tears to accept their money, but the reply was, " You are too late!   We have paid for all the printing matter we can possibly circulate before the end.   We have hired several power presses to run night and day; we do not want any more money."   An eye witness testified to me that he saw men lay thousands of dollars on the desk before the publisher of the *Voice of Truth,* and in anguish of spirit beg of him to take it and use it.   The reply was, "You are too late!   We don't want your money now!   We can't use it!"   Then they asked, " Cannot it be given to the poor?"   The answer was the same, " We have made provision for the immediate wants of all such that we can reach."   In distress of mind the men took away their money, declaring that the frown of God was upon them for their lack of faith, and for the covetousness which had led them to withhold means from the cause of God when it was needed and would have been gladly used.

Guardians Appointed

The character and principles of those who left their crops standing unharvested and their shops desolate, to scatter the printed page or to talk and pray with the people from house to house, were beyond criticism.   The people questioned not that such men and women believed every word they said, and withal, such a power attended them that the honest hearted could not gainsay nor resist their words. Thousands were by this means led to believe the truth, and sought and found God's mercy.

The scoffing sinner and the worldly professor, however, decided that this work of scattering advent publications must be stopped. These men who were taking a township or a whole county and going from house to house with this advent doctrine, and neglecting their business and families, must be beside themselves, they said, and must therefore have guardians placed over them. The alleged evidences of an unsound mind exhibited by the believers (being simply labor for the salvation of their fellow-men, without testimony that the families were suffering because of the leaving of their business), were insufficient proof of insanity; consequently but few persons were placed under guardianship. Judging by the glibness with which opponents of the present day speak of the fact, one would think there were many instances; yet in all my labors as an Adventist minister, covering a period of over fifty-six years, I have met with only two cases of " Millerites " who were placed under guardians. A brief notice of these may not be out of place.

His Own Guardian

The first occurred in the State of New York, less than thirty miles from where I lived. A man accepted the advent doctrine who was worth about $100,000. He gave about half of this sum to his wife and children, who were not with him in the faith. The remainder he considered was his to use as he saw fit; and as some of it went into the advent cause, his children raised objections, and counseled with a judge, pleading that a guardian be appointed over their father. After the judge had explained to them the duties and power of a guardian in managing the property, he asked them to nominate whom they wished him to appoint. After consulting together for a time, they decided that they knew of no man with whom they dare trust the property, and reported to the judge that they had selected their father as his own guardian. The judge turned to the man and said, " Mr. ———, your children have chosen you as the proper person to manage your own property. Your affairs stand just the same as before you were brought into court." [8]

A Ludicrous Situation

The other case was that of Stockbridge Howland, of Topsham, Me. He was one of the best mechanics in all that section of country, a master workman in the construction of mills and bridges. In this "midnight cry" movement, Mr. Howland went on horseback over several townships, scattering advent papers and tracts from house to house, greatly to the annoyance of opponents and scoffers, who complained that in this tract distribution he neglected his business. So they at once secured the appointment of a guardian, who found more to do than he anticipated, as Mr. Howland sent to him all tax collectors, and in fact every one who came with accounts to be paid; "for," said he, "I am not considered competent to do any business." Soon afterward the county wished to construct a bridge over the Kennebec River,— a bridge that would stand the torrent of raging waters and floating ice in the time of spring freshets. The county commissioners and selectmen of the town decided that Stockbridge Howland was the man for the work. When they came with specifications and a contract for him to build the bridge, he said, ironically, "Gentlemen, you will have to go to my guardian. You know I am not considered competent to care for my own business, and do you come to me to build a bridge!" The situation was a little too ludicrous for sensible men, and the guardianship suddenly ended. Suffice it to say that his persecutors afterward made the most humble acknowledgments for the unjust and uncalled-for course they had taken.

[3] Although well acquainted with the person and the facts, I am not at liberty to give the name.

CHAPTER XI

THE SECOND ANGEL'S MESSAGE

AND there followed another angel, saying, Babylon is fallen, is fallen, that great city, because she made all nations drink of the wine of the wrath of her fornication," [1]

" Then the master of the house being angry said to his servant, Go out quickly into the streets and lanes of the city, and bring in hither the poor, and the maimed, and the halt, and the blind." [2]

The Lord through his ministers had stirred the world with the message, " The hour of his judgment is come," — a message on which all his professed people might have united if they would. This was the first call to the marriage " supper." It had been declared " to them that were bidden." [3] As this call was set aside with various excuses, a second call was given, corresponding to the second angel's message. [4] By this call the Lord separated a people to go forth to the end of time with the advancing light of his truth.

The Second Call to the Marriage Supper

The second message — the one following the judgment hour cry — says, " Babylon is fallen, is fallen, that great *city,* because she made all nations drink of the wine of the wrath of her fornication." And the second call to the supper reads, " Go ye out quickly into the streets and lanes of the *city,* and bring in hither the poor, and the maimed, and the halt, and the blind." In each of these scriptures the Lord's

[1] Rev. 14: 8.   [2] Luke 14: 21.   [3] Luke 14: 17.
[4] Luke 14: 21; Rev. 14: 8.

professed people are called a "city." With their conflicting, confused creeds they are called "Babylon." By another scripture referring to the last times, we see that just before the Lord's coming his people are called out of "Babylon:" "Babylon the great is fallen, is fallen, and is become the habitation of devils, and the hold of every foul spirit, and a cage of every unclean and hateful bird. . . . Come out of her, my people, that ye be not partakers of her sins, and that ye receive not of her plagues." [5]

"Remember How Thou Hast Heard"

In the address to the Sardis church we read, "Remember therefore how thou hast received and heard, and hold fast, and repent. If therefore thou shalt not watch, I will come on thee as a thief, and thou shalt not know what hour I will come upon thee." [6] The Sardis church seems to have been brought out by the Reformation, after the dark period of the work of "Jezebel" — the apostate church. The church of Sardis was told that she had been a *live* church; but when she heard and rejected the doctrine of the Lord's coming, she placed herself where she was liable to be overtaken by that event as by a "thief in the night." So, it is stated by the apostle Paul in 1 Thess. 5: 1 - 5, will be the condition of those who cry, "Peace and safety," when the Lord's coming is near. Those who follow the light of truth are called the "children of the day," and the Lord will not come on them as a thief.

In this prophetic description of the seven churches, we see the fall of the Sardis church is immediately followed by the Philadelphia, or (as the word signifies) *brotherly love,* church. Such, indeed, were the 50,000 believers who, by the second angel's message, were brought out from all the varied churches, and united in one bond of brotherly love on the great cardinal truth of the immediate advent of Christ.

[5] **Rev. 18:** 2 - 4.   [6] Rev. 3: 3.   For a full exposition of the seven churches, see "Thoughts on Daniel and the Revelation."

How the Second Message was Proclaimed

The *Midnight Cry* of Sept. 12, 1844, contains a statement made by Elder J. V. Himes respecting the second angel's message, and the circumstances which led to the proclamation of the same. His letter is dated, McConnelsville, Ohio, Aug. 29, 1844, and reads:—

" When we commenced the work with Brother Miller in 1840, he had been lecturing nine years. During that time he stood almost alone. But his labors had been incessant and effectual in awakening professors of religion to the true hope of God's people, and the necessary preparation for the advent of the Lord; as also the awakening of all classes of the unconverted to a sense of their lost condition, and the duty of immediate repentance and conversion to God, as a preparation to meet the Bridegroom in peace at his coming. Those were the great objects of his labors. He made no attempt to convert men to a sect or party in religion.

" When we were persuaded of the truth of the advent at hand, and embraced the doctrine publicly, we entertained the same views, and pursued the same course among the different sects, where we were called, in the providence of God, to labor. We told the ministers and churches that it was no part of our business to break them up, or to divide and distract them. We had one distinct object, and that was to give the ' cry,' the warning of the judgment ' at the door,' and persuade our fellow-men to get ready for the event. . . . The ministry and membership who availed themselves of our labors, but had not sincerely embraced the doctrine, saw that they must either go with the doctrine, and preach and maintain it, or in the crisis which was right upon them, they would have difficulty with the decided and determined believers. They therefore decided against the doctrine, and determined, some by one policy and some by another, to suppress the subject. This placed our brethren and sisters among them in a most trying position. Most of them loved their churches, and could not think of leaving. But when they were ridiculed, oppressed, and in various ways cut off from their former privileges and enjoyments, and when the ' meat in due season ' was withheld from them, and the siren song of ' peace and safety ' was sounded in their ears from Sabbath to Sabbath, they were soon weaned from their party predilections, and arose in the majesty of their strength, shook off the yoke, and raised the cry, ' Come out of her, my people.

In a Trying Position

" This state of things placed us in a trying position, (1) Because we were right at the end of our prophetic time, in which we expected the Lord would gather all his people *in one;* and (2) we had always preached a different doctrine: and now that the circumstances had changed, it would be regarded as dishonesty in us if we should unite in the cry of separation and breaking up of churches that had received us and our message. We therefore hesitated, and continued to act on our first position, until the church and ministry carried the matter so far that we were obliged, in the fear of God, to take a position of defense for the truth and the down-trodden children of God.

Apostolic Example for Our Course

" ' And he went into the synagogue, and spake boldly for the space of three months, disputing and persuading the things concerning the kingdom of God. But when divers were hardened, and believed not, but spake evil of that way before the multitude, he departed from them, and separated the disciples, disputing daily in the school of one Tyrannus.' [7] It was not until ' divers were hardened ' and ' spake evil of that way [the Lord's coming] before the multitude,' that our brethren were moved to come out and separate from the churches. They could not endure this ' evil speaking ' of the ' evil servants,' and the churches that could pursue the course

[7] Acts 19: 8, 9.

of oppression and 'evil speaking' toward those who were looking for the 'blessed hope,' were to them none other than the daughters of the mystic Babylon. They so proclaimed them, and came into the liberty of the gospel. And though we may not all be agreed as to what constitutes Babylon, we are agreed in the instant and final separation from all who oppose the doctrine of the coming and kingdom of God at hand. We believe it to be a case of life and death. It is death to remain connected with those bodies that speak lightly of or oppose the coming of the Lord. It is life to come out from all human tradition, and stand upon the word of God, and look daily for the appearing of the Lord. We therefore now say to all who are in any way entangled in the yoke of bondage, 'Come out from among them, and be ye separate, saith the Lord, and touch not the unclean thing; and I will receive you, and will be a Father unto you, and ye shall be my sons and daughters, saith the Lord Almighty.' " [8]

Unaccountable Opposition

Wm. Miller thus speaks of the conflict which existed at that time between the churches and the Adventists:—

"It is most unnatural and unaccountable that the Christian churches should exclude this doctrine and their members for this blessed hope. I know some of the Baptist churches say they do not exclude them for their faith, but for their communion with the advent believers. Then if it is not for their faith in a coming Saviour, why am I excluded from their pulpits, who have never communed with any but a Baptist church? It is a false plea. But this cannot be the plea of the Methodists and Presbyterians; for they believe in mixed communion. What do they exclude for? I heard of some being excluded for 'hymning' second advent melodies; others for insanity, when all the insanity proved against them was, they were watching for Christ. O God, 'forgive them, for they know not what they do.' "

[8] 2 Cor. 6: 17, 18.

Storrs on the Attitude of the Churches

George Storrs spoke of the attitude of the churches toward the Adventists, on this wise: —

"Which of them, at this moment, are not saying, ' I sit as a queen ' ?   And which of them are not pleasing themselves with the idea that some day *they* are to effect the conquest of the world, and that it is to be subjected to their faith? Which of them will suffer a soul to remain among them *in peace,* that openly and fearlessly avows his faith in the advent at the door?   Are not the terms of remaining among them undisturbed, that you ' wholly refrain ' from a *public* expression of faith in the coming of the Lord this year, whatever your convictions may be on the subject, and however important you may feel it to cry, ' Fear God, and give glory to him, for the hour of his judgment is come '? "

Mansfield's Testimony

L. D. Mansfield, writing from Oneida, N. Y., March 21, 1844, thus testifies: —

" God is moving upon the minds of his dear children who are waiting for the Lord from heaven, and leading them not only to heed the angel ' having the everlasting gospel to preach, saying, The hour of his judgment is come,' but to obey the subsequent command, ' Come out of her, my people! ' I am more fully persuaded than ever before, that the religious organizations of the present day constitute no small portion of that Babylon which is to be thrown down with violence, and found no more at all. . . . It seems to me, however, that in some of the organizations the resemblance to the little horn is most striking.   Some instances will illustrate the matter.

The Mob Spirit Manifest

" A brother who had labored very successfully in this region, in proclaiming the coming of the Lord, made an appointment to lecture at a certain place at a given time. The Lord so ordered it that he was sixteen miles from the appointment, but a —— minister was present, at the head of a mob, with tar and feathers, for the purpose of applying them to that servant of the Most High God. This same minister commenced a protracted meeting soon after, but all was as cold and icy as the glacier of the North — no souls awakened or converted. At length the minister said he believed he should ' have to take the anxious seat.'

"A class-leader in this village said to his class since we have been holding meetings here, that if any man should come into his house and say he believed Christ would come this year, he would turn him out of doors."

Duty to the Churches

We will at this point introduce a testimony from an address to the advent conference of believers assembled in Boston, Mass., dated May 31, 1844, and signed by Wm. Miller, Elon Galusha, N. N. Whiting, Apollos Hale, and J. V. Himes. They say: —

"Upon our duty to the churches we may also say a word. The danger here, as in most other cases, appears to us to be in the extremes. The first form of the danger is that of allowing the authority of the church with which we may be associated to impose silence upon us in such a question of duty. We have no doubt thousands have brought themselves into condemnation before God by yielding to the unscriptural claims of their churches in this matter, who, if they had been decided and faithful, would now be in a much more safe condition, and more useful, though they might also be called to suffer.

"The second form of danger is that of yielding to a spirit of revenge against the churches on account of their injustice toward us, and of waging an indiscriminate warfare against all such organizations. As to the duty of the Adventists, in reference to the churches with which they may be associated, if we were called upon to do it, we could give no directions which could be of general application. They must act in the fear of God, as the circumstances of the case require.

"We should, however, be decided in doing our duty, in testifying for the truth on all proper and suitable occasions. And if by taking this course we give offense to the churches, and they threaten us with expulsion unless we remain silent (though if we see fit to dissolve our relation to the church amicably, it may be the better way), *let us do our duty*, and when we are expelled, be patient in suffering the wrong, and be willing with our Master to 'go forth without the gate, bearing his reproach.'"

From these quotations respecting the action of the churches toward those giving the second angel's message, it can be readily seen how, as the first result of giving this second call to the "supper," those who were gathered into one spiritual fold are spoken of as the "maimed," "the halt," and "the blind," which strongly suggests the ill treatment they had received from the "smiting" of their "fellow-servants," from whom they had been separated.

A Separate People Chosen to Receive New Truths

The purpose of the Lord can be clearly discerned in bringing out a distinct people under the proclamation of the second angel's message — the second call to the "supper" — and the "midnight cry." Precious truths for the last days were to be searched out and proclaimed — a work which could not be done in "creed-bound" churches any more than the heralding of the gospel to the world could be accomplished by the apostolic church while retaining a connection with the Jewish sects. God called for separation there, [9] and he also called for separation of the advent believers from those who would seek to hold them in the circle of their creeds.

[9] Acts 13: 46.

Storr's "Six Sermons"

Soon after this coming out we note that the light came to the advent bands on the subject of future punishment, as set forth in the pamphlet, "Six Sermons," by George Storrs, taking the position that man by nature is mortal; that the dead are unconscious between death and the resurrection; that the final punishment of the ungodly will be total extinction; and that immortality is a gift of God, to be received only by faith in our Lord Jesus Christ.

Thousands of the Adventists accepted this doctrine of man's nature, but not all of them. The rejection of it brought no confusion among them, as it was regarded as a matter of belief simply, and no test of moral standing; hence the united effort to warn the world of the near approach of Christ was unbroken. It did, however, have the effect to stir up the ire of the churches against them.

Unable to Refute the "Six Sermons"

The Methodist minister in the town where I lived, and who had previously joined in preaching the advent doctrine in 1843, received the "Six Sermons," read it, and admitted to his church members that he was unable to refute the doctrine; but on finding that many of his church members were accepting it, he advised others not to read the book, as they "would believe the doctrine if they read it." In the month of September, 1844, after this minister returned from the annual conference, he arose in his pulpit and publicly renounced the advent doctrine, and humbly asked the pardon of the church for ever inviting the lecturers to speak in the house.

Tried for Heresy

This action on the part of the minister was soon followed by an effort to deal with the advent believers for heresy; but as they were allowed to plead their cases from the Bible, no victory was gained by the church. Several were excluded from this church because their course was not in harmony with the discipline, and many others withdrew because of this exclusion of members whose faith could not be shown to be contrary to the Scriptures. Thus the advent doctrine was forever shut out of the church where hundreds had found the Saviour and been made happy in God.

What was done in my native town was also enacted in hundreds of other churches throughout the country. Those who were thus treated by their former brethren found much consolation in the words of the prophet Isaiah: "Hear the word of the Lord, ye that tremble at his word: Your brethren that hated you, that cast you out for my name's sake, said, Let the Lord be glorified; but he shall appear to your joy, and they shall be ashamed." [10]

Wrath of the Wicked Displayed

As the day drew near on which the Lord was expected, the believers became more earnest in their labors, and the wicked raged and scoffed the more fiercely, as will be seen by the following statement made by the editor of the *Midnight Cry* of Oct. 31, 1844: —

"The effect that this movement produced upon the wicked, also greatly served to confirm us in our belief that God was in it. When God's children were met together to prostrate and humble themselves before him, and to prepare for his appearing, as it became a company of sinners to do, who could only be saved by grace, the wicked manifested the greatest malice. When we had given no notice of our meetings save in our own paper, nor had invited the public there, the sons of Belial crowded into them, and caused much disturbance. On the evening of Saturday, the 12th instant [Oct. 12, 1844], we held no meeting at the tabernacle, that the sexton [janitor], might have an opportunity to cleanse the house for the Sabbath [Sunday]. But the mob broke into the house, and refused even that privilege. The

[10] Isa. 66: 5.

mayor, however, unsolicited, promptly interfered, and expelled them.

" At our meetings on the Sabbath following, after the tabernacle was filled, a dense crowd occupied the street in. front of the building, many of them being enraged that any should believe in the advent of the Lord. In the evening, on account of the excitement of the populace, no meeting was held; yet the street was filled with the mob at an early hour; but the prompt interference of the mayor and his efficient police cleared the street, after sending a few to the watch-house. We could only liken the conduct of the mob to that which surrounded the door of Lot, on the evening pending the destruction of Sodom. . . . This movement on their part was so sudden, simultaneous, and extensive, that its manifestation on the first day of the Jewish seventh month strengthened us in our opinion that this must be the month."

Scoffers Put on Ascension Robes

On the 22nd of October, 1844, the day the twenty-three hundred days terminated, at Paris, Maine, while the believers were assembled in the house of worship, engaged in solemn prayer to God, in expectation that the Lord would come that day, the scoffing mockers gathered around the house, singing songs in burlesque.. Two of these rowdies put on long white robes and climbed upon the house top, sang songs, and mocked those in the house who were praying and waiting for the Lord to come.

It is probable that from this circumstance originated the falsehoods circulated about Adventists' putting on ascension robes; for notwithstanding advent papers have offered rewards as high as $500 for one authentic instance where an Adventist put on an ascension robe in 1844, and thus waited for the Lord to come, not one case has ever been produced.

Hazen Foss's Vision, 1844

About this time there lived in Poland, Maine, a young man by the name of Hazen Foss, who firmly believed the Lord would come on the tenth day of the seventh month. He was a man of fine appearance, pleasing address, and quite well educated. A few weeks before the "midnight cry" ended, the Lord came near and gave him a vision, in which he was shown the journey of the advent people to the city of God, with their dangers. Some messages of warning were given to him, which he was to deliver, and he had also a view of the trials and persecution that would consequently follow if he was faithful in relating what had been shown him. He, like Mr. Foy, was shown three steps by which the people of God were to come fully upon the pathway to the holy city. Being a firm believer in the Lord's coming "in a few more days" (as they then sang), the part of the vision relating to the three steps onto the pathway was to him unexplainable; and being naturally of a proud spirit, he shrunk from the cross, and refused to relate it. The vision was repeated the second time, and in addition he was told that if he still refused to relate what had been shown him, the burden would be taken from him, and be given to one of the weakest of the Lord's children, one who would faithfully relate what God would reveal. He again refused. Then a third vision was given, and he was told that he was released, and the burden was laid upon one of the weakest of the weak, who would do the Lord's bidding.

Foss Fails to Relate His Vision

This startled the young man, and he decided to relate what had been shown him, and accordingly gave out his appointment. The people crowded together to see and hear. He carefully related his experience, how he had refused to relate what the Lord had shown him, and what would result from his refusal. "Now," said he, "I will relate the vision." But alas! it was too late: he stood before the people as dumb as a statue, and finally said in the deepest agony, "I cannot remember a word of the vision." He wrung his hands in anguish, saying, "God has fulfilled his word. He has taken the vision from me," and in great distress of mind said, "I am a lost man." From that time he lost his hope in Christ, and went into a state of despair. He never attended an Adventist meeting again, and had no personal interest in religion. His demeanor in many respects, to say the least, has been that of one deprived of the gentle influence of the Spirit of the Master, of one "left to his own ways, to be filled with his own doings." In this condition of mind he died in 1893.

Foss's Vision Related by Another

About three months from the time he failed to recall his vision, he heard from an adjoining room a vision related by another. The meeting was held in a dwelling-house where he was. He was urged to come into the meeting, but refused to do so. He said the vision was as near like that shown him as two persons could relate the same thing. And thus was known what he saw but could not remember when trying to relate it. On getting a view of the person afterward, he said, "That is the instrument on whom the Lord has laid the burden."

Sadly Disappointed

The tenth day of the seventh month, Jewish time (Oct. 22, 1844), at last came. It found thousands upon thousands who were looking to that point for the consummation of their hopes. They had made provisions for nothing earthly beyond that date. They had not even cherished the thought, "if it doesn't come," but had planned their worldly affairs as they would if they had expected that day to end the period of their natural lives. They had warned and exhorted the wicked to flee from the wrath to come, and many of these *feared* that the message might prove true. They had counseled and prayed with their relatives, and had bidden good-bye to such of them as had not given their hearts to God. In short, they had bidden adieu to all earthly things with all the solemnity of one who regards himself as about to appear face to face with the Judge of all the earth. Thus, in almost breathless anxiety, they assembled at their places of worship, expecting, momentarily, to hear " the voice of the archangel and the trump of God," and to see the heavens ablaze with the glory of their coming King.

The hours passed slowly by, and when at last the sun sank below the western horizon, the Jewish tenth day of the seventh month was ended. The shades of night once more spread their gloomy pall over the world; but with that darkness came a pang of sadness to the hearts of the advent believers, such in kind as can only find a parallel in the sorrow of the disciples of our Lord. as they solemnly wended their way to their homes on the night following the crucifixion and burial of him whom but a little while before they had triumphantly escorted into Jerusalem as their King.

CHAPTER XII

THE DISAPPOINTMENT--THE BITTER BOOK

TOOK the little book out of the angel's hand, and ate it up; and it was in my mouth sweet as honey: and as soon as I had eaten it, my belly was bitter. And he said unto me, Thou must prophesy again before many peoples, and nations, and tongues, and kings. And there was given me a reed like unto a rod: and the angel stood, saying, Rise, and measure the temple of God, and the altar, and them that worship therein." [1]

In scriptural language, the "eating" of a book represents the reception of truth in order to communicate it to others, as is seen in Ezekiel, where the prophet is shown "a roll of a book," and it was said to him, "Eat this roll, and go speak unto the house of Israel." After eating the roll, he says, "Then did I eat it; and it was in my mouth as honey for sweetness." [2]

The prophet Jeremiah uses this same figure: "Thy words were found, and I did eat them; and thy word was unto me the joy and rejoicing of mine heart." [3] From this language we learn that the "sweetness" of the book while eating it represents the joy and satisfaction experienced by those who thus feed on the word of the Lord.

The Book Sweet, then Bitter

The book mentioned in Revelation 10, of which it is said that to the eater it was sweet as honey, but as soon as eaten was "bitter" (or, as some translate, "as soon as I had di-

[1] Rev. 10: 10, 11; 11: 1. [2] Eze. 3: 1 - 3. [3] Jer. 15: 16.

gested it, in my stomach it was *picra*"[4]), was that book from which the angel announced, on the authority of him who made heaven, earth, and sea, " Time shall be no longer." Eating this book, then, must represent the joyful acceptance of the *time* proclamation. The sudden bitterness of the morsel to those who ate it must represent the sad contrast in their experience after the *time* of the book is expired, and they find themselves sorely disappointed in their expectations.

The Time Proclamation a Sweet Morsel

The proclamation of the time in 1844 was indeed joyful news to those who believed, and who, without a doubt, expected so soon an eternal deliverance from all the ills, woes, and sorrows of this sinful world. The thought that in a few short weeks they should be glorified, immortalized, and be in the golden city of God, with their King, was indeed soul-inspiring. As expressed by one who had that experience, " Those who sincerely love Jesus can appreciate the feelings of those who watched with the most intense interest for the coming of their Saviour. . . . We approached this hour with a calm solemnity. The true believers rested in a sweet communion with God, an earnest of the peace that was to be theirs in the bright hereafter. Those who experienced this hope and trust can never forget those precious hours of waiting."

The peculiarly trying position of those who, on the eleventh day of the seventh month, found themselves still in this dark world of trial and temptation, where they must meet the scorn, sneers and ridicule of those whom a few hours before they had exhorted to get ready to meet their Lord, finds a fitting illustration in the case of Mary as she " stood without at the sepulcher weeping; " and when accosted by the angels with the question, " Woman, why weepest thou? " said to them, " Because they have taken away my Lord, and I know not where they have laid him." [5]

[4] Picra — a most disagreeable, bitter preparation of alcohol, aloes, and gum myrrh.
[5] John 20: 13.

Disappointed, but not Discouraged

Those who passed through this trying scene said of it: "We were perplexed and disappointed, yet did not renounce our faith. We felt that we had done our duty; we had lived up to our precious faith; we were disappointed, but not discouraged. We needed unbounded patience, for the scoffers were many. We were frequently greeted by scornful allusions to our former disappointment. 'You have not gone up yet; when do you expect to go up?' and similar sarcasms were often vented upon us by our worldly acquaintances, and even by some professed Christians, who accepted the Bible, yet failed to learn its great and important truths. Mortality still clung to us; the effects of the curse were all around us. It was hard to take up the vexing cares of life that we thought had been laid down forever."

Compared with the Disappointed Disciples

The feelings of such, when compared with their joy and rejoicing of a few hours previous, must have been to them like the pungent bitterness of picra. The world around supposed, as no doubt the masses did after Christ's crucifixion, that the believers would now renounce their faith, and join in scoffing at their own supposed folly. They very soon learned to their astonishment that the love of the Lord's appearing was not easily eradicated from the affections of those who had truly consecrated themselves to God.

"Sat not with the Mockers"

The course these earnest ones did pursue, and their feelings, are well defined by the words of the prophet Jeremiah, where he says, "Thy words were found, and I did eat them; and thy word was unto me the joy and rejoicing of mine heart: for I am called by thy name, O Lord God of hosts. I sat not in the assembly of the mockers, nor rejoiced: I sat alone because of thy hand; for thou hast filled me with indignation. Why is my pain perpetual, and my wound incurable, which refuseth to be healed? Wilt thou be altogether unto me as a liar, and as waters that fail?" [6]

James White on the Disappointment

A few brief quotations from some of these disappointed, yet hopeful ones, will give a good idea of the situation. The first is from Elder James White, who labored very successfully in 1843 and 1844. He says:—

"The disappointment at the passing of the time was a bitter one. True believers had given up all for Christ, and had shared his presence as never before. They had, as they supposed, given their last warning to the world, and had separated themselves, more or less, from the unbelieving, scoffing multitude. And with the divine blessing upon them, they felt more like associating with their soon-expected Master and holy angels, than with those from whom they had separated themselves. The love of Jesus filled the soul, and beamed from every face, and with inexpressible desires they prayed, 'Come, Lord Jesus, and come quickly,' but he did not come.

"But God did not forsake his people. . . . And with especial force and comfort did such passages as the following to the Hebrews, come home to the minds and hearts of the tried, waiting ones: 'Cast not away therefore your confidence, which hath great recompense of reward. For ye have need of patience, that, after ye have done the will of God, ye might receive the promise. For yet a little while, and he that shall come will come, and will not tarry. Now the just shall live by faith; but if any man draw back, my soul shall have no pleasure in him. But we are not of them who draw back unto perdition; but of them that believe to the saving of the soul.' [7] The points of interest in this portion of Scripture are these: —

"1. Those addressed are in danger of casting away their confidence in that in which they have done right.

[6] Jer. 15: 16 - 18.   [7] Heb. 10: 35 - 39.

"2. They had done the will of God, and were brought into that state of trial where patience was necessary.

"3. The just at this time were to live by faith, not by doubting whether they had done the will of God, but faith, in that in which they had done the will of God.

"4. Those who should not endure the trial of faith, but should cast away their confidence in the work in which they did the will of God, and drew back, would take the direct road to perdition." [8]

From N. Southard, Editor of the "Midnight Cry"

In the *Midnight Cry* of Oct. 31, 1844, about ten days after the close of the twenty-three hundred days, the following was published from the pen of the editor: —

"In view of all the circumstances attending this movement, the blessed effects it has produced on the minds of God's children, and the hatred and malice his enemies have displayed, we must regard it as the true 'midnight cry.' And if we have a few days in which to try our faith, it is still in accordance with the parable of the ten virgins; for when they had all arisen and trimmed their lamps, there was still to be a time when the lamps of the foolish virgins would be going out. This could not be till after the passing of the tenth day; for till that time their lamps would burn. There must, therefore, be a passing by of that day, for the foolish to give up their faith, as there must have been of 1843, for the tarrying time. A little delay is therefore no cause for disappointment, but shows how exact God is in the fulfilment of his word. Let us therefore hold fast the profession of our faith without wavering; for he is faithful who has promised."

From Joseph Marsh, Editor of the "Voice of Truth"

In the *Voice of Truth* of Nov. 7, 1844, we read: —

"We cheerfully admit that we have been mistaken in the nature of the event we expected would occur on the

[8] "Life Sketches," pp. 107 - 109.

tenth day of the seventh month; but we cannot yet admit that our great High Priest did not on that day accomplish all that the type would justify us in expecting. We now believe he did."

It was expected by the Adventists that on the tenth day of the seventh month, 1844, the twenty-three hundred days would end, and that on that day Christ would complete his priestly work and come to earth to bless his people. Later investigation has demonstrated that it was the beginning of his work of cleansing the heavenly sanctuary that took place on that day, and not the completion of his work as a priest. [9] Instead of regarding the work of cleansing the sanctuary as any part of Christ's work as a priest, it was claimed that the cleansing of the sanctuary was to be the purification of the earth by fire at Christ's coming. If not the whole of it, at least the land of Canaan would be cleansed at that time.

The Sanctuary Believed to be the Earth

This idea is brought out in an article by Geo. Storrs, in the *Midnight Cry* of April 25, 1844. He asks, "What is the sanctuary to be cleansed? My previous views have been that it was the whole earth. That it is a part of the earth I still believe. But what part? is the inquiry I shall endeavor to answer."

He quotes the promise to Abraham, the establishment of the same to Isaac, and its renewal to Jacob, and then quotes the song of Moses, composed by Miriam after the passage of the Red Sea, in which they sang: "Thou shalt bring them in, and plant them in the mountain of thine inheritance, in the place, O Lord, which thou hast made for thee to dwell in, in the sanctuary, O Lord, which thy hands have established." [10]

If the reader will carefully compare the above text with the record of its fulfilment made by the psalmist, he will see that it does not state that even the land of Palestine is

[9] No one at that time had any idea of a sanctuary in heaven.

[10] Ex. 15: 17.

the sanctuary. David says, when speaking of the Lord's leading the children of Israel: " He brought them to the border
of his sanctuary, even to this mountain, which his right hand
had purchased." [11] In the song at the Red Sea it is said
of the land of Canaan, that it was the place he had made
to " dwell in, in the sanctuary." So in this quotation from
the psalms, the Mount Moriah, where the sanctuary was
built, is only called ' the *border* of his sanctuary." But in
this same psalm it is said, " He chose the tribe of Judah,
the Mount Zion which he loved. And he *built* his sanctuary
like high palaces, like the earth which he hath established
forever." [12]

Cleansing the Sanctuary Thought to be Purifying the Earth

In the article above referred to, after quoting the supposed proof that the earth, or at least the land of Palestine,
was the sanctuary, the elder next proceeds to inquire, " How
will the sanctuary be cleansed? " In the words of the prophet
Micah, he replies, " For, behold, the Lord cometh forth out
of his place, and will come down, and tread upon the high
places of the earth. And the mountains shall be molten under
him, and the valleys shall be cleft, as wax before the fire,
and as the waters that are poured down a steep place." [13]

With the idea, commonly accepted at that time, that the
earth was the sanctuary, the reader will readily see why they
supposed, without a doubt, that at the end of the twenty-three
hundred days the Lord would come and purify the earth in
the manner described by Micah. In all the opposition raised
against the Adventists, not an opponent even intimated that
the cleansing of the earth by fire was not the event to take
place as the cleansing of the sanctuary, at the end of the
twenty-three hundred days.

The Apostles Disappointed, Yet Fulfilled Scripture

This is not the only instance where people have done the
will of the Lord, fulfilled scripture, and yet have been dis-

[11] Ps. 78: 54.   [12] Ps. 78: 68, 69.   [13] Micah 1: 3, 4.

appointed in their expectations simply because they did not understand the nature of the event to transpire. Thus it was with the apostles of Christ. When he was seated on the colt, riding into Jerusalem, they shouted as they remembered the words of the prophet: [14] " Shout, O daughter of Jerusalem: behold, thy King cometh unto thee; he is just, and having salvation; lowly, and riding upon an ass, and upon a colt the foal of an ass." [15]   It was so needful that there should be shouting on that occasion that had they held their peace, the very stones would have cried out. [16]   The disciples supposed that Christ, then and there, was going to ascend the throne of David as a temporal king (" we trusted that it had been he which should have redeemed Israel " [17]), and so they shouted, " Blessed be the kingdom of our father David, that cometh in the name of the Lord." [18]   How much shouting would there have been on that occasion had they understood that within a week Christ would be dead in Joseph's tomb, surrounded by the Roman guard? How much of giving " glory " to God and of consecration would there have been with the Adventists in 1844 had they understood that the cleansing of the sanctuary at the end of all prophetic time was to occupy a series of years before the Lord would come?

No Mistake in Reckoning the 2300 Days

As this people carefully looked over their reckoning of the period, they found no defect; but the Lord did not come, neither was the earth cleansed by fire. What did it mean? Of a surety they knew that the Lord had been with them in the great movement; but now they were in suspense. Their confidence in the Lord was unshaken. They knew he would not forsake them. The light would come from some source. The trying question before them is stated in the words of Jeremiah already referred to, " Wilt thou be altogether unto me as a liar, and as waters that fail? " Faith did not cherish this doubt, for the words of the Lord by the prophet Habak-

[14] John 12: 16.   [15] Zech. 9: 9.   [16] Luke 19: 40.
[17] Luke 24: 21.   [18] Mark 11: 10.

kuk respecting the vision occurred to their minds, "At the end it shall speak, and not lie." [19]   The expression already quoted from the editor of the *Voice of Truth* well sets forth their position: " We cannot yet admit that our great High Priest did not on that very day accomplish all that the type would justify us in expecting."

Light on the Sanctuary Discovered

Hiram Edson, of Port Gibson, N. Y., told me that the day after the passing of the time in 1844, as he was praying behind the shocks of corn in a field, the Spirit of God came upon him in such a powerful manner that he was almost smitten to the earth, and with it came an impression, " The sanctuary to be cleansed is in heaven." He communicated this thought to O. R. L. Crosier, and they together carefully investigated the subject.   In the early part of 1846 an elaborate exposition of the sanctuary question from a Bible standpoint, written by Mr. Crosier, was printed in the *Day Star,* a paper then published in Canandaigua, N. Y.   In that lengthy essay it was made to appear that the work of cleansing the sanctuary was the concluding work of Christ as our high priest, beginning in 1844 and closing just before he actually comes again in the clouds of heaven as King of kings and Lord of lords.

Churches Seeking Lost Members

The tenth day of the seventh month had passed, and the churches thought they were going to have an easy time regaining lost members, who had been separated from them under the " midnight cry " and the second angel's message; but in this they were greatly disappointed, as will be shown by the following reply to the importunities to return to their former organizations, as given in the *Midnight Cry* of Dec. 26, 1844:—

" But what are the facts?   They well know that in the great mass of these churches the prominent themes are, ' The

[19] Hab. 2: 3.

world's conversion,' 'a thousand years' millennium,' and 'the return of the Jews to Palestine,' before the personal advent of the Saviour. Those that go back to sit under the lullaby songs of such unscriptural, unreasonable doctrines, do it with eyes open; and such a course on their part will be 'going back,' indeed.

"Having become 'free' in a scriptural sense, it is much more safe to 'press forward' than either to 'go back' or to 'draw back,' especially at this time, when the crown of glory is so soon to be given to the faithful in Christ Jesus."

The course of the churches in putting off the coming of the Lord by the advocacy of the above unscriptural doctrines, suggested to the Adventists these words of the prophet Ezekiel: "Son of man, behold, they of the house of Israel say, The vision that he seeth is for many days to come, and he prophesieth of the times that are far off." In the same connection is found the reply which the Adventists used, "Therefore say unto them, Thus saith the Lord God: There shall none of my words be prolonged any more, but the word which I have spoken shall be done, saith the Lord God." [20]

"Thou Must Prophesy Again"

Those who "ate" the book, and gave the "time" proclamation, deemed their work for the world was done; hence the declaration that they must *again* teach nations, and tongues, and kings. Another part of the work, hitherto unseen, must now be accomplished,— that of presenting to the people the real character of the temple of God in heaven and its altar service. The command to measure the temple [21] is needful in order to gain a knowledge of the nature of the event to transpire at the close of the prophetic time, and thus an explanation be given of the words, "Then shall the sanctuary be cleansed."

Notice that the angel of this time proclamation came from heaven, and before his work is completed he gives a com-

[20] Eze. 12: 27, 28.
[21] In a measurement where no figures are given as the result, it is character, and not dimensions, that is involved.

mission to teach the people again. The message, then, which is to explain the sanctuary question, to give confidence to the disappointed ones, and at the same time furnish them a " reed," or " rod," or rule, by which the people of God can try their moral standing before him, must bear evident marks that it is heaven born, and not of human origin.

Prejudice Barred Access to the People

The existing prejudice against the advent doctrine was an almost impassable barrier to the people; and to try to teach them again without clear and positive light as to the cause of the disappointment, would be useless. The Adventist believers themselves needed to have their own souls inspired anew with a heavenly commission, before the people could be correctly taught; and how could this be accomplished? Could it be done by merely human wisdom? or would those who had experienced the deep work of the Spirit of God under the late movement, be satisfied with simply human reasoning? Nothing but a work like that of the " third angel's message " [22] could lift them out of their perplexities; and this, step by step, as they could receive it, was duly inaugurated, bearing most convincing proofs that it was of heavenly origin.

Like Sheep without a Shepherd

Here was the great advent body, in one sense, as sheep without a shepherd, thousands of whom only a few weeks previously had separated themselves from all churches and creeds, no human organizations being responsible for their spiritual welfare. They had no earthly counselors in whom they could confide; in God alone was their trust.

They were confident, however, of one thing, and this to them was like an anchor,— the *time* proclamation was right. [23] But as a people they were in a position where, unless God should guide and keep them, they were liable to accept false

[22] Rev. 14: 9 - 12.

[23] By the most careful review of their reckoning of the 2300 days, they could find no mistake, neither yet can any be found.

explanations, or lose "patience" and give up faith in their past experience. This some did; while others, with an eye of faith fixed on him whom their souls loved, earnestly inquired, "Watchman, what of the night? Watchman, what of the night? The watchman said, The morning cometh, and also the night: if ye will inquire, inquire ye: return, come." [24]

J. N. Andrews on the Disappointment

Elder J. N. Andrews, one who passed through this experience in 1844, thus speaks of the disappointment: —

"Those were disappointed who expected the Lord in 1843 and in 1844. This fact is with many a sufficient reason for rejecting all the testimony in this case. We acknowledge the disappointment, but cannot acknowledge that this furnishes a just reason for denying the hand of God in this work. The Jewish church were disappointed when, at the close of the work of John the Baptist, Jesus presented himself as the promised Messiah. And the trusting disciples were most sadly disappointed when he whom they expected to deliver Israel was by wicked hands taken and slain. And after his resurrection, when they expected him to restore again the kingdom to Israel, they could not but be disappointed when they understood that he was going away to his Father, and that they were to be left for a long season to tribulation and anguish. But disappointment does not prove that God has no hand in the guidance of his people. It should lead them to correct their errors, but it should not lead them to cast away their confidence in God. It was because the children of Israel were disappointed in the wilderness, that they so often denied divine guidance. They are set forth as an admonition to us, that we should not fall after the same example of unbelief." [25]

Truth Has a Baptism of Unpopularity

It seems to be the Lord's plan to place important truths in an unpopular channel where it will be a cross [26] to accept

[24] Isa. 21: 11, 12.   [25] "The Three Messages of Rev. 14: 6 - 12," pp. 32 - 35.
[9] Matt. 16: 24.

J. N. ANDREWS

and obey them. This is especially true in these last days.
Peter, speaking of that time when the end of all things will
be " at hand," and when the " judgment " shall " begin at the
house of God," says, " Beloved, think it not strange concerning the fiery trial which is to try you, as though some strange
thing happened unto you: but rejoice, inasmuch as ye are partakers of Christ's sufferings; that, when his glory shall be revealed, ye may be glad also with exceeding joy. If ye be
reproached for the name of Christ, happy are ye; for the
spirit of glory and of God resteth upon you: on their part he
is evil spoken of, but on your part he is glorified." [27]

When the truth has received its baptism of unpopularity,
to accept it requires more grace than simply to follow the
faith of the masses. Hypocritical pretenders see no great
inducement to accept a truth which requires action, like row-
ing up stream " 'gainst wind and tide." Thus the truth
becomes a test to the loyal, honest-hearted, sincere, and conscientious.

We have before shown that the prophecy of the advent
movement calls for a disappointment. It came; and thus, in
the providence of God, the acceptance of that message had
its cross.

[27] I Peter 4: 7, 17, 12 - 14.

CHAPTER XIII

TOKENS OF DIVINE GUIDANCE

ATH God assayed to go and take him a nation from the midst of another nation, by temptations, by signs, and by wonders, and by war, and by a mighty hand, and by a stretched-out arm, and by great terrors, according to all that the Lord your God did for you in Egypt before your eyes? Unto thee it was showed, that thou mightest know that the Lord he is God; there is none else beside him." [1]

It was thus that the Lord wrought in taking a people from the midst of a heathen nation, that he might lead them out where he could *speak* his law to them, and where he could hand it down to them graven in tables of stone. These wonders were not performed to gratify their curiosity; but that they might know of a certainty that he who had " done great things in Egypt; wondrous works in the land of Ham, and terrible things by the Red Sea," [2] and had spoken to them from amid the fire and smoke of Sinai's burning top, was none other than the living and true God, the Maker of all things.

Moses' Call from the Burning Bush

Moses himself could not have moved the Israelites to leave Egypt by simply saying to them, " As I was tending the flocks in the desert, I had thoughts of sympathy for you in your bondage, and I am now come down to lead you out of Egypt, as I assayed to do when I slew the Egyptian just before I fled to the land of Midian."

[1] Deut. 4: 34, 35. [2] Ps. 106: 21, 22.

It took the burning bush that consumed not, and an audible voice proceeding from the midst of the flames, to convince even Moses that he was the one to " go and lead the people out of Egypt." It was in this wonderful manner that he received his commission, his high and holy calling, a revelation of which would at once arrest the attention of his brethren, and prepare their minds for what should follow, and thus lead them to accept Moses, under God, as their leader.

If ever there was a time since the Saviour's resurrection when his sorrowing and disappointed followers needed to be comforted by his presence and cheering words, it was at that time when some of the sad and persecuted believers were holding on by steadfast faith after the "midnight cry" of 1844; and if in mercy God ever communicated directly to sorrowing souls, it would seem that it would certainly be at such a time, and to such a people.

The Presence of the Lord Promised

He who is not limited in ways or means of working, and who placed the gifts of the Spirit in his church " when he ascended up on high," [3] promised to be with his followers in preaching the gospel, " even unto the end of the world."

All the way along the Lord has been ready to show forth his power and his gifts with those who fully sought him. Did he not say in giving the gospel commission, " These signs shall follow them that believe: In my name shall they cast out devils; they shall speak with new tongues; they shall take up serpents; and if they drink any deadly thing, it shall not hurt them; they shall lay hands on the sick, and they shall recover "? [4]

Gifts of the Spirit During the Reformation

There were some wonderful displays of the Lord's power and manifestations of the gift of prophecy during the Reformation of the sixteenth century, and in the times following.

[3] Eph. 4: 8 - 15.　　　[4] Mark 16: 17, 18.

D'Aubigné speaks of the prophecies of John Huss. Charles Buck, in his "Religious Anecdotes," tells of the prophesying of George Wishart, in 1546. John Wesley, in his works, tells of the prophecies of Jonathan Pyrah, and their fulfilment. Elder J. B. Finley, in his autobiography, tells of a remarkable vision and healing in his own person, in the summer of 1842. The *Christian Advocate* (Methodist) published an interesting account of a remarkable vision and its results, as given to Doctor Bond, of that church, during his ministry. These were tokens to those humbly seeking the Lord, that he had not changed, and that he still would speak to his people through the prophetic gift.

The Remnant Church to Have the Spirit of Prophecy

There are plain and specific statements in the Scriptures that the Lord will specially manifest the gifts of his Spirit, and especially the gift of prophecy, among the people who will be found waiting for his coming. The first text that we call attention to is found in the letter to the Corinthians, and reads: "I thank my God always on your behalf, for the grace of God which is given you by Jesus Christ; that in everything ye are enriched by him, in all utterance, and in all knowledge; even as the testimony of Christ was confirmed in you: so that ye come behind in no gift; waiting for the coming of our Lord Jesus Christ; who shall also confirm you unto the end, that ye may be blameless in the day of our Lord Jesus Christ." [5]

In the revelation we read of the "remnant"— the last gospel church: "The dragon was wroth with the woman [church], and went to make war with the remnant of her seed, which keep the commandments of God, and have the testimony of Jesus Christ." [6] What is the "testimony of Jesus," we inquire, which the last church is to *have,* and which in its confirmation prepares the way for the manifestation of all the gifts of the Spirit? To this question we find an answer in the testimony of the angel to John on the isle of Patmos:

[5] 1 Cor. 1: 4 - 8.   [6] Rev. 12: 17.

" I fell at his feet to worship him. And he said unto me, See thou do it not: I am thy fellow-servant, and of thy brethren that have the *testimony of Jesus:* worship God: for the testimony of Jesus is the spirit of prophecy." [7]

This definition given by the angel shows that it is the " spirit of prophecy " manifest in the church that is waiting for Christ that prepares the way for all the gifts, and that war is made on the " remnant " church for having that gift among them.

Paul's Testimony on the Gifts

Paul's letter to the Thessalonians shows that the day of the Lord — the final day of executive judgment — will come upon the masses " as a thief in the night; " but that it will not thus overtake the Lord's faithful children because they are " children of light, and the children of the day." Among his admonitions to that *watching* people he says, " Quench not the Spirit. Despise not *prophesyings.* Prove all things; hold fast that which is good." [8]

Of the Greek word *propheteias,* here rendered prophesyings, Greenfield, in his Greek Lexicon, says, " The exercise of the gift of prophecy, in this sense, 1 Thess. 5: 20." With this also agree the lexicons of Parkhurst, Robinson, and Liddell and Scott. This, then, is a plain testimony that the true gift of prophecy will be with the church waiting for Christ's second coming. The admonition is not to despise the gift, but to *prove* it; finding the *good* manifestation, to " hold fast " to it. [9]

A Fulfilment of the Promise

We have noted heretofore how the Lord began to manifest the gift of prophecy during the proclamation of the first and second angels' messages. This gift has been more fully developed since the close of the twenty-three hundred days.

---

[7] Rev. 19: 10.   [8] 1 Thess. 5: 5, 19 - 21.

[9] For a full canvass of the Bible testimony on the perpetuity of spiritual gifts, see " Prophetic Gift in the Gospel Church," a pamphlet of 120 pages, to be obtained from any of our publishing houses.

The Lord chose his own instrument for this purpose, selecting as his agent one who had not only surrendered all for him, but whose life trembled in the balance, " the weakest of the weak." [10] Within two months after the passing of the time, Miss Ellen G. Harmon, of Portland, Maine, then only about seventeen years of age, began to receive revelations from the Lord.

As I have had opportunity to converse with those living at Portland at the time of the first vision, and was also acquainted with Mrs. Haines, at whose house Miss Harmon had her first vision, I will relate the facts as they were given me by those persons.

Miss Harmon was at that time in a very critical condition of health. For a number of weeks she had scarcely been able to speak above a whisper. One physician had decided that her trouble was dropsical consumption. He said her right lung was decayed, and the left one considerably diseased, and that her heart was affected. He said he did not think she could live but a very short time at most, and was liable to drop away at any time. It was with great difficulty that she could breathe when lying down. At night she obtained rest only by being bolstered up in the bed in an almost sitting posture. Frequent spells of coughing and hemorrhages from the lungs had greatly reduced her physical strength.

Miss Harmon's First Vision

At the time she had her first vision she was staying at the home of Mrs. Haines. It was in the morning, and they were engaged in family worship. There were five persons present, all sisters in the faith. Others had prayed, and Miss Harmon was praying in a whisper, when the power of God came down in a most wonderful manner, manifestly affecting all who were present, and in a moment she was lost to all that was transpiring around her — she was in vision.

In the next meeting she related to the believers in Port- and what had been shown her. They had full confidence that

[10] As shown to Hazen Foss. See page 182.

it was from the Lord. There were about sixty at that time in Portland who indorsed it as the work of the Lord. There was a power that attended the vision, as well as the relation of it, that could emanate only from the Divine. A solemn sense of eternal interests was constantly upon her, and she seemed to be filled with an unspeakable awe that one so young and feeble as she should be chosen as an instrument through whom the Lord would communicate light to his people. She stated that while in the vision she seemed to be surrounded by radiant angels in the glorious courts of heaven, where all is joy and peace, and that it was a sad change to awaken to the unsatisfying realities of this mortal life.

Synopsis of the First Vision

The following brief synopsis of her first vision, as related by her to the believers in Portland, will give some idea of the character of all of them : —

"While praying, the power of God came upon me as I had never felt it before. I was surrounded with light, and was rising higher and higher from the earth. I turned to look for the advent people in the world, but could not find them, when a voice said to me, 'Look again, and look a little higher.' At this I raised my eyes, and saw a straight and narrow path, cast up high above the world. On this path the Advent people were traveling to the city, which was at the farther end of the path. They had a bright light set up behind them at the first end of the path, which an angel told me was the 'midnight cry.' This shone all along the path, and gave light for their feet, that they might not stumble. And if they kept their eyes fixed on Jesus, who was just before them, leading them to the city, they were safe. But soon some grew weary; they said the city was a great way off, and they expected to have entered it before. Then Jesus would encourage them by raising his glorious right arm, and from his arm came a bright light, which waved over the advent people, and they shouted, Hallelujah! Others rashly denied the light behind them, and said that it was not God that had led them out so far. The light behind these went out, leaving their feet in perfect darkness, and they stumbled and got their eyes off the mark, and lost sight of Jesus, and fell off the path down into the dark and wicked world below. Soon we heard the voice of God like many waters, which gave us the day and hour of Jesus' coming. The living saints knew and understood the voice, while the wicked thought it was thunder and an earthquake. When God spake the time, he poured on us the Holy Spirit, and our faces began to light up and shine with the glory of God, as Moses' did when he came down from Mount Sinai." [11]

Description of Mrs. White's Condition While in Vision

Before we trace further the thrilling account of this wonderful manifestation of the Spirit of God, I will state some facts relative to the visions. The first time I saw Mrs. E. G. White (formerly Miss Harmon) was in October, 1852. On that day I saw her in a vision that lasted over one hour. Since that time I have had the privilege of seeing her in vision about fifty times. I have been present when physicians have examined her while in this state, and I esteem it a pleasure to bear testimony to what I have seen and know. I trust a narration of the facts in the case may not be care-lessly cast aside for the random suppositions of those who have never seen her in this condition.

In passing into vision she gives three enrapturing shouts of " Glory! " which echo and re-echo, the second, and especially the third, fainter, but more thrilling than the first, the voice resembling that of one quite a distance from you, and just going out of hearing. For about four or five seconds she seems to drop down like a person in a swoon, or one having lost his strength; she then seems to be instantly filled with superhuman strength, sometimes rising at once to her feet and walking about the room. There are frequent move-

[11] " Early Writings, Experience and Views," pp. 30 - 32.

MRS. E. G. WHITE

ments of the hands and arms, pointing to the right or left as her head turns. All these movements are made in a most graceful manner. In whatever position the hand or arm may be placed, it is impossible for any one to move it. Her eyes are always open, but she does not wink; her head is raised, and she is looking upward, not with a vacant stare, but with a pleasant expression, only differing from the normal in that she appears to be looking intently at some distant object. She does not breathe, yet her pulse beats regularly. Her countenance is pleasant, and the color of her face as florid as in her natural state.

Compared to That of Daniel

Her condition as to breathing, loss of strength, and being made strong as the angel of God touches her, all agree perfectly with the description given by the prophet Daniel of his own experience in vision when he says: " Therefore I was left alone, and saw this great vision, and there remained no strength in me; for my comeliness was turned in me into corruption, and I retained no strength." " For how can the servant of this my lord talk with this my lord? for as for me, straightway there remained no strength in me, neither is there breath left in me. Then there came again and touched me one like the appearance of a man, and he strengthened me, and said, O man greatly beloved, fear not: peace be unto thee; be strong, yea, be strong. And when he had spoken unto me, I was strengthened, and said, Let my Lord speak; for thou hast strengthened me." [12]

TESTIMONIALS OF EYE-WITNESSES

M. G. Kellogg, M. D.

As to Mrs. White's condition while in vision, a few statements from eye-witnesses may be in place. The first is from M. G. Kellogg, M. D., who refers to the first vision given in Michigan, May 29, 1853, at a meeting held in Tyrone, Livingston County. He says: —

[12] Dan. 10: 8, 17 - 19.

"Sister White was in vision about twenty minutes or half an hour. As she went into vision every one present seemed to feel the power and presence of God, and some of us did indeed feel the Spirit of God resting upon us mightily. We were engaged in prayer and social meeting Sabbath morning at about nine o'clock. Brother White, my father, and Sister White had prayed, and I was praying at the time. There had been no excitement, no demonstrations. We did plead earnestly with God, however, that he would bless the meeting with his presence, and that he would bless the work in Michigan. As Sister White gave that triumphant shout of 'Glory! g-l-o-r-y-! g-l-o-r-y-!' which you have heard her give so often as she goes into vision, Brother White arose and informed the audience that his wife was in vision. After stating the manner of her visions, and that she did not breathe while in vision, he invited any one who wished to do so to come forward and examine her. Dr. Drummond, a physician, who was also a First-day Adventist preacher, who (before he saw her in vision) had declared her visions to be of mesmeric origin, and that he could give her a vision, stepped forward, and after a thorough examination, turned very pale, and remarked, '*She doesn't breathe!*'

"I am quite certain that she did not breathe at that time while in vision, nor in any of several others which she has had when I was present. The coming out of the vision was as marked as her going into it. The first indication we had that the vision was ended, was in her again beginning to breathe. She drew her first breath deep, long, and full, in a manner showing that her lungs had been entirely empty of air. After drawing the first breath, several minutes passed before she drew the second, which filled the lungs precisely as did the first; then a pause of two minutes, and a third inhalation, after which the breathing became natural." Signed, "M. G. Kellogg, M. D., Battle Creek, Mich., Dec. 28, 1890."

F. C. Castle

We give the following statement from an individual who witnessed a medical examination of Mrs. White while in vision at Stowe, Vermont, in the summer of 1853. He says : —

" A physician was present, and made such examination of her as his wisdom and learning dictated, to find the cause of the manifestation. A lighted candle was held close to her eyes, which were wide open; not a muscle of the eye moved. He then examined her in regard to her pulse, and also in regard to her breathing, and there was no respiration. The result was that he was satisfied that it could not be accounted for on natural or scientific principles." Signed, " F. C. Castle."

D. H. Lamson

The following testimonials relate to an examination made while Mrs. White was in vision, in a meeting held in the home of Elder James White, on Monroe Street, Rochester, N. Y., June 26, 1854 : —

" I was then seventeen years old. It seems to me I can almost hear those thrilling shouts of ' G-l-o-r-y ! ' which she uttered. Then she sank back to the floor, not falling, but sinking gently, and was supported in the arms of an attendant. Two physicians came in, an old man and a young man. Brother White was anxious that they should examine Sister White closely, which they did. A looking-glass was brought, and one of them held it over her mouth while she talked; but very soon they gave this up, and said, ' She doesn't breathe.' Then they closely examined her sides, as she spoke, to find some evidence of deep breathing, but they did not find it. As they closed this part of the examination, she arose to her feet, still in vision, holding a Bible high up, turning from passage to passage, quoting correctly, although the eyes were looking upward and away from the book.

" She had a view of the seven last plagues. Then she saw the triumph of the saints, and her shouts of triumph I can seem to hear even now. To these facts I freely testify." Signed, " Elder D. H. Lamson, Hillsdale, Mich., Feb. 8, 1893."

Mrs. Drusilla Lamson

Another testimonial is given respecting the same medical examination from Mrs. Drusilla Lamson, widow of Elder Lamson's cousin, and matron of Clifton Springs, N. Y., Sanitarium. Speaking of the meeting of June 26, 1854, she says :—

" I remember the meeting when the trial was made, namely, to test what Brother White had frequently said, that Sister White did not breathe while in vision, but I cannot recall the name of the doctor who was present. . . . It must have been Doctor Fleming, as he was the doctor called sometimes for counsel. He is, however, now dead. I can say this much, that *the test was made,* and *no sign of breath* was visible on the looking-glass." Signed, " Drusilla Lamson, Clifton Springs, N. Y., March 9, 1893."

Still another testimony from one who was present on the above-mentioned occasion : —

David Seeley

" This is to certify that I have read the above testimonials of David Lamson and Mrs. Drusilla Lamson, concerning the physician's statement when examining Mrs. E. G. White while she was in vision, June 26, 1854. I was present at that meeting, and witnessed the examination. I agree with what is stated by Brother and Sister Lamson, and would say further that it *was* Doctor Fleming and another younger physician who made the examination. After Mrs. White rose to her feet, as they have stated, quoting the texts of Scripture, Doctor Fleming called for a lighted candle. He held this candle as near her lips as possible without burning, and in direct line with her breath in case she breathed. There was not the slightest flicker of the blaze. The doctor then said, with emphasis, '*That settles it forever, there is no breath in her body.*'" Signed, "David Seeley, Fayette, Iowa, Aug. 20, 1897."

Mr. and Mrs. A. F. Fowler

The following statements relate to an examination made while Mrs. White was in vision in Waldron's Hall, Hillsdale, Mich., in the month of February, 1857. Doctor Lord, a physician of Hillsdale of fifty years' practice, made a most careful examination, concerning which I present the following testimonials: —

"We were present when (in February, 1857) Sister E. G. White had a vision in Waldron's Hall, Hillsdale. Dr. Lord made an examination, and said, 'Her heart beats, but there is no breath. There is life, but no action of the lungs; I cannot account for this condition.'" Signed, "A. F. Fowler, Mrs. A. F. Fowler, Hillsdale, Mich., Jan. 1, 1891."

C. S. Glover

Here is given another statement concerning the same vision: —

"I was present when Sister White had the above-named vision in Waldron's Hall, Hillsdale. In addition to the above statement, I heard the doctor say that Sister White's condition in vision was 'beyond his knowledge.' He also said, 'There is something supernatural about that.'" Signed, "C. S. Glover, Battle Creek, Mich., Jan. 19, 1891."

Mr. and Mrs. Carpenter

Here is a third statement on the same case: —

"This is to certify that we were present in Waldron's Hall, Hillsdale, Mich., in February, 1857, when Mrs. E. G. White had a vision, and while in that condition was examined by Dr. Lord, and we heard his public statement respecting the case, as given above by Brother and Sister Fowler." Signed,

14

"W. R. Carpenter, Eliza Carpenter, Noblesville, Ind., Aug. 30, 1891."

D. T. Bourdeau

Your attention is next called to a test applied while Mrs. White was in vision at Buck's Bridge, St. Lawrence County, N. Y.: —

"June 28, 1857, I saw Sister Ellen G. White in vision for the first time. I was an unbeliever in the visions; but one circumstance among others that I might mention convinced me that her visions were of God. To satisfy my mind as to whether she breathed or not, I first put my hand on her chest sufficiently long to know that there was no more heaving of the lungs than there would have been had she been a corpse. I then took my hand and placed it over her mouth, pinching her nostrils between my thumb and forefinger, so that it was impossible for her to exhale or inhale air, even if she had desired to do so. I held her thus with my hand about ten minutes, long enough for her to suffocate under ordinary circumstances; she was not in the least affected by this ordeal. Since witnessing this wonderful phenomenon, I have not once been inclined to doubt the divine origin of her visions." Signed, "D. T. Bourdeau, Battle Creek, Mich., Feb. 4, 1891."

A Spirit Medium Doctor Testing the Vision

I will mention another medical examination that I witnessed at Parkville, St. Joseph County, Mich., Jan. 12, 1861.

At the close of an exhortation given by Mrs. White to a large congregation that had assembled at the Adventist meeting-house, the blessing of God rested upon her in a remarkable degree, and she was taken off in vision while seated in her chair. There was present a Doctor Brown, a hale, strong man physically, a spirit medium. He had said that her visions were the same as spirit mediumship, and that if she had one where he was, he could bring her out of it in one minute. An invitation was given for any who desired to do so to come forward, and by examination satisfy themselves as to her condition while in vision. The doctor came forward, but before he had half completed his examination, he turned deathly pale, and shook like an aspen leaf. Elder White said, "Will the doctor report her condition?" He replied, "She does not breathe," and rapidly made his way to the door. Those at the door who knew of his boasting said, "Go back, and do as you said you would; bring that woman out of the vision." In great agitation he grasped the knob of the door, but was not permitted to open it until inquiry was made by those near the door, "Doctor, what is it?" He replied, "*God only knows; let me out of this house;*" and out he went.

It was evident that the spirit that influenced him as a medium was no more at rest in the presence of the power that controlled Mrs. White in vision than were the demoniacs in the days of the Saviour, who inquired, "Art thou come hither to torment us before the time?" [13]

A similarity is seen in this circumstance to that recorded in the experience of Daniel the prophet. As he went into vision by the Spirit of the Lord, the Chaldeans who were present — heathens who knew not that Spirit — were greatly terrified, and "fled to hide themselves." [14]

Miss Harmon Bidden to Relate Her Visions

About one week after her first vision, at a meeting held in her father's house, Miss Harmon had a second vision in which she was bidden to make known to others what had been revealed to her. She was in great perplexity to know how she could do the Lord's bidding. Her health was so poor that she was in actual bodily suffering, and to all appearance had but a short time to live. She was but seventeen years of age, small and frail, unused to society, and naturally so timid and retiring that it was painful for her to meet strangers. She prayed earnestly for several days,

[13] Matt. 8: 29.   [14] Dan. 10: 7.

and far into the night, that this burden might be removed, and laid upon some one else more capable of bearing it. But the light of duty never changed, and the words of the angel sounded continually, " Make known to others what I have revealed to you."

While in this perplexed state of mind, Miss Harmon attended another meeting held at her father's house. In this meeting the company all united in earnest prayer for her, and once more she consecrated herself to the Lord, and felt willing to be used to his glory. While praying, the thick darkness that had enveloped her, scattered; and as she afterward said, a bright light, like a ball of fire, came toward her, and as it fell upon her, her strength was taken away, and she seemed to be in the presence of Jesus and the angels. Again it was repeated, " Make known to others what I have revealed to you." She said that she earnestly begged that if she must go and relate what the Lord had shown her, she might be kept from exaltation. Then an angel told her that her prayer was answered, and that if she should be in danger of exaltation she would be afflicted with sickness. The angel said to her, " If ye deliver the message faithfully, and endure unto the end, ye shall eat of the fruit of the tree of life, and drink of the river of the water of life."

Miss Harmon's Visit to Poland, Maine

Miss Harmon had been shown that she must go to Poland, Maine, and narrate her vision. The day after this third vision, unexpectedly to all, her brother-in-law drove up to the door of her father's house, and proposed to take her to Poland. While there she held a meeting in which she related the vision. Hazen Foss, [15] being in despair, could not be induced to attend the service, but with his ear near to the door outside, he heard her recount her vision, and said, " The vision she has related is as near like what was shown to me as two persons could describe the same thing." The next morning he unexpectedly met Miss Harmon, and told her to

[15] See Chapter XI, pp. 182, 183

be " faithful in bearing the burden, and in relating the testimonies the Lord should give her, and she would not be forsaken of God." To others he said, " That is the instrument on whom the Lord has laid this burden." He surely ought to know, as he had seen the person in the vision in which he was told that the burden was " taken from " him.

Miss Harmon's work from that time was in going from place to place in the New England States, relating what had been shown her. In some instances she was told, in vision, where to go, and also told what difficulties she would meet. Her messages were, especially, reproofs for those who were drifting into the doctrine of the spiritual advent of Christ, and encouraging all to hold on to the past experience.

She says of her experience: " Some refrained wholly from labor, and disfellowshiped all those who would not receive their views on this point. . . . God revealed these errors to me in vision, and sent me to his erring children to declare them; but many of them wholly rejected the message, and charged me with conforming to the world. On the other hand, the nominal Adventists charged me with fanaticism, and I was falsely, and by some wickedly, represented as being the leader of the fanaticism that I was actually laboring to do away." [16] Of this we shall learn more fully in the succeeding chapter.

[16] " Early Writings," page 17.

CHAPTER XIV

THE SHUT DOOR

"WHILE they went to buy, the bridegroom came; and they that were ready went in with him to the marriage: and the door was shut."[1]

The coming of the Bridegroom introduced in this parable is not the coming of Christ to the earth, but to the marriage. The marriage is an event that takes place before the Lord's coming. It is expressed in the Gospel recorded by Luke thus: "Let your loins be girded about, and your lights burning; and ye yourselves like unto men that wait for their Lord, when he will return from the wedding; that when he cometh and knocketh, they may open unto him immediately."[2]

Receiving a Kingdom Called a Marriage

The coming of the Bridegroom to the marriage is represented in Dan. 7:13, 14, where Christ comes to the Father to receive his kingdom. In ancient times the coming of a king to his capital city to receive his throne and kingdom was called a marriage. This event — the receiving of the capital city as the bride — was celebrated with the pomp and show of a real marriage. So when Christ receives from the Father in heaven his kingdom, he is said to be married to his bride — the New Jerusalem (Rev. 21:9); and this is called in the parable "*the marriage.*"

After the close of the twenty-three hundred days, Oct. 22, 1844, the Advent people, who compared events in their experience with the facts connected with an Eastern marriage, said, "Christ has gone in to the marriage." As they received

[1] Matt. 25:10.   [2] Luke 12:35, 36.

clearer light on the nature of the event to take place at the end of the twenty-three hundred days, their faith followed Christ in the work upon which he had entered; so by faith, they " went in with him to the marriage."

"I Will Return"

In a view given Miss Harmon, in 1845, of Christ passing from the first to the second apartment of the heavenly sanctuary, we find these words: " ' Wait here; I am going to my Father to receive the kingdom; keep your garments spotless, and in a little while I will return from the wedding and receive you unto myself.' Then a cloudy chariot, with wheels like flaming fire, surrounded by angels, came where Jesus was. He stepped into the chariot, and was borne to the holiest, where the Father sat." [3]

Mercy after the Door is Closed

The shut door of this parable seems to have reference to an event that occurs before the actual coming of the Son of man in the clouds of heaven; for *after* the door is shut, the other virgins come and knock, and are told to " watch " because they know not the day nor the hour of his coming. Again, this door is shut *after* the wise virgins go in with the Bridegroom to the marriage.

It would seem from the language used in this parable of the virgins that after the going in to the marriage there is still opportunity for even the " foolish " virgins to make an acceptable preparation to meet the Bridegroom. They are commanded to " watch." Watching and waiting are features connected with the true preparation to meet the Lord. It would appear, therefore, that mercy is not withdrawn when the door in this parable is closed.

Not the Door of Luke 13:25-28

In the past, errors have been made in confounding the door spoken of in this parable with the door mentioned in

[3] " Early Writings," page 46.

Luke 13 : 25 - 28, which reads, " When once the master of the house.is risen up, and hath shut to the door, and ye begin to stand without, and to knock at the door, saying, Lord, Lord, open unto us ; and he shall answer and say unto you, I know you not whence ye are. . . . Depart from me, all ye workers of iniquity. There shall be weeping and gnashing of teeth, when ye shall see Abraham, and Isaac, and Jacob, and all the prophets, in the kingdom of God, and you yourselves thrust out." It is very evident from the above language that when this door is shut, the fate of those shut out is decided. The kingdom of God has then come ; for they shall *see* the saved *in the kingdom.* On the contrary, in the parable of the virgins the Lord has not yet come into his kingdom, but has gone to his Father to receive his kingdom.

A Closed Door in the Typical Service

Those who by faith followed Christ in his work, after the close of the period of twenty-three hundred days — Oct. 22, 1844 — saw that when the day of atonement came in the typical service the high priest closed the door of the outer apartment and opened the door into the holy of holies, there to perform his work of blotting out the sins confessed in the sanctuary ; and that even so Christ, our high priest, had closed the door of the outer apartment of the heavenly temple, and opened that apartment in which was seen " the ark of his testament." [4]

Who Were in Error ?

At this date there were those among the Adventist believers who had not yet received clear light on the sanctuary service of Christ, their attention not yet having been called to the third angel's message. These erred in confounding this outer door of the sanctuary with the shut door in Luke 13 : 25 - 28. However, these were not Seventh-day Adventists. But *who* they were, and *how* that doctrine originated, and *what* circumstances led to such conclusions, we shall endeavor to show.

[4] Rev. 11: 19.

The people who had separated themselves from the nominal churches under the proclamation of the advent message, as well as those from whom they had thus separated, are addressed in the testimony to the fifth and sixth of the seven churches of the Revelation. The admonition to the fifth, the Sardis, church reads, " Remember therefore how thou hast received and heard, and hold fast, and repent. If therefore thou shalt not watch. I will come on thee as a thief, and thou shalt not know what hour I will come upon thee." [5] From this language it is evident that the persons thus addressed had heard the proclamation of the Lord's coming. They had professedly received it, but were now about to renounce the same.

The Philadelphia Church

The Philadelphia church, the sixth state of the gospel church, is next mentioned. This church represents the people who had been brought out under the proclamation of the first and second messages of Revelation 14. To this church the Lord says, " Behold, I come quickly: hold that fast which thou hast, that no man take thy crown." [6] They are still further addressed in the following words: " These things saith he that is holy, he that is true, he that hath the key of David, he that openeth, and no man shutteth; and shutteth, and no man openeth: I know thy works: behold, I have set before thee an open door, and no man can shut it; for thou hast a little strength, and hast kept my word, and hast not denied my name." [7]

What is the Shut Door of this Parable?

What is to be understood by the *open* and *shut* door in the scripture just quoted? We think a satisfactory answer to the question may be found in the accompanying explanation: While there were those among the Adventists who had received advanced light, and were teaching that the Saviour had changed his service from the first to the second apartment

[5] Rev. 3: 3.   [6] Rev. 3: 11.   [7] Rev. 3: 7, 8.

of the heavenly sanctuary, and were correctly presenting the open and shut door question to those who would hear, another class opposed this truth, and were trying to establish faith in the doctrine that the open door was closed, and the closed door open. In doing this they were hedging up the way, or hindering the work, of the Lord's servants here on earth. The doors of the heavenly sanctuary are opened and closed by the power of Christ — " He that openeth, and no man shutteth." In the address to the Philadelphia church, the people who hold fast, keep the word, and do not deny his name, gain a victory that opens a door that no man can shut. This undoubtedly refers to the door of access to the people, which door men, seemingly (as we shall see), had effectively *shut;* but as a recognition of their steadfastness, the Lord sets before the faithful an " open door " that *no man can shut.*

A Door of Utterance

Many instances are given in the Scriptures in which a *door* is used in this sense. Paul, in writing to the Corinthians, says, "A great door and effectual is opened unto me, and there are many adversaries." [8] Again, in his second letter to the Corinthians, he says, " When I came to Troas to preach Christ's gospel, and a door was opened unto me of the Lord, I had no rest in my spirit, because I found not Titus my brother." [9] He also made request of the Colossians on this wise: "Continue in prayer, and watch in the same with thanksgiving; withal praying also for us, that God would open unto us a door of utterance, to speak the mystery of Christ, for which I am also in bonds." [10]

From these scriptures it appears that openings for the proclamation of the truth are called *open doors;* and from the words spoken to the Philadelphia church it would seem that at the time this people were called out, men were making strenuous efforts to close the door of utterance against them. As the Philadelphia church passed through the trial, holding fast to his " word " and " name," the word of the Lord to

[8] I Cor. 16: 9.   [9] 2 Cor. 2: 12, 13.   [10] Col. 4: 2, 3.

them was, that he would place before them *an open door* that no man could shut.

The Situation after Oct. 22, 1844

Having the case before us as stated in the words of prophecy, let us take a retrospective view of the situation as events developed. As has already been presented, down to April, 1844, churches were opened to the proclamation of the advent message, the calls for laborers being more numerous than could be supplied by the living preachers. After the disappointment, in the spring of 1844, those who had not in sincerity embraced the doctrine, turned to opposing it. When, in the summer of 1844, as the second angel's message of Revelation 14 and the " midnight cry " (Matthew 25) were given, there arose the most bitter persecution of those who still dared affirm their faith in the near coming of the Lord. These opponents sought by various means to suppress the subject, and in every way possible to hinder the work of those who still proclaimed " the hour of his judgment is come." William Miller said of this opposition, " It is the most unnatural and unaccountable." So determined was the opposition near the close of the twenty-three hundred days that Geo. Storrs said of it, " We have done with the nominal churches and all the wicked, except so far as this cry may affect them."

After the close of the period, as the opposition and scoffing from the wicked was doubly and trebly intensified, William Miller said of the situation, " We have done our work in warning sinners, and in trying to awake a formal church. God in his providence has *shut the door*." [11]

The General Hardness of Sinners

This course of the scoffing world not only hardened sinners against the advent doctrine, but the testimony of those in the nominal churches was this: " When we call to mind how ' few and far between ' cases of true conversion are, and the almost unparalleled impertinence and hardness of sinners,

[11] *Advent Herald.* Dec. 11, 1844.

we almost involuntarily exclaim, ' Has God forgotten to be gracious? or is the door of mercy closed?' " [12]

From another worker we read still further of the situation after the close of the prophetic period: " It was then next to impossible to obtain access to unbelievers, the disappointment in 1844 had so confused the minds of many, and they would not listen to any explanation of the matter." [13]

All Doors of Access to Unbelievers Closed

Such a condition seemed, for the time being, to *shut* the *door* of access to any but those who still held fast their faith and hope in the soon coming of Christ.   As the *door of utterance* appeared so completely *closed,* and the Adventist people saw that there was a *shut door* in the parable applying to their experience, it can be readily seen how they arrived at the conclusion that there was no more mercy for sinners: or, as some expressed it, that " the door of mercy was closed," especially if they thought the shut door in this parable and the shut door in Luke 13 were the same.   If the people utterly refused to hear, thus hardening the heart, how could they be converted?

Who First Taught the False Shut Door?

The question now arises, *Who* began the teaching of the doctrine of " no mercy for sinners "? *who* believed it? and *who* rejected it?   As an answer to the first question, we will call attention to the report of a visit made by J. V. Himes in the spring of 1845, to the State of Maine.   He says:—

" Brother Joseph Turner and others took the ground that we were in the great Sabbath — that the six thousand years had ended — consequently no Adventist should perform any more manual labor.   To do so would surely, in their estimation, result in their *final destruction.*

" While waiting in this position of idleness as to worldly manual labor, a new light, as it was thought, shone upon

[12] Circleville, Ohio, *Religious Telescope,* 1844.
[13] Mrs. E. G. White, in *Advent Review,* Nov. 20, 1883.

Brother Turner's mind, viz., that *the Bridegroom* HAD COME —
that he came on the tenth day of the seventh month of the
Jewish year last past — that the marriage then took place —
that all the virgins then, in some sense, went in with him
to the marriage, and the *door was shut!* — none of these could
be lost, and none without could be saved. Thus all the spiritual affairs of this mighty globe were finished." [14]

Who Stoutly Opposed the False Theory?

Elder Turner began teaching his " no-more-mercy " doctrine in Paris, Maine, and for a little time had quite a following
in that section of country. As there was such a complete
shut door of *access* to the people outside of Adventists, whether
professor or nonprofessor, many quite naturally drifted into
Turner's view of the subject.

Lest the term Adventists should be misunderstood, we
will hereafter speak of this people as First-day Adventists;
and it was many of this class that were accepting Mr. Turner's
views. They had not as yet seen or heard the Sabbath truth,
neither had they heard of the third angel's message. It is
of these that Mrs. White speaks thus in one of her publications:—

"After the passing of the time of expectation in 1844,
Adventists still believed the Saviour's coming to be very near;
they held that they had reached an important crisis, and that the
work of Christ as man's intercessor before God had ceased.
Having given the warning of the judgment near, they felt that
their work for the world was done, and they lost their burden
of soul for the salvation of sinners, while the bold, blasphemous
scoffing of the ungodly seemed to them another evidence that
the Spirit of God had been withdrawn from the rejecters of his
mercy. All this confirmed them in the belief that probation
had ended, or, as they expressed it, 'the door of mercy was
shut.' As has been stated, Adventists were for a short time
united in the belief that the door of mercy was shut." [15]

[14] Elder Himes's report of labors in Maine, in the *Morning Watch,* New York
City, June 6, 1845.
[15] " Spiritual Gifts," Vol. IV, page 271.

In this quotation Mrs. White states the position taken by the First-day Adventists. She does not even intimate that she believed it. As shown above, the doctrine was first taught by Joseph Turner, at Paris, Maine. Mrs. White (then Miss Harmon) met Joseph Turner at the above-named place in the early spring of 1845, and heard him declare his doctrine of "no more manual labor for Adventists, and no more mercy for sinners," and plainly told him he was "teaching a false doctrine; that there was still mercy for sinners, and for those who had not understandingly rejected the truth."

Opposed to the "No-Mercy" Theory

J. N. Andrews, who resided in Paris, Maine, in 1844 and 1845, and who was fully conversant with the course of the people there, as well as with that of Joseph Turner, who taught that there was no more mercy for sinners, says of Miss Harmon's position on the subject at that time, " Instead of the visions' leading them to adopt this view, it corrected those upon it who still held to it." [16]

Miss Harmon made a second visit to Paris, Maine, in the summer of 1845. Concerning this visit I will quote from Mrs. Truesdail, who then resided in Paris. She says: —

"During Miss Harmon's visit in Paris, Maine, in the summer of 1845, I stated to her the particulars concerning a dear friend of mine whose father had deprived her of attending our meetings, consequently she had not rejected light. She smilingly replied, 'God has never shown me that there is no salvation for such persons. It is those only who have had the light of truth presented to them and knowingly rejected it.' " [17]

She also speaks respecting a third visit of Miss Harmon to Paris, in 1846, as follows: —

Another Reproof of the False Theory

"Another occasion worthy of mention was a vision given in 1846, in Paris, Maine. Miss Harmon was shown that when

[16] Letter of J. N. Andrews, September, 1874.
[17] Mrs. Truesdail's letter of Aug. 17, 1875.

Satan could not prevent the honest-hearted from doing their
whole duty, he would exert his skill in pushing them beyond
duty. One good sister had been telling the churches that
God had rejected them because they had rejected the message
sent from heaven to save them. Sister Harmon was shown
that there was no truth in her message, as there were many
in the churches who would yet embrace the truth; that the
good angels would yet go to work for souls in those churches,
and when they did thus, they [the angels] would leave this
sister, with her message [meaning her " no-mercy " message],
outside the door." [18]

No Contradiction

As there are those who are very zealous in trying to
prove that Mrs. White once taught the theory of " no more
mercy for sinners," but now teaches the contrary, I will present testimonials from those acquainted with her work from
1845, respecting her labors for the conversion of sinners.
The following is a statement from Ira Abbey, of Brookfield, Madison County, State of New York:—

" Between the years 1846 and 1850, Brother and Sister
White came to our house, and were very zealous for the
children and those that had not rejected the truth. They
labored for unconverted souls, and never do I remember of
hearing Sister White say that there was no hope of the
backsliders and those that had not rejected the truth." [19]

First-day Adventist Testimony

As to what the First-day Adventists of New England
know about the extreme *shut door* doctrine, let the following
letter testify: —

" August 5 to 9, 1891, I held a debate with Elder Miles
Grant, at Brookston, a city of about 30,000 inhabitants. The
debate was in the large tent, and was presided over by Mr.
John Barbour, once president of the city council. This city

[18] Mrs. Truesdail's letter of Jan. 27, 1891.   [19] Letter of Ira Abbey, March,
1885, quoted in *Review and Herald* of April 7, 1885.

is about twenty miles from Boston. The debate was on the Sabbath question, but Mr. Grant tried to drag into the debate the matter of Sister White's experience in this work. He charged that ' she was shown, way back in 1844, that probation was passed, and there was no more mercy for sinners."

" In reply, I told him that the First-day Adventists took that position, nearly all of them, at one time, before we separated from them, and that instead of Mrs. White's favoring the position at all, one of the first things she was shown was that that position was ' false,' and that there *was* still mercy for sinners. I said, ' This is so, and Elder Grant knows that it is so.' As I said this, numbers of the First-day Adventist people before me [that class constituted quite a portion of the large tent full] nodded their heads in emphatic and positive assent to the statement. Suffice it to say that Elder Grant did not mention that point again in the debate."

Signed " Geo. E. Fifield, South Lancaster, Mass., Dec. 6, 1895."

Mrs. White Ever Seeking the Salvation of Sinners

That Mrs. White has labored for the conversion of sinners from 1844 to the present time, is further proved by these facts: She and Elder White held a meeting in Albert Belden's house, at Rocky Hill, Conn., commencing April 20, 1848. In this meeting labor was put forth for some from the world. Elder White and his wife manifested special interest for such souls. On this point we will give the testimony of one of this class who received baptism at the hands of Elder White. John Y. Wilcox, writing from Kensington, Conn., Feb. 22, 1891, says: —

" I was brought into the truth at the time meetings were held in the unfinished chamber of Brother A. Belden's house, Rocky Hill, Conn. My receiving the light of present truth was under the labors of Brother and Sister White. I was baptized soon after by Brother White. But for the encouragement and strength I received from them I don't know as I would ever have dared to think or feel that I was accepted of the Lord. They were deeply interested for me, and labored to help me."

Elder White said of that meeting in a letter to Stockbridge Howland, Topsham, Maine, "Brother Bates presented the commandments in a very clear light, and their importance was urged home by very powerful testimonies. The word had effect to establish those already in the truth, and to awaken those not fully decided."

Labor for Sinners in Oswego, N. Y.

In 1849 Elder James White and his wife labored in Oswego, N. Y. In those meetings Hiram Patch and a Miss Benson, who were engaged to be married, were converted to God and the present truth.

In March, 1850, meetings were again held in Oswego. In the *Present Truth* for April, Elder White, in speaking of those meetings, said: "A very interesting work is now going on among the children of the remnant in this city. Their salvation has been the principal subject in our meetings for the last two Sabbaths, and God has wonderfully blessed us. The truth has had a good effect upon us as well as upon our children. In the evening following the last first day, we had a meeting for their special benefit, and the Spirit of the Lord was poured out in our midst. The children all bowed before the Lord, and seemed to feel the importance of keeping the commandments, especially the fifth, and seeking salvation through Jesus Christ. This was one of the most interesting meetings that I ever witnessed."

In the *Present Truth* of November, 1849, Elder White published an account of a number who were converted and baptized; and in the last number of this paper in 1850 there is an account of a meeting held at Waitsfield, Vt., and of the attendance of Heman Churchill, who had just been *converted* from the world. He is spoken of in the article as " brother." How could that be if there was no more mercy for sinners?

15

Testimony of Twenty-one Witnesses

In this connection we give a testimonial signed, in 1888, by twenty-one individuals, each of whom was in the advent movement in the year 1844, and was conversant with the rise of the third angel's message. All were in the message prior to 1851, most of them having been connected with the Seventh-day Adventists almost from the rise of the message: —

" We, the undersigned, having been well acquainted with the advent movement in 1844 at the passing of the time, and having also embraced the truth of the third angel's message as early as 1850, hereby cheerfully subscribe our names to the following statement concerning the shut-door doctrine held by believers in the third angel's message from the time of its rise to the last mentioned date, and onward.

" They believed, in harmony with Rev. 3:7, 8 and other scriptures, that at the close of the twenty-three hundred days of Dan. 8:14, Christ closed his work in the first apartment of the heavenly sanctuary, and changed his· ministration to the most holy, and·entered upon the work of the judgment, changing his relation in this respect to the plan of salvation. Here was a door opened and a door shut.

" They believed that those who had the clear light upon the first angel's message, and turned against it, bitterly opposing it, were rejected of God. But they did *not* believe that those who had not had the light or those who had not come to years of accountability previous to 1844, if they should seek God with honest hearts, would be rejected.

" While they believed with William Miller and the great mass of Adventists *immediately* after the passing of the time, that their work for the world was done, and that the Lord would come *very* soon, yet after the light upon the sanctuary and the third message explained their disappointment, they did *not* believe that mercy was past save for those who had rejected the light."

Signed, "J. B. Sweet, South Saginaw, Mich.; Samuel Martin, Westrindge, N. H.; Ira Abbey, North Brookfield, N. Y.; Mrs. R. B. Abbey, North Brookfield, N. Y.; Mrs. Diana Abbey, North Brookfield, N. Y.; Mrs. L. B. Abbey, North Brookfield, N. Y.; Heman S. Guerney, Memphis, Mich.; Ann E. Guerney, Memphis, Mich.; William Gifford, Memphis, Mich.; Mrs. Mary S. Chase, Battle Creek, Mich.; S. M. Howland, Battle Creek, Mich.; Mrs. F. H. Lunt, Battle Creek, Mich.; Mrs. Melora A. Ashley, Battle Creek, Mich.; Mrs. Caroline A. Dodge, Battle Creek, Mich.; Mrs. Sarah B. Whipple, Battle Creek, Mich.; Mrs. Uriah Smith, Battle Creek, Mich.; Mrs. Paulina R. Heligass, Moline, Kan.; R. G. Lockwood, St. Helena, Cal.; Mrs. R. G. Lockwood, St. Helena, Cal.; Reuben Loveland, North Hyde Park, Vt.; Mrs. Belinda Loveland, North Hyde Park, Vt.

A Vision Misconstrued.

An effort has been made to construe a vision given to Mrs. White, at Topsham, Maine, March 24, 1849, as teaching this erroneous doctrine — no more mercy for sinners. This view was given just as the "Rochester knockings" (Spiritualism) was being introduced. Mrs. White saw that the mysterious signs and wonders and false reformations would increase and spread. These reformations were not reformations from error to truth (she did not say there would never be such reformations, but that the kind shown her where they were using human influence were such), but from bad to worse; for those who professed a change of heart had only wrapped about them a religious garb which covered up the iniquity of a wicked heart. Some appeared to be really converted, thus being enabled to deceive God's people; but if their hearts could have been seen, they would have appeared as black as ever.

She then said: " My accompanying angel bade me look for the travail of soul for sinners as used to be. I looked, but could not see it; for the time of their salvation is past." [20]

The claim has been made that this vision taught that there was no more mercy for sinners, but we ask, How could that be when she had opposed that doctrine from the very time Joseph Turner first taught it in the spring of 1845, and had all the way along been laboring earnestly for the conversion and salvation of sinners?

In " Supplement to Experience and Views," published in 1853, Mrs. White says, " The false reformations' referred to on page 37, are yet to be more fully seen. This view relates more particularly to those who have heard and rejected the light of the advent doctrine. They are given over to strong delusions. Such will not have the ' travail of soul for sinners ' as formerly." [21]

Opponents claim to know more about what Mrs. White was viewing in this vision than she herself did. Let us examine it a moment in connection with their version of it; viz., that she was viewing the condition of sinners instead of the revivalists. So she looked *at* the sinners to find a " travail of soul *for* sinners, but could not see it." Who ever found a travail of soul *for* sinners by simply looking *at* the sinners? But, we inquire, what about the persons mentioned in the above testimony who were simply using human influence and mesmerism to gain converts, and calling it the work of the Spirit of God? Are these opponents, who were so anxious to show that Mrs. White taught the extreme " shut door " theory, ready to admit that these revivalists were holy people, and gaining genuine converts?

It is evident to every candid mind that the class of persons addressed in this connection were those who professed to have this travail of soul, while they had rejected light and truth, and were using mesmerism to gain converts. Such could not have a genuine travail of soul for sinners when they

[20] " Early Writings," page 37.
[21] " Early Writings, Experience and Views," second page of Supplement.

themselves were subjects of damnation; for "the time of *their* [their own] salvation is passed."

From Mrs. White's vision of March 24, 1849, some persons have tried to draw the conclusion that it taught that there was no more mercy for sinners; but we have already shown that in 1845, in Paris, Maine, she taught that there was mercy for all who had not knowingly and understandingly rejected light and truth. In a vision given in the same place in 1846, it was shown that the Lord had a "people in the churches who had not rejected the truth." To those individuals who thought differently, a reproof was given, saying that angels of God would yet work for such, and when they did work, those who were denouncing them would be left outside.

Again, in April, 1848, Elder White and his wife were laboring at Rocky Hill, Conn., for the conversion of sinners. All of which goes to prove that the vision of March 24, 1849, harmonizes with the one given in Paris, Maine, in 1846, and with the course pursued by these servants of God in April, 1848.

A False Revivalist Defeated.

This vision was first published in Connecticut, in the year 1849. A minister was working very earnestly there to secure converts, even professing to have the gift of tongues. He was striving to gain an influence over the little company of Sabbath-keepers at Rocky Hill. One of these he called a "dear saint of the Lord." In his presence Mrs. White had a vision showing the deceptive nature of his work, and that his "dear saint" was taking a course not in harmony with the seventh commandment. This lady "saint" denied the charge, and the minister made a strong plea, seeking to gain sympathy for the "poor saint of the Lord," as he called her. In the night following, this young woman had an attack of cholera morbus, and thought she was going to die. She sent for Mrs. White, and confessed that what had been shown concerning her was true; that she was guilty of just what Mrs. White had stated. So this false worker failed in deceiving that company, and the nature of his work was exposed, which suddenly closed his efforts in that place.

Another False Revivalist in Oswego, N. Y.

As a further illustration of the principle set forth in the above testimony, and to show how Elder White and his wife still labored in 1849-50 for the conversion of sinners, we give the following facts, which were related to me by Elias Goodwin and others of the early members of the church in Oswego, State of New York: —

There was then (1849) residing in the place a young man by the name of Hiram Patch. He was betrothed to a young lady to whom he was soon afterward married. They were unconverted persons, but were attending the meetings held by Elder White and his wife, and were almost persuaded to become Christians. At this time a revival was started in one of the churches in Oswego, not by the ministry, but by a prominent lay member, a treasurer of the county funds. This man appeared very zealous, and professed to have a great burden for sinners. He would wring his hands as he prayed for the unconverted, being apparently in the greatest distress because of their lost condition.

Mr. Patch and his affianced went to these revival meetings, and were in doubt how to decide. They were present on one occasion when Mrs. White had a vision in which she was pointed to Hosea 5:6, 7, which reads, " They shall go with their flocks and with their herds to seek the Lord; but they shall not find him; he hath withdrawn himself from them. They have dealt treacherously against the Lord; for they have begotten strange children: now shall a month devour them with their portions." She was shown that those who were conducting this revival were not right with God, and that they had no real burden of soul for sinners.

A Prediction of Failure

Then she said to Mr. Patch, " I was told to say to you that in this case the statement of the text will be literally fulfilled. Wait a month, and you will know for yourself the character of the persons who are engaged in this revival, and who profess to have such a great burden for sinners." Mr. Patch said, " I will wait."

Within a fortnight from the time this vision was given, the said treasurer, who claimed such anguish of soul for sinners, in his affected agony burst a blood-vessel in his stomach, and had to be taken to his bed through loss of blood. The affairs of the treasurer's office had to be taken hold of by the sheriff of the county, who with one of the constables looked at the balance called for on the treasurer's book, and then counted up the money preparatory to taking charge of the business, when, lo, there was a shortage in the money to the amount of an even $1,000.

To the sheriff and constable it seemed impossible that a man so earnest in a revival could be guilty of having taken the money. They thought he must have paid it out, and forgotten to make the proper entry on the book; or perhaps he had deposited it in the bank, and it did not appear in the account in the safe. At all events, they must seek of him a satisfactory explanation, but it must be done with caution; for if he had the money, he would undoubtedly make an effort to conceal it. It was therefore arranged that one of them should go on before and secrete himself in the shed back of the house, so as to watch the back door in case any demonstrations were made, while the sheriff should enter the front door. When the sheriff approached the house and entered the front door, he discovered the dress of a woman just leaving the back door. The man in the shed saw the woman go quickly to a snow-bank, dig a hole in the snow, and deposit something there, which she covered with the snow, and returned to the house.

The sheriff came to the bedside of the treasurer, and after making inquiries as to his condition of health, hinted at their perplexities in the office, suggesting that he could probably explain the difficulty. The man, greatly agitated, raised his hand toward heaven, and calling God to witness, said he knew nothing about the money. Just then the wife stepped in, and wanted to know what was the matter, and why her husband was so much excited. The man replied, " They think we have their money." The woman then lifted her hands in like manner, and called God to witness that they had not the money, and, furthermore, knew nothing about it. Just as she had finished this sentence, the constable, who had hastened from his hiding-place to the snow-bank as she went into the house, interfered, with these words, " Madam, what is this: I saw you rush from the house, and deposit this in the snow-bank, and here it is, the missing sack of money, marked upon it $1,000."

As might be expected, that revival suddenly collapsed Mr. Patch and his intended, after learning the character of the one conducting the revival, took their position for the truth, and united with the Seventh-day Adventists, of which church they remained worthy members to the day of their death.

This vision, as is clearly seen, was given in the interest and for the special benefit of the unconverted, and resulted in the conversion of sinners, while its immediate bearing was upon those who were themselves sinners and rejected of the Lord because of their hypocrisy. They had " dealt treacherously against the Lord; " professing to have great travail of soul for sinners, they only begat " strange children."

A Hypocritical Worker in Camden, N. Y.

Among other places visited by Elder and Mrs. White during the winter of 1849-50, was the town of Camden, N. Y., about forty miles from Oswego, where they were still living. Of this meeting, Mrs. White says: " Previous to going, I was shown the little company who professed the truth there, and among them I saw a woman who professed much piety, but who was a hypocrite, and was deceiving the people of God." [22]

In January, 1884, while laboring in the State of New York, I learned the following particulars from Mr. Preston, who was a resident of Camden at the time of the above-mentioned conference, and with whom Elder White and his wife tarried during the meeting: —

"This woman taught extreme views on the subject of sanctification, saying there was a state of perfection to be attained where a person would be entirely above the law of God; and she claimed to have reached that perfect state. With this doctrine of holiness she was troubling the minds of some of our people at Camden. Sister White was shown that with all this woman's pretended holiness, her heart was black with sin, and in life she was corrupt.

"While in this place, Sister White was given another vision, in the presence of this woman, who appeared to have a great burden of soul for the unconverted; but Sister White told her it was not a genuine travail of soul for sinners, because her own course of life was such that she did not herself stand right in the sight of God. 'So,' said Mr. Preston, 'what is called the Camden vision applied definitely and especially to the case of that woman, and not to the condition of sinners generally, and we so undersood it at the time.'"

After Mrs. White had related her vision, the woman arose, and said, "God knows my heart, and if you could see it, you would see that it is pure and clean." Thus the meeting closed. Not long after, however, the woman was taken seriously ill, and thought she was dying. Said she, "I must see Sister White; I have a confession to make to her. I told her I was a good woman, that I was pure. It is not so. I am a wicked woman. This man that I am living with is not my husband. I left a good husband in England, and one little child, and ran away with this man. We were never

<hr>

[22] "Life Sketches," page 265.

married. I have been professing to be a doctor, and have been selling medicine that I swore in court cost me $1 a bottle, but it only cost me twelve cents a bottle. I also swore that a cow we sold to a poor man cost us $30, when it only cost us $20." [23]

To such hypocritical pretenders do the words of Mrs. White respecting " travail of soul for sinners " apply, and not to sinners in general. Taking into consideration the facts presented above, showing that the doctrine of " no more mercy " for sinners was fully condemned from the first of its being preached in the spring of 1845; and that Mrs. White has labored earnestly for the conversion of sinners all the way along since that date, who can believe that in 1850, when her work entitled " Experience and Views " was published, she meant to teach that there was " no more salvation for sinners "?

A No-Mercy Man

Even as late as the year 1848, there remained here and there an individual who held that there was no more mercy for sinners. These, however, were not Seventh-day Adventists. One of this class, by the name of Sweet, resided in the city of Rochester, N. Y. Just after I had made a public profession of religion, and had been baptized among the First-day Adventists, I was attending a tent meeting in Canandaigua, N. Y., conducted by Elders J. C. Bywater and Geo. W. Burnham. This man Sweet was present, and expressed very serious doubts as to the genuineness of my religious experience, because he " thought it not possible now for sinners to be converted."

[23] The account given by Mr. Preston respecting the Camden meeting confirms the statement made in " Life Sketches," pages 265 - 268, while it also gives the above particulars not mentioned there.

CHAPTER XV

INCREASING LIGHT AND GREATER WONDERS

ALL to remembrance the former days, in which, after ye were illuminated, ye endured a great fight of afflictions; partly, whilst ye were made a gazing-stock both by reproaches and afflictions; and partly, whilst ye became companions of them that were so used." [1]

The period of time from the disappointment in 1844 until the clear light respecting the sanctuary and the third angel's message was brought out, was one of peculiar trial. Adventists who still persisted that they were right in the past movement, were indeed a "gazing-stock" to those who supposed the message to be an entire failure; and for this cause they were subjects of great reproach. This they could cheerfully endure while they held on to the Lord by faith, and shared the presence of his Holy Spirit.

Two Special Points of Attack

Satan had two special points of temptation for the Adventist people. The first was to cause those who were firm in the belief that prophetic time was ended, to believe that Christ's second coming was a spiritual coming, and that in some way he made this advent at the end of the twenty-three hundred days. The second was to induce those who were wavering with reference to their past experience, to give it all up. So while the truth in regard to the sanctuary and the third angel's message was being gradually unfolded from the Scriptures, the messages of the Spirit of God, through the gift of prophecy,

[1] Heb. 10: 32, 33.

confirmed the past movement, calling it " a bright light which God set up at the head of the pathway, to shine all the way along to the city, and pointed to the scripture evidences that the second advent of Christ is to be literal and personal, and could not therefore be the event at the end of the " days."

Wonderful Manifestations

Should the Lord speak to his people by visions in these last days, would we not expect that in the manifestation itself there would be evident tokens of the divine?   These tokens are apparent in the visions of Mrs. E. G. White.   The phenomenon of the visions themselves, as shown in Chapter XIII, is simply miraculous; but there are many wonderful features connected with her earlier views, which you will notice as you further peruse this work; and could we expect it to be otherwise in a gift of this character designed of God to attract the attention of the people, and lead them to say, like Moses, " I will turn aside, and see this great sight "?   The simple statement of a poor, sickly, feeble girl, apparently on the brink of the grave, that the Lord had given her a vision, would not have been enough to do this.   The wonderful manifestations connected with the visions did create an interest in them, and a call was made for the girl to go from place to place and relate what the Lord had bidden her to make known to others.

Remarkable Demonstrations in the Third Vision

I will here state some facts respecting her third vision, the one given in her father's house, mentioned in Chapter XIII, page 212, as related to me by Mrs. White's father and mother, by her sister, Mrs. Sarah Belden, and others.

In the room where the vision was given, there was lying on the bureau a very large family Bible.   It was one of an edition printed in Boston by Joseph Teale, in the year 1822. The book is eighteen by eleven inches, four inches in thickness, and weighs a little over eighteen pounds.   While in vision, she arose, and took this heavy Bible on her left arm, the book lying open, and held it out at right angles with her body; and then for over half an hour, with her right hand, turned from place to place, and pointed to different texts of Scripture, which she repeated while her eyes were looking upward, and in an opposite direction from the book. Her sister Sarah (afterward the wife of Stephen Belden), or, at times, some other person present, looked at every text to which her finger pointed, and saw clearly that in every instance she was repeating the scripture upon which her finger was resting. Mother Harmon said her daughter Ellen in her natural condition " was unable, for lack of strength, to lift that heavy Bible from the bureau; but in the vision she held it as easily, apparently, as though it were only a pocket Testament."

Here, indeed, was a wonder! — a delicate girl, weighing only seventy pounds, holding a heavy Bible for over half an hour in a position in which a strong man could not hold it for two minutes; again, turning from place to place to texts of Scripture which proved in every instance to be the text she repeated, while her eyes were turned upward and in an opposite direction from the book; and lastly, a voice emanating from a person with no movement of the lungs or breath in the body, and repeated correctly the designated texts of Scripture,— this surely is above the charge of being produced by human agency, or as being the effect of disease. Those who saw it regarded it as most clearly a manifestation of the Spirit of Him who spake from the burning bush. Such manifestations as these in Miss Harmon's third vision, where known, carried convincing proof that a power more than finite was in the visions.

The Topsham Vision

Very soon after this occurrence the company of Adventists at Topsham, some thirty miles northeast of Portland, Maine, hearing of the Lord's dealings with Miss Ellen G. Harmon, invited her to that place. The invitation was accepted, and thus her first visit was made to Topsham. The

Adventist meetings at that time were held in the house of Mr. Curtiss. Mrs. Frances Lunt (formerly Miss Frances Howland), of Oakland, Cal., gave me the following statement, dated Jan. 19, 1890:—

"I, with my father's family, attended the meetings of Sister Harmon in Topsham, in 1845, and during these meetings she had a vision. It was the first time we ever saw her in vision. One of those old-fashioned Bibles [the Teale Family Bible, weighing eighteen pounds] was owned by Brother Curtiss. This big Bible was taken from the bureau by Sister Harmon while in vision, and texts of Scripture were pointed out by her as she turned from leaf to leaf, while her eyes were looking upward, and away from the book. The texts she repeated were either words of instruction, encouragement, or reproof. Another peculiarity of the manifestation at that time was the position of the book. It was held on her open hand at an angle of forty-five degrees, and no one else was able to hold any book at a similar angle without its slipping at once from the hands; but Sister Harmon held this Bible at that angle for several minutes, as firmly as though it was stuck to her hand, she passing meanwhile from one to another in the room."

Mrs. Truesdail's Testimony

Another statement respecting this same vision is from Mrs. M. C. Truesdail, of Trenton, Mo., dated Jan. 27, 1891. She says:—

"I was fifteen years old in 1845, and was present at the time of Sister Harmon's first visit to Topsham, when she had the vision at the house of Brother Curtiss, where she took up the great family Bible and held it up in a position in which none of the others could hold a book on the hands without its slipping off at once.

"Sister Harmon was in vision over two hours. It was the most wonderful manifestation of the power of God I ever witnessed, and I have seen her in vision more than one

dozen times. These were always occasions of deep solemnity
and self-examination, but this exceeded them all. O! how
we trembled as the Majesty of heaven instructed us through
his feeble instrument; as she read to us passages so comforting and appropriate in our trying position; such as Heb. 2:
2, 3; James 5:7, 8; Heb. 10:35, 39; 1 Peter 1:7; Luke 12:
32 - 37, besides many others, holding the large family Bible
so high that I was obliged to stand on a chair to read where
she was pointing. I do not think Sister Harmon was over
two inches the taller."

Such manifestations convinced the candid that some power
more than human was controlling the humble instrument, and
calls came from various parts of New England for her to
come and deliver her testimony.

Manual Labor a Sin

Soon after this Miss Harmon was instructed, in vision,
to visit Paris, Maine, where were individuals who believed it
a sin to follow manual labor. Elder Stephens, of Woodstock,
Maine, was the leader in this error, and exerted a strong
influence over others. He had previously been a Methodist
preacher, and was considered a humble, faithful Christian.
He had won the confidence of many by his zeal for the truth,
and his apparently holy living, which caused some to believe
him specially directed of God. The Lord gave Miss Harmon
a reproof for him. She stated that he was going contrary
to the word of God in abstaining from labor, in urging his
errors upon others, and in denouncing all who did not receive
them. He rejected all the evidences which the Lord gave to
convince him of his error, and refused to acknowledge his
wrongs. He followed impressions, and went weary journeys,
walking great distances, where he would only receive abuse,
and considered that in all this he was suffering for Christ's
sake. His reason and judgment were laid aside.

Concerning the testimony of Miss Harmon and the outcome of the case, I will quote from a letter received from

Mrs. M. C. Truesdail, who then resided in Paris, Maine. After giving some particulars in harmony with the above, she says:—

"Confessions came from all except their leader, Jesse Stephens. Sister Harmon warned him that unless he humbled himself by confessing his errors, he would soon end his career. All understood this to be a *prediction* that he would in some way commit suicide."

The following is the sequel in his case:—

"After his little flock left him, he became melancholy, and soon after lost his reason, refusing to eat anything cooked by the wicked. He had not heard of my return from Massachusetts when I carried him his dinner. He inquired, as he reached out his skeleton hand through a small opening in a window, 'Did God send you with this, Sister Marion?' Noticing my hesitating reply, he refused to taste it. His pitiful condition, confined in a small room at his brother's (an unbeliever), reminded me of the warning which had been so kindly sent him from heaven, and which he so stubbornly rejected. He was taken to his family two days after this sad visit, where he soon ended his life by suicide, making a rope of his bedclothes." [2]

A Prediction Fulfilled

In the summer of 1845, by invitation of Otis Nichols, Miss Harmon visited Massachusetts, her sister Sarah accompanying her. They made their home with the family of Mr. Nichols. He and his wife would go with their carriage, and take them to different places to hold meetings, where Miss Harmon delivered her testimonies. Thus she was able to visit Boston, Roxbury, and Carver. At the time of their second visit to Boston, Mass., a very interesting incident occurred.

There was in Boston and vicinity a company of fanatical persons who also held that it was a sin to labor, their principal message being, "Sell that ye have, and give alms."

[2] From Mrs. M. C. Truesdail's letter, Jan. 27, 1891.

They said they were in the jubilee, that the land should rest, and that the poor must be supported without labor. Sargent, Robbins, and some others were leaders. They denounced the visions as being of the devil, because their own errors had been shown. They were severe upon all who did not believe with them.

While Miss Harmon and her sister were visiting at the house of Mr. Nichols, Sargent and Robbins came from Boston to obtain a favor of him, and said they had come to have a visit, and to tarry over night with him. Mr. Nichols replied that he was glad they had come, for Misses Sarah and Ellen Harmon were in the house, and he wished them to become acquainted with them. They changed their minds at once, and could not be persuaded to come into the house. Mr. Nichols asked if Ellen could relate her message in Boston, and if they would hear, and then judge. "Yes," said they, "come into Boston next Sabbath [meaning Sunday, as *they* had not yet received the Sabbath]; we would like the privilege of hearing her."

Mr. Nichols related this to me at his house, in Dorchester, in 1858. He said that he had made all his calculations to go to Boston on Sabbath morning with his carriage to take Miss Harmon to the proposed meeting. That evening, during family prayers, she was taken off in vision. After coming out of it, she said, "Brother Nichols, I am not going to Boston to-morrow; the Lord has shown me that I must go to Randolph. He has a work for me to do there." Mr. Nichols had a great regard for his word. He had promised to take her to Boston the next day, and he anxiously inquired, "What shall I do with my word to Sargent and Robbins?" "Never mind that," said Miss Harmon, "the Lord has bidden me go the other way." "Well," said Mr. Nichols, "I do not understand it." "The Lord showed me that we would understand it when we get there," said Miss Harmon. "Well," said Mr. Nichols, "there is no way for you to get there unless we go and take you, but I do not know how I will explain

16

matters to the brethren in Boston." Mr. Nichols further stated to me that " Sister Harmon saw their hypocrisy in the vision, that there would be no meeting in Boston on the Sabbath, that Sargent, Robbins, and others opposed would meet with the large company at Randolph (thirteen miles from Boston) on the Sabbath; and that we must meet the opposers at Randolph, at their meeting on the Sabbath, and there she would have a message given her for them, which would convince the honest, the unprejudiced ones, whether her visions were of the Lord or from Satan." Instead of going to Boston and then to Randolph, making a distance of twenty-two miles, they went direct to Randolph, arriving there about meeting time. There they found the very ones who had agreed to meet them in Boston. Mr. Nichols then said, " I understand it now."

This effort of Sargent and Robbins to evade Miss Harmon's testimony, and the manner in which she was directed so as to meet them, had great influence on the minds of some who were present. Of the meeting itself, I will quote the account as given by Mr. Nichols :—

Remarkable Demonstrations

" Sister Ellen was taken off in vision with extraordinary manifestations, and continued talking in vision with a clear voice, which could be distinctly understood by all present, until about sundown. Sargent, Robbins, and French were much exasperated, as well as excited, to hear Sister Ellen talk in vision, which they declared was of the devil; they exhausted all their influence and bodily strength to destroy the effect of the vision. They would unite in singing very loud, and then alternately would talk and read from the Bible in a loud voice, in order that Ellen might not be heard, until their strength was exhausted, and their hands would shake so they could not read from the Bible, but amidst all this confusion and noise, Ellen's clear and shrill voice, as she talked in vision, was distinctly heard by all present. The opposition of these men continued as long as they could talk and sing, notwithstanding some of their own friends rebuked them, and requested them to stop. But said Robbins, You are bowed to an idol: you are worshiping a golden calf.'

" Mr. Thayer, the owner of the house, was not fully satisfied that her vision was of the devil, as Robbins declared it to be. He wanted it tested in some way. He had heard that visions of Satanic power were arrested by opening the Bible and laying it on the person in vision, and asked Sargent if he would test it in that way, which he declined to do. Then Mr. Thayer took a heavy, large quarto family Bible which was lying on the table, and seldom used, opened it, and laid it open upon the breast of Ellen while in vision, as she was then inclined backward against the wall in the corner of the room. Immediately after the Bible was laid upon her, she arose upon her feet, and walked into the middle of the room, with the Bible open in one hand, and lifted up as high as she could reach, and with her eyes steadily looking upward, declared in a solemn manner, ' The inspired testimony from God,' or words of the same import. And then, while the Bible was extended in one hand, and her eyes looking upward, and not on the Bible, she continued for a long time to turn over the leaves with her other hand, and place her finger upon certain passages, and correctly utter their words with a solemn voice. Many present looked at the passages where her finger was pointed, to see if she spoke them correctly, for her eyes at the same time were looking upward. Some of the passages referred to were judgments against the wicked and blasphemers: and others were admonitions and instructions relative to our present condition.

Her Longest Vision, over Six Hours

" In this state she continued all the afternoon until near sunset, when she came out of vision. When Ellen arose in vision upon her feet, with the heavy open Bible in her hand,

and walked the room, uttering the passages of Scripture, Sargent, Robbins, and French were silenced. For the remainder of the time they were troubled, with many others; but they shut their eyes, and braved it out without making any acknowledgment of their feelings." [3]

Miss Harmon's Marriage

August 30, 1846, Miss E. G. Harmon and Elder James White were united in marriage, and together they labored for the advancement of the message. During the year 1847 their labors were mostly confined to Maine and Massachusetts.

The first Sabbath in April, there was given to Mrs. White a most interesting view, at the home of Stockbridge Howland, Topsham, where the meetings were then usually held. This vision is the one mentioned in " Early Writings," where she had a view of the sanctuary and its furniture, the time of trouble, the saints fleeing from the cities, the wicked surrounding them, their deliverance at the voice of God, the jubilee, the Lord's coming in the cloudy chariot, etc. It may be well to notice some of her movements while in this vision.

Many Bibles Used in a Vision

Mrs. Frances Lunt (daughter of S. Howland), on the 19th of January, 1890, said to me: " There was at the side of the room where the meetings were held, a table upon which were a number of books of various kinds, among which were several Bibles of ordinary size. While in vision, Mrs. White rose to her feet, went to the table, picked up a Bible without touching another book, and holding it open above her head with her left hand, with the index finger of the right hand pointed to the text of Scripture she was repeating as she stood before the person for whom it was designed, and then placed the open book on the chest of the person before whom she repeated the scripture. Returning to the table, she took another Bible, and in the same manner repeated another text of Scripture and placed the open Bible on the chest of the

[3] " Early Writings," pages 77 - 79.

James White

individual she was addressing. This act was repeated to about half a dozen persons; after which in a graceful manner, she took her seat in a chair, while her eyes were all the while looking upward and away from the book."

Of this Mrs. Truesdail says: "I was present [April, 1847] when Sister White went to the table and picked up one Bible after another from among the books that were on the table, laying the Bible on the breast of the one for whom she had a text of Scripture. This was done while her eyes were uplifted toward heaven. On this occasion she held the Bible above her head while speaking to me; and then she placed it upon my breast. The passage given me was 2 Cor. 6: 17." [4]

In a letter from Mrs. Frances Lunt, she gives the names of three persons who were present on this occasion, and on whom the Bibles were laid while Mrs. White talked to them on the text for each, and among the names was that of Mrs. Truesdail.

First Work was among Advent Believers

The work of Miss Harmon, under the guidance of the prophetic gift, from January, 1845, to the spring of 1846, almost eighteen months, was with the "believers" in Christ's near coming, with whom she had previously associated. After the close of the twenty-three hundred days (Oct. 22, 1844), until the cause of their disappointment and the nature of the event that then occurred should be understood, there would be danger of the believers' drifting into erroneous views, or of giving up entirely their past experience. Her message was to such: "The past movement was of God. Hold fast your faith. The Lord has still a work for his people. Study the Bible. Search the word, and you will find the light."

This instruction is in harmony with the Lord's plan. His purpose has ever been that his special messages for his people should, in their time, be brought forth from his word, and

[4] Mrs. M. C. Truesdail's letter, Jan. 27, 1891.

then the gift of prophecy comes in "secondarily," to confirm and build up the believers.

A striking illustration of this fact is found in the case of Cornelius as recorded in the Acts of the Apostles. An angel of God appeared to him and gave him a vision in his own house. That angel well knew the truths of the gospel, and could have taught it to Cornelius, but he was sent to minister to one who was an heir of salvation in giving Cornelius a vision. He assured him that his devotions and consecration were accepted by the Lord. He did not preach the gospel to him, but simply told him to call for Peter, who was lodging with Simon the tanner, at Joppa. Peter came, and from the Scriptures proclaimed to Cornelius the gospel of Christ.

Position of the Gift of Prophecy

At this point it may be well to note the order of the development of the gifts, as the Lord has marked it out in his word. Paul refers to this in his letter to the Corinthians, where he says, "God hath set some in the church, *first* apostles, *secondarily* prophets." [5]

When looking at the apostle's statement respecting the relation of these gifts in the gospel work, we see at once why this order is observed. When comparing these gifts, Paul says: "Wherefore tongues are for a sign, not to them that believe, but to them that believe not: but prophesying serveth not for them that believe not, but for them which believe." [6] The Lord's order is that his special messages to the world shall be brought from his word; and accordingly he moves men to search the Scriptures, and go forth as apostles, burdened with the Lord's messages, proclaiming them from the Bible, which has stood the test of ages. As believers are raised up, the gift of prophecy comes in "secondarily," accomplishing its part "for the perfecting of the saints, for the work of the ministry, for the edifying of the body of Christ." [7]

[5] 1 Cor. 12: 28.   [6] 1 Cor. 14: 22.   [7] Eph. 4: 12.

CHAPTER XVI

THE THIRD ANGEL'S MESSAGE

HE third angel followed them, saying with a loud voice, If any man worship the beast and his image, and receive his mark in his forehead, or in his hand, the same shall drink of the wine of the wrath of God, which is poured out without mixture into the cup of his indignation; and he shall be tormented with fire and brimstone in the presence of the holy angels, and in the presence of the Lamb; and the smoke of their torment ascendeth up forever and ever: and they have no rest day nor night, who worship the beast and his image, and whosoever receiveth the mark of his name. Here is the patience of the saints: here are they that keep the commandments of God, and the faith of Jesus." [1]

The Most Solemn Warning in the Bible

This is the most solemn warning that the Bible contains, and it is certain that the record of our world's history presents no testimony that this message has been heard in the past. The fact that the first and second angels of this series have been proved to belong to the present generation, most clearly establishes the point that this message does not belong to past ages.

Said Elder J. V. Himes in 1847:—

" The fourteenth chapter [of Revelation] presents an astounding cry, *yet to be made,* as a warning to mankind in that hour of strong temptation. Verses 9 - 11. A denunciation of wrath so dreadful cannot be found in the book of

[1] Rev. 14: 9 - 12

God, besides this.   Does it not imply a strong temptation, to require so terrific an admonition? " [2]

The Temple Opened — the Ark Seen

J. N. Andrews said of this message, " The opening of the holiest of all in the temple of heaven by which the ark is seen, is an event that takes place under the sounding of the seventh angel.   And as the ministration of our great High Priest is changed to that apartment at the termination of the twenty-three hundred days, we understand that the opening of the temple is marked by the termination. of that period as represented by the proclamation of the first angel.   The entrance of our High Priest to the most holy place to minister before the ark of God, calls the attention of the church to the commandments of God contained within that ark.   The commandments of God have been shining out from the heavenly sanctuary since that time.

Change of the Sabbath

" It is a fact beyond dispute that the fourth commandment, some ages since, was changed from the rest-day of the Lord to the pagan festival of Sunday.   This change was made in express contradiction of the Holy Scriptures, which everywhere recognize the seventh day as the only weekly Sabbath of the Lord.   It was accomplished by the great apostate, who Daniel predicted should 'think to change times and laws.'   This power is essentially the same as the beast which was to be worshiped by all the world.   And it is a fact of deep interest that this commandment which has been so long trodden down, is now being vindicated, and the people of God are beginning to keep it with the other nine.   Thanks be to God that he is preparing the remnant for their final conflict with the dragon, and for admittance through the gates into the holy city.   Rev. 12:17; 22:14.   The vindication of the fourth commandment in opposition to the Sabbath of the

[2] " Facts on Romanism," page 112.

apostasy, and the preaching of all the commandments of God is a striking testimony that the present is the period of the saints' patience, and of the warning of the third angel." [3]

Attention has been called in previous chapters to the first and second of these messages, as fulfilled in the great second advent proclamation down to Oct. 22, 1844. The scripture at the opening of this chapter reads, " The third angel followed them," that is, followed the first and second angels. It will perhaps be of interest, in this connection, to call attention to the rise of the third message.

The First Adventist Sabbath-Keepers

During the " midnight cry," in 1844, the Lord began to lead the minds of his people to the keeping of the seventh-day Sabbath. This doctrine, among Adventists, arose on this wise: Rachel Preston, a Seventh-day Baptist, moved to Washington, N. H., where there was a church of Adventists. She accepted the advent doctrine, and that church, composed of about forty members, through her missionary labors accepted the Sabbath of the fourth commandment.[4] This led to inquiry upon that subject. In the *Cry* of Sept. 5, 1844, we read, " Many persons have their minds deeply exercised respecting a supposed obligation to observe the seventh day." This statement was contained in an editorial, in which a faint effort was made to establish the claims of Sunday-keeping. The subject was continued in the number of September 12, where we find the following significant statement, which led to serious and close study by many:—

The Seventh Day the Only Law-appointed Day

" Last week we found ourselves brought to this conclusion: *There is no particular portion of time which Christians are required by law to set aside as holy time.* If this conclusion is incorrect, then we think *the seventh day* is the *only day* for the observance of which there is any *law.*"

[3] " The Three Angels of Rev. 14: 6 - 12." pages 125, 126.
[4] Rachel Preston died at Vernon, Vt., Feb. 1, 1868, aged 59 years.

T. M. Preble's Essay

The attention of the Adventists as a body was called to the Sabbath question by an essay on the subject from T. M. Preble, dated Feb. 13, 1845, and published in the *Hope of Israel,* Portland, Maine, Feb. 28, 1845. After showing the claims of the Bible Sabbath, and the fact that it was changed to Sunday by the great apostasy, he remarks: " Thus we see Dan. 7 : 25 fulfilled, the little horn changing ' times and laws.' Therefore it appears to me that all who keep the first day for the Sabbath are the pope's Sunday-keepers and God's Sabbath-breakers." [5]

J. B. Cook on the Sabbath Question

Soon after this there appeared in print an article from J. B. Cook, in which he showed that there is no Scriptural evidence for keeping Sunday as the Sabbath, and he used this terse expression: " Thus easily is *all* the wind taken from the sails of those who sail, perhaps unwittingly, under the pope's Sabbatic flag."

Although Sabbath-keeping by these two men was of short duration, they had set a ball rolling that could not easily be stopped. The catch phrases, " pope's Sunday-keepers," " God's commandment-breakers," and " sailing under the pope's Sabbatic flag," were on the lips of hundreds who were eager to know the truth of this matter. Elder Joseph Bates, of Fairhaven, Mass., had his attention thus arrested, and he accepted the Sabbath in 1845.

Joseph Bates Accepts the Sabbath

His experience was on this wise: Hearing of the company in Washington, N. H., that were keeping the Sabbath, he concluded to visit that church, and see what it meant. He accordingly did so, and on studying the subject with them he saw they were correct, and at once accepted the light on the Sabbath question. On returning to New Bedford, Mass., he

[5] Andrews's " History of the Sabbath," page 506, edition of 1887.

met, on the bridge between New Bedford and Fair Haven,
a prominent brother, who accosted him thus, " Captain Bates,
what is the news? " Elder Bates replied, " The news is
that the seventh day is the Sabbath of the Lord our
God." " Well," said the man, " I will go home and read my
Bible, and see about that." So he did, and when next they
met, this brother had accepted the Sabbath truth and was
obeying it.

The First Book on the Sabbath

Elder Bates at once began to preach this truth from
State to State. He soon saw that a book, or even a tract,
on the Sabbath question would be a great help to him in his
work, and his soul was moved by the Spirit of God to write
and publish something on this subject. But how it could
be done without money, was the question, as all that he had
was a York shilling (twelve and a half cents). It may be of
interest to the reader to relate his experience in this matter
just as he told it to me in 1855.

Four Pounds of Flour

He said that while in prayer before God, he decided to
write the book, and felt assured that the way would open
to publish it. He therefore seated himself at his desk, with
Bible and concordance, to begin his work. In the course of
an hour, Mrs. Bates came into the room and said, " Joseph,
I haven't flour enough to make out the baking," and at the
same time mentioned some other little articles that she needed.
" How much flour do you lack? " asked Captain Bates.
" About four pounds," was her reply. " Very well," replied
he. After she had left the room, he went to a store near by,
purchased the four pounds of flour and the other articles,
brought them home, and again seated himself at his writing
desk. Presently Mrs. Bates came in and saw the articles on
the table and exclaimed, " Where did this flour come from? "
" Why," said the captain, " isn't there enough? You said

you wanted four pounds." "Yes," said she, "but where did you get it?" "I bought it," said he; "is not that the amount you wanted to complete the baking?" "Yes," continued Mrs. Bates, "but have *you*, Captain Bates, a man who has sailed vessels out of New Bedford to all parts of the world, been out and bought *four* pounds of flour?" "Yes, was not that the amount you needed to complete the baking?" "Yes," said Mrs. Bates, "but have you bought *four pounds (!)* of flour?"

Eleven Thousand Dollars Spent for the Truth

Another trial soon followed. When Captain Bates left the sea, he sold out his interest in a ship for $11,000, but now he had spent his all to advance the cause of truth. Up to this date Mrs. Bates did not know his true financial condition, but he felt that he must now acquaint her with it, so he calmly said, "Wife, I spent for those articles the last money I have on earth." With bitter sobs Mrs. Bates inquired, "What are we going to do?" The captain arose, and with all the dignity of a captain directing his vessel, said, "I am going to write a book; I am going to circulate it, and spread this Sabbath truth before the world." "Well," said Mrs. Bates, through blinding tears, "what are we going to live on?" "The Lord is going to open the way," was Captain Bates's smiling reply. "Yes," said Mrs. Bates, "the Lord is going to open the way! That's what you always say," and bursting into tears she left the room.

An Unexpected Supply

After Captain Bates had continued his work for half an hour, the impression came to him to go to the post-office, as there was a letter there for him. He went, and sure enough there was a letter. In those days the postage on letters was five cents and prepayment was optional. The writer of this letter had for some reason failed to pay the postage. And here again Captain Bates was humbled, as he was obliged

JOSEPH BATES

to tell the postmaster, Mr. Drew, with whom he was well acquainted, that he could not pay the postage, as he had no money; but he said, " Will you let me see where it is from? " " Take it along," said the postmaster, " and pay some other time." " No," said the captain, " I will not take the letter out of the office until the postage is paid." While he had the letter in his hand, he said, " I am of the opinion that there is money in this letter," and turning to the postmaster, he asked, " Will you please open it? If there is money in it, you can take the postage out; if not, I will not read it." The postmaster complied with his request, and lo! it contained a ten-dollar bill. He found, by reading, that the letter was from a person who said the Lord so impressed his mind that Elder Bates was in need of money that he hastened it to him; and in the haste he probably forgot to pay the postage.

After paying the postage, he went to a provision store, bought a barrel of flour for $4, besides potatoes, sugar, and other necessary articles. When giving orders where they were to be delivered, he said, " Probably the woman will say they don't belong there, but don't you pay any attention to what she says; unload the goods on the front porch."

He then went to the printing office and made arrangements for publishing one thousand copies of a tract of about one hundred pages, with the understanding that as the copy was furnished the printers were to put it in type as rapidly as possible, sending proofs to him. He was to pay for the work as fast as he received the money, and the books were not to be taken from the office until the bills were all paid.

Captain Bates knew well there was no money due him, but he felt it his duty to write this book, believing that the Lord would move on the hearts to send the money when it was needed. After purchasing paper, pens, etc., thus giving time for the household supplies to go in advance of him, he went to the head of the street leading to his house. On seeing that the articles were there, he went into the house by the back entrance, and seated himself again at his desk. Mrs.

Bates came in and said excitedly, " Joseph, just look out on the front porch! Where did that stuff come from? A drayman came here and would unload it. I told him it didn't belong here. but he would unload it." "Well," said Captain Bates, " I guess it's all right." "But," said Mrs. Bates, " where did it come from?" "Well," said the Captain, "the Lord sent it." "Yes," said Mrs. Bates, "the Lord sent it; that's what you always say." He then handed the letter to his wife, saying, "Read this, and you will know where it came from." She read it, and again retired for another cry, but it was of a different character from the first; and on returning she humbly asked his pardon for her lack of faith.

Money Coming for the Book

As the work of writing and printing progressed, Captain Bates received money from time to time through the mail and otherwise, sometimes from persons he had never met. As he received the money, it was passed over to the printers, and applied on the book account. Finally the day came when the books were all printed, and from a source unexpected by Brother Bates the balance of the account was met; thus the books were not delayed even a day in their circulation.

Last Bill Paid

H. S. Gurney, of Memphis, Mich., told me in March, 1884, that he, on the very morning Elder Bates's book was completed, received $100 on an outlawed note from a man who declared he would never pay him. Having received this money, he esteemed it a pleasure to spend a portion of it in paying the last bill on the Sabbath tract of Elder Bates. "But," said Mr. Gurney, " Brother Bates never knew to the day of his death *who* paid the balance of the book bill." This experience of Elder Bates in printing the Sabbath truth seemed to say to our people from the very beginning of publishing the truth on the Sabbath question, " Go forward in this line of work, and expect God's providence to open the way as you advance."

Elder Bates Skeptical of the Visions

The following statement, abridged from " Life Sketches," will show how the gift of prophecy and the Sabbath reform were united : —

While on a visit to New Bedford, Mass., in 1846, Miss Harmon became acquainted with Elder Joseph Bates. He had early embraced the advent faith, and was an active laborer in the cause. He was a true Christian gentleman, courteous and kind. He treated Miss Harmon as tenderly as though she were his own child. The first time he heard her speak, he manifested deep interest, and after she had ceased, he arose and said, " I am a doubting Thomas. I do not believe in visions. But if I could believe that the testimony the sister has related to-night was indeed the voice of God to us, I should be the happiest man alive. My heart is deeply moved. I believe the speaker to be sincere, but I cannot explain in regard to her being shown the wonderful things she has related to us."

Miss Harmon Accepts the Sabbath

Elder Bates was keeping the Sabbath, and urged its importance. Miss Harmon did not at that time feel its importance, and thought Elder Bates erred in dwelling upon the fourth commandment more than upon the other nine. But the Lord gave her a view of the heavenly sanctuary. The temple of God was opened in heaven, and she was shown the ark of God with the mercy-seat covering it. Two angels stood, one at either end of the ark, with their wings spread over the mercy-seat, and their faces turned toward it. This, her accompanying angel informed her, represented all the heavenly host looking with reverential awe toward the law of God which had been written by the finger of God. Jesus raised the cover of the ark, and she beheld the tables of stone on which the ten commandments were written. She was amazed as she saw the fourth commandment in the very center of the ten precepts, with a soft halo of light encircling it. The angel said, " It is the only one of the ten which defines the living God who created the heavens and the earth and all things that are therein. When the foundations of the earth were laid, then was also laid the foundation of the Sabbath." She was shown that if the true Sabbath had been kept, there would never have been an infidel or an atheist. The observance of the Sabbath would have preserved the world from idolatry.

The fourth commandment has been trampled upon, therefore we are called to repair the breach in the law, and to plead for the downtrodden Sabbath. The man of sin, who exalted himself above God, and thought to change times and laws, brought about the change of the Sabbath from the seventh to the first day of the week. In doing this he made a breach in the law of God.

Just prior to the great day of God a message is sent forth to warn the people to come back to their allegiance to the law of God which anti-Christ has broken down. Attention must be called to the breach in the law by teaching and example. She was also shown that the third angel of Revelation 14, proclaiming the commandments of God and the faith of Jesus, represents the people who receive this message, and raise the voice of warning to the world to keep the commandments of God and his law as the apple of the eye, and that in response to this warning many would embrace the Sabbath of the Lord. [6]

This experience of Miss Harmon and Elder Bates was in harmony with the Lord's method of working. The attention of both Miss Harmon and Elder White was called to the Sabbath question by Elder Bates, who presented to them from the Scriptures the claims of the unchangeable law of God. Although Miss Harmon had been blessed with special manifestations from the Lord for about eighteen months, nothing

[6] " Life Sketches," pages 236 - 238.

on this subject had been previously shown her. Now the Lord's time had come, as believers were being raised up to keep his law, to impart light to them through the gift of prophecy, and thus, by his own way of working, the third angel's message, " the commandments of God, and the testimony of Jesus Christ," were brought together.

Beginning of the Third Angel's Message

From that time the third angel's message, as connected with the other two, began to be proclaimed. The Sabbath truth, as connected with the ark of God and the light developing with reference to the sanctuary, confirmed what had been previously shown,—that the past advent movement was right, and in the order of the Lord. They could now understand more fully than ever before the meaning of the " three steps up on to the pathway to the city of God."

Elder Bates Accepts the Visions as from God

In the month of November, 1846, a conference was held in Topsham, Maine, at which Elder Bates was present. At that meeting Mrs. White (Miss Harmon's marriage to Elder James White has been previously noticed) had a vision which was the cause of Elder Bates's becoming fully satisfied as to their divine origin. He was a man who had followed the sea for fifty years, filling all positions from cabin-boy up to master and owner of vessels. His understanding of astronomy was such that, as he told me, he could tell very nearly where he was upon the sea, as to latitude and longitude, by his observation of the celestial bodies. Such a one would naturally be interested in talking about astronomy.

In conversation with him, he told me how he became convinced of the divine origin of the visions. He said he tried to talk with Mrs. White one day about the stars, but he soon found she knew nothing about astronomy; in fact, as she told him, she did not know as she had ever looked into a book treating on that subject. She had no inclination to converse upon that topic, and turned the conversation by talking about the new earth, and what had been shown her in vision respecting it.

The "Opening Heavens"

In the previous year, April 19, 1845, the *Illustrated London News* had published something of great interest to astronomers from Lord Rosse, respecting the wonderful discoveries he had made through his monster telescope, especially a view of what astronomers call "the gap in the sky." One evening, at the conference above mentioned, at the house of Mr. Curtiss and in the presence of Elder Bates, who was yet undecided in regard to these manifestations, Mrs. White, while in vision, began to talk about the stars, giving a glowing description of rosy-tinted belts which she saw across the surface of some planet, and added, "I see four moons." "Oh," said Elder Bates, "she is viewing Jupiter!" Then having made motions as though traveling through space, she began giving a description of belts and rings in their ever-varying beauty, and said, "I see seven moons." [7] Elder Bates exclaimed, "She is describing Saturn." Next she said, "I see six moons," and at once began a description of the "opening heavens," with its glory, calling it an opening into a region more enlightened. Elder Bates said that her description far surpassed any account of the opening heavens he had ever read from any author.

While she was talking and still in vision, he arose to his feet, and exclaimed, "O how I wish Lord John Rosse was here to-night!" Elder White inquired, "Who is Lord John Rosse?" "Oh," said Elder Bates, "he is the great English astronomer. I wish he was here to hear that woman talk astronomy, and to hear that description of the 'opening heavens. It is ahead of anything I ever read on the subject." From that

---

[7] In "'Rise and Progress," it says she saw eight moons to Saturn. This change was made after the proofs went out of my hands. More moons to both Jupiter and Saturn have *since* been discovered.

evening Elder Bates became fully satisfied that the visions of Mrs. White were outside of her knowledge and control. This and the character of the reproof and instruction given, satisfied him that they were from God.

This phenomenon in the heavens thus described by Mrs. White in that vision, is a matter rarely mentioned by astronomical writers. Hugins, the first discoverer of it, gives the following description: —

A Glorious Light in the Sword of Orion

"Astronomers place three stars close together in the sword of Orion; when I viewed the middlemost with a telescope, in the year 1656, there appeared in the place of that one twelve other stars; among these, three that almost touch each other, and four more besides appeared, twinkling as through a cloud, so that the space about them seemed much brighter than the rest of the heaven, which, appearing wholly blackish, by reason of the fair weather, was seen as through a curtain opening, through which one had a free view into another region which was more enlightened."

William Herschel says of this opening in the sky: —

"If its diameter at this distance subtend an angle of 10°, which it nearly does, its magnitude must be utterly inconceivable. It has been calculated that it must be two trillions of times the dimensions of the sun."

Lignter than the Sun

Thomas Dick, the philosopher, thus speaks of this luminous nebulæ: —

"Were we placed as near it as one half the distance of the nearest star, great as that distance is, from such a point it would exhibit an effulgence approximating to that of the sun; and to beings at much nearer distance it would fill a large portion of the sky, and appear with a splendor inexpressible. But the ultimate design of such an object, in all its bearings and relations, may perhaps remain to be evolved during the future ages of an interminable existence; and, like many other objects in the distant spaces of creation, it excites in the mind a longing desire to behold the splendid and mysterious scenes of the universe a little more unfolded." [8]

Elder Bates, in concluding an article upon the subject, said: —

"Thus we see from all the testimony adduced (and we could give much more, were it necessary), that here is a most wonderful and inexplainable phenomenon in the heavens; a *gap* in the sky more than eleven billion and three hundred and fourteen [11,000,000,314] miles in circumference. Says the celebrated Hugins, 'I never saw anything like it among the rest of the fixed stars — a free view into another region more enlightened.'"

Another Testimony on the Planet Vision

Again we quote from Mrs. Truesdail, who was present on the occasion of the giving of the vision referred to. She says: —

"Sister White was in very feeble health, and while prayers were offered in her behalf, the Spirit of God rested upon us. We soon noticed that she was insensible to earthly things. This was her first view of the planetary world. After counting aloud the moons of Jupiter, and soon after those of Saturn, she gave a beautiful description of the rings of the latter. She then said, 'The inhabitants are a tall, majestic people, so unlike the inhabitants of earth. Sin has never entered here.' It was evident from Brother Bates's smiling face that his past doubts in regard to the source of her visions were fast leaving him. We all knew that Captain Bates was a great lover of astronomy, as he would often locate many of the heavenly bodies for our instruction. When Sister White replied to his questions, after the vision, saying that she had never studied or otherwise received knowledge in this direction, he was filled with joy and happiness. He praised God,

[8] "Dick's Sidereal Heavens," page 96.

and expressed his belief that this vision concerning the planets was given that he might never again doubt." [9]

A Vicious Horse Suddenly Tamed

Shortly after this meeting in Topsham, another striking incident occurred in connection with the visions, which I will relate as told me by Elder Bates: —

Elder White had the use of a partly broken colt and a two-seated market wagon, which was constructed without a dash-board, but had a step across the front of the wagon, and an iron step from the shafts. It was necessary that extreme care be taken in driving the colt, as in case the lines or anything touched his flanks he would instantly kick furiously, and he had to be held in continually with a taut rein to keep him from running. This colt belonged to a party to whose place they wished to go, and as Elder White had been used to managing unbroken colts, he thought he would have no serious trouble with this one. Had they known, however, that during its frantic demonstrations it had previously killed two men, one by crushing him against the rocks by the roadside, he might have been less confident.

On this occasion there were four persons in the wagon, Elder White and his wife upon the front seat, and Elder Bates and Israel Damon on the back seat. While Elder White was giving his utmost care to keep the horse under control, Mrs. White was conversing about the truth, when the power of God came down upon the company, and she was taken off in vision, seated in the wagon. The moment she shouted " Glory ! " as she went into vision, the colt suddenly stopped perfectly still, and dropped his head. At the same time Mrs. White arose, while in this state, and with her eyes looking upward, stepped over the front of the wagon, down on to the shafts, with her hands on the colt's haunches. Elder Bates called out to Elder White, " The colt will kick that woman to death." Elder White replied, " The Lord has the colt in charge now ; I do not wish to interfere." The colt stood as

[9] Mrs. Truesdail's letter of Jan. 27, 1891.

gentle as an old horse. By the roadside the bank rose up some six feet, and next to the fence was a grassy place. Mrs. White, with her eyes still upward, not once looking down, went up the bank on to the grassy plot, then walked back and forth for a few minutes, talking and describing the beauties of the new earth. Then, with her head in the same posture, she came down the bank, walked up to the wagon, stepped up on to the steps, with her hand on the rump of the colt, and so up on to the shafts, and into the wagon again. The moment she sat down upon the seat she came out of vision, and that instant the horse, without any indication from the driver, started up, and went on his way.

While Mrs. White was out of the wagon, Elder White thought he would test the horse, and see if he was really tame or not. At first he just touched him with the whip; at other times the horse would have responded with a kick, but now there was no motion. He then struck him quite a blow, then harder, and still harder. The colt paid no attention to the blows whatever, but seemed as harmless as the lions whose mouths the angels shut the night Daniel spent in their den. " It was a solemn place," said Elder Bates, " and it was evident that the same Power that produced the visions, for the time being subdued the wild nature of the colt.

If this vision was simply the result of some of her bodily infirmities, the query naturally arises, Was the horse afflicted in like manner?

Israel Damon's Testimony

I will give here, as corroborating the account given me by Elder Bates, the following statement: —

·" About twenty years ago, just after I had commenced the observance of the Sabbath, Israel Damon related to me the circumstances of Sister White's having the vision while he, Elder Bates, and Elder White and his wife were riding in the light wagon behind the refractory colt. I have to-day read the above description of the occurrence, as written out by Elder Loughborough, and it agrees precisely with what Elder Damon told me." Signed, " R. S. Webber, Battle Creek, Mich., Feb. 9, 1891."

Elder Bates's Testimony on the Visions

Elder Bates states his own experience thus:—

" Although I could see nothing in them that militated against the word, yet I felt alarmed and tried exceedingly, and for a long time unwilling to believe that it was anything more than what was produced by a protracted debilitated state of her body.

" I therefore sought opportunities in presence of others, when her mind seemed free from excitement (out of meeting), to question and cross-question her, and her friends who accompanied her, especially her elder sister, to get, if possible, at the truth. During the number of visits she has made to New Bedford and Fairhaven since, while at our meetings, I have seen her in vision a number of times, and also in Topsham, Maine; and those who were present during some of those exciting scenes know well with what interest and intensity I listened to every word, and watched every move, to detect deception or mesmeric influence. And I thank God for the opportunity I have had with others to witness these things. I can now confidently speak for myself. I believe the work is of God, and is given to comfort and strengthen his ' scattered,' ' torn,' and ' peeled people,' since the closing up of our work . . . in October, 1844. The distracted state of ' Lo, here's! ' and ' Lo, there's! ' since that time has exceedingly perplexed God's honest, willing people, and made it exceedingly difficult for such as were not able to expound the many conflicting texts that have been presented to their view. I confess that I have received light and instruction on many passages that I could not before clearly understand. I believe her to be a self-sacrificing, honest, willing child of God." [10]

" The author *does not* ' obtain the sentiments ' of her visions ' from previous teachings or study.' When she re-

[10] "A Word to the Little Flock," page 21.

ceived her first vision, December, 1844, she and all the band in Portland, Maine (where her parents then resided), had given up the 'midnight cry' as being in the past. It was then that the Lord showed her in vision the error into which she and the band in Portland had fallen. She then related her vision to the band, and they acknowledged their seventh-month experience to be the work of God." [11]

How the Three Messages Were Regarded in 1847

The following from Elder James White, written in April, 1847, will show how the three messages were then regarded:—

" All classes of second advent believers agree that the angel brought to view in the sixth and seventh verses of this chapter (Revelation 14), represents the advent message to the church and world. . . . The work of the second angel was to show to the advent host that Babylon had fallen. And as a large portion of them did not learn this fact until the power of the 'midnight cry' waked them up just in time for them to make their escape from the churches before the tenth day came, it follows that since the seventh month, 1844, the third angel's message was, and still is, a warning to the saints to 'hold fast,' and not go back, and 'receive' the marks which the virgin band got rid of during the second angel's cry.

" And has not the true message for God's people, since the seventh month, 1844, been just such a warning? — It certainly has. . . . The twelfth verse reads, 'Here is the patience of the saints: here are they that keep the commandments of God and the faith of Jesus.' Where did you see them, John?— Why, ' here,' during the third angel's message. As the patient, waiting time has been since the seventh month, 1844, and as the class that keep the Sabbath, etc., have appeared since that time, it is plain that we live in the time of the third angel's message." [12]

[11] "A Word to the Little Flock," page 22.
[12] *Idem.*, pages 10, 11, Brunswick, Maine, May, 1847.

CHAPTER XVII

THE TRUTH ADVANCED UNDER DIFFICULTIES

"A S a shepherd seeketh out his flock in the day that he is among his sheep that are scattered; so will I seek out my sheep, and will deliver them out of all places where they have been scattered in the cloudy and dark day." [1]

Those who up to this time (1847) had accepted the third angel's message, were poor in this world's goods, and consequently could do but little financially for the spread of the message. Elder White and his wife and Elder Bates saw the importance of personal labor among the scattered brethren, and also the necessity of preparing reading matter to place in the hands of the people, as an aid in leading them to the knowledge of the truth. Elder Bates was aided much in presenting the Sabbath question by his tract on that subject, as he went to different localities, and by the circulation of the same through the mail. He labored with the utmost perseverance.

A Young Sister's Sacrifice for the Truth

At one time, having no money to pay his fare, he was about to start on foot to go from Massachusetts to New Hampshire. Just then he received a letter from a young sister who had engaged to do house-work at $1 per week that she might have something with which to help the cause. After working one week, she was so impressed with the thought that Elder Bates needed money that she went to her employer and obtained advanced pay so as to enable her to send him at once

[1] Eze. 34: 12.

265)

$5. With this he paid his fare to New Hampshire, by public conveyance. At every place he had good meetings, and many souls accepted the truth.

Housekeeping with Borrowed Furniture

In order to show the spirit of sacrifice which actuated the early pioneers in this message, we note the following from Mrs. White's statement of their situation in the winter of 1857-58, when they occupied rooms in the spacious home of S. Howland, Topsham, Maine, where with borrowed furniture they set up housekeeping:—

"We were poor, and saw close times. My husband worked at hauling stone on the railroad, which wore the skin on his fingers through, and the blood started in many places. We had resolved not to be dependent, but to support ourselves, and have wherewith to help others. But we were not prospered. My husband worked very hard, but could not get what was due him for his labor.

Elder White Cutting Cord-Wood

"My husband left the railroad, and with his ax went into the woods to chop cord-wood. With a continual pain in his side he worked from early morning till dark to earn about fifty cents a day. He was prevented from sleeping nights by severe pain. We soon received letters from brethren in different States inviting us to come and visit them; but as we had no means to take us out of the State, our reply was that the way was not open before us.

"We received a letter from Brother Chamberlain, of Connecticut, urging us to attend a conference in that State. We decided to go if we could obtain the means. Husband settled with his employer, and found that there was ten dollars due him. With half of this I purchased articles of clothing which were much needed, and then patched my husband's overcoat, even piecing the patches, making it difficult to tell the original cloth in the sleeves. We had five dollars left to take us to

Dorchester, Mass. Our trunk contained nearly everything we possessed on earth. But we enjoyed peace of mind and a clear conscience, and this we prized above earthly comforts.

" We called at the house of Brother Nichols, and before we left, Sister Nichols handed my husband five dollars, which paid our fare to Middletown, Conn. We were strangers in that city, and had never seen one of the brethren in the State. We had but fifty cents left. My husband did not dare to use that to hire a carriage, so he threw the trunk upon a pile of boards, and we walked on in search of some one of like faith. We soon found Brother Chamberlain, who took us to his house."

Conference at Rocky Hill, Conn.

This conference was held at Rocky Hill, the meeting room being a large, unfinished chamber in Brother Belden's house. The following extract from a letter written by Elder White to S. Howland, gives some interesting particulars respecting the meeting : —

" April 20 [1848], Brother Belden sent his wagon to Middletown for us and the scattered brethren in that city. We arrived at his place [Rocky Hill] about four in the afternoon, and in a few minutes in came Brethren Bates and Gurney. We had a meeting that evening of about fifteen. Friday morning the brethren came in until we numbered about fifty. These were not all fully in the truth. Our meeting that day was very interesting. Brother Bates presented the commandments in a clear light, and their importance was urged home by powerful testimonies. The word had effect to establish those already in the truth, and to awaken those not fully decided." [2]

Invited to Oswego County, N. Y.

As the result of the circulation of Elder Bates's tract among the Adventists, persons in other States began the observance of the Sabbath. Hiram Edson, of Port Gibson, N. Y.,

[2] " Life Sketches," page 245.

wrote inviting Elder and Mrs. White and others to attend a conference of Sabbath-keepers in Volney, Oswego County, in August, 1848. He said that the brethren were generally poor, and he could not promise that they would do much toward defraying expenses. Elder White had received $40 as the result of labor performed in the hay field. A part of this was spent in purchasing clothing which was greatly needed, and the remainder paid their way to Volney and return.

This conference in western New York was held in Mr. Arnold's carriage house. There were about thirty-five persons present, all that could be collected in that part of the State, but hardly two of these were agreed. Each was strenuous for his own views, declaring that they were according to the Bible. All were anxious to advance their sentiments and to preach them. They were told that Elder White and his wife had not come so great a distance to hear them, but had come to teach them the truth. Mr. Arnold held that the one thousand years of Revelation 20 were in the past, and that the one hundred and forty-four thousand mentioned in Revelation were those raised at Christ's resurrection.

Mr. Arnold Objects to Ordinances

As the emblems of our dying Lord were before this company, and as they were about to commemorate his sufferings, Mr. Arnold arose and said he had no faith in what they were about to do,— that the Lord's supper was a continuation of the passover, to be observed but once a year.

These strange differences of opinion rolled a heavy weight upon Mrs. White. She well knew that Mr. Arnold was in error, and great grief pressed upon her spirits, for it seemed that God was dishonored. Some feared that she was dying; but Elders Bates, White, Chamberlain, Gurney, and Edson prayed for her, and the Lord mercifully heard the prayers of his servants, and she revived. The light of heaven rested upon her, and she was soon lost to earthly things. While in this state, she was shown some of the errors of those present, and also truth in contrast with these errors, showing that these discordant views, which they claimed were according to the Bible, were only according to their opinions of the Bible, and that they must yield their errors, and unite upon the third angel's message. The meeting ended gloriously; truth gained the victory. Those who held these strange diversities of opinion confessed their errors, and united upon the present truth of the third angel's message, and God greatly blessed them.

A Vision with Wonderful Use of the Bible

The following account of this meeting was given by Mr. Alexander Ross, Jan. 4, 1884, who was one of the thirty-five composing the little gathering. He said: —

" Sister White, while in vision, arose to her feet and took the family Bible upon her left hand; the book was one of ordinary size. While holding it open, high up, without looking toward it, with her right hand she would turn from text to text, and placing her finger on the scripture, would repeat the same. I looked at many of the texts to see if she was repeating the one to which she pointed. Myself or some of the company looked at them all. In every case she not only repeated the text to which she pointed, but she did so while her eyes were looking upward and in an opposite direction from the Bible. It was these scriptures which she repeated that overthrew the false theories of Sabbath-keepers assembled at Volney, in August, 1848, and caused us to unite upon the truth."

Indeed, one must have been hard to convince who did not renounce error of doctrine corrected under such circumstances, by plain texts quoted from the Bible, and in this remarkable manner. This company of Sabbath-keepers in Oswego County, after their errors had thus been corrected, and they had become united upon the truth, went forth from that meeting to spread the light to others. The results surely bore the evidence of being the work of God. Satan is ever ready to divide, distract, and scatter, by whatever means he can employ. "God is not the author of confusion, but of peace, as in all churches of the saints." [3]

Miraculous Cases of Healing

After the conference before mentioned, meetings were held in Madison County, Port Gibson, Port Byron, and in New York City. Following these was a general meeting in Connecticut. At some of these places the Lord came very near to his servants, and the healing power of the Great Physician came upon the sick in answer to the earnest prayers of his people as they followed the rule laid down in the Epistle of James. [4] Even persons pronounced hopeless by physicians were healed of their diseases. Incidents of such a character have often been experienced at various times since 1845.

Pioneers Endure Hardness

Elder White, in the *Review and Herald* of Feb. 5, 1880, when speaking of those pioneer days, said: —

" In our early labors we have suffered hunger for want of proper food, and cold for want of proper clothing. We deprived ourselves of even the necessaries of life to save money for the cause of God. While *at the same time* we were wearing ourselves fearfully in order to accomplish the great amount of work that seemed necessary to be done in writing, editing, traveling, and preaching from State to State."

The year 1848 was memorable, not only in the advent history, but politically. The truths of the third angel's message were very well defined, and the way was opening in different directions for the advancement of the work. At this time events in the moral and political world were assuming a shape calculated to arouse anew the attention of the

[3] 1 Cor. 14: 32.   [4] Jer. 5: 14, 15.

students of prophecy. Not only was there great confusion among the nations of the Old World, but at Hydesville, Wayne Co., N. Y., began the manifestations of modern Spiritualism, which Bible students said must be the " spirits of devils, which are to gather the nations of the earth to the battle of the day of the Lord."

Confusion of Nations in 1848

On the 21st day of February, 1848, when the courtiers of Louis Phillippe, of France, were gathered around him, he said: " I was never more firmly seated on the throne of empire than I am to-night." In the twilight of the next evening, wearing a " pea jacket," disguised as a hackney coachman, he fled outside the walls of the city of Paris seeking a refuge for his personal safety. The cause of this great and sudden change is said to have been the result of some movement on his part favoring the papal usurpation, which offended his subjects and his soldiers. He had on that day completed, in the city of Paris, a grand military review of the French army; and when their arms were stacked, he retired to the palace, when suddenly a small boy jumped upon a cannon, waving a tri-colored flag, crying, "DOWN WITH THE POPE! DOWN WITH THE POPE!!" The soldiers taking up the cry, it passed swiftly up and down the lines, gaining strength as it went, until connected with it was the cry, "AND DOWN WITH THE KING!" In a few hours all Paris was a scene of wild confusion. The soldiers, with guns in hand, accompanied by a mob, were rushing for the king's palace. He, on being informed of the turmoil, hastened to escape under disguise.

Nations that were Involved in the Struggle

The commotion and unrest of France spread rapidly to other countries. Prussia, Hanover, Sardinia, Sicily, Naples, Venice, Lombardy, Tuscany, and Rome caught the same mob spirit. Within three months all Europe was astir, and over thirty empires and kingdoms were in the greatest disorder. Thrones were burned in the streets, kings and emperors were fleeing and hiding for fear of losing their lives. Politicians predicted that there would be a general revolution of the governments of the world.

Many of the Adventist ministers who had not as yet heard of the third angel's message, saw this confusion, and supposed it must be the rallying of the nations for " the battle of the great day of God Almighty." [5]

Sealing Message Discovered

Just at this time the Seventh-day Adventists were learning from the Scriptures that the Sabbath of the fourth commandment was the *sign,* or *seal,* of the living God, and that the time had arrived for the proclamation of the *sealing message* of Rev. 10: 1 - 4, and they were devising ways and means of getting this message before the people. While the seventh-day people were preparing for this work, the First-day Adventists were saying, " You are *too late* with your *sealing message,* for the battle of the great day and the Lord's actual coming are right upon us."

Turmoil Suddenly Quieted Down

Some three months later, the outburst among the nations quieted down ; not, however, by a settlement of their grievances, but in a manner that journalists themselves could not explain. Of this trouble, Horace Greeley, in the New York *Tribune,* said : " It was a great wonder to us all what started so suddenly that confusion among the nations ; but it is a greater wonder still what stopped it."

Senator Choate on the Situation in the Old World

We come down to 1851, and find Senator Choate, in a speech before the United States Congress, referring to the

[5] Rev. 16: 13 - 15.

state of affairs in the Old World, and saying: "What that state and aspect exactly is, that shadows, clouds, and darkness appear to rest upon, you entirely appreciate; how wholly unsettled. It has seemed to me as if the prerogatives of crowns, and the rights of men, and the hoarded up resentments of a thousand years were about to unsheath the sword for a conflict in which blood shall flow, as in apocalyptic vision, 'to the bridles of the horses,' and in which a whole race of men shall pass away; in which the great bell of time shall sound out another hour; in which society itself will be tried by fire and steel, whether it be of nature and of nature's God or not."

"Testimony" of Nov. 18, 1848

While those claiming that this stir among the nations in 1848 was to usher in the coming of the Lord, met with a sad disappointment, how was it with Seventh-day Adventists who claimed that the time had now come for the "seal of the living God" to be presented to the people? In reply we quote from a tract published by Elder Joseph Bates in the month of January, 1849. In speaking of a circumstance that occurred Nov. 18, 1848, he says: —

"A small company of brethren and sisters were assembled in a meeting in Dorchester, near Boston, Mass. Before the meeting commenced, some of us were examining some of the points in the sealing message; some difference of opinion existed about the correctness of the view of the word 'ascending,' etc., and whereas we had made the publishing of the message a subject of prayer at the Topsham [Maine] conference a little previous, and the way to publish appeared not sufficiently clear, we therefore resolved unitedly to refer it all to God. After some time spent in earnest prayer for light and instruction, God gave Sister White the following in vision." We quote the words as they were spoken by her while in vision:—

18

Words Spoken in the Vision

"Where did the light break out? Let thine angel teach us where the light broke out. It commenced from a little, when thou didst give one light after another. The testimony and commandments are linked together, they cannot be separated; that comes first the ten commandments, by God. He was well pleased when his law began to come up in strength, and the waste places began to be built up. Out of weakness it has become strong from searching his word. The test upon it has been but a short time. It's the seal! It's coming up! It arises, commencing from the rising of the sun. Like the sun, first cold, grows warmer and sends its rays. When that truth arose, there was but little light in it, but it has been increasing. O the power of these rays! It grows in strength. The greatest weight and light is on that truth, for it lasts forever, when the Bible is not needed. It arose there in the east; it began with a small light, but its beams are healing. O how mighty is that truth; it's the highest after they enter the goodly land, but it will increase till they are made immortal. It commenced from the rising of the sun, keeps on its course like the sun, but it never sets.

"The angels are holding the four winds. It is God that restrains the powers. The angels have *not* let go, for the saints are not all sealed. When Michael stands up, this trouble will be all over the earth. Why, they are just ready to blow. There's a check put on because the saints are not sealed. Yea, publish the things thou hast seen and heard, and the blessing of God will attend. Look ye! That *rising* is in *strength,* and grows brighter and brighter." [6]

After coming out of this vision Mrs. White said to her husband, "I have a message for you. You must begin to print a little paper and send it out to the people. Let it be small at first; but as the people read they will send you means with which to print, and it will be a success from the first.

[6] "A Seal of the Living God," pages 24 - 26.

From this small beginning it was shown to me to be like streams of light that went clear round the world."

Doubtful from a Human Standpoint

These predictions were made in 1848 concerning the *rise* and *spread* of the Sabbath truth. To look at the situation from a human standpoint at that time, *reason* would say, " That prediction can never be fulfilled." One man remarked to one of our laborers soon after the prediction was made, " It will take you 144,000 years to do what you propose." " What! " they would say, " three preachers — Elder White and wife, and Elder Bates — all penniless, with less than one hundred adherents, all of whom are destitute of money, going forth with a few hundred copies of an eighty-page tract on the Sabbath question, to give a warning message to all the world! *Preposterous assumption!* " While those thus reasoning said, " *Impossible!* " faith in the message and the testimony of assured success said, " In the name of Israel's God it *will* be done! and trusting in his strength it *must* be done! "

How the First Seventh-day Adventist Paper was Printed

From the time the testimony was borne concerning the publishing work, many prayers were offered by those observing the seventh day, that the Lord would open the way for the printing of a " little paper." The great lack was money with which to secure the publication of the first number. In the month of June, 1849, Elder White had the opportunity of mowing forty acres of timothy grass, with a hand scythe, at seventy-five cents per acre ; and thus he was enabled to produce the first number of the little journal. It may not be out of place to insert at this point a facsimile of the first page of the little sheet. The reader will observe in the first column the words of Elder White, where he says, " The way has not been opened to commence the work until now." And you can also see that it was his self-sacrificing that " opened the way."

Mrs. White's Account of the First Papers

Mrs. White says of the beginning of the publishing work: —

" My husband began to publish a small sheet at Middletown, eight miles from Rocky Hill, Conn., and often walked this distance and back again, although he was then lame. When he brought the first number from the printing office, we all bowed around it, asking the Lord, with humble hearts and many tears, to let his blessing rest upon the feeble efforts of his servant. He then directed the paper to all those who he thought would read it, and carried it to the post-office in a carpet-bag. Every number was taken from Middletown to Rocky Hill, and always before preparing them for the post-office they were spread before the Lord, and earnest prayers, mingled with tears, were offered to God that his blessing would attend the silent messengers. Very soon letters came bringing means to publish the paper, and the good news of many souls embracing the truth." [7]

Prediction of Support of Paper Fulfilled

It is with feelings deeper than mere interest that we present this the first page of the first paper published by Seventh-day Adventists. The whole volume of *The Present Truth* consisted of eleven numbers of eight pages, two columns each. The reading matter on the page measured four and five-eighths by eight inches. Numbers 1 and 4 were printed in July, August, and September, at Middletown, Conn. Numbers 5 to 9 were printed at Oswego, N. Y., and are dated December, 1849, March, April, and May, 1850. Number 11 is dated November, 1850, and was printed at Paris, Maine. In Number 6 Elder White said, " While publishing the first four numbers more than enough money came in to pay for

[7] " Life Sketches," page 260.

THE PRESENT TRUTH.

PUBLISHED SEMI-MONTHLY—BY JAMES WHITE.

Vol.1.   MIDDLETOWN, CONN JULY, 1849.   No. 1.

" The secret of the Lord is with them that fear him; and he will shew them his covenant "—Ps. xxv. 14.

" WHEREFORE, I will not be negligent to put you always in remembrance of these things, though ye know them, and be established in the PRESENT TRUTH." 2 Pet. i: 12.

It is through the truth that souls are sanctified, and made ready to enter the everlasting kingdom. Obedience to the truth will kill us to this world, that we may be made alive, by faith in Jesus. " Sanctify them through thy truth; thy word is truth." John xvii: 17. This was the prayer of Jesus. "I have no greater joy than to hear that my children walk in truth." 3 John iv.

Error, darkens and fetters the mind, but the truth brings with it freedom, and gives light and life. True charity, or LOVE, "rejoiceth in the truth." Cor. xiii: 6. " Thy law is the truth." Ps. cxix: 142.

David describing the day of slaughter, when the pestilence shall walk in darkness, and destruction waste at noon-day, so that, "a thousand shall fall at thy side and ten thousand at thy right hand," says—

" He shall cover thee with his feathers, and under his wings shalt thou trust; his TRUTH shall be thy SHIELD and BUCKLER." Ps. xci: 4.

The storm is coming. War, famine and pestilence are already in the field of slaughter. Now is the time, the only time to seek a shelter in the truth of the living God.

In Peter's time there was present truth, or truth applicable to that present time. The Church have ever had a present truth. The present truth now, is that which shows present duty, and the right position for us who are about to witness the time of trouble, such as never was. Present truth must be oft repeated, even to those who are established in it. This was needful in the Apostles day, and it certainly is no less important for us ,who are living just before the close of time.

For months I have felt burdened with the duty of writing, and publishing the present truth for the scattered flock, but the way has not been opened for me to commence the work until now. I tremble at the word of the Lord. and the importance of this time. What is done to spread the truth must be done quickly. The four Angels are holding the angry nations in check but a few days, until the saints are sealed, then the nations will rush, like the rushing of many waters. Then it will be too late to spread before precious souls, the present saving, living truths of the Holy Bible. My spirit is drawn out after the scattered remnant. May God help them to receive the truth, and be established in it. May they haste to take shelter beneath the "covering of Almighty God," is my prayer.

The Weekly Sabbath Instituted at Creation, and not at Sinai.

" And on the seventh day GOD ended his work which he had made ; and he rested on the seventh day from all his work which he had made. And GOD blessed the seventh day, and sanctified it: because that in it he had rested from all his work which GOD created and made." Gen. ii: 2, 3.

Here GOD instituted the weekly rest or Sabbath. It was the seventh day. He BLESSED and SANCTIFIED that day of the week, and no other ; therefore the seventh day, and no other day of the week is this day, sanctified time.

GOD has given the reason why he blessed and sanctified the seventh day. " Because that in it he had rested from all his work which GOD had created and made." He rested, and set the example for man. He blessed and set apart the seventh day for man to rest from his labor, and follow the example of his Creator. The Lord of the Sabbath said, Mark ii: 27 " The Sabbath was made for man." Not for the Jew only, but for MAN, in its broadest sense ; meaning all mankind. The word man in this text, means the same as it does in the following texts. " Man that is born of a woman is of few days and full of trouble." Job xiv. 1. " Man lieth down and riseth not, till the heavens be no more." Job xiv: 12,

No one will say that man here means

(277)

the papers. It has been used in paying our expenses. to the meetings we have attended." During the year 1849, under the influence of these papers, and the pioneer labors of Elder Bates, many accepted the message in Vermont, Michigan, and other States.

In contrast with the unpromising situation of the work in 1848, we will consider a few facts as they exist in 1905, and thus be enabled better to judge respecting the final outcome of this cause, whether those were right who opposed the humble beginning of the message, or the God of heaven who spake through his handmaid of the " *increasing* " strength of the " *sealing* " work.

Progress of the Publishing Work

This truth is now being proclaimed and printed in about forty of the leading languages of the world. Instead of three ministers, there are, counting those that are ordained and the licentiates, over 600, besides hundreds of others working as physicians, Bible workers, teachers, and medical missionaries. The literature of the denomination is represented in over half a hundred different periodicals, which are printed in nearly a score of publishing houses located in Europe, Asia, Africa, North and South America, the islands of the Pacific, and Australia. In these publishing houses there are printed over eleven hundred different books, pamphlets, and tracts. To obtain a copy of each, with the periodicals for one year, would require about $340. Instead of simply one hundred adherents, there are not far from 100,000 who are rejoicing in this truth. Truly this message, like the sun, is " *arising*," and we may say, in the language of the testimony of 1848, " O the *power* of these rays! "

The Condition of the Nations

While the message has been thus advancing, what has been the condition of the nations? From that time down, in the public journals, we have often been treated to statements concerning the general war that is soon to be in Europe. While there has been strife here, and an outbreak there, the general " whirlwind " is held back,— the " four winds " are not permitted to blow all at once, " until the servants of God are sealed." That the elements of strife and war are there, but do not break out because they are held in check, is evident to all.

Henry Ward Beecher, not long before his death, called the maintaining of such large armies in Europe, " drawing the life-blood beforehand, for fear it would be spilt." The situation among the nations, with their grudges and animosities, and their threatening attitude toward one another, he compared to a " dead lock," caused by a group of men pointing daggers at each other's breasts, not one of whom dared to strike, for fear of being struck. " But," said he, " some one of them will soon see the favorable time to strike, and then the general mêlée will come."

Comparison of War Implements

Since 1848 implements of war have been constructed compared with which the *best* of that time would now be counted as mere toys. The " Peace Association " of America, in making its call for peace services on Peace Sunday,— Dec. 15, 1895,— said : " Now while there is a decided advancement in civilization, on the other hand there are greater preparations for war among the nations than ever before."

General Miles on War Preparations

General Nelson A. Miles, in a speech at a mass-meeting in Washington, D. C., Jan. 12, 1904, said :—

" In this enlightened age of progress and intelligent, refined civilization we would be glad to believe that the burdens and dangers of war have been lessened ; yet strange as it may seem, there never has been a time in the world's history when so much wealth was squandered in preparation for war, nor when so many millions of trained, skilled, and disciplined men, armed with the most destructive weapons, were taken from the avenues of peaceful industry, as at the present time."

But the whirlwind of war still delays, while the *sealing work* goes on.

CHAPTER XVIII

PROVIDENCE OF GOD IN THE PUBLISHING WORK

THEN shall we know, if we follow on to know the Lord; his going forth is prepared as the morning." [1]

Up to the month of June, 1849, the labors of Elder White and his wife and Elder Bates were confined to the New England States. At this time Miss Clarissa Bonfoey, of Middletown, Conn., joined Elder White's family. A short time previous to this, her mother died, leaving her everything necessary for housekeeping on a small scale. By this means Elder White was enabled again to set up housekeeping; and this he did in a part of Mr. Belden's house at Rocky Hill, Conn.

Beginning of Modern Spiritualism

On March 24, 1849, a general meeting was held at Topsham, Maine. On that Sabbath a vision was given to Mrs. White, the subject of which was of the greatest importance. Perhaps a better understanding of the view will be obtained by getting before the mind a general idea of the situation at that time.

In the latter part of March, 1848, in Hydesville, Wayne Co., N. Y., began the "mysterious noises," or what afterward developed into the "spirit rappings." This first occurred in the house of the Fox family. In the latter part of the summer, the family moved to Rochester, N. Y., where, in Corinthian Hall, public demonstrations were made, and the girls were subjected to the closest examination by committees composed

[1] Hosea 6: 3.

of ladies and gentlemen selected from the best citizens for that purpose. While the great majority of the people looked upon the rappings as a humbug, or some sleight-of-hand trickery, the most credulous had but little idea that it would grow to any great proportions.

Predictions Concerning Spiritualism

In the vision above mentioned, Mrs. White saw that the mysterious knocking in Rochester and other places, was the power of Satan, and that such things would be more and more common; and that they would be clothed in a religious garb, to lull the deceived to greater security, and to draw the minds of God's people, if possible, to those things, and cause them to doubt the teachings of the Holy Spirit.

But few, if any, at that time had the faintest idea that Spiritualism would spread over the earth as then predicted, or that it would ever assume to be a religion, with its regularly organized churches and pastors.

Prediction Fulfilled

The fulfilment of the prophecy, however, is apparent when we consider their membership, which is reported to be 10,-000,000 in the United States alone. As to their present religious garb, we give the following from the *Review and Herald,* Washington, D. C., Nov. 12, 1903: —

"At the recent convention of the National Association of Spiritualists, held in this city, a new ritual was adopted. Provision was made for the 'ordination' of pastors or ministers, and a company of believers in Spiritualism was recognized as a 'church.' This will be seen by reading the following section from the new ritual: —

"'No pastor or minister shall be settled over a church or society without first having been formally inducted into office by what has been known from the earliest ages of religious history as the service of ordination. No person can become a candidate for ordination until he has received a call to the pastorate of some church or society, or been appointed missionary by some State Spiritualist Association, incorporated as a religious body in the State in which it is located, or by the National Spiritualist Association of the United States of America. All persons who are candidates for pastorates or for missionary work must have been for at least three years in full fellowship with some Spiritualist church or society, and for at least two years a licentiate, commissioned by a State or the National Association as a trial speaker. Pastors settled for less than one full calendar year shall be ineligible for ordination.' "

Elder White in Oswego, N. Y.

As the publishing work was located in Oswego, N. Y., Elder White changed his residence from Connecticut to this place in the fall of 1849, and here was held, the same year, on November 3, a conference of believers. Of their labors following, Mrs. White says: —

" We then decided that it was our duty to labor in the State of New York. My husband felt a burden upon him to write and publish. We rented a house in Oswego, borrowed furniture from our brethren, and began housekeeping. There my husband wrote, published, and preached. It was necessary for him to keep the armor on at every moment, for he often had to contend with professed Adventists who were advocating error, preaching definite time, and were seeking to prejudice all they could against our faith." [2]

Second Advent Review Published

In the autumn of 1850 it was deemed advisable to make another change; accordingly Elder White moved to Paris, Maine, where the first volume of the *Second Advent Review and Sabbath Herald* was published as a semi-monthly, consisting of thirteen numbers, each containing eight two-column

[2] " Life Sketches," page 265.

pages, the size of the printed page being seven and one-eighth by ten and one-fourth inches. The first number was dated the following November, and the last number, June 9, 1851.

The enlarged size of the paper over *Present Truth* was a very good index to the proportionate spread of the truth, the increase of laborers in the cause, and of supporters of the work. As the terms of the paper were gratis, it was expected that the friends of the cause would aid in its publication, and this they did. Although the believers were composed mostly of people in moderate circumstances, they aided as the Lord had prospered them, and did according to their ability to push on the car of truth.

J. N. Andrews Begins Preaching

About this time J. N. Andrews, who resided in Paris, Maine, began his public labors as a minister of the gospel and a writer on religious topics. In the *Review* for May, 1851, he had an article occupying over five pages on the subject of the three messages. In this he applied the prophecy of the two-horned beast of Revelation 13 to the United States, taking the position, on the strength of the prophecy alone, that the enforcement of Sunday as the Sabbath would be the point on which a union of church and state would finally be founded in this nation. His argument rested wholly upon the prophecy, as no movement at that time pointed very strongly in that direction, the strongest expression that could be found favoring it being a statement from Dr. Durbin, taken from the *Christian Advocate and Journal,* which said : —

" When Christianity *becomes* the moral and spiritual life of the state, the state is bound, through her magistrates, to prevent the open violation of the holy Sabbath, as a measure of self-preservation."

THE FIRST PRESS

Selling Farms to Aid the Work

It was about this time that such men as Hiram Edson, of New York, and Cyrenius Smith, of Jackson, Mich., were led to sell their farms, each worth $3,500, and rent farms for their own use, that they might have means to help in different enterprises that should arise in the prosecution of the work of the message.

Removal of the Publishing Work to Saratoga

In 1851, Elder White moved from Paris, Maine, to Saratoga Springs, N. Y., and here again, with borrowed furniture, he set up housekeeping, and published the second volume of the *Advent Review*, the first number bearing date of August 5 of the same year. This volume consisted of fourteen numbers, and was issued semi-monthly. The last number was published March 23, 1852. The name of the paper was slightly changed from that of the *Second Advent Review*, as in Vol. I, to the *Advent Review and Sabbath Herald*, the name which in its eighty-second volume it still retains. The size of the journal was increased to three columns, eight pages, the printed page measuring eight and one-fourth by eleven and three-fourths inches.

It will be seen from the increased size of what was and is still the denominational journal, that every change was for the better, showing a reasonable degree of prosperity, and giving marked evidence that the work of the third angel " had come to stay."

Publishing in Rochester — Owning a Hand-Press

On May 6, 1852, the first number of Volume III of the *Advent Review and Sabbath Herald* was published in Rochester, N. Y., and was printed on a press and with type owned by Seventh-day Adventists. Hiram Edson had advanced means to purchase a Washington hand-press, with type and material for fitting up the office. He was to receive his pay as donations should come in from the friends of the truth. That hand-press stood in the office of the *Review and Herald* at Battle Creek, Mich., until consumed in the fire, Dec. 30, 1902. It was at that time regarded as the best proof-press in the office. In Number 12, Vol. III, Oct. 14, 1852, an announcement was made that the cost of fitting up the office with this press and material was $652.93, and the receipts for that purpose up to that date were $655.84. Of these twelve numbers of the paper, 2,000 copies of each number had been issued and circulated gratuitously.

The Youth's Instructor Started

In August there was begun in the Review office the publication of the *Youth's Instructor,* a monthly. Now it is a weekly, with four times the reading matter in each number that it contained at that time.

Uriah Smith Connects with the Office

In 1853 Elder Uriah Smith began his labors in the office of the *Review and Herald,* where he held a responsible position for half a century. That year (1853) it was for the first time stated in the *Review and Herald* that those who desired to do so could buy our publications by paying the cost price. To all others the printed matter was free, as the deficit was met by the donations of the liberal and willing hearted. In 1854 it was announced that the price of the *Review* semimonthly was $1.00 a year. In that same year, at a tent-meeting held in McComb County, Michigan, in the month of July, an effort was made to sell our publications. During this meeting $50 worth of books were sold. Elder White, in speaking of this effort, said, through the *Review,* " This shows that our books can be sold."

Call for $500 Tract Fund

In the *Review* of Oct. 12 and Dec. 24, 1854, calls were made for a $500 tract fund to enable the office to furnish minis-

G. W. AMADON   L. O. STOWELL   WARREN BACHELLER   URIAH SMITH

The " First Press " as it stood in the Review office, with the same men who worked in the office at Rochester, N. Y.

ters with tracts for free distribution in connection with their labors, and also for a " relief fund of $500 for the office, that the *Review* might be published regularly each week, instead of missing, occasionally, a week for lack of funds."

J. P. Kellogg and Henry Lyon Sell Their Farms

It was during this period that J. P. Kellogg, of Tyrone, and Henry Lyon, who lived near Plymouth, Mich., sold their farms, each worth about $3,500, for the sole purpose of having means to use in advancing the work; and thus did two more Michigan brethren step forward at an opportune time, with ready means and willing hearts to lift where help was most needed. The former engaged in the manufacture of brooms in Jackson, Mich., while the latter moved to Battle Creek, and labored at the carpenter's trade to sustain his family.

All Our Papers and Books for $3.00

At the end of Volume VI, June, 1855, one could get the *Review* and the *Instructor* for one year, besides a complete set of all the pamphlets, tracts, and a hymn book, such as was then used,— twenty-six pamphlets and tracts, all told,— for the sum of $3.00. The established price of the *Instructor* was twenty-five cents for twelve numbers.

Review Office Invited to Michigan

In the month of April, 1855, Elder White and his wife again visited Michigan, and held meetings at several places. On the 28th and 29th of the same month a conference convened at Battle Creek, during which it was voted by the brethren in Battle Creek to invite Elder White to move the Review office from Rochester to Battle Creek. Dan Palmer, Cyrenius Smith, J. P. Kellogg, and Henry Lyon agreed to furnish $300 each, without interest, making a sum of $1200, to purchase a lot and erect a publishing office. Accordingly they secured a lot on the southeast corner of West Main and Washington Streets, and erected thereon a two-story wooden building 20 x 30 feet in size, with twenty-foot posts.

First Meeting-House in Battle Creek

During the same season the first Seventh-day Adventist meeting-house in Battle Creek was erected, 18 x 24 feet in size. This plain building, boarded up and down, and battened, stood near the northwest corner of Van Buren and Cass Streets.

In Our First Printing Office

The first number of the *Review* published in Battle Creek in an office owned by Seventh-day Adventists was dated Dec. 4, 1855. The price of the paper was then established at $1.00 per volume of twenty-six numbers; but donations were solicited to send the paper free to the worthy poor. From this time forward Elders Waggoner and Cottrell were almost constant contributors to the columns of the *Advent Review*.

In the *Review* of Dec. 18, 1855, the publishing committee made a statement which to the present workers in the office may sound strange. It read thus: "We do not see why those who labor in the office should not receive a reasonable compensation for their services. The editor only receives one half what he could get elsewhere." It may be well to mention that common wages then were not one half what they are at the present time, and that half pay then was not more than one third or one fourth what the office pays for similar labor now. The workers in the office at that time made the gift of half the worth of their services that the gospel of present truth might be published.

Call for Power-Press and Engine

In the *Review* of March 19, 1857, the suggestion was first made that a power-press and engine was needed and should be obtained for the printing of the papers, tracts, and books. As reported April 2, the decision was made to buy an Adams power-press, and seven men pledged $100 each toward its purchase. In the following issue a statement was made that the press and engine would cost some $2,500, and pledges had already been raised to $1,700.

In an editorial from Elder White in the *Review* of Aug. 13, 1857, is this encouraging statement: " Our office is free. There is a general book fund of $1,426, now invested in books. The new power-press is in operation and works beautifully, and the prospect is fair that it will soon be running by steam power, and all paid for. Our tent operations are far better sustained than formerly."

First Report of Book Sales

Oct. 29, 1857, it was reported in the *Review* that the book sales for the two previous years was $1,287.91, which was the first report of the kind made up to this date. It was a token of advancement in the cause, hence a source of encouragement, as it showed that the truth was gaining in strength, and " like streams of light making its way around the world."

Review Office a Safe Deposit

In the *Review* of Aug. 13, 1858, the idea was first advanced to our people of making the office a place of deposit for surplus means. Persons who had money for which they had no immediate use could make the office a depository, drawing it at any time upon order as they might need it, and thus give the office the benefit of its use. This suggestion being acted upon, it afforded still greater financial strength to the work.

From that time to this (1905), no person has ever yet lost a dollar thus loaned to our publishing houses, or failed to get his money when called for. The candid, thoughtful ones have come to regard our offices of publication a safer place even to deposit their surplus means than banks, which so often fail. Banks have worldly credit, while our publishing houses

19

have the strength of the whole denomination for their " backing."

Seventh-day Adventist Publishing Association Organized

The Seventh-day Adventist Publishing Association was organized May 3, 1861, and circulars were sent out soliciting subscriptions to the capital stock at $10 per share. In two weeks it was announced that $4,080 in stock had already been subscribed.

Beginning with June 11 of that year, the *Review* was published by the Seventh-day Adventist Publishing Association. The first office building erected by the association was located on the southeast corner of Main and Washington Streets, on the site from which the old frame building was removed to Kalamazoo Street. This structure was two stories high, of solid brick walls. It was in the form of a Greek cross, and fronted north on Main Street. The extreme measure east and west was 44 feet, by north and south, 72 feet.

First Publications in Other Tongues

Step by step the message advanced, and each aggressive movement tended to strengthen and consolidate the work. At this time our publishing house issued five pamphlets in foreign languages, three in the Danish-Norwegian and two in French; thus a beginning was made in printing for foreign countries.

With the continual increase of membership there was a steady and continued growth in finances. This is indicated by the report in the *Review* of May 16, 1863, where the secretary of the association gave a statement of the total receipts as follows: —

Received in shares and donations to the Association to date	$10,374.13
Received from Rochester office	700.00
Received for additional material	300.00
Received on book fund	1,355.00
Received for power-press and engine	2,500.00
Total	$15,229.13

The secretary further states: " By a safe estimate of the property of the association, its value is decided to be not less than $20,000 which is nearly $5,000 more than it has cost the friends of the cause. This speaks well for the integrity and faithfulness of Brother White and those who have been associated with him in the Review office.

" E. S. WALKER, *Secretary.*"

Transfer of the "Review" to the Association

The publishing work having been brought to these results by the trying labors and sacrifices of Elder White, the profits arising therefrom virtually belonged to him; for the gain was really his self-denial, his business tact, and careful management. But instead of claiming it, or any part of it, he cheerfully passed it all over to the church; and more than this, when the association, after its organization, voted that he should have $6 per week for his services rendered, he only accepted $4 per week.

A Paper on the Pacific Coast

In the *Review* of April 21, 1874, was an article from Elder White, in which, speaking of the work on the Pacific Coast, he stated that there would soon be demanded the establishment of a weekly paper devoted to the interests of the cause upon that coast. A short time after this the way opened for purchasing a small quantity of type and material in Oakland, with which, in the month of June, a semi-monthly publication was begun, called the *Signs of the Times.*

Raising Means

After printing six numbers of the *Signs,* Elder White returned East, requesting the California Conference to make provision for the publication of the paper. At the General Conference, Aug. 15, 1874, a proposition was made to the Eastern brethren to raise $6,000 with which to purchase press, engine, and type for the *Signs* office, if the brethren on the Pacific Coast would raise $4,000 to secure a site and erect a suitable building for an office.

Elder Geo. I. Butler, at that time a member of the General Conference Committee, attended the camp-meeting at Yountville, Cal., and presented the proposition to the brethren. On Oct. 11, 1874, they responded to the call by pledging the sum of $19,414 in coin.

The Pacific Press Established

On Feb. 2, 1875, Elder James White and his wife, accompanied by Elder J. H. Waggoner and other efficient workers, arrived in Oakland. On the 12th of the same month a special session of the California Conference was called, to take into consideration a location upon which to erect buildings for the office of the *Signs of the Times*. After due deliberation, the decision was made to secure lots on the west side of Castro St., between 11th and 12th Sts. The same day Elder White and John Morrison purchased these lots, taking deeds in their own names, with the understanding that when the Association should be formed, they would deed over to it as much of the land as should be deemed necessary for the use of the corporation.

April 1, 1875, the Pacific Seventh-day Adventist Publishing Association was formed in Oakland, its capital stock being fixed at $28,000. The central portion of the lots on Castro St. was, according to agreement, deeded over to the association, and a building was at once constructed by O. B. Jones, of Battle Creek, Mich., the form and size of which was the same as that of the office erected in Battle Creek, except that the one in Oakland was constructed of wood instead of brick. This building being ready for occupancy, the *Signs of the Times* was moved into its new quarters on Friday, Aug. 27, 1875.

Removal to Mountain View

In this building the publication of periodicals and books was successfully carried forward until 1904, when arrangements were made to move the printing plant into the country. The reason for making this change is given by the manager of the Pacific Press in these words: " For years the management of the Pacific Press Publishing Company have felt that the land now occupied by their publishing house is too valuable, and the land surface too cramped, in the heart of a large city in a residence district, for factory purposes, and that it is wisdom in many ways to seek some rural place where land is less valuable, where homes in healthy surroundings could be secured by employees, with space sufficient for gardens, fruit trees, and breathing room; and where shipping advantages would be good. Such a place has been found and secured in the village of Mountain View, Santa Clara County, thirty-nine miles south of San Francisco, a place which combines many of the advantages of the city with the benefits of a healthy country life."

Printing Begun in Foreign Lands

Indicating the spread of the truth, we note that from 1875 to 1878 the printing work was begun in Basel, Switzerland, and in Christiana, Norway.

In the autumn of 1875 a report was given in the *Review* of book sales at the Review and Herald office alone, for seven years, from 1868 to 1875, amounting to $85,644.54, nearly six-fold increase over the seven preceding years, and the sales for all four of the offices (Michigan, California, Switzerland, and Norway), for three years, from 1875 to 1878, was $98,163.73.

A statement was made in the *Review* of October 17, 1878, that all the books, pamphlets, and tracts printed by the Review office previous to 1864 amounted to 50,058,000 pages. From

1864 to 1878 the number of pages was 158,130,951, **or a total of** 208,188,951 pages.

The Youth's Instructor Made a Weekly

Up to Jan. 1, 1879, the *Youth's Instructor* had been published monthly, but at this date, as it entered upon its thirty-first year, it was issued weekly; and thus its usefulness was increased fourfold.

What Elder White Turned over to the Association

In the *Review* of Jan. 23, 1879, are some statements made by Elder White respecting his connection with the cause, which it is proper to introduce here, as they shed more light on the sacrifices made in the publishing work. The quotation reads :—

" When, in 1861, the Publishing Association was instituted at Battle Creek, Mich., we gave our list of subscribers and the right to republish all our works (since decided to h've been worth $10,000) to the association, leaving us worth only $1,000; and we continued our labor as editor, manager, and preacher at $6 per week.

" In 1866, when we returned to the Review office, after severe sickness, we found the managers paying ten per cent. on thousands, and the capital stock reduced to $32,000;[3] but in four years, with the blessing of God, the debts were paid, the stock raised to $75,000, and we [the association] had $5,000 in the banks."

Standing of the Publishing House in 1880

In the *Review* of Jan. 15, 1880, Elder Butler says: —

" Our publishing house (Battle Creek) has recently been enlarged by the erection of a central portion between the two eastern buildings, thus materially increasing the capacity and convenience of the whole. Facilities exist for electrotyping and stereotyping, and doing the best binding. In fact,

[3] $3,000 below stock paid in, and donations.

it is stated by those who ought to know, that it is the most perfect and complete publishing house in the State of Michigan."

Notwithstanding this enlargement, it became necessary, before the close of the summer, to construct a new building south of the main building, for a press-room. To this room the five power-presses of the association were removed. One of these presses was of larger size than any heretofore used in the office. One of the same size and style had also just been placed in the office of the *Signs of the Times,* Oakland, Cal.

In the *Review* of May 17, 1881, referring to the success of the publishing work at the central publishing house in Battle Creek, Elder White said :—

" Take the amount of debts of the Seventh-day Adventist Publishing Association from a careful invoice of the property, and there is left in real and personal property not less than $105,000. Of this, all our people have given in shares, donations, and legacies, the sum of $34,432.17, and a few faithful men and women who have devoted their lives to the work, have added [not in donations, but by sacrifice and careful management] $70,567.83."

The Canvassing Work Inaugurated

Beginning with the year 1881 our people made a new venture, and entered into the canvassing work for the sale of our publications. As no accurate reports were made by the canvassers, of their sales, until the year 1884, our report for that period is made up from the reported sales of the four publishing houses. According to their figures the sales for five years were $221,248.69. As the influence of the work extended from our missions in Central Europe and the Scandinavian countries, the demand for publications in foreign languages increased.

Book Sales for Ten Years

From 1884 to 1894, a period of ten years, the sale of our large bound books was quite largely accomplished by the canvassers. Their sales for this period were $4,031,391.26. During this time our work was further extended by the establishing of publishing houses in Australia; Tahiti, Pacific Islands; Helsingfors, Finland; Hamburg, Germany; and at other places. The canvassers' sales for the year 1895, hard as the times were that year, were, as reported, a total of $357,467.23, making a grand total, including the sales we have already mentioned, of $4,816,773.73.

Sales for Fifty Years $11,000,000

To ascertain the whole amount of sales from 1854 to Jan. 1, 1896, we must still add the figures of the sale of trade books, pamphlets, tracts, and charts, as reported by all the publishing houses for the above ten years, which amount is $3,458,278.23; giving a grand total for the book sales of the denomination for twenty-two years of $8,275,051.96. To state it in another form: The sales for thirty years (1854 to 1884) were $424,915.24, and for the next twelve years following, to Jan. 1, 1896, $7,850,136.72. Notwithstanding the force in the canvassing field has for the last eight years decreased, it is a safe estimate to say that from 1854 to the present time (1905) more than $11,000,000 worth of Seventh-day Adventist publications have been sold.

Printing in about Forty Languages

The progress of the message in printed form is apparent when we consider that a beginning has been made in about forty of the leading languages, as the Arabic, Armenian, Basuto, Bohemian, Bulgarian, Bengali-India, Chinese, Danish, English, Esthonian, Finish, French, Fijian, Greek, German, Dutch, Hungarian, Hawaiian, Italian, Icelandic, Japanese, Kaffir, Lettish, Lavonian, Maori, Polish, Portuguese, Roumanian, Russian, Servian, Spanish, Swedish, Tahitian, Tongan, Welsh, etc. In these various countries and nationalities are active workers who are advancing the truths of the third message.

The number of books, pamphlets, and tracts printed in the different languages is over eleven hundred and eighty-seven. To secure a copy of each, and the eighty-seven periodicals of the denomination [4] in different tongues for one year, would require about $340.

Location of the Twenty Publishing Houses

Twenty publishing houses of the Seventh-day Adventists are located as follows: Avondale, Australia; Battle Creek, Mich. (2); Basel, Switzerland; Christiana, Norway; Copenhagen, Denmark; Cape Town, South Africa; Calcutta, India; College View, Nebraska; Hamburg, Germany; Helsingfors, Finland; London, England; Melbourne, Australia; Montreal, Canada; Nashville, Tennessee; Oakland, California; South Lancaster, Massachusetts; Stockholm, Sweden; Tocubaya, Mexico; Washington, D. C. Besides these publishing houses, our people are printing papers and tracts in Hong Kong, China; Tokio, Japan; Cairo, Egypt; South America; and in the Fiji Islands.

Issuing the First Pamphlet

For a moment we will take a retrospective glance at the facilities with which the pioneers had to work. In the fall of 1853, in the making up of the first book printed on the Washington press — "The Sanctuary," — after a "bee" of sisters had folded and gathered the signatures preparatory to stitching them, the writer stabbed them with a pegging awl; and after the covers had been put on, Uriah Smith pared them with a straight-edge and a sharp penknife. This was done because of a lack of proper machinery to do that part of the work.

[4] See list of the 87 in General Conference "Year Book" of 190

No farther back than 1861 all the literature of the denomination was printed on one Adams power-press, driven by a two-horsepower engine. Now, in the different offices of publication, there are more than forty steam-power presses running constantly, printing present truth. These offices employ a total of over five hundred persons to carry on the work, while hundreds of canvassers are in the field selling the books among the people.

In the year 1862 a full set of all the publications issued by Seventh-day Adventists could be purchased for the sum of $7.50; in 1904, as has been shown, it would require $340 to procure a complete set. Surely something more than human devising has wrought in producing these results.

The rise of the publishing work among the Seventh-day Adventists, as predicted in 1848, has indeed been like the progress of the sun, " Grows warmer — sends its rays " — " Keeps on its course like the sun, but it never sets."

Move by Faith — Elder Stone's Testimony

The zeal and earnestness of those who 'have pressed forward in the work of the third angel's message is well expressed in the *Review* of Feb. 5, 1884, by Elder Albert Stone, one of the pioneers in the cause, who lived to the ripe age of ninety years :—

" The early history of the cause was a day of small things, and the means employed seemed insufficient for the work. But the men and women of faith have known from the beginning that the strong arm of the Lord was enlisted in this work. They have known that the time set to favor Zion had come, and that the Lord had set his hand to gather his people. They saw that the Lord was at the helm, and that the Gospel Ship, freighted with the remnant church and her cargo of restored truth, tried faith, and perfect love, would come safely into harbor."

CHAPTER XIX

"BY THEIR FRUITS YE SHALL KNOW THEM"

E gave some, apostles; and some, prophets; and some, evangelists; and some, pastors and teachers; for the perfecting of the saints, for the work of the ministry, for the edifying of the body of Christ; till we all come in the unity of the faith, and of the knowledge of the Son of God, unto a perfect man, unto the measure of the stature of the fulness of Christ." [1] ·

When the Saviour placed the gifts of his Spirit in the church, to accomplish, "as it pleased him," the work of the Lord until the perfect day should come, he did not leave his people to guess whether a manifestation was from heaven, or from evil spirits, but he gives rules by which we might know whether the spirit was of God or not. Even in these last days, when, as predicted by the prophet Joel, the Lord was to pour out his Spirit upon all flesh, and both sons and daughters should prophesy, [2] Paul says the people should not despise prophesyings, but should "prove all things," and "hold fast that which is good." [3]

How else can such manifestations be tested but by comparing them with the Scripture rules for discerning the work of God's Spirit? Everything that is above the comprehension of finite minds is not necessarily from God, for the Bible declares that in the last days Satan will work miracles, to deceive the world, that he may gather them to the battle of that great day of God Almighty. [4] It is then by a careful comparison of the manifestation with the Bible rules that a

---

[1] Eph. 4: 11 - 13.   [2] Joel 2: 28, 29.   [3] 1 Thess. 5: 20, 21.
[4] Rev. 16: 14.

true spiritual gift may be known. The same care is requisite in this, that men of the world use in detecting counterfeit money.

Detecting Counterfeit Money

In the Detroit *Bank Note Reporter* of April, 1863, Mr. Preston gave five rules for detecting counterfeits, and declared that any person who would make a rigid inspection of every bill that came into his possession, according to these rules, need never fear of being deceived.

There is no surer way to prove a prophetic gift than by comparing it with the description of such gifts as were manifested in Scripture times, and testing it by the rules therein given. The Scriptures thoroughly furnish us unto all good works (2 Tim. 3: 16, 17), and give a correct record of the manifestations of the gift of prophecy, and how the true work of the Spirit of God may be known from the workings of Satan, with his spurious gifts.

RULES FOR DISCERNING TRUE GIFTS

The Lord has given in his word at least seven distinct rules by which genuine manifestations of the Spirit of God may be distinguished from the working of Satan.

Rule One — Special Instruction

The prophet Isaiah, in speaking of affairs existing in the last days, says: " Bind up the testimony, seal the law among my disciples. And I will wait upon the Lord, that hideth his face from the house of Jacob, and I will look for him. . . . And when they shall say unto you, Seek unto them that have familiar spirits, and unto wizards that peep and that mutter; should not a people seek unto their God? for the living to the dead? To the law and to the testimony; if they speak not according to this word, it is because there is no light in them." [5]

[5] Isa. 8· 16· 20.

In this Scripture, attention is called to a people engaged in restoring the *seal* to God's law — a people who are waiting upon the Lord, engaged in his service. They are looking for him; that is, they are looking for his coming — this, too, in a time when spirits professing to be spirits of the dead are asking the people to seek to them. Some heed their call, and seek to the dead for knowledge; but the Lord invites his people to seek him. That is virtually saying that if they seek him he will give them special instruction. They need not seek to the dead, who can give them no information; for "neither have they any more a portion forever in anything that is done under the sun;" and "the dead know not anything." [6]

In the above scripture a rule is given by which all communications are to be tested,— "if they speak not according to this word, it is because there is no light in them." All communications from the Lord will speak in harmony with his *word* and his *law*.

Applying this rule to the writings of Mrs. White, I would say that during the last fifty-two years I have carefully read her testimonies, comparing them with the law of God and the testimony of the Bible, and I find the most perfect harmony between the two. Her instructions do not come in to give any new revelation to take the place of the Scripture, but rather to show us *where* and *how*, in these times, people are liable to be led astray, to be led from the word. The position that the testimonies of Mrs. White occupy can be best told in what she herself has written respecting them: —

"The word of God is sufficient to enlighten the most beclouded mind, and may be understood by those who have any desire to understand it. But, notwithstanding all this, some who profess to make the word of God their study are found living in direct opposition to its plainest teachings. Then, to leave men and women without excuse, God gives

[6] Eccl. 9: 6, 5.

plain and pointed testimonies, bringing them back to the word that they have neglected to follow.

" The word of God abounds in general principles for the formation of correct habits of living, and the testimonies, general and personal, have been calculated to call their attention more especially to these principles. . . . You are not familiar with the Scriptures. If you had made God's word your study, with a desire to reach the Bible standard and attain Christian perfection, you would not have needed the testimonies. . . .

" The Lord designs to warn you, to reprove, to counsel, through the testimonies given, and to impress your minds with the importance of the truth of his word. The written testimonies are not to give new light, but to impress vividly upon the heart the truths of inspiration already revealed. . . . Additional truth is not brought out, but God has, through the testimonies, simplified the great truths already given, and in his own chosen way brought them before the people, to awaken and impress the mind with them, that all may be without excuse. . . .

" The testimonies are not to belittle the word of God, but to exalt it, and to attract minds to it, that the beautiful simplicity of truth may impress all. . . . If the people who now profess to be God's peculiar treasure would obey his requirements, as specified in his word, special testimonies would not be given to awaken them to their duty, and impress upon them their sinfulness and their fearful danger in neglecting to obey the word of God." [7]

Rule Two — True Prophets

We have already learned that all true prophets will speak in harmony with the law of God and the testimony of his word. The apostle John gives another rule describing the teaching of true prophets. He says: " Beloved, believe not every spirit, but try the spirits whether they are of God: because

[7] " Testimony for the Church," No. 33, pages 101 - 105.

many false prophets have gone out into the world. Hereby know ye the Spirit of God: Every spirit that confesseth that Jesus Christ is come in the flesh is of God: and every spirit that confesseth not that Jesus Christ is come in the flesh is not of God: and this is that spirit of antichrist, whereof ye have heard that it should come; and even now already is it in the world." [8]

Note carefully the foregoing scripture. It does not say that whosoever confesseth that Jesus Christ " *did* come in the flesh," " but *is come in the flesh;* " that is, that he comes, by his Spirit, and dwells *in us,* in response to our faith. This, in fact, is the central truth of the gospel, " Christ in you, the hope of glory." [9]

The practical theme found in all the writings of Mrs. White is the necessity of Christ as an indwelling Saviour if we would make any advancement in the heavenly way. Her writings teach the necessity of Christ first, *last,* and *all the time.* As an illustration of this fact, attention is called to her book, " Steps to Christ," of which more than one hundred thousand copies have been sold in the English language, to say nothing of the thousands of copies in the eighteen foreign languages in which it is now printed. A Presbyterian minister, having read the book, ordered over three hundred copies for his church-members and friends, and said, " This book was written by some one who is well acquainted with the Lord Jesus Christ."

Rule Three — False Prophets

John gives a rule for detecting false prophets: " They are of the world: therefore speak they of the world, and the world heareth them." [10] The teaching of false prophets will pander to the carnal heart, instead of exalting the self-denying and cross-bearing way. False prophets will teach " smooth things," instead of exalting the " Holy One of Israel." [11] Any one who reads even a few pages of Mrs.

[8] 1 John 4: 1 - 3.   [9] Eph. 3: 17; Col. 1: 27.
[10] 1 John 4: 5.   [11] Isa. 30: 10, 11.

White s writings can see that they are in the line of self denial and cross-bearing, and not of a nature to please a worldly, carnal heart.

Rule Four — Suffering and Patience

In tracing this subject still further, we will take, as a *fourth* rule, the words of the apostle James: " Take, my brethren, the prophets. who have spoken in the name of the Lord, for an example of suffering affliction, and of patience." [12] When we read of the experience of those ancient prophets we learn that one of the greatest of their trials was to see Israel reject, or go contrary to, the plain testimonies borne to them. A brief study of those times will show at once the character of both true and false prophets. " Thus saith the Lord of hosts, Hearken not unto the words of the prophets that prophesy unto you: they make you vain: they speak a vision of their own heart, and not out of the mouth of the Lord." [13]

There is nothing in the writings of Mrs. White to make the reader *vain;* but, as expressed by another, " I have received great spiritual benefit times without number from the testimonies. Indeed, I never read them without feeling reproved for my lack of faith in God, lack of devotion, and lack of earnestness in saving souls." Surely, then, the effect of Mrs. White's testimonies is vastly different from that of the teachings of false prophets, as described by Jeremiah.

The prophet tells us also *how* false prophets will teach: " They say still unto them that despise me, The Lord hath said, Ye shall have peace; and they say unto every one that walketh after the imagination of his own heart, No evil shall come upon you." [14]

As to the nature of Mrs. White's teaching in her testimonies, I will quote the following words from a careful reader: " I have read all her testimonies through and through, most of them many times, and I have never been able to find one

[12] James 5: 10.   [13] Jer. 23: 16.   [14] Verse 17.

immoral sentence in the whole of them, or anything that is not strictly pure and Christian; nothing that leads any one from the Bible or from Christ; but there I find the most earnest appeals to obey God, to love Jesus, to believe the Scriptures, and to search them constantly. Such nearness to God, such earnest devotion, such solemn appeals to live a holy life, can only be prompted by the Spirit of God."

A careful observer of her testimonies from the first writes: " In the matter of plain and faithful dealing, without fear or favor, I desire to bear witness that there has been no lack. If base and evil motives were the controlling power in this work, flattering words would fill the place of searching testimonies and faithful reproofs. Plainness of speech, faithful reproofs for wrong, words of compassion and encouragement for trembling souls who feel their need of the Saviour, and for the erring who seek in humility to put away their faults,— these are the things that have entered largely into her labors. The testimony of Mrs. White, reproving wrongs in the case of many persons whom she had seen in vision, has been borne with great faithfulness, and with the most excellent effect." [15]

Rule Five — True Prophecies are Fulfilled

There is a statement made by Moses relative to true and false prophets, found in the eighteenth chapter of Deuteronomy. He says: " How shall we know the word which the Lord hath not spoken? When a prophet speaketh in the name of the Lord, if the thing follow not, nor come to pass, that is the thing which the Lord hath not spoken, but the prophet hath spoken it presumptuously; thou shalt not be afraid of him." [16]

The same thing is also found in the following scriptures: " Who is he that saith, and it cometh to pass, when the Lord commanded it not?" [17]   Of the prophet Samuel it was said, " All that he saith cometh surely to pass." [18]   " When the

[15] J. .N. Andrews, in the *Review* of December, 1867.   [16] Deut. 8: 21, 22.
[17] Lam. 3: 37.   [18] I Sam. 9: 6.

20

word of the prophet shall come to pass, then shall the prophet be known, that the Lord hath truly sent him." [19]

It is now over fifty-three years since the writer first saw Mrs. E. G. White in prophetic vision. During these years many prophetic statements have been made by her relative to things that would take place. Some of these predictions relate to events already fulfilled, and some are in process of fulfilment, while others are still future. As to those relating to past or present events, I know not of a single instance of failure. Some of her predictions have already been noted. Others will appear in succeeding chapters as we continue our narrative.

Rule Six — Miracles not a Test of a True Prophet

It has been affirmed by many theological writers, and stated in commentaries on the Scriptures, that the sign of a true prophet is the working of miracles. We have yet to learn from the Scriptures a rule of this character.

If the working of miracles is proof of a true prophet, then the " false prophet " mentioned in Rev. 19: 20 would be declared after all a *true* prophet; for it is said, " The beast was taken, and with him the false prophet that *wrought miracles* before him, with which he deceived them that had received the mark of the beast." The same power is spoken of again in Rev. 13: 14, as deceiving " them that dwell on the earth by the means of those *miracles* which he *had power to do* in the sight of the beast." By the same application of this rule, we should be driven to the conclusion that even Satan is a true prophet. Certain spirits who will do a special work under the sixth of the seven last plagues are called " the spirits of devils, *working miracles,* which go forth unto the kings of the earth and of the whole world, to gather them to the battle of that great day of God Almighty." [20]

If the proof of a true prophet is to be found in the miracles he performs while out of vision, we should find but few

[19] Jer. 28: 9.   [20] Rev. 16: 14.

of the Bible prophets who would stand the test, especially
if the decision is to rest upon what is recorded concerning
their works. It is true that miracles are recorded as being
wrought by some of the prophets, as in the case of Elijah,
Elisha, and Paul. But who has found a record in the Bible
of the miracles of Isaiah, Jeremiah, Daniel, Hosea, Joel, Amos,
etc.? Yet these were true prophets of the Lord, and are
shown to be such by the rules the Lord has given as the
test of a true prophet.

That the working of miracles is *not* the test of a true
prophet is clearly seen by reading the scripture record of John
the Baptist. That he was a prophet is shown by the prediction of his father, Zacharias, in relating the vision God had
given him respecting the son that should be born to him:
" And thou, child, shalt be called the *prophet* of the Highest:
for thou shalt go before the face of the Lord to prepare his
ways." [21] Our Saviour himself recognized John as that very
prophet who should prepare the way before him; for of John
he said: " But what went ye out for to see? a prophet? Yea,
I say unto you, and much more than a prophet. This is he,
of whom it is written, Behold, I send my messenger before thy
face, which shall prepare thy way before thee. For I say unto
you, Among those that are born of women there is not a
greater prophet than John the Baptist? " [22]

Here, then, is a plain statement of the Saviour that John
was a prophet. Let us apply the test of miracle-working and
see the result. In the Gospel as written by John the evangelist,
we have these words: "And many resorted unto him [Christ]
and said, John did *no miracle;* but all things that John spake
of this man were true." [23] This statement alone is a complete
refutation of the claim that the sign of a true prophet is the
working of miracles.

This rule given in Deuteronomy 13 : 1 - 3, which we de-
nominate as rule *six* in our present enumeration, is to guard
against running after anything wonderful or miraculous until

[21] Luke 1: 76.   [22] Luke 7: 26 - 28.   [23] John 10: 41.

we have first carefully noticed whether its tendency is to greater nearness to the Lord or to a drawing away from him. This text virtually tells us to apply *all* the rules, especially to see if it is in harmony with God and his law.

This sixth rule teaches that if a miracle is wrought by a pretender, there will be seen with it, when carefully tested, a departure from the sacred truths of God's word, and a lowering of the standard to meet a heart inclined to shun the way of self-denial. The Lord permits such a pretender to arise, and his course is a test to the true child of God, giving him an opportunity to weigh carefully the tendency or motive of said miracle-worker. Those who cling to God's word, instead of being captivated by the false miracle-worker, come forth strong in God as the result of such experience.

In these evil days, when many are claiming to be " faith healers," " divine healers," " Christian Science healers," etc., it would be well to apply closely the scriptural rules; for it will need divine rules, and the illumination of the Holy Spirit, to enable us clearly to discern the intent and purpose of some of these " healers," so subtle is their work ; while on the other hand are those who openly disregard God's law and his truth for this time. In some instances these pretended " healers " have raged like men filled with madness at even a mention of the law of God. As surely as the Lord has a message proclaiming his holy law, so surely are the men destitute of the movings of the Holy Spirit who rail against his law, and thrust from their presence those who even mention it.

Rule Seven — Their Fruits

" Beware of false prophets, which come to you in sheep's clothing, but inwardly they are ravening wolves. Ye shall know them by their fruits. Do men gather grapes of thorns, or figs of thistles? Even so every good tree bringeth forth good fruit ; but a corrupt tree bringeth forth evil fruit. A good tree cannot bring forth evil fruit, neither can a corrupt tree bring forth good fruit. Every tree that bringeth not forth good fruit is hewn down, and cast into the fire. Wherefore by their fruits ye shall know them." [24]

These words of our Saviour recognize the fact that the gift of prophecy would exist in the gospel age. If no true prophets were to be connected with the work, and every prophetic manifestation was to be from an evil source, would he not have said, " Beware of prophets "? The fact that he tells us so definitely how each kind may be known is the best of evidence that in the work of the Comforter, the Holy Spirit, in showing " things to come " (John 16: 13), would be the true gift of prophecy. This rule, which in our enumeration we have called rule seven, is an infallible one. Christ did not say ye *may* know them by their fruits, but, positively, " by their fruits *ye shall know them.*"

We inquire, What is the fruit to be seen in the work of genuine gifts of the Spirit of God? The answer is found in the statement of Paul respecting the purpose of the Lord in placing the gifts in the church: " Wherefore he saith, When he ascended up on high, he led captivity captive, and gave gifts unto men. . . . And he gave some, apostles; and some, prophets; and some, evangelists; and some, pastors and teachers; for the perfecting of the saints, for the work of the ministry, for the edifying of the body of Christ; till we all come in the unity [" into the unity," margin] of the faith, and of the knowledge of the Son of God, unto a perfect man, unto the measure of the stature of the fulness of Christ." [25]

Apply this rule to the prophetic gift that has been connected with the third angel's message from its rise, and what is the result?— We find that the continual instruction given through Mrs. White has been in the line of unity and harmony, admonishing to " counsel together," and to " press together," to be in unison with Christ, thus insuring true fellowship and union with one another.

[24] Matt. 7: 15 - 20.   [25] Eph. 4: 8 - 13.

Some of the opponents of this work have tauntingly said, "If it was not for the visions of Mrs. White, which you have among you, your cause would have gone to pieces long ago." It is replied, "That is true; because from that source the Lord has given counsel, caution, and light, and thus dissensions have been removed, and the work has prospered." So what they designed as a thrust against the gift is in reality testimony that its fruit is that of the true gift of prophecy.

For sixty years and more have the manifestations of the gift of prophecy through Mrs. White been tested by these seven rules, and in every particular they have met the specifications required of a true prophecy.

CHAPTER XX

SACRIFICES IN THE EARLY WORK

"GATHER my saints together unto me; those that have made a covenant with me by sacrifice. And the heavens shall declare his righteousness: for God is judge himself." [1]

In the *Review and Herald* of June 3, 1902, we read: "Those who enter the work at the present time know comparatively little of the self-denial and self-sacrifice of those upon whom the Lord laid the burden of his work at its beginning. The experience of the past should be told them again and again; for they are to carry forward the work with the same humility and self-sacrifice that characterized the true workers in the past."

Again, in "Testimonies for the Church," Vol. VII, these words are found: "We are nearing the end of this earth's history, and the different lines of God's work are to be carried forward with much more self-sacrifice than has yet been manifested." [2]

The circumstances under which Elder Bates was moved out, in 1845, to write and publish his first book on the Sabbath question, have already been referred to. Also reference has been made to the trying situation of Elder James White, when, in 1849, he began the publication of the paper called *The Present Truth*.

A Pamphlet on the Opening Heavens

After the vision given to Mrs. White in Topsham, Maine, in the fall of 1846, when some of the planets were shown her,

[1] Ps. 50: 5, 6.   [2] Page 240.

Elder Bates prepared the manuscript for a pamphlet on "The Opening Heavens." But ready means for its publication was greatly needed. To meet this demand, a sister residing in Massachusetts, who had just completed and laid a new rag carpet, took it up and sold it, and gave the proceeds to Elder Bates, which enabled him to publish his second book.

A Pamphlet on the Sealing Work

After the view of the sealing work, given in Dorchester, Mass., Nov. 18, 1848, Elder Bates wrote a third pamphlet, entitled, "A Seal of the Living God." Here again he was confronted with the problem of no money for printing. A young widow, learning of the situation, sold a small home which she possessed in the country, and gave to Elder Bates half of the amount she received for it. Thus was he again enabled to pay for the printing of a book.

Demands of the Publishing Work

In 1851-52 the *Advent Review and Sabbath Herald* was printed at Saratoga Springs, N. Y. Here Mr. Thompson furnished Elder White and his wife house room free; and with borrowed furniture they were again privileged to set up housekeeping.

At this time believers in the present truth were increasing, and with this increase there was a demand for the personal labors of Elder and Mrs. White. This, with the work of editing, created a demand for office help. Just at that time others were impressed to assist in the literary work. As an illustration of how the Lord works in response to the faith of his people, and raises up workers in the time of need, we give the experience of a devoted sister, Mrs. Rebecca Smith, of West Wilton, N. H.: —

After the passing of the time, her son Uriah and daughter Annie R. desired greatly to attend school, that they might fit themselves for teaching. The mother feared the children were drifting away to the world, and, in fact, her fears were not wholly groundless. The parental love of the mother was reciprocated by the children.

Uriah Smith at Phillips' Academy

From 1848 to 1851 the son attended Phillips' Academy in Exeter, N. H., where the students were taken through the first year of a college course, so that on entering college they would be one year in advance. This course he finished. In 1851 he labored to earn money with which to attend college, but as his employer failed in business, he lost his money, and in consequence the long-cherished plan of a college course was abandoned.

Miss Smith at a Ladies' Seminary

While Uriah was at the academy, his sister was attending a young ladies' seminary in Charlestown, Mass. Her course there was nearly finished, and as she was soon to leave school, an offer was made to herself and her brother to teach in an academy at Mt. Vernon, N. H., for three years, at $1,000 a year, with board and room.

About this time the mother embraced " present truth." Her prayers were now, if possible, more earnest and fervent than ever in behalf of her children. Elder Bates visited West Wilton, and before him Mrs. Smith laid the case of her children, and their conversion was made a subject of prayer. Elder Bates was expecting in a few days to hold meetings in Somerville, Mass., at the house of Paul Folsom, and Mrs. Smith was to write to her daughter, inviting her to attend the meeting. In the meantime, Elder Bates and the mother were to pray that God would move upon her heart to go to the meeting.

Two Dreams Fulfilled

Elder Bates had never been in the room where the meeting was to be held, and therefore knew nothing of its situation.

The night before the meeting, he dreamed of being in the room, and that every seat was occupied except the one just by the door. He also dreamed that he changed his subject from that on which he intended to speak, and spoke on the sanctuary question; that they had sung the first hymn, prayed, and sung the second hymn, and he had just opened his Bible and was reading, "Unto two thousand and three hundred days, then shall the sanctuary be cleansed," pointing to the figure of the sanctuary on the chart, when the door opened, and a young lady entered and took her seat in the vacant chair. He also dreamed that the person was Annie R. Smith, and that she at once became interested, and embraced the truth.

Elder Bates's meeting was on the Sabbath (Saturday), and as there was no school that day, Annie said, "Just to please my mother, I'll go." The night before that Sabbath she dreamed that she went, and was late; that on arriving at the door the first hymn had been sung, prayer offered, and they were just concluding the second hymn; that as she entered, she observed that every chair was occupied but the one by the door; that a tall, noble, pleasant speaker was pointing to a chart such as she had never seen before, and was repeating, "Unto two thousand and three hundred days, then shall the sanctuary be cleansed." She dreamed that what he said greatly interested her, and that it was the truth.

She started for the meeting in ample time, but missed the way, so failed to get there until the singing of the last of the second hymn. When she entered, everything was exactly as she had seen it in the dream, and the identical man of her dream was repeating, in the same manner, the text from Dan. 8: 14. It struck conviction to her heart at once.

Elder Bates had not thought of his dream until she entered the door and took her seat. He had prepared to talk on another subject, but his mind would rest on the sanctuary question. While he was repeating the text, his dream flashed into his mind, and silently he prayed for help to speak to the hearts of his hearers. He had great freedom in explaining the passing of the time, with which Annie was familiar. Then he set forth the truth of the third angel's message and the Sabbath.

Annie Smith Accepts the Truth

As he closed the meeting, he stepped up to Annie, and said, " I believe this is Sister Smith's daughter of West Wilton. I never saw you before, but your countenance looks familiar. I dreamed of seeing you last night." Then Annie told her dream. She left the meeting with feelings and aspirations all changed, having there and then accepted the truth of the Sabbath.

She went back to the seminary, packed her trunk, and went home. On learning of Elder White's cares in publishing, and of his labors in preaching, she felt that God called her to go and help him in his office work. In August, 1851, when the paper was moved from Paris to Saratoga Springs, N. Y., Miss Smith went there as one of the workers.

A Sacrifice and a Consecration

In the *Review*, Vol. II, No. 7, are a few lines from her pen expressing her feelings after having given up her former plans for her humble, unpretentious work. She says: " I trust I have forsaken all to follow the Lamb whithersoever he leads the way. Earth has entirely lost its attractions. My hopes, joys, affections, are now all centered in things above and divine. I want no other place than to sit at the feet of Jesus, and learn of him — no other occupation than to be in the service of my heavenly Father — no other delight than the peace of God which passeth all understanding."

Sister Annie's help in the office as proof-reader, etc., was timely. For three years she labored faithfully and effectively, receiving only board and clothing. At the end of this period consumption had marked her for its victim. During the ravages of this lingering and fatal disease she wrote some beautiful poems, the sweetest of all being, "Home Here and Home in Heaven," the preface to which, written the day before her death, July 26, 1855, so well expresses the graces of simplicity and humility so largely developed in her character that we cannot refrain from giving it in full: —

> "I thanked my God, that, while below,
>   This pleasing task to me was given;
> And when my numbers ceased to flow,
>   I bent the knee and looked to heaven.

> "Let none this humble work assail,
>   Its failings to expose to view;
> Which sprung within Misfortune's vail,
>   And neath the dews of sorrow grew."

Housekeeping under Difficulties

In April, 1852, Elder White moved from Saratoga Springs to Rochester, N. Y. It was in this city, at 124 Mt. Hope Avenue, that they for the first time set up housekeeping with articles purchased instead of borrowed. But such was their anxiety to make the publishing work a success, in order that the paper might be regularly published, and thus the truth be spread abroad, that they denied themselves of many of the common comforts of life.

The manner in which they began housekeeping at this time, you can read in the following private letter written by Mrs. White to S. Howland's family, April 16, 1852: —

" We are just getting settled here in Rochester. We have rented an old house for $175 a year. We have the press in the house. Were it not for this, we should have to pay $50 a' year for office room. You would smile, could you look in upon us and see our furniture. We have bought two old bedsteads for twenty-five cents each. My husband brought me six old chairs, no two of them alike, for which he paid one dollar, and soon he presented me with four more old chairs, without any seating, for which he paid sixty-two cents for the lot. The frames were strong, and I have been seating them with drilling. Butter is so high we do not purchase it, neither can we afford potatoes. We use fruit sauce in the place of butter, and turnips for potatoes. Our first meals were taken on a fire-board, placed upon two empty flour barrels. We are willing to endure privations if the work of God can be advanced. We believe the Lord's hand was in our coming to this place. There is a large field for labor, and few laborers. Last Sabbath our meeting was excellent. The Lord refreshed with his presence."

Liberality of the Believers

In the first number of the *Review,* printed in Rochester, May 6, 1852, speaking of the removal from Saratoga to Rochester, Elder White said: " The brethren have provided means to sustain the paper beyond our expectations. And although our expenses in moving from Saratoga Springs, and commencing the paper in this city, have been considerable, yet we are free from debt."

Sacrifice of the Laborers

In a business note in Number 12, October 14, we read: " The office is not in debt, however, for this reason: Brethren Belden and Stowell who have worked in the office the past six months, have received but a trifle more than their board. Others engaged in the same work have received no more than they have. It will certainly be a pleasure for all the friends of present truth to help make up the deficiency in the receipts, that those who have labored hard, especially in our absence, in the midst of sickness, in publishing the *Review and Herald,* may have comfortable support."

Accessions in Rochester, N. Y.

During the summer of 1852, when the publishing work was fairly started in Rochester, Elder White and his wife took a three months' trip, with horse and carriage, as far east as Bangor, Maine, holding meetings and visiting scattered Sabbath-keepers on the way. Before their return, beginning September 26, Elder J. N. Andrews gave a series of discourses at 124 Mt. Hope Avenue. At this time eight First-day Adventists accepted present truth, the writer being one of the number.

Oswald Stowell Healed

One Friday evening in October, Elder White and his wife arrived home from their eastern tour. The next day (Sabbath) we saw them for the first time, in the Sabbath meeting. At the time of this meeting Oswald Stowell, the pressman, was suffering from a very severe attack of pleurisy, and had been given up by his physician to die. The doctor said he could " do nothing for him." During the service Oswald was in an adjoining room, and in great physical agony. At the close of the meeting he sent in a request that prayers be offered for him. With others I was invited to engage in a season of prayer. We bowed by his bedside, and while prayers were being offered, Elder White anointed him with oil " in the name of the Lord." There was a sensible presence of the Spirit of God, and he was instantly healed. When we arose from prayer he was sitting up in bed, striking his sides, which before had been so painful, and saying, " I am fully healed. I shall be able to work the hand-press to-morrow." Two days after this he did work it.

Mrs. White's Vision before the Rochester Company

The same blessing that healed Brother Stowell fell in still greater measure upon Mrs. White, and as Elder White turned to look at her, he said, " Ellen is in vision ; she does not breathe while in this condition. If any of you desire to satisfy yourselves of this fact, you are at liberty to examine her." She remained thus in vision about one hour and twenty minutes.

While in that condition she spoke words, and sometimes distinct sentences; yet by the closest scrutiny no breath could be discerned in her body.

Vision on the Course of an Absent Member

After Mrs. White came out of this vision, she bore testimony as to what she had seen. Before the return of Elder White and his wife from their eastern journey, one of our number had left the city, and was traveling on business in the State of Michigan. He was not, therefore, present at this meeting, and had never seen Elder White or his wife. In relating her vision, Mrs. White told us, among other things, what she saw concerning a man who, while he was traveling and away from home, had much to say about the law of God and the Sabbath, but was at the same time breaking one of the commandments. She said he was a person whom she had never met, yet she believed she would see him sometime, as his case had been unfolded to her. Not one of our number, however, supposed him to be any one with whom we were acquainted.

About six weeks from the time of the above vision, the brother previously mentioned returned from Michigan. As soon as Mrs. White looked upon his countenance, she said to one of the sisters, " That is the man I saw in the vision, of whom I told you." The vision being related to this brother, in the presence of his wife and several other persons. Mrs. White said to him, " As Nathan said to David, ' Thou art the man.' " He then did just what Paul said some persons would do when reproved for their sins by the gift of prophecy: " But if all prophesy, and there come in one that believeth not, or one unlearned, he is convinced of all, he is judged of all: and thus are the secrets of his heart made manifest; and so falling down on his face he will worship God, and report that God is in you of a truth." [3] After listening to the rehearsal of his wrong-doings by Mrs. White, this brother dropped upon his

[3] 1 Cor. 14: 24, 25.

knees before his wife, and with tears said to her, and to the few present, " God is with you of a truth," and then made a full confession of his course while in Michigan, in violating the seventh commandment, as revealed at the time of its occurrence, over five hundred miles away.

Thus a few weeks' time gave us a strong confirmation of the testimonies. Not only were we led to say that they were produced by some supernatural power, but that they were from a source which in no uncertain terms reproved men for sin.

Uriah Smith Connects with the Review Office

It was during the publication of Volume III of the *Review* that Uriah Smith began the observance of the Sabbath, and became connected with the Review office, in which he was writer and editor for so many long years. His first production published in the paper was a poem entitled, " The Warning Voice of Time and Prophecy," which appeared March 17, 1853.

Elder Smith first heard the third angel's message at a conference held in Washington, N. H., Sept. 10 to 12, 1852. Returning home to West Wilton, he carefully studied what he had heard, and began the observance of the seventh day the first Sabbath in December, 1852. He became connected with the Review office in Rochester, N. Y., May 3, 1853, where he and his sister Annie labored for their board and clothing, instead of teaching in an academy for $1,000 per year and their board. Such were, in kind, some of the sacrifices made to establish the work of the third angel's message in its early days.

Ordained a Minister

About the year 1863 Elder Smith began to exercise his gift in public speaking. In 1866 he was ordained as a minister of the gospel, after which time he labored much in campmeetings and conferences in the various States from the At-

URIAH SMITH

lantic to the Pacific, as well as in pastoral labors in the Battle Creek church, which was his home church. After the opening of the Battle Creek College, he taught more or less in the Biblical department of that institution. In the interest of the *Review and Herald* he crossed the Atlantic Ocean, in the year 1894, visiting different countries in Europe. While in Syria he contracted a fever from the effects of which he never fully recovered.

Fifty Years of Untiring Labor

From 1853 to 1903, half a century, Elder Smith had an almost constant editorial connection with the *Advent Review and Sabbath Herald;* and for a greater part of that time he had the entire editorial management of the paper. Even on the day of his death, when smitten down by a paralytic stroke, he was on his way to the office with matter which he had prepared for print. He also contributed several important volumes to the literature of the denomination. Among these works are " Thoughts on Daniel and the Revelation," " Nature and Destiny of Man," an enlarged volume on the " Sanctuary and Twenty-three Hundred Days," " The Marvel of Nations," " Modern Spiritualism." The first of these volumes was mostly written between the hours of nine o'clock P. M. and midnight, after the day's editorial and office work was completed.

Elder Smith's Death

His was a useful life well spent. He rests from his labors, having fallen asleep in Jesus March 6, 1903. But of him it can be truly said, " His works follow him," and though dead, he yet speaketh.

21

CHAPTER XXI

THE GUIDING HAND IN THE WORK

 WILL instruct thee and teach thee in the way which thou shalt go." [1]

To him who makes the Lord his trust, his care is continually manifest. There are times, however, when this care is more especially realized, such as special deliverances from evils and dangers, seen and unseen, and direct providential openings for the extension of his truth. It is of these themes that this chapter treats.

The First Vision in Michigan

In the month of May, 1853, Elder White and his wife visited Michigan. It was the first time they had been west of Buffalo, N. Y. The last Sabbath in May they were at Tyrone, and at that place Mrs. White was shown in vision the different companies of Sabbath-keepers in the State, with warnings as to the influences that were liable to work against them. On June 2, in Jackson, she wrote eight pages of foolscap, stating some of the things which had been shown her. She gave me a pencil copy of the vision, on condition that I would furnish her a plain copy written with pen and ink.

A Woman who Professed Holiness

Among other things shown, there was described the case of a woman who was trying to intrude herself among our people. She said this woman professed great holiness. Mrs. White had never met her, and had no knowledge of her except that which was imparted to her in this vision. She not only

[1] Ps. 32: 8.

told the woman's mode of procedure, but also that when she should be reproved she would put on a sanctimonious look, and say, " The—Lord—knows—my—heart." She said this woman was traveling about the country with a young man, while her husband, an old man, was at home working to support them in their evil course. Mrs. White said that the Lord had shown her that " notwithstanding the woman's pretentions to holiness, she and the young man were guilty of violating the seventh commandment." With the written description of this case in my pocket, I waited with some anxiety to see how matters would turn.

The Meeting in Vergennes, Mich.

We had meetings in Jackson, Battle Creek, Bedford, and Hastings, and then came to Vergennes, Kent Co., which proved to be the place where the woman lived. We arrived at the place where we were to tarry for the night, on June 11, a little before the Sabbath. Our stopping place was the home of an Elder White who had formerly been a minister of the Christian denomination. As this was a newly settled country, preparations had been made for our meetings in a large, newly built barn, three miles farther on, and the woman seen in vision, as it proved, lived still two miles beyond the place of meeting.

Testimony to the Fanatic

June 12, at 10:30 A. M., we assembled in the barn for meeting. Mrs. White sat at the left end of the rostrum, I sat next to her, Elder Cornell next to me, and Elder White was at the right of the rostrum, speaking. After he had been talking about fifteen minutes, an old man and a young man came in together, and sat down on the front seat next to the rostrum. They were accompanied by a tall, slim, dark-complexioned woman, who took her seat near the door. After a short discourse by Elder White, Mrs. White arose and introduced her remarks by speaking of the care ministers should have that they mar not the work committed to them, using the text, " Be ye clean that bear the vessels of the Lord." She said it was not God's order to call a woman to travel about the country with any other man than her husband. Finally she plainly said, " That woman who sat down a short time since near the door claims that God has called her to preach. She is traveling with this young man who just sat down in front of the desk, while this old man, her husband — God pity him! — is toiling at home to earn means which they are using to carry on their iniquity. She professes to be very holy, — to be sanctified, — but, with all her pretense to holiness, God has shown me that she and this young man are guilty of violating the seventh commandment."

All present knew that Mrs. White had never seen these individuals until they came into the barn. Picking them out and delineating their character in the manner she did, had its influence upon the minds of those present, and increased their confidence and confirmed their faith in the visions.

The Words Uttered as Predicted

As Mrs. White bore her testimony, there was an anxious looking toward Mrs. Alcott, the woman reproved, to see how she received what was said, and what she was going to do and say. Had she been innocent of the charge made against her, it would naturally be expected of her to rise up and deny the whole thing. If guilty, and grossly corrupt, she might be none too good to deny it all, even though she knew it to be true. Instead of this, she did just what the testimony said she would do when reproved. She slowly rose to her feet, while every eye was fixed upon her, and putting on a sanctimonious look, slowly said, " The—Lord—knows—my—heart," and sat down without uttering another word. She had said just what the testimony said she would say, and said it in the same manner.

Guilt Acknowledged

True, God knew their hearts, and they knew themselves to be guilty of the charge; for afterward the young man said to Mr. Gardner, a resident of the same place, who .closely questioned him concerning the matter, "Mr. Gardner, what Mrs. White said about us was too true;" and the woman, after telling Mrs. Wilson, at Greenville, in 1862, that she "would not dare to say a word against Sister White lest she should be found fighting against God," admitted that what was shown about her and the young man was true.

The Messenger Party

During the fall of 1853 a few disaffected ones in Michigan joined together and began the publication of a sheet called the *Messenger of Truth*. The mission of this sheet and its conductors seemed to be to tear down and defame instead of to build up. Many falsehoods were inserted in its pages, which annoyed us in our work in the message; and as it was our first experience with such an open attack, we thought it our duty to refute their slanderous statements. Doing this occupied time that should have been spent in advancing the truth committed to our trust, and suited well the purposes of Satan, who was undoubtedly the instigator of this opposition. And thus the state of affairs continued until the evening of June 20, 1855, when Elder White and his wife, Elder Cottrell, and myself had just closed a meeting in Oswego, N. Y. We had been annoyed in our meeting by one Lillis, who came in and circulated those slanderous documents among the people. Again the question as to our duty in this matter came up. All previous efforts at answering their falsehoods had only resulted in their manufacturing more.

Advice and Prediction

At a prayer-meeting held that evening at the house of John Place, in the city of Oswego, Mrs. White was given a vision in which she was shown that if we would keep at our work, preaching the truth, regardless of any such people as the " Messenger party," they would go to war among themselves and their paper would go down, and when that should happen we would find that our ranks had doubled. Believing this testimony to be from the Lord, we began at once to act in harmony with it.

Collapse of the Messenger Party and Paper

The cause of truth advanced rapidly, while the " Messenger party " got into trouble among themselves. In a brief space of time the party were scattered, many of their leaders having given up the Sabbath. Their paper soon ceased for lack of support, and he who had acted, for a time, as editor, turned his attention to teaching school; but not having learned first to govern himself, he failed utterly in governing his pupils. In attempting to correct one of the lads in his school, he drew a revolver, which snapped, but failed to fire. To escape lynching, he was obliged to flee in the night to Canada.

Effect on the Advent Cause

At this time there existed a greater state of harmony and unity among our people than ever before; and as efforts were made to push out with the message, the way opened in every direction.

In No. 10, Vol. XI, of the *Review*, Jan. 14, 1858, the editor, in speaking of the result of the Messenger work, said: "At the time of the disaffection, when the effort was made to break down the *Review*, the church property at the office was valued at only $700. Since then it has increased to $5,000. Then there were about one thousand paying subscribers, now there are two thousand, besides quite a ' free ' list."

As we had now reached the time (1858) when the " Messenger party " split and scattered, and the *Messenger* ceased to exist, the above figures are significant. As the number of paying subscribers to the *Review* had exactly doubled, so the number of believers had more than doubled. Thus the prediction made through Mrs. White in June, 1855, was fulfilled.

Tent-meetings First Suggested

It was our custom in the early days of the message to hold meetings in school-houses when no better place was attainable. In a building of this kind, on one occasion, such a crowd of people came together that two school-houses of that size could not have held them. To be heard by all, the speaker stood in an open window and spoke to those in the house and to a larger audience seated in their carriages and on the grass. It was the sight of this large assembly that led to the consideration of holding tent-meetings.

First Tent-meeting in Battle Creek, Mich.

Therefore on May 22, 1854, it was decided by Elder James White and others in council, that it would be a feasible plan to use tents for meetings. At that time large tents were very rarely used for other purposes than circuses, menageries, and shows of various kinds. Michigan was the first State in which Seventh-day Adventists made the venture in that line of working. The first tent-meeting opened in Battle Creek, June 10, 1854. At the present time this mode of holding meetings in the summer season has grown to great proportions.

Camp-meetings Suggested

In the year 1868 another aggressive step was taken. The propriety of holding camp-meetings was duly considered, and the decision was reached that this would be an excellent way to accommodate the large gatherings of our people at general meetings. Having a large tent for public services and smaller family tents, the people would be made comfortable, and thus a number of days could be spent profitably in counsel and worship.

The First Camp-meeting at Wright, Mich.

The first camp-meeting was held in Wright, Mich., Sept. 1 - 7, 1868. These important general gatherings of our people have grown to that extent that over half a hundred camp-meetings are held each year in various parts of the field. Not in America only are these camp-meetings held, but in Europe, Australia, New Zealand, and South Africa.

The largest assembly of this character ever held by our people was in the year 1893, at Lansing, Mich. In that large gathering there were 3,400 living in over 500 family tents. Over 150,000 yards of canvass were represented in the construction of the various tents in the camp.

Deliverance from a Railway Disaster

The day after the decision was made to purchase our first 60-foot tent (May 23, 1854), Elder White and his wife, being then in Jackson, Mich., were to start on their journey for Wisconsin, where they were to labor for a time. We spent the afternoon at the house of D. R. Palmer, only a short distance from the station. Several times in the afternoon Elder White spoke saying, " I feel strangely in regard to starting on this trip; but, Ellen, we have an appointment out, and we must go. If I had not an appointment, I should not go to-night."

As night came on, near the time of the arrival of the train, we had a season of prayer. All seemed led out to pray for the safety of Elder White and his wife on this journey. As we arose, Elder White expressed his faith that the Lord would have a care for them and keep them.

At eight o'clock I went with them to the train to assist in securing seats and adjusting their parcels. We went into one car with high-backed seats, called in those days a " sleeping car." Mrs. White said, " James, I can't stay in this car. I must get out of here." I helped them in getting a seat in the middle of the next car. Mrs. White sat down with her

parcels in her lap, but said, " I don't feel at home on this train."
The bell rang, and bidding them a hasty " Good-by," I soon
left for Cyrenius Smith's, to tarry for the night.

About ten o'clock we were all much surprised to hear
Elder White, whom we supposed was well on the way toward
Chicago, knocking for admittance. He said the train had run
off the track three miles west of Jackson; that most of the
train, with the engine, was a total wreck; but while a number
had been killed, he and Mrs. White had escaped uninjured.
He soon secured a horse and carriage, and in company with
Abram Dodge, went for Mrs. White, whom the Elder had
carried some distance in his arms, over a wet, marshy tract
of land and across a small stream of water, to a place of safety,
away from the scene of disaster.

Early the next morning I went with Mr. Dodge to view
the wreck. At a point where the road crosses the track
obliquely, an ox had lain down to rest directly on the track.
The engine had no cow-catcher, and so on striking the animal
it was thrown from the track to the left. At the first shock
of the engine's striking the ground, the baggage car, containing Elder White's trunk of books, jumped entirely clear
from the track and was uninjured; at the same time the
passenger car in the rear of the train was uncoupled from the
rest of the train without human aid, and quietly stopped upon
the track. The engine and tender ran on the ground off the
track some six or eight rods, when the engine struck an oak
stump some three feet in diameter. The force of the train
was such that the engine was turned over bottom side up,
and the back of the tender swung round across the track.
The main body of the train, going with full force, struck
this wreck of the engine, thus producing a second shock.
The first car that struck the engine was an express car,
which was crushed into kindling wood. It, with its contents,
was a mass of rubbish piled upon and around the tender.
The next was a second-class car, containing eighteen passen-

gers, of whom one was killed and all the rest were more or less injured. This car was split in two by the sleeping car running through it. The fore part of the sleeper was broken in pieces, and the seat in which Mrs. White did not feel free to stay was completely crushed.

Evidence of Divine Deliverance

As we viewed the wreck, and then the car in which Elder White and his wife were riding at the time of the accident, standing quietly by itself, some fifteen rods away from the wreck, we felt to say in our hearts that God heard prayer, and who knows but he sent his angel to uncouple that car, that his servants might escape unharmed? More especially did this thought impress our minds when the brakeman said that he did not uncouple it, and furthermore, that no one was on the platform when it occurred, and that it was a mystery to himself and to all the train-men how it was done; and what was still more mysterious to them, the link and bolt were both unbroken, and the bolt with its chain was lying on the platform of the wrecked car as though placed there by a careful hand.

By the evening of the 24th the track was so far cleared of the rubbish that the trains ran as usual, and Elder and Mrs. White again entered the cars and made a safe passage to their appointment in Wisconsin.

Opponents Reproved

It was not all " smooth sailing " with ancient Israel. They had foes without who were seeking to impede their progress at every step. The " mixt multitude " and unconsecrated ones within the camp were ready tools, through whom Satan sought to stir up discontent, strife, murmuring, and rebellion. The fact that God's prospering hand was with the confiding ones, and that victory attended their efforts, was proof that this people had found grace in his sight — that the hand of the Lord was leading them.

So in the rise and progress of the third angel's message; its advancement has not been because the truths presented have been something congenial to the natural heart of man. On the contrary, the very central truth of the message — the Sabbath of the Lord — conflicts with selfish, worldly interests, separating those who obey it from the business of the world two days in a week. The cause of present truth has had its external foes, determined and persistent in their efforts to overthrow the work. Of them it may be said, in the words of the psalmist, "If it had not been the Lord who was on our side, now may Israel say; if it had not been the Lord who was on our side, when men rose up against us; then they had swallowed us up quick, when their wrath was kindled against us." [2]

Selfish and discontented persons within our ranks have arisen from time to time, telling what great things would be done when their purposes were accomplished; but like a will-o'-the-wisp their lights have long since gone out. The cause of present truth, meanwhile, had been surely and steadily making its way round the world, gaining in stability and strength with every advance movement.

Elders Stephenson and Hall

During the summer of 1855 Elders Stephenson and Hall endeavored to create a rebellion in the State of Wisconsin. It was well known by the leading brethren that they had desired to try all other points of our faith by their "Age-to-Come" doctrine, and were quite anxious that Seventh-day Adventists should be taught the doctrine of probation after Christ's second coming.

Prediction Concerning Them

Nov. 20, 1855, Mrs. White was given a view of their course, with a prediction respecting its final outcome in these words: "Think ye, feeble man, that ye can stay the work of .

[2] Ps. 124: 1 - 3.

God? Feeble man, one touch of his finger can lay thee prostrate. He will suffer thee but a little while."

Our opponents have said that here was a vision which declared that these men were soon to die, and as they lived for several years, the vision had not been fulfilled. There is nothing in the vision about their dying. They were shown in the capacity of men seeking to stay the work of the third angel's message. While they were informed how easy a thing it would be for God to stop them, it is added, " He will suffer thee but a little while." What did they do? — Instead of succeeding in their warfare, as they had expected, they seemed to be left to grope their way in darkness. In a few weeks they entirely gave up the Sabbath, and turned to oppose it. They had hoped to form an "Age-to-Come " party, with themselves as leaders. Instead of succeeding in this, by giving up the Sabbath they entirely lost their hold upon our people. Thus by their own course they completely defeated what they were first designing to do. Our people said, " Indeed, God has ' suffered them but a little while.' "

A Sad Termination of Life

As to the outcome of these two men, it may be well to give some statements respecting their sad fate, that were made by their own brethren, "Age-to-Come " believers, with whom they were associated after leaving the Sabbath. Thirty-seven years ago Mr. Hall became somewhat demented (occasioned by softening of the brain), the cause of this condition being the loss of quite an amount of property by fraud on the part of others. He labored under the delusion that if he should go out-of-doors he would flatten out, or down to the earth. He is harmless, but, of course, for these long years has been entirely unfitted for ministerial work in any capacity. [3]

Elder Stephenson has been dead about sixteen years. For several years before his death he was of unsound mind (insane), though not dangerous to others. Before becoming

[3] These facts last noted were stated by his family to Brother Frederickson, of Dakota, in April, 1892.

thus, under the liberty which he supposed he had with the no-law theory that he had espoused, he•left his own wife, a woman against whom no stain of virtue was claimed (he could get a divorce only by employing a dishonest lawyer), and married another woman much younger than his former wife. This act was such a flagrant violation of morality that his own " Age-to-Come " brethren discountenanced his course, and would not permit him to preach for them any more.

The statements of their own brethren respecting the last days of these men express the deepest pity; yet they are the unvarnished facts, which are given without malice or prejudice. With this we leave our readers to draw their own conclusion with reference to the physical application of the testimony.

Elder J. H. Waggoner Accepts the Message

In the year 1852 Elder J. H. Waggoner, who had been conducting a county paper in Wisconsin, accepted present truth, and in the following year gave himself fully to the work of the ministry. In 1857 he wrote two very important pamphlets of about two hundred pages each. The first of these was entitled, " The Nature and Tendency of Modern Spiritualism," and the second, " A Refutation of the Age-to-Come." The former has not only been a means of saving many from falling into that snare of Satan, but, with God's blessing, it has opened the eyes of many who knew not what to make of these modern manifestations.

His " Refutation of the Age-to-Come " is a most complete *exposé* of the false theories of probation for sinners after the second coming of our Lord. It is so complete a refutation of that doctrine that it has not only not been answered, but no attempt at a reply has ever yet come under our observation. The book sets forth, in a most clear and concise manner, the position of Christ as a priest on his Father's· throne (his Melchisedec priesthood) during the present dispensation, and the position he will occupy on his own throne, in his future eternal kingdom,— a throne with which no mediatorial priesthood will be connected.

Still later Elder Waggoner wrote a third pamphlet of about the same size, entitled, "The Atonement in the Light of Reason and Revelation." About the year 1884 this was revised and enlarged to a volume of some 400 pages. It is a clear and concise treatise upon the subject indicated by its title.

From this time he was closely connected with the publishing work, both as writer and editor. He also continued his ministerial labors, his last years being spent in Europe.

April 17, 1889, he suddenly passed away at Basel, Switzerland, just after having completed his last book, "From Eden to Eden." On the 16th he did a full day's work of writing, and made this entry in his diary, "Did a hard day's work." From the report of his case made by European brethren, the following particulars are obtained: —

" On the morning of the 17th, at about half past five, he fell dead in his kitchen, without a moment's warning, of paralysis of the heart. He had been working very hard to finish up the English edition of his new book, and he expected to start for London on the following Sunday, to labor in connection with the work there, previous to returning to America the coming summer."

From 1854 Elder Waggoner had been constantly and prominently before the public in defense of the truth, both in the pulpit and in the press. At the time of his death he was nearly sixty-nine years of age. He was buried in Basel, April 20. Thus fell at his post of duty another of the early workers in the cause.

Faith Healing

In the early spring of 1858 Mrs. White had been greatly afflicted for a number of days, being confined to her bed in an almost helpless condition. One evening, near midnight, she fainted; the family tried all the means in their knowledge to restore her to consciousness, but failed in their effort. She remained in this condition for over half an hour, when Elder Andrews and myself were hastily summoned by Elder White to join in a season of prayer. In answer to earnest petitions offered at her bedside, the Lord mercifully restored her to consciousness, and raised her up to usual health. While offering praises to God she was taken off in vision, still lying in bed. Some of the things shown her in this view can be read in " Testimony for the Church," No. 5.

Remarkable Physical Manifestation

A peculiar physical manifestation was connected with this vision, to which we call special attention. Elder White and myself were sitting at one side of the bed, and Elder Andrews at the other side. Her hands were alternately clasped over her breast or moved with her arms in her usual free and graceful manner toward the different scenes she was viewing. The upper portion of her body was raised from the bed, so that there was a space of some eight or nine inches between her shoulders and the pillow. In other words, the body from the hips upward was flexed at an angle of about thirty degrees. And in that position she remained during the continuance of the vision, which was thirty minutes. No one could naturally assume that posture, unsupported by hands and arms, much less hold himself there for that length of time. Here again was proof that some power over which she had no control was connected with the vision.

Another Prediction

The first of October, 1858, a general meeting was held by Elder and Mrs. White and the writer, in Rochester, N. Y. From this meeting the writer accompanied them on a tour through the State of New York and the New England States. One Sabbath Mrs. White was given a vision in which she was shown, among other things, that at some place on our contemplated journey Satan was going to make a powerful attack upon her, and that Elder White and myself must hold on for her by faith, and the Lord would deliver.

Mrs. White's Affliction

Here again was a prophecy of what would transpire. The sequel will show how accurately it was fulfilled. The first Sabbath after the Rochester meeting we were at Roosevelt, and the next Sabbath in Brookfield, Madison County. The week following we held meetings in the commodious kitchen of Mr. Ballou, at Mansville, Jefferson County. While journeying by train from Brookfield to Mansville, Mrs. White's face became inflamed just under the eyes. This was so painful that by the time we reached Mansville she was obliged to take her bed. The inflammation increased for two days, depriving her of sleep, as well as preventing her from taking any part in the meetings. Her head was swollen so that both eyes were closed, and her face was so disfigured that it no longer looked like that of a human being. Amid all this racking pain, and extreme nervousness, caused by loss of sleep, the enemy was striving hard to cause her to murmur against God. Thus things continued to the close of the appointed meetings.

After the meetings had closed Elder White said to me, " Brother John, this is the very attack of Satan upon my wife of which we were warned in Rochester. You remember the promise was there made that if we would take hold together and hold her up by faith, not letting go for a moment when the struggle came, the power of the enemy would be broken, and she would be delivered. Let us go in at once and have a praying season."

Deliverance as Predicted

We went immediately into the room where Mrs. White was confined to her bed, and engaged in earnest prayer for her,

J. H. WAGGONER   (See page 333)

while the brethren in the room where we had been holding meetings remained in silent prayer. In about ten minutes after we began to pray the power of the Lord came down and filled the room. Mrs. White was instantly relieved from all pain, and at once called for food. This was about five o'clock in the afternoon. By seven o'clock the swelling had all disappeared upon her face, and she attended the meeting that evening, to all appearance as well as ever.

At the request of the citizens a discourse was given in the evening on the " Saints' Inheritance," at the close of which Mrs. White gave an exhortation. While Elder White was out of doors with his little boy, W. C., she was taken off in vision before that large assembly. Some of the things shown to her at that time may be read in the closing article of Testimony Number 5, dated Mansville, N. Y., Oct. 21, 1858.

The relief obtained by Mrs. White on the occasion above referred to was as effectual as had been predicted in the view given at Rochester. No difficulty of the kind occurred again on that journey, and we had a glorious victory for the truth at every place.

Prediction of the American Civil War

On Sabbath, the 12th of January, 1861, just three months to a day before the first gun was fired on Fort Sumter (which was really the opening of the war which resulted in the liberation of 4,000,000 African slaves in America), the Seventh-day Adventist meeting-house in Parkville, Mich., was dedicated. The service was attended by Elder White and his wife, Elders Waggoner, Smith, and the writer. At the close of the discourse by Elder White, Mrs. White gave a stirring exhortation, after which she took her seat in a chair. In this position she was taken off in vision. The house was crowded with people, and it was indeed a solemn place. After coming out of the vision she arose, and looking about the house, said: —

22

"There is not a person in this house who has even dreamed of the trouble that is coming upon this land. People are making sport of the secession ordinance of South Carolina, but I have just been shown that a large number of States are going to join that State, and there will be a most terrible war. In this vision I have seen large armies of both sides gathered on the field of battle. I heard the booming of the cannon, and saw the dead and dying on every hand. Then I saw them rushing up engaged in hand-to-hand fighting [bayoneting one another] Then I saw the field after battle, all covered with the dead and dying. Then I was carried to prisons, and saw the sufferings of those in want, who were wasting away. Then I was taken to the homes of those who had lost husbands, sons, or brothers in the war. I saw their distress and anguish."

Then looking slowly around the house she said, "There are those in this house who will lose sons in that war."

Mrs. Ensign's Testimony Concerning the Visions

As a confirmation of the above fact, and as proof that the prediction was made on the day stated, and as an illustration of how the congregation understood it and circulated it, the following testimony is given : —

"This certifies that I was living in St. Joseph County, Michigan, in January, 1861, about six miles from Parkville. I was not an Adventist. On the 12th day of that month a number of my neighbors went to Parkville to attend meetings. When they came home they told me that there was a woman at the meeting that was in a trance, and who said that there was a terrible war coming on the United States; that large armies were going to be raised on both sides, in the South as well as in the North, and there would be many who would suffer in prisons; and pinching want would be felt in many families in consequence of losing husbands, sons, and brothers in the war; and that there were men in the house who would lose sons in that war." Signed, "Martha V. Ensign, Wild Flower, Fresno County, California, Jan. 30, 1891."

In connection with the prediction of that fearful war, Mrs. White further stated that Seventh-day Adventists "would be brought into strait places in consequence of the war, and that it was the duty of all to earnestly pray that wisdom might be given them to know what to do in the trying times before them."

Magnitude of the Civil War

At the time of the giving of the vision the Northern people generally had but little, if any, conception of the pending war. Even President Lincoln, three months after (April 12, 1861), when several States had joined South Carolina in her secession ordinance, and the first gun was fired on Fort Sumter, called for only 75,000 men, and these for the short term of three months.

The total number of troops enrolled on the Union side during the war was 2,859,132. The Encyclopedia Britannica says that "the Confederate army numbered, at the beginning of 1863, about 700,000 men," but that it is difficult to ascertain just how many they had enrolled in all. It estimates their death roll at "about 300,000 men." Some of the late encyclopedias place the loss on the Union side (of those killed in battle, or who died of wounds or diseases contracted in the field or in prisons) at 359,528. Of the debt on the Union side the Britannica says: —

"The debt reached its maximum Aug. 31, 1865, amounting to $2,845,907,626.56. Some $800,000,000 of revenue had also been spent, mainly on the war; States, cities, counties, and towns had spent their own taxation and accumulated their own debts for war purposes; the payments for pensions will probably amount to $1,500,000,000 in the end. The expense of the Confederacy can never be known, the property destroyed by the Federal armies and by Confederate armies can hardly be estimated ; and the money value ($2,000,000,000) of the slaves in the South was wiped out by the war. Altogether, while the cost of the war cannot be exactly calculated, $8,000,000,000 is a moderate estimate." [4]

Another Confirmation of the Vision

As to the prediction concerning the men in the Parkville meeting-house losing sons in the war, I will simply state that in the autumn of 1883 I met the elder of the Parkville church, who was also the elder in January, 1861, when the vision was given, and asked him if he remembered the expression made by Mrs. White in relating the vision concerning the war. " Yes," said he, " I do." " Will you tell me how many you know who were in the house that day who lost sons in the war? " He at once recalled the names of five, and said, " I know these were there, and that they lost sons in the war ; and if I were at home, where I could talk with my people, I could give you more names. I think," he continued, " there were five more, besides these that I have mentioned."

Four years and more of persistent fighting on the part of the South, until nearly half of all the mustered forces were lost by death in battle or from sickness, shows a striking fulfilment of the above prediction.

Slavery and the War

In relating a vision given her Jan. 4, 1862, Mrs. White said : —

" Thousands have been induced to enlist with the understanding that this war was to exterminate slavery ; but now that they are fixed, they find that they' have been deceived, that the object of this war is not to abolish slavery, but to preserve it as it is."

[4] " Encyclopedia Britannica " (ninth edition), Vol. XXIII, page 780.

The foregoing was given at a time when the soldiers were required to aid in the work of returning to their masters all slaves who had escaped into the Union lines, and the soldiers are represented as saying, "If we succeed in quelling this rebellion, what has been gained?" They answer discouragingly, "Nothing. That which caused the rebellion is not removed. The system of slavery, which has ruined our nation, is left to live and stir up another rebellion." These words, taken from Testimony No. 7, where a thrilling account of the war is given in full, under the head of "Slavery and the War," do not state that slavery would never be abolished, but represent the situation as the soldiers then viewed it. A little farther along in the same testimony is a prediction as follows : —

Prediction of Success to the North

"And yet a national fast is proclaimed! Saith the Lord, 'Is not this the fast that I have chosen, to loose the bands of wickedness, to undo the heavy burdens, and to let the oppressed go free, and that ye break every yoke?' When our nation observes the fast which God hath chosen, then will he accept their prayers as far as the war is concerned; but now they enter not into his ear."

Those who are familiar with the history of the war are aware of the defeats, disasters, delays, etc., connected with the efforts of the North to conquer the Southern forces up to the time the emancipation proclamation was made — Jan. 1, 1863. Then how rapid were the conquests from that time to the close of the war! How evident, to those who were watching the progress of the work, was the fulfilment of that prediction of Jan. 4, 1862. After the burdens were lifted, the bondage was loosened and the yoke broken from the slave! How evident that God heard the prayers of his people, and favored the effort to close the war when they chose the fast pleasing to him!

Ex-Governor St. John's Testimony

In a speech by Ex-Governor John P. St. John, of Kansas, in Ottawa, Ill., to which I listened on the afternoon of June 29, 1891, he made the following statement: —

"I was never so disappointed as I was when the [Confederates] whipped us at Bull Run. But it was all a part of God's plan. Had we whipped the [Confederates], the politicians would have hatched up a peace, and the Union would have been continued with slavery, and we would have had it to-day. For two years the [Confederates] had the advantage; but after Lincoln issued the famous emancipation proclamation we had swung round to God's side, and could not lose."

CHAPTER XXII

ORGANIZATION

"F OR this cause left I thee in Crete, that thou shouldest set in order the things that are wanting, and ordain elders in every city, as I had appointed thee." [1]

In the advancement· of the third angel's· message twelve years had passed (from 1846 to 1858) before our people seemed to realize a necessity for any more formal association than simply the belief of the truth and Christian love. Although the Lord had spoken to his people upon this subject through the gift of prophecy, it seemed to require some adverse experiences to arouse them fully to a sense of the necessity of the organization of conferences and churches and associations for the management of the temporalities of the cause.

Opposition to Organization

In a foot-note on page 12 of " Supplement to Experience and Views," published in 1853, Elder James White says: —

" After the time passed in 1844 there was great confusion, and the majority were opposed to any organization, holding that it was inconsistent with the perfect liberty of the gospel! Mrs. White was always opposed to every form of fanaticism, and early announced that some form of organization was necessary to prevent and correct confusion. Few at the present time can appreciate the firmness which was then. required to maintain her position against the prevailing anarchy."

[1] Titus 1: 5.

The union which has existed among Seventh-day Adventists has been greatly fostered and maintained by her timely warnings and instructions.

George Storrs on Organization

The following from George Storrs, written in 1844, will show what was taught concerning organization to those who had separated themselves from the churches under the advent proclamation : —

" Take care that you do not seek to organize another church. No church can be organized by man's invention but what it becomes Babylon *the moment it is organized.* The Lord organized his own church by the strong bonds of love. Stronger than that cannot be made ; and when such bonds will not hold together the professed followers of Christ, they cease to be his followers, and drop off from the body as a matter of course." [2]

Order in Apostolic Times

Seventh-day Adventists, as before stated, were without a formal organization of any kind for many years, not even having a church organization. Any person who had moral courage to accept the truth and obey it under the outside pressure of opposition which then existed, was considered honest and worthy of Christian love and fellowship. There came a time in the days of the apostles when it became necessary to " set in order the things that were wanting." [3] About 65 A. D. Titus was authorized to " ordain elders in every city " where there were believers, and Timothy received quite full instructions on the subject. [4]

Elder White on Organization

The following from Elder James White upon the subject of organization and discipline appeared in the *Review* of Jan. 4, 1881 : —

[2] *Midnight Cry,* Feb. 15, 1844.   [3] Titus 1: 5 - 9.   [4] 1 Tim. 3: 1 - 15.

" Organization was designed to secure unity of action, and as a protection from imposture. It was never intended as a scourge to compel obedience, but rather for the protection of the people of God. Christ does not drive his people; he calls them. ' My sheep hear my voice, I know them, and they follow me.' Our Living Head leads the way, and calls his people to follow.

" Human creeds cannot produce unity. Church force cannot press the church into one body. Christ never designed that human minds should be moulded for heaven by the influence of other human minds. ' The head of every man is Christ.' His part is to lead, and to mould, and to stamp his own image upon the heirs of eternal glory. However important organization may be for the protection of the church, and to secure harmony of action, it must not come in to take the discipline from the hands of the Master.

Unity Between Two Extremes

" Between the two extremes of church force and unsanctified independence we find the grand secret of unity and efficiency in the ministry and in the church of God. Our attention is called to this in a most solemn appeal from the venerable apostle Peter to the elders of his time: ' The elders which are among you I exhort, who am also an elder, and a witness of the sufferings of Christ, and also a partaker of the glory that shall be revealed: feed the flock of God which is among you, taking the oversight thereof, not by constraint, but willingly; not for filthy lucre, but of a ready mind; neither as being lords over God's heritage, but being ensamples to the flock. And when the Chief Shepherd shall appear, ye shall receive a crown of glory that fadeth not away. Likewise, ye younger, submit yourselves unto the elder. Yea, all of you be subject one to another, and be clothed with humility; for God resisteth the proud, and giveth grace to the humble.

Humble yourselves therefore under the mighty hand of God, that he may exalt you in due time.' [5]

Simplicity and Form of New Testament Organization

" Those who drafted the form of organization adopted by Seventh-day Adventists labored to incorporate into it, as far as possible, the simplicity of expression and form found in the New Testament. The more of the spirit of the gospel manifested, and the more simple, the more efficient the system.

" The General Conference takes the general supervision of the work in all its branches, including the State conferences. The State conference takes the supervision of all the branches of the work in the State, including the churches in the State. And the church is a body of Christians associated together with the simple covenant to keep the commandments of God and the faith of Jesus.

Church Officers are Servants

" The officers of a local church are servants of that church, and not lords, to rule over it with force. ' He that is greatest among you shall be your servant.' [6] These officers should set examples of patience, watchfulness, prayer, kindness, and liberality to the members of the church, and should manifest a good degree of that love to those whom they serve that is exhibited in the life and teachings of our Lord."

The First Testimony on Order

In the supplement to " Experience and Views," published in 1853, some special instruction is given upon the subject of gospel order. On page fifteen we read the following : —

" The church must flee to God's word, and become established upon gospel order, which has been overlooked and neglected. This is indispensably necessary to bring the church into the unity of the faith."

[5] 1 Peter 5: 1 - 6.   [6] Matt. 23: 11.

Order Needed Near the End

In a testimony given Dec. 23, 1860, we read: "As we near the close of time, Satan comes down with great power, knowing that his time is short. Especially will his power be exercised upon the remnant. He will war against them, and seek to divide and scatter them, that they may grow weak and be overthrown. The people of God should move understandingly, and should be united in their efforts. They should be of the same mind, of the same judgment; then their efforts will not be scattered, but will tell forcibly on the upbuilding of the cause of present truth. Order must be observed, and there must be union in maintaining order, or Satan will take advantage of them." [7]

Order of the Angels to be Imitated

In Testimony No. 14, published in 1868, we read: "The more closely we imitate the harmony and order of the angelic host, the more successful will be the efforts of these heavenly agents in our behalf. If we see no necessity of harmonious action, and are disorderly, undisciplined, and disorganized in our course of action, angels, who are thoroughly organized and move in perfect order, cannot work for us successfully. They turn away in grief, for they are not authorized to bless confusion distraction, and disorganization.

God a God of Order Still

"Has God changed from a God of order? No; he is the same in the present dispensation as in the former. Paul says, 'God is not the author of confusion, but of peace.' He is as particular now as then. And he designs that we should learn lessons of order and organization from the perfect order he instituted in the days of Moses for the benefit of the children of Israel." [8]

[7] "Testimony for the Church," Vol. I, page 210.
[8] Testimonies, Vol. I, pages 649. 653.

Christ's Prayer for Order

In a testimony written in 1882 we see the same sentiment expressed in these words, " That union and love might exist among his disciples was the burden of our Saviour's last prayer for them prior to his crucifixion. . . . ' Neither pray I for these alone, but for them also which shall believe on me through their word; that they all may be one; as thou, Father, art in me, and I in thee, that they also may be one in us; that the world may believe that thou hast sent me.' " [9]

Danger of Individual Independence

In 1885 this testimony was given: " One point will have to be guarded, and that is *individual independence.* As soldiers in Christ's army, there should be *concert of action* in the various departments of the work." [10]

Satan Delights to Overthrow Order

In a special testimony published in 1895 we read, " O how Satan would rejoice to get in among this people, and disorganize the work at a time when thorough organization is essential, and will be the greatest power to keep out spurious uprisings, and refute claims not endorsed by the word of God. We want to hold the lines evenly, that there shall be no breaking down of the *system* of regulation and order."

Commendation of Ministers

One of the first points to be considered in establishing order among our people, in harmony with the testimonies just quoted, was some mode of recognizing those who preached the message. From 1850 to 1861 the plan adopted was that of giving the ministers who had proved their gift, and were evidently approved of the Lord, and in harmony with all the work, a card recommending them to the fellowship of the Lord's people everywhere, simply stating that they were approved in the work of the gospel ministry. These cards were

[9] Testimony No. 31, pages 232, 233.   [10] Testimony No. 33, page 62.

dated and signed by two of the leading ministers, known by our people to be leaders in the work.

Ministerial Support

In the winter of 1858-59 instruction was given to the effect that the Bible contained a complete system for the support of the ministry, and that if our people would study the subject from a scriptural standpoint they would find that system. Accordingly a Bible class was held in Battle Creek, over which Elder J. N. Andrews presided. After careful and prayerful study of the Scriptures, an article was prepared and published in the *Review* of Feb. 3, 1859, presenting a plan that embraced the principle of tithing. An address on that subject was submitted to a large gathering of our people, assembled in a general meeting in Battle Creek, Mich., June 6, 1859, and unanimously adopted by a vote of the entire assembly.

The Established Order Commended

In Testimony No. 6, 1861, the Lord thus spoke, through Mrs. White, concerning the system that had been adopted by Seventh-day Adventists: "Rob not God by withholding from him your tithes and offerings. It is the first sacred duty to render to God a suitable proportion. Let no one throw in his claims and lead you to rob God. Let not your children steal your offerings from God's altar for their own benefit.

The Tithing System to Develop Character

"This tithing system, I saw, would develop character, and manifest the true state of the heart. If people have this matter presented before them in its true bearing, and they be left to decide for themselves, they will see wisdom and order in the tithing system."

In this manner a system of finance was established among Seventh-day Adventists, for supporting the work of the ministry, and it is now in use by our people all over the world.

In the *Review* of July 21, 1859, as the result of instruction previously given through the Testimonies, it was first suggested that each State hold an annual meeting in which a careful planning of the work be made; and thus avoid the confusion which too commonly existed in the manner of ministerial labor, and that order and system be observed in our work. This suggestion really looked forward to the formation of State conference organizations.

Holding Church Property

As the message advanced and numbers increased, there naturally followed an accumulation of property, which led to the consideration of legally holding church property. In an article from Elder White, found in the *Review* of Feb. 23, 1860, we read the following:—

" We hope, however, that the time is not far distant when this people will be in that position necessary to be able to get church property insured, hold their meeting-houses in a proper manner, that those making wills, and wishing to do so, can appropriate a portion to the publishing department. We call upon our preachers and leading brethren to give the matter their attention. If any object to our suggestions, will they please write out a plan on which we as a people can act? "

Legal Organization Endorsed

During the summer of this year, there was more or less friendly discussion of this subject in the *Review*. And in a general gathering of representatives of our people from Michigan and several other States, held in Battle Creek from September 28 to October 1, there was a candid consideration of the subject, and a full and free discussion of legal organization for the purpose of holding the office and other church property — meeting-houses, etc. This discussion is found at length in the *Review*, Vol. XVI, Nos. 21, 22, and 23, issued October 9, 16, and 27, 1860.

As the result of the deliberations at this gathering, it was voted unanimously to legally organize a publishing association, and in order that such a corporation might be formed as soon as practicable, a committee of five was elected by the conference assembled.

A Denominational Name

This conference also took into consideration the subject of a name by which our people should be called. This again called forth a diversity of opinions, some pleading for one name and some for another. The " Church of God " being proposed, it was objected to on the ground that it gave none of the distinctive features of our faith, while the name " Seventh-day Adventists " would not only set forth our faith in the near coming of Christ, but would also show that we were observers of the Seventh-day Sabbath. So unanimous was the assembly in favor of the latter name that when put to vote, only one man voted against it, and he soon afterward withdrew his objection.

The Name Approved

In Testimony No. 6, we read: " No name which we can take will be appropriate but that which accords with our profession, and expresses our faith, and marks us as a peculiar people. . . .

" The name Seventh-day Adventist carries the true features of our faith in front, and will convict the inquiring mind. Like an arrow from the Lord's quiver, it will wound the transgressors of God's law, and will lead to repentance toward God and faith in our Lord Jesus Christ." The effect of the testimony was to settle forever this question in the minds of the believers.

The Office of a True Gift

Is not this the special province of a manifestation of the gifts of God's Spirit? Paul said they were placed in the church " for the perfecting of the saints, for the work of the ministry, for the edifying of the body of Christ: till we all, come in the unity of the faith," etc. [11]   How appropriate, that after the believers have prayerfully and in humility sought for light, the Spirit should speak and say, " This is the way; your conclusions are correct; " and then " edify " the church still further, as in this case, by telling them the practical bearing of the question, and some of the good results that will accrue from their decisions.

Church Organization

In an address delivered by Elder White before the General Conference in Battle Creek, in April, 1861, and published in the *Review,* June 11, 1861, he introduced the idea of a more complete organization of our churches. By invitation, nine ministers held a Bible class to seek light upon the subject, and were requested by the Conference to publish in the *Review* the results of that investigation. After presenting the Scriptural testimony on church order and church officers, the topic of equal representation from the several States in the General Conference was considered, as well as proper and equal representation of churches in the State conferences. In reality this was the first introduction of the idea of having duly elected delegates to general associations on some equal ratio that might be agreed upon.

Michigan State Conference Organized

Oct. 6, 1861, the Michigan Conference was organized by the election of a chairman, a secretary, and an executive committee of three. By vote of the conference it was recommended that the churches enter into organization, adopting the following as a church covenant:—

" We, the undersigned, hereby associate ourselves together as a church, taking the name Seventh-day Adventists; covenanting to keep the commandments of God and the faith of Jesus Christ."

[11] Eph. 4: 12, 13.

Ministers' Credentials

At this conference it was first decided that credentials should be granted to all Seventh-day Adventist ministers in this State who were in good standing, and that ministers should carry papers consisting of a certificate of ordination, and credentials signed by the chairman and clerk of the conference, which credentials should be renewed annually.

It was also voted that a committee be selected to prepare an address setting before our people the mode of procedure in organizing churches. This address was published in the *Review* of Oct. 15, 1861.

Delegates' Credentials

In the month of September, 1862, the Michigan Conference held its first session in Monterey. Here for the first time was presented the idea of receiving churches into the conferences as members were voted into churches. As seventeen churches in the State had already been organized, these were, by vote, taken into the conference; and all members of these churches who were present were accepted as delegates.

Ministers' Salaries

It was at this conference, too, that the plan was adopted of paying ministers a certain sum per week for services rendered. The ministers on their part were required to report the time spent in labor in the conference, with their receipts and expenses; and the conference receiving this report was to make proper settlement.

Credentials First Presented by Delegates

May 20, 1863, the General Conference was held in Battle Creek, Mich. It was the first session of that body in which the delegates bore credentials from their respective States. The representation was not, however, on a numerical basis.

23

The States represented on this occasion were Michigan, Wisconsin, Iowa, Minnesota, New York, and Ohio.

General and State Conference Constitutions

May 21, a constitution was adopted by the General Conference, and on the same day a State constitution was recommended to the State conferences. It was adopted in a session of the Michigan Conference. These constitutions provided a numerical basis for delegate representation in the State conferences and in the General Conference. The State constitution, there recommended, is about the same as that used now by our seventy-two local conferences throughout the world.

At the time of the General Conference, in the spring of 1864, a recommendation was first made to the State conference that an Auditing Committee of laymen who had not been in the employ of the conference during the year, be selected to act with the executive committee in auditing and settling accounts with ministers. Thus step by step, as necessity required, order was established in the work and cause of God.

Thus we have briefly traced the steps that led to the formal organization of the work. This was done when the denomination was very small compared with what it is at the present time.

When the General Conference was fully organized, in 1863, the whole number of delegates was not so large as we now have annually in some of the small local conferences.

Object of Organization

The object to be accomplished by organization was that the property of the body might be lawfully held and legally managed; and that the laborers in the work might move in harmony, without confusion, because their movements were with counsel, and, therefore, without distraction. The same principles adopted in our organization up to 1864 were incorporated into the work as it enlarged and extended to other countries and nationalities.

General Organizations Formed

As the message advanced, the following general organizations were formed, the officers of which were elected at the regular sessions of the General Conference:—

The General Conference Association — a legal body of twenty-one members, to hold the title to the property of the various institutions in America and other countries.

The Foreign Mission Board — to superintend and extend mission work outside of organized conferences.

The International Tract Society — whose province was the distribution of reading matter, and correspondence, seeking to open up new missions.

The Religious Liberty Association — its special field being to aid those persecuted for conscience' sake, and to circulate literature on the principles of religious liberty.

The International Sabbath-School Association — the object of which was the building up and advancement of the Sabbath-school work in all fields.

The Medical Missionary and Benevolent Association — its work relating to the training of physicians and nurses, the conducting of sanitariums, homes for orphans, the aged, etc.

The Field Occupied up to 1868

Up to 1868 our field of operations included that portion of the United States east of the Missouri River and north of the parallel of latitude corresponding with the southern line of Missouri. At that time the General Conference Committee had only three members, the president of the conference being one of the members. The eight local conferences were all under the supervision of the General Conference, which had its headquarters at Battle Creek, Mich.

Why Re-organization was Necessary

As the message extended to other lands, a necessity arose for a re-organization of the entire field. Hence, steps were taken in 1897 pointing in that direction; but the work of re-arranging has been more thoroughly accomplished during the last four years, in which time a European General Conference has been organized, with an executive committee of fourteen members; and the original General Conference, with its headquarters at Washington, D. C., has an executive committee of twenty-eight members, representing all the various interests of the message, and taking the place of some of the general associations, which have been discontinued.

Organized Standing Jan. 1, 1903

The following from the General Conference Year Book of 1904 gives some interesting statistical facts up to Jan. 1, 1903: —

At that time our organized work consisted of two General Conferences, comprised of fourteen Union Conferences, seventy-two local Conferences, and forty-two missions. These are distributed as follows: Local Conferences in North America, forty-nine; outside of North America, twenty-three. Union Conferences in America, eight; in other countries, six. Mission fields in America, including Alaska, Hawaii, and New Foundland, five; missions outside of America, thirty-seven, located as follows: Twelve in Europe; four in Africa; three in Asia; two in South America; two in South Africa; and the remainder in Central America, Mexico, West Indies, and the Pacific Islands. Connected with these missions are sixty-seven ordained and licensed ministers and one hundred and thirty-one churches.

Unity in Diversity

It is a source of encouragement to know that these different organizations in various countries and nationalities are all united in the promotion of the one great cause of truth and the salvation of men. Not in the mere formal machinery of organization do we trust, but in God, the author of order. With his blessing upon the united and harmonious action of his workers we may realize how good and pleasant it is to have " all things done decently, and in order."

CHAPTER XXIII

HEALTH INSTITUTIONS

BELOVED, I wish above all things that thou mayest prosper and be in health, even as thy soul prospereth."[1]

On Sabbath, June 6, 1863, Elder White and his wife attended a tent-meeting held by Elders Cornell and Lawrence in Otsego, Mich. Mrs. White was there given a vision which opened before her the subject of health reform. From that time, articles on health and healthful living were published in the *Review,* and she began to write what had been revealed to her on health. Some of this appeared in Testimony No. 11, and in a work entitled, "How to Live."

The subject of healthful living and its proper relations to physical, mental, and spiritual development, was brought prominently before the people. In the *Review* of Oct. 25, 1864, Elder J. N. Andrews made the following important suggestions on the subject: —

J. N. Andrews on Healthful Living

"To leave off every injurious article of food, and to lead lives of temperance under the influence of good instruction and of conscience toward God, are among the things most essential to good health. Our bodies are the temples of the Holy Spirit. That we may truly glorify him in our bodies as in our spirits, how requisite that we possess in full vigor all the powers of our physical being! Thank God that this subject is now being especially set before our people. Health

[1] 3 John 2.

and strength are among the things most valuable to us, and of greatest consequence to those who shall witness the grand events of the time of trouble."

The subject of Bible hygiene and Christian temperance was advocated, not only through the columns of the *Review,* but by our ministers.

At the General Conference, May 20, 1866, the following instruction was given through Mrs. White (the same is found in Testimony No. 11) : —

A Health Institution to be Provided

" I was shown that we should provide a home for the afflicted, and those who wish to learn how to take care of their bodies that they may prevent sickness. . . .

" As unbelievers shall resort to an institution devoted to the successful treatment of disease, and conducted by Sabbath-keeping physicians, they will be brought directly under the influence of the truth. By becoming acquainted with our people and our real faith, their prejudice will be overcome, and they will be favorably impressed. By thus being placed under the influence of truth, some will not only obtain relief from bodily infirmities, but will find healing balm for their sin-sick souls.

Prediction of Results

"As the health of invalids improves under judicious treatment, and they begin to enjoy life, they have confidence in those who have been instrumental in their restoration to health. Their hearts are filled with gratitude, and the good seed of truth will the more readily find a lodgment there, and in some cases will be nourished, spring up, and bear fruit to the glory of God. One such precious soul saved will be worth more than all the means needed to establish such an institution. . . .

" Some who go away restored, or greatly benefited, will be the means of introducing our faith in new places, and raising the standard of truth where it would have been impossible to gain access had not prejudice first been removed from minds by a tarry among our people for the object of gaining health."

It was decided by a unanimous vote of our people assembled, that as soon as practicable a health institution should be opened in or near Battle Creek, and that it should be under the medical management of Dr. H. S. Lay, who had, in addition to his former medical education, spent over a year at an Eastern water-cure to learn the hydropathic methods of treating disease.

Site for a Sanitarium Purchased

The establishing of such an institution at that time looked like a great undertaking; and had it not been for this encouraging testimony concerning the result, there would have been some delay in taking hold of the work. Instead of delay, however, only a few days passed after the close of the conference before the spacious dwelling house of Judge Graves, with eight acres of land, constituting his beautiful place of residence in West Battle Creek, was purchased. Adjoining this building a two-story addition was at once constructed to serve as bath-rooms. In these buildings the Health Reform Institute was opened.

In the *Review* of June 19, 1866, the first general call for stock in the institution was made. In the same number of the paper a statement was made that stock had already been subscribed by the churches of Battle Creek, Mich., and Olcott, N. Y., to the amount of $2,625, or 105 shares of $25 each. As there was no law in the State of Michigan under which a corporation for managing health institutions could be formed, the property was held in trust for a time, until an incorporation could be effected.

A Health Journal Started

The first of August there was also begun by the managers the publication of a monthly health journal, sixteen pages with cover, in magazine form. This was called the *Health Reformer*. This journal is still continued, under the name *Good Health*, and is now the leading health magazine of the world. This journal not only treated on health and temperance principles, but was also a means of advertising the health institution, which was formally opened for patients and boarders on the 5th of September, 1866. So here was the institution, purchased, equipped, and in running order less than four months from the time the subject was first mentioned to our people; and the sum of $11,000 was subscribed to stock, a large proportion of which was already paid.

A Medical Corporation Organized

During the winter of 1866-67 a law was passed by the Michigan Legislature under which a corporation for managing the health institution could be formed. May 17, 1867, this step was taken, by-laws were adopted, and the real estate and other property passed over to duly elected trustees. The whole amount of stock subscribed up to that date was $26,100, of which $18,264.87 was paid. The institution had a competent corps of physicians and helpers, and the buildings were nearly full of patients, several of whom had already embraced our faith, having learned of us as a people and of the truth after coming to the institution.

Healthful Dress

In all ages and in all countries the natural heart is susceptible to the influence of the world, with its pride of life, its follies and fashions. The year 1863, in our own land, when the health and dress question was shown to Mrs. White, was not an exception, as will be seen by the infatuation of the ladies in following the prevailing fashion of wearing hoops, the dimensions of which made many of them look as if walking in an inverted balloon. About the same time two other extremes in dress were introduced which excited much discussion. A brief notice of these will, perhaps, prepare the reader to better understand a testimony given by Mrs. White on the subject of dress, found in " Testimony for the Church," No. 10.

Extremes in Dress Condemned

The first extreme was that of wearing dresses made with a trail, or train, from ten inches to half a yard or more in length, according to the fancy of the wearer. These were often left to drag upon the ground, and were denominated by the gentlemen as " street sweepers." The second extreme was exactly the opposite, and was in a style as nearly like that worn by the men as possible. This fashion was adopted by those following in the wake of Miss Bloomer, and hence was called the " bloomer dress." Finally the name was changed to the " American Costume." Conventions were held from place to place by the advocates of this costume, and many of our sisters were in favor of adopting it. Some did wear it.

A Testimony on the Dress Question

Concerning what was shown Mrs. White on the dress question, I will quote a few paragraphs from Testimony No. 11: —

" God's loyal people are the light of the world and the salt of the earth, and they should ever remember their influence is of value. Were they to exchange the extreme long dress for the extreme short one, they would, to a great extent, destroy their influence. Unbelievers, whom it is their duty to benefit and seek to bring to the Lamb of God, would be disgusted. Many improvements can be made in the dress of women in reference to health without making so great a change as to disgust the beholder.

The Reform Dress

" The form should not be compressed in the least with corsets and whale-bones. The dress should be perfectly easy, that the lungs and heart may have healthy action. The dress should reach somewhat below the top of the boot, but should be short enough to clear the filth of the sidewalk and street, without being raised by the hand. A still shorter dress than this would be proper, convenient, and healthful for women when doing their housework, and especially for those who are obliged to perform more or less out-of-door labor.

The Body to be Evenly Clothed

"Whatever may be the length of the dress, their limbs should be clothed as thoroughly as are the men's. This may be done by wearing lined pants, gathered into a band and fastened about the ankle, or made full and tapering at the bottom; and these should come down long enough to meet the shoe. The limbs and ankles thus clothed are protected against a current of air. If the feet and limbs are kept comfortable with warm clothing, the circulation will be equalized, and the blood will remain pure and healthy, because it is not chilled or hindered in its natural passage through the system."

The length of this dress was presented as a commendable medium between the dress with a trail and the American costume. It was not said that any one *must* put it on, but that they must *not* take a course to cut off their influence, and disgust those they should help. It was not said that they *must* clothe their ankles in the *manner* here described, but that it *might* be done in that way. If the same object is accomplished in some other manner, as with long undersuits and knitted leggins, it would be in perfect harmony with that testimony.

Five Points Essential to Healthful Dress

It will be noticed that in the style of dress recommended there are five points essential to healthful clothing, viz.: —

1. Discarding corsets and all compression of the waist.

2. Dispensing with all bands on arms or limbs that would hinder the free circulation of the blood.

3. Clothing all parts of the body equally, especially the feet and ankles.

4. Suspending the skirts from the shoulders, and in no case allowing them to hang upon the hips, with bands.

5. The length of the dress.

The first four points are now advocated by every intelligent physician, and as to the fifth, the trail and the extreme short dress are now both discarded.

Mrs. Jenness-Miller on Dress

During the year 1890 Mrs. Jenness-Miller, of New York, in the most scientific hygienic dress journal of the age, advocated that women shorten their dresses little by little, so as not to make too abrupt a change, until they are brought up to about the top of a lady's boot,— just the length that Testimony No. 11 advocated.

Dr. Trall's Endorsement

In 1868 it was arranged for Dr. R. T. Trall, of the Hygieotherapeutic College of Florence Heights, N. J., to give a week's course of lectures before our ministers in Battle Creek, Mich., the last of May. During the course the doctor was the guest of Elder White. Mrs. White did not attend the lectures, but as the doctor would ride out daily in the carriage with Elder White and his wife and Elder J. N. Andrews, it was understood that he was to listen to her ideas of hygiene, disease and its causes, the effects of medicines, etc. She simply talked what had been shown to her in vision, not telling, however, the source whence she derived her knowledge. The doctor stated that medical science was in harmony with the ideas expressed by her. Elder Andrews told me that on concluding the conversation of the second day the doctor asked Mrs. White where she graduated in medical science. He was surprised on learning that she had never studied these things, but was giving him the result of what had been shown to her in Ostego,

Mich., June 6, 1863. He assured her that her ideas were all in the strictest harmony with physiology and hygiene, and that on many of the subjects she went deeper than he ever had. After about five days of such rides and talks the doctor wanted to know of Elder White why he was invited to leave his college to lecture before the ministers in Battle Creek. Said he, " Mrs. White is just as well prepared to give them the needed instruction in hygiene as I am."

Medical Science Approves

Her numerous writings on the various branches of practical hygiene have been for years before the public, and many of them are now compiled in a volume entitled " Christian Temperance and Bible Hygiene." Some of the best educated physicians have declared, after a careful examination of these writings, that medical science is in perfect accord with them. With her they are not the result of study, but simply the writing out of what the Lord has revealed to her in vision.

Dr. Kellogg's Testimony

As a testimonial of how the researches of medical science accord with what was opened in vision before Mrs. White in 1863, I will quote from the preface to " Christian Temperance " words written by J. H. Kellogg, M. D., who stands at the head of the world-famous sanitarium of Battle Creek, Mich. He says : —

" 1. At the time the writings referred to first appeared, the subject of health was almost wholly ignored, not only by the people to whom they were addressed, but by the world at large.

" 2. The few advocating the necessity of a reform in physical habits, propagated in connection with the advocasy of genuine reformatory principles the most patent, and in some instances, disgusting errors.

" 3. Nowhere and by no one was there presented a systematic and harmonious body of hygienic truths, free from patent errors and consistent with the Bible and the principles of the Christian religion.

" Under these circumstances the writings referred to made their appearance. The principles taught were not enforced by scientific authority, but were presented in a simple, straightforward manner by one who makes no pretense to scientific knowledge, but claims to write by the aid and authority of the divine enlightenment.

The Principles Have Stood the Test

" How have the principles presented under such peculiar circumstances and with such remarkable claims stood the test of time and experience? is a question which may very properly be asked. Its answer is to be found in facts which are capable of the amplest verification. . . . The principles which a quarter of a century ago were either entirely ignored or made the butt of ridicule have quietly won their way into public confidence and esteem, until the world has quite forgotten that they have not always been thus accepted. New discoveries in science and new interpretations of old facts have continually added confirmatory evidence, until at the present time every one of the principles advocated more than a quarter of a century ago is fortified in the strongest possible manner by scientific evidence.

Proof of the Divine Origin of the Visions

" It certainly must be regarded as a thing remarkable, and evincing unmistakable evidence of divine insight and direction, that in the midst of confused and conflicting teachings, claiming the authority of science and experience, but warped by ultra notions and rendered impotent for good by the great admixture of error,— it must be admitted to be something extraordinary, that a person making no claims to scientific knowledge or erudition should have been able to organize, from the confused and error-tainted mass of ideas advanced by a few writers and thinkers on health subjects, a body of hygienic principles so harmonious, so consistent, and so genuine that the discussions, the researches, the discoveries, and the experience of a quarter of a century have not resulted in the overthrow of a single principle, but have only served to establish the doctrines taught." Dated, " Battle Creek, Mich., 1890."

The Health Institution Enlarged

Under the management of J. H. Kellogg, M. D., who became connected with the institution as physician-in-chief in 1876, it was found that the demand for treatment was so great that in the spring of 1877 more room must be provided. The name of the institution was in 1876 changed from Health Reform Institute to the Medical and Surgical Sanitarium, and in 1878 a new main building was erected.

This structure was 136 x 46 feet in size, four stories above the basement. It was heated throughout by steam, and lighted by gas. Shortly after its opening it was nearly filled with patients and guests.

Up to that time what had been predicted in 1866 by the testimony of Mrs. White respecting the institution had been most strikingly fulfilled. Scores had already accepted the light of present truth whose attention had first been called to this people by their coming to the institution in pursuit of health.

Rural Health Retreat

In the *Signs of the Times* of Nov. 22, 1877, M. G. Kellogg, M. D., half-brother of J. H. Kellogg, announced that he had secured grounds on the side of Howell Mountain, two and a half miles northeast from St. Helena, Napa County, Cal., and was about to erect a building to be called the " Rural Health Retreat," located by the side of Crystal Springs. During the winter of 1877-78 a building was erected, and was opened for the treatment of patients in the early part of 1878.

This health retreat, like the parent institution, the sanitarium in Battle Creek, has not only grown in proportions, but has also been a place where very many have been brought to the knowledge and acceptance of the message.

The Pacific Health Journal

The summer of 1885 was quite an eventful period of progress in the cause of the third angel's message. The first of May the Rural Health Retreat at St. Helena was placed under the medical management of a regularly graduated physician. In the month of June was begun the bimonthly issue of the *Pacific Health Journal and Temperance Advocate,* a 24-page magazine under the editorial supervision of Elder J. H. Waggoner. By these agencies new life came to the health institution, which, instead of losing, as in previous years, began to show, from year to year, a net profit in its workings of from $2,000 to $4,000 per year, until the year which closed April, 1891, it showed a net gain of over $12,000.

At the meeting of the Rural Health Retreat Association, at St. Helena, 1887, the following statement was made in reference to the finances of the institution: May 1, 1885, the net worth of the institution was only $5,322.76, or $2,547.24 less than all the stock that had been issued up to that date. In other words, the institution had consumed all of its earnings and $2,547.24 of its capital stock. April 1, 1887, the value of the institution above all its debts was $21,372.64, or a gain in twenty-three months of $16,049.88. Of this sum, stock had been taken to the amount of $5,280, and donations had been made to the institution to the amount of $2,497.60; so on the workings of the institution there was a net gain of $8,272.28. About this time the *Pacific Health Journal* was issued as a 32-page monthly, with a cover, and was found to be of still greater service in advancing the interests and principles of the institution.

Charitable Work

In the *Medical Missionary* for January, 1891, speaking of the Battle Creek Sanitarium, Dr. J. H. Kellogg said:—

"The charity treatment administered during the quarter of a century which the institution has existed amounts to considerable more than $100,000, several times more than the capital stock originally invested.

"In addition to the charity work referred to, the institution has sent out lecturers, nurses, instructors in cooking schools, and other persons who have been trained for various lines of missionary work."

A Plea for the Orphans

At the General Conference, March 8, 1891, Dr. Kellogg made a very earnest plea in behalf of the orphans. He said: "I find myself appointed 'a delegate at large,' and I am going to represent the unrepresented — the orphans, who have no one to care for them."

Mrs. Haskell's $30,000 Gift

In the *Home Missionary* for January, 1892, a strong plea was made for means with which to provide a home for the orphan children. In that journal were the names of those whose pledges for the home amounted to $17,716 — too small an amount, the promoters of the enterprise thought, for so large an undertaking, hence a delay in the execution of the work was feared. But He who sees the end from the beginning, and who owns the "cattle upon a thousand hills," so ordered events that a wealthy lady not of our faith, Mrs. Caroline E. Haskell, of Chicago, widow of Mr. Frederick Haskell, on hearing of this contemplated work of charity, at once placed at the disposal of the building committee the sum of $30,000, with the simple stipulation that it be wholly used in building an orphanage according to the plans previously outlined, that it be conducted in a broad and liberal spirit,

24

and that the institution be called the *Haskell Memorial Home* in memory of her deceased husband.

With means thus furnished the Medical Missionary and Benevolent Association was enabled, during the year, to erect and open the building as an orphans' home. This building was dedicated Jan. 25, 1894. For much of the time since that date the family, consisting of orphans, helpers, and teachers, has averaged one hundred.

The James White Memorial Home

Besides the care and support of these orphans, this association has the management of another charitable institution, called the James White Memorial Home, where more than a score of aged and homeless people are cared for and made comfortable.

Medical Missionaries

In this line of work, another aggressive step was taken when the training of medical missionaries was undertaken. In commendation of this effort for the uplifting of humanity, Mrs. White, when writing from Preston, Australia, Sept. 16, 1892, said:—

" I could wish that there were one hundred in training where now there is one. It ought to be thus. Both men and women can be more useful as medical missionaries than as missionaries without a medical education."

The number taking a course of instruction preparatory to entering a life service of this character has been largely augmented since the above was written.

Growth of the Health Work

In the *Medical Missionary* for January, 1894, is a brief statement setting forth interesting facts respecting the growth of the health work. It reads as follows:—

" The Health Reform Institute was organized in 1866.
. . . A modest frame house was purchased, a private residence
in a pleasant and healthful location on the higher grounds
of Battle Creek, one of the growing cities of Michigan. Two
doctors, two bath attendants, one nurse (untrained), three
or four helpers, one patient, and any amount of inconven-
iences, and a great deal of faith in the future of the institution and the principles on which it was founded — this was
the beginning of the present enterprise. It was known as
the Health Reform Institute.

" On the site of the original cottage there now stands
a building 312 feet long and 100 feet deep, six stories high,
which accommodates three hundred guests, furnished with
every appliance that modern science can suggest for the care
and restoration of the sick. Ten physicians, most of whom
are specialists in their respective lines, constitute the medical
faculty. Nurses and other helpers form a family of more than
three hundred, and the patronage of the institution represents
every State in the Union, and many guests from other lands.
Its doors are always open to the missionary, home or foreign,
of whatever name, and the family is rarely without one or
more of these guests.

The Sanitarium Hospital

" The hospital was erected in 1888, a building 100 x 60
feet, five stories high. Three of the upper floors of the
building are used for the surgical department of the sanitarium, patients' rooms, and wards. Offices for the charitable
work of the institution are also found here. Twenty cot-
tages, several of which are heated by steam, and lighted,
like the main building, with electricity, cluster about it, and
are filled with either patients or students. A school for the
training of medical missionary nurses was organized July 1,
1884. During the first six months thirty-five students were
enrolled."

Prediction of Workers Going Forth

In speaking of the health institution located at St. Helena, Cal., Mrs. White, in a communication written from Tramelan, Switzerland, Feb. 6, 1887, says:—

" God has said that if the men connected with this institution would walk humbly and obediently, doing the will of God, it would live and prosper; and from it would be sent forth missionaries to bless others with the light God has given them. These will in the spirit of Jesus demolish idols in high places; they will unveil superstition, and plant truth, purity, and holiness where now are cherished only error, self-indulgence, intemperance, and iniquity."

We quote these words, as they apply with equal force to other like institutions.

Success in Health Work Promised

In a special testimony given to the church in 1891, we read: " God's blessing will rest upon every effort made to awaken an interest in health reform; for it is needed everywhere. There must be a revival in regard to this matter; for God purposes to accomplish much through this agency."

The American Medical Missionary College

Step by step the light advanced on the rational mode of treating disease until in June, 1895, a demand was created for the organization of a medical educational institution. In compliance with this demand, the American Medical Missionary College was organized for the special purpose of training physicians to work under the Seventh-day Adventist Medical Missionary and Benevolent Association, in home and foreign fields. The inauguration exercises were held in Battle Creek, Sept. 30, 1895, and the college was opened the following day, October 1, with a class of forty students.

In the college announcement we read: " The college is incorporated in Chicago, under the laws of the State of Illinois. The course of study will be as thorough as that of the best medical schools in the United States. The instruction will be given partly in Chicago, and partly in Battle Creek, Mich."

Concerning those preparing for medical missionary work we read the following in the *Medical Missionary* of August, 1895: "The class of nurses now in training at the Battle Creek Sanitarium Training-School for Nurses numbers over 250; every one of these who is now competent to engage in medical missionary work has a position assigned him. Nurses are wanted for the South Sea Islands, India, the West Indies, South America, twenty-five or thirty for the Southern States of the United States, and for our large cities."

Growth of the Medical Missionary Work

At the graduating exercises of the Sanitarium Missionary Nurses' class, held in the Tabernacle, Nov. 5, 1895, Dr. Kellogg said:—

"A dozen years ago, at an exercise of this kind, two nurses graduated. At the present time there is a corps of between three and four hundred nurses. There are nineteen physicians at the sanitarium, and twenty-two at similar institutions, more or less connected with the sanitarium, and under the supervision of the Medical Missionary and Benevolent Association. Fifty-three of our nurses are in different foreign countries,— in Sweden, Old Mexico, Gold Coast of Africa, Australia, South Africa, Denmark, India, New Zealand, Samoa, and British Guiana. There are sixty-three medical students now in training. Forty-one of these are here, twenty-two at the University of Michigan and other schools. Twenty-two nurses graduate here to-night who are fully prepared to go forth as approved nurses."

In tracing the growth of our health institutions to 1902, we find the Battle Creek Sanitarium, with its medical college and training school for nurses, to be the largest institution of the kind in the world owned by Seventh-day Adventists.

The Main Buildings Burned

On the night of Feb. 18, 1902, the large main building, with its fine equipments, and the commodious hospital, were consumed by fire. There were four hundred invalids and guests in the buildings at the time, but through the heroic efforts of the doctors, nurses, and helpers, and with the special protection of the Lord, these were all gotten out of the buildings without serious injury.

The New Sanitarium

Another building, larger and more substantial than the former, has been erected on the site of the old buildings. The corner-stone of the present structure was laid May 12, 1902, and the building was dedicated May 31, 1903. The managers of the institution say of the new edifice that " it is as solid and enduring as a building can be made with iron, stone, brick, and cement.

" The equipment of the institution is in all particulars the most modern, complete, sanitary, convenient, and substantial to be obtained ; and it is believed that, as it now stands, completed, the Battle Creek Sanitarium offers facilities and conveniences for invalids which are certainly not surpassed.

" The aim of the managers of the institution has been to gather together in one place and under favorable conditions, all the new methods and appliances for the treatment of the sick which are recognized in rational medicine, and to utilize those methods in a conscientious and intelligent manner."

Many Sanitariums to be Established

The light communicated to this people is that the Lord would have many sanitariums, moderate in size, distributed over the world, rather than to have a few mammoth institutions. We are glad to note that a beginning has been made in opening small sanitariums in various parts of the world, especially during the last decade. In the General Conference Year Book for 1904 is a list of over half a hundred of these smaller institutions.

List of Sanitariums

While it might be a matter of interest to relate the circumstances which have led to the establishment of these, we must, in our limited space, content. ourselves with a list of the countries where they are located, and the number in each country. We find in the United States, 35; Great Britain, 3; Germany, 1; Switzerland, 1; Denmark, 1; Norway, 1; Sweden, 1; South Africa, 1; Australia, 2; New Zealand, 1; Island of Samoa, 1; Old Mexico, 1; India, 1; Japan, 1.

List of Treatment Rooms

Besides these sanitariums there are twenty-two treatment rooms, seventeen of which are in the United States; one in Jaffa, one in Jerusalem, Palestine; one in Guadalajara, Old Mexico; one in Kimberley, South Africa; and one in Rockampton, Australia. In addition to these there are twenty-six vegetarian restaurants where people can obtain pure hygienic food, and also receive more or less instruction respecting the proper mode of living.

These statistics respecting the progress of health reform principles show how the Lord can " accomplish a great work through this agency." as divinely predicted in 1866; and they also show, as foretold in 1863, how " the principles of health reform " may act a part in " fitting up a people for translation at the coming of the Lord." So may these health institutions increase to a hundred-fold, and soon accomplish that for which they were appointed and designed.

CHAPTER XXIV

OTHER PREDICTIONS FULFILLED

 ONSIDER now from this day and upward, from the four and twentieth day of the ninth month, even from the day that the foundation of the Lord's temple was laid, consider it. Is the seed yet in the barn? yea, as yet the vine, and the fig-tree, and the pomegranate, and the olive-tree, hath not brought forth: from this day will I bless you." [1]

The sure and steady advancement of the third angel's message from its first inception may well be compared with the prosperity that attended Zerubbabel from the day he laid the foundation stone of the temple.

A Forbidding Prospect

When the Jewish people, with empty purse and granaries, were called to build the Lord's temple, it looked to all human appearance as a forbidding prospect. When by faith they obeyed the call, and took hold of the work willingly, God's prospering hand was manifest to them. As we trace the experiences in the rise of this third message, we discern the guiding hand with those who choose his way. Although affliction be their lot, still God's care for his people and his work is always made clear to those who trust in him.

Testimony Delineating Character

On Nov. 24, 1862, two meetings were held at the same hour in the house of William Wilson, of Greenville, Mich.,

[1] Haggai 2: 18, 19.

for the purpose of organizing two churches for those who had accepted the Sabbath truth in that vicinity. The meeting for the Greenville church was conducted by Elder White and his wife in one room, while Elder Byington and myself had charge of a meeting in another room for the West Plains church. While we were engaged in the preliminary work in one room, we could hear the voice of Mrs. White as she bore her testimony in the other room. We were meeting with some difficulties in our work, when just at the opportune time Mrs. White opened the door, and said, " Brother Lough-borough, I see by looking over this company that I have testimonies for some of the persons present. When you are ready, I will come in and speak." That being just the time we needed help, she came in. Aside from Elder Byington and myself, she knew the names of only three persons in the room. The others were strangers, whom she had never seen, only as they had been presented to her in vision.

Mr. Pratt's Life Described

As she arose to speak, she said: " You will have to excuse me in relating what I have to say, if I describe your persons, as I do not know your names. As I see your countenances, there comes before me what the Lord has beer pleased to show me concerning you. That man in the corner with one eye [some one spoke, saying, " His name is Pratt "] makes high professions, and great pretensions to religion, but he has never yet been converted. Do not take him into the church in his present condition, for he is not a Christian. He spends much of his time idling about the shops and stores, arguing the theory of the truth, while his wife at home has to cut the fire-wood, look after the garden, etc. He makes promises in his bargains that he does not fulfill. His neighbors have no confidence in his profession of religion. It would be better for the cause of religion, for him, in his present condition, to say nothing about it."

Brother Barr Made Glad

She continued, saying, " This aged brother [as she pointed to him, some one said, " Brother Barr "] was shown me in direct contrast with the other man. He is very exemplary in his life, careful to keep all his promises, and provides well for his family. He hardly ventures to speak of the truth to his neighbors, for fear he will mar the work and do harm. He does not see how the Lord can be so merciful as to forgive his sins, and thinks himself unfit even to belong to the church." She then said to him, " Brother Barr, the Lord bade me say to you that you have confessed all the sins you knew of, and that he forgave your sins long ago, if you would only believe it." The look of sadness on the brother's countenance quickly fled. He looked up with a smile, and said, in his simplicity, " Has he? " " Yes," responded Mrs. White, " and I was told to say to you, ' Come along, and unite with the church; and as you have opportunity, speak a word in favor of the truth; it will have a good effect, as your neighbors have confidence in you.' " He responded, " I will."

Then she said, " If Mr. Pratt could, for a time, take a position similar to that which Brother Barr has been occupying, it would do him good."

Thus was one cause of our difficulty in organizing removed. Before her testimony was borne, we could not get Mr. Barr to consent to unite with the church; while on the other hand, we found about every one was opposed to receiving Mr. Pratt; still no one felt free to tell why he opposed.

A Family Jealousy Healed

She next addressed a man having a sandy complexion, who sat on one side of the room; and then pointed to a thin-featured woman on the extreme opposite side, addressing them as husband and wife. She delineated some things that transpired in their former lives, before either of them had made any profession of the truth. She said these things had been magnified by Satan before the mind of the woman until she was driven to insanity. " I saw," said Mrs. White, " that this woman had been one year in the insane asylum; but since recovering her reason, she has permitted these same jealous feelings to trouble her mind, greatly to the grief of her husband, who has done everything in his power to show his wife that he was true to her, and that she had no reason to hold him off in the manner she does."

In a moment the wife rushed across the room, and on her knees begged her husband to forgive her. The individuals were almost strangers in that part of the country, and their former history was unknown. Those best acquainted with them, however, were aware that an estrangement existed between them, but the cause they knew not.

Similar to Elisha and Hazael

After Mrs. White had borne her testimony, the work of organizing the church was soon completed. Mr. Barr came heartily into the organization, while Mr. Pratt was left out. The moment the meeting closed, the latter said, with considerable vehemence, " I tell you what, there is no use trying to go with this people and act the hypocrite; *you can't do it.*"

The delineation of character, as in the above instance, forcibly reminds us of a similar case recorded in the days of Elisha the prophet:[2] Benhadad, King of Syria, had sent his servant Hazael to Elisha to inquire whether he should recover of his sickness. Elisha had had a view of Hazael's case, and as the man came before him, and he looked on his countenance, all came vividly to his mind.

Elder White Stricken with Paralysis

On Wednesday, August 16, 1865, Elder White, as a result of excessive labor and loss of sleep, had a stroke of paralysis. As health institutions among our people had not yet been

[2] 2 Kings 8: 7 - 15.

established, he was taken to Dansville, N. Y., to a health institution called, " Our Home on the Hillside." His wife and the writer were with him there from September 14 to December 7. As he received but little relief from the treatments given in the institution, we went to the hospitable home of Bradly Lamson, Lake View, Rochester, N. Y., where we remained about three weeks. Here we were glad to meet Elder J. N. Andrews, who had just returned to that city, after having spent several months in Maine.

Prayer for Elder White

The families of Elder Andrews and Mr. Orton joined with us every afternoon in a praying season with and for Elder White. This continued until December 25. While the outside world was full of gaiety and feasting on that Christmas day, it was observed by the Rochester church as a day of fasting and prayer for Elder White. We had meetings in both the forenoon and afternoon, at the house of Elder Andrews, New Main St., and in the evening those who had been previously praying with Elder White, met with him again at the house of Mr. Lamson.

The Vision Given Christmas Night

The meeting that evening was a powerful one. Elder White was greatly blessed, and Mrs. White was given a wonderful vision, in which many things were shown her. Among these were instructions to Elder White how to proceed that he might carry out his faith in God, who had so evidently reached down his hand to work for him that he might regain his health.

Satan's Attack Predicted

To those who had been praying for Elder White, Mrs. White said: "Satan's purpose was to destroy my husband, and bring him down to the grave. Through these earnest prayers his power has been broken. I have been shown that

Satan is angry with this company who have continued for three weeks praying earnestly in behalf of this servant of God, and he is now determined to make a powerful attack upon them. I was told to say to you, ' Live very near to God, that you may be prepared for what may come upon you.' "

J. T. Orton's Premonitions

On the first day of January, 1866, Elder White and his family started by train for Battle Creek, Mich. I remained in western New York the rest of the winter. From the very evening that the vision was given, Mr. J. T. Orton was impressed that his life was in danger, and yet he knew not from what source. This impression he expressed to several. On Sunday evening, March 4, he returned to Rochester from Parma, where he had been attending a two days' meeting, in company with Mr. E. B. Sanders (now, 1905, residing in San Jose, Cal.), whom he requested to keep on the lightest street as they walked through the city, " for," he said, " I feel all the while as though some one is going to try to kill me." And yet he did not seem to have any idea who it was that wanted to take his life.

I returned to Rochester from Parma, March 7, and stopped with Mr. Lamson, son-in-law of Mr. Orton. On the 8th he and Mrs. Orton visited with us, when we made arrangements to go the next morning by train to Lancaster, Erie Co., where I was to perform the marriage ceremony for his only son. The day was spent pleasantly by us, yet it was a solemn day.

Murder of J. T. Orton

They left Mr. Lamson's at 5 P. M., and at 7 : 30 P. M. a messenger came, informing us of a brutal attack that had been made on Mr. Orton by some unknown person, in his own barn, while caring for his horses. We hastened to the place, and found that he had been cruelly beaten over the head with an iron-bound cartstake, and was unconscious. He died at 12 : 35 that night. To this day it is unknown who committed the cruel deed. It certainly was not done for money, as his watch in his pocket was untouched, as was also his purse, which contained $45. This was a heavy shock to Mrs. Orton, from the effects of which she never recovered. Her bodily health rapidly failed, and she did not long survive her husband.

Prediction Made that Christmas Fulfilled

In a few months from that memorable Christmas evening, six out of the nine who engaged in that three weeks of prayer were in their graves. And thus was another prediction most strikingly fulfilled.

Relief to the Despairing

In the early morning of Dec. 12, 1866, Elias Stiles, of North Liberty, Ind., came to my home, requesting me to go with him to that place to administer relief, if possible. to James Harvey, who was in despair, and feeling that there was no hope in his case. Knowing that Mrs. White had had a very extensive view in the last vision given, and that many cases were shown to her prophetically, I said to him, " It may be that Sister White has seen something about his case, and if so, and if she will write it out, it will be more forcible than anything I could say to him."

We at once called upon her, and without a word being spoken to her of Mr. Harvey's condition, I asked, " Sister White, have you had any light in any of the visions given you concerning the case of Brother James Harvey? " " Yes," said she, " I have, and I have felt for a few days as though I ought to write it out, and send it to him." She then began to tell us what she had seen. I said, " I am going to see him in the morning, and if you will write out what has been shown to you, I will take it to him." With this understanding, we left her, and in the evening we called again. She had completed the writing, and favored us by reading it aloud.

Testimony for James Harvey in Despair

The testimony stated clearly that Mr. Harvey would be brought into a feeble condition of health, and that Satan would seek to crowd him into despair, and try to make him think there was no mercy for him, and no hope in his case; but she saw he had done all in his power to rectify the mistakes of his past life, and that God had forgiven him; and furthermore, when he should be tempted to destroy himself, she was shown that angels of God were hovering around him and pointing him to hope in God and heaven. There were many like words of comfort and encouragement in the testimony.

With this document in my possession, we went the next morning to North Liberty. On the way, Mr. Stiles told me that Mr. Harvey wanted to see me, but he said that I would have no word of hope for him; that, when I should meet him, I would agree with him that his case was hopeless, that he was a lost man; and then, like Eli of old, when he was told that the ark of God was taken, he should fall over backward and die.

We arrived at Mr. Harvey's about 3 P. M. When I met him, I said, " Brother Harvey, how are you?" In a most lamentable strain he replied, "Lost! *lost!!* LOST!!!" " No! you are *not* lost. There is hope in your case!" said I. When he saw that I thus answered him, he said, in a modulated tone, " I have thought for three weeks that there was no hope for me, and that I was lost; and to-day, as I was coming into town from the farm, and passing over the bridge at the mill-pond, something seemed to say to me, ' You *are* lost! There is *no hope* for you! Jump into the mill-pond and drown yourself!' I thought to do such a thing would bring reproach on the cause of Christ, and so I was restrained from destroying myself."

Deliverance Came Quickly

"Well, Brother Harvey, you are not lost!" I said. "I have a testimony here direct from heaven, saying that you *are not lost!*" He replied, "Then I will hear it." I then read the testimony to him, after first stating that not one word had been told Mrs. White of his state of mind until after she had written out what had been shown her, and the writing had been placed in my hands. As I completed the reading, his face lighted up with a smile as he said, "Then there is hope in my case. I do believe in the Lord."

Following the reading, we had a praying season, from which he arose a changed and happy man. He told us that that writing described the workings of his mind for the last three weeks more accurately than he could possibly have done it. Thus the love of God was shown in lifting this brother, by this means, out of despair.

Field of Labor Enlarged

Up to the year 1868, the Seventh-day Adventists' field of labor had been confined to the United States, and to that portion of it north of the southern boundary of Missouri and east of the Missouri River. At a meeting to consider the fields and the distribution of labor, during a session of the General Conference which was held in Battle Creek, Mich., May 28, it was decided to send two laborers and a sixty-foot tent to California. Elder D. T. Bourdeau and the writer arrived in San Francisco July 18 of that year.

Opening of the California Mission

One thing I wish to notice in connection with the opening of the California mission, which well illustrates the practical utility of the gift of prophecy. Paul, in speaking of spiritual gifts, including the gift of prophecy, says they are " for the perfecting of the saints, for the work of the ministry, for the edifying of the body of Christ." [3] Surely the most feasible way to perfect saints is to point out to them their errors, so that they may put them away, and be washed from their sins in the precious blood of our Lord Jesus Christ. To this end, aid through the gift of prophecy in the work of the ministry has all the way along been manifested in connection with the cause of present truth, pointing out to the servants of the Lord the defects in their *manner* of labor, and how, by a different mode, they could be more efficient in the conversion of souls.

Testimony on How to Labor in California

Shortly after our arrival in California we received a letter from Mrs. White, in which she related a vision given her in Battle Creek on the Friday evening of June 12,— a day that we had spent at Lancaster, N. Y., before starting for California. She had never been in California, and had no personal knowledge of the habits of the people. In fact, at that time she had never been west of the Missouri River. Any knowledge she possessed concerning things there was derived from what the Lord was pleased to reveal to her.

In the instruction in her letter, she delineated the liberal ways of the people of California, and what would be the effect of labor among them on a close, " pennywise " plan. In preaching to the people of California, they must be approached in something of the liberal spirit in which they work, and yet not in a spendthrift manner.

The Predicted Success Came

As I now look back over the last thirty-seven years since the work was first started in California, and take in the situation then, with the condition of the people, and the manner in which we would have conducted our work but for the tes-

[3] Eph. 4: 12.

25

timony received, and as I witness the results of following the
instruction given, I can say that our cause advanced more in
three months than it would have done in one year had we not
been helped " in the work of the ministry " by the instruction
received through the gift of prophecy. Up to the spring
of 1871, as the result of the efforts in Sonoma County, five
churches of Sabbath-keepers had been raised up.

The First Tent-Meeting in San Francisco

In June the same year, we erected our tent for the first
time, in San Francisco. As Elder Bourdeau had returned to
the East, another laborer from Michigan was sent to take
his place. He arrived on June 17, and at once united with
me in labor in the city. After a few weeks' effort in the tent,
we continued our meetings to Dec. 1, 1871, in hired halls. As
the result of this labor over fifty accepted the message in San
Francisco.

Internal Trials in California

Until this date our trials in California had been more from
outside opposition, but now arose an unlooked-for test of faith
for our people of a different character. An associate laborer
persisted in a course of action which I was confident would
subject himself and the cause to reproach. We had some
bitter enemies in the city, who were watching our every movement, and were ready to use any unwise action to our injury.
It became, therefore, extremely necessary to heed the apostle's admonition to " shun every appearance of evil."

Dangerous Independence

I did not claim that the brother had committed actual sin in
his course of action, but I reasoned that our enemies would
make capital of what he claimed to be innocent. He took the
position that he had a right to " do as he pleased " in the
matter, especially when it was admitted there was no sin in

what he was doing. Thus things went on until Jan. 23, 1872, when I went from Sonoma County to San Francisco to see what could be done to check matters there.

By this time our enemies were making use of his course as I had feared, and he was taking the position that it was " none of their business," that he would show them that he had a mind of his own, and could walk the streets *as* he pleased, and *with whom* he pleased, without being subject to their remarks. I tried, by private labor, to show him that such a course of action would not answer, and that such an independent spirit would end in evil. He had his friends, who strongly sympathized with him, some of whom began to take a position which would subject him to still greater censure. A large portion of the church saw the evil of his waywardness, and were ready to second the efforts I was making to save the cause from dishonor.

Investigation Meeting Appointed

Thus matters stood on Sabbath, January 27, when it was decided that there must be an investigation of the case, and some decisive action taken by the church, to save them from the stigma that this defiant spirit was likely to produce. A meeting was appointed, to begin Sunday, January 28, at 9 A. M., for the consideration of the situation, and our duty as a church in reference to the same. To all appearances a division of that church was inevitable. I spent much of that night in prayer to God, that he would work in our behalf.

A Written Confession

On the morning of the 28th, as I started for the meeting, I met the fellow-laborer on the sidewalk, near my boarding place, weeping. Said he, " Brother Loughborough, I am not going to the meeting to-day."

" Not going to the meeting? " said I ; " the meeting relates to your case."

" I know that," said he, " but I am all wrong. You are right in the position you have taken in reference to me. Here is a letter of confession I have written to the church; you take it and read it to them. It will be better for you, and better for those who might be inclined to sympathize with me, if I am not there."

" What has occasioned this great change in you since yesterday?" I inquired.

A Wonderful Vision Received

He replied, " I went to the post-office last night, after the Sabbath, and received a letter from Sister White, from Battle Creek, Mich. It is a testimony she has written out for me." Handing it to me, he said, " Read that, and you will see how the Lord sees my case."

He requested me to say to the church that he had received a testimony from Sister White, reproving him for his conduct, and that he accepted it, as it was the truth.

Convincing Nature of the Vision

This was part of a view given to Mrs. White at Bordoville, Vt., Dec. 10, 1871. She began to write the part relating to this brother's case Dec. 27, 1871, but for some reason the completion of the document was delayed until Jan. 18, 1872, at which time it was finished and mailed from Battle Creek. It then required about nine days to get letters overland from Michigan to California.

In vision many things are shown her prophetically. It was so in this instance. At the time of the vision there was but a shadow of what was actually developed when the testimony arrived in San Francisco. It will be seen, from a comparison of dates, that the culmination of the case in San Francisco came after the written testimony left the former place. Our brethren in San Francisco saw at once that no person could have written to Battle Creek and communicated the intelligence to Mrs. White in time for her to write this letter, for the state of things did not then exist.

This fact was of great weight with the brethren there, convincing them that there was divine power with that vision. I had not written a line to Elder White or his wife concerning the state of things in San Francisco, and the fellow-laborer declared that he had written nothing; and the brethren said, "If he had written, he would not have told the things that were brought out concerning himself."

How the Vision was Written

When we afterward learned, from the other end of the line, concerning the writing out and mailing of the testimony, it was still further evident that the Lord who gave the vision had a care over the time of its being written and forwarded to its destination, so that it would reach there just at the right time.

At a very early hour on the morning of Jan. 18, 1872, Mrs. White was awakened with the above testimony vividly impressed upon her mind. The impression was as distinct to her as though audibly spoken, "Write out immediately that testimony for California, and get it into the very next mail; it is needed." This being repeated the second time, she arose, hastily dressed, and completed the writing. Just before breakfast she handed it to her son Willie, saying, "Take this letter to the post-office, but don't put it into the drop. Hand it to the post-master, and have him be sure to put it into the mail bag that goes out this morning." He afterward said that he thought her instructions a little peculiar, but he asked no questions, and did as he was bidden, and "saw the letter go into the mail bag."

Proof of Divine Guidance

Knowing our situation in San Francisco at that time, you will readily see the importance of getting that letter into that very mail. In those days we had only one overland mail per day. Had the letter come Sunday night, the 28th, instead of Saturday night, the 27th, there would doubtless have been a sad rupture in the church. Had it come several weeks earlier, even just after the vision was given, the church would not so readily have seen its force.

Here was a testimony which bore evident marks of the Lord's hand, not only in that it arrived at a proper time to effectually correct the existing errors, but, being humbly accepted and acted upon by the brother, it exerted a mighty influence to bring unity and stability into that young church.

Manner of Writing out the Visions

This instance serves also as an illustration of her own statement respecting the manner of writing out what she has seen. Of this she says: " I have been aroused from my sleep with a vivid sense of subjects previously presented to my mind; and I have written, at midnight, letters that have gone across the continent, and arriving at a crisis, have saved a great disaster to the cause." [4]

[4] Testimony No. 33, page 113.

CHAPTER XXV

EDUCATIONAL INSTITUTIONS

"GET wisdom, get understanding; forget it not; neither decline from the words of my mouth. Forsake her not, and she shall preserve thee; love her, and she shall keep thee. Wisdom is the principal thing; therefore get wisdom: and with all thy getting get understanding." [1]

Prof. G. H. Bell's School

The educational work of the denomination has at the present time attained to comparatively large proportions. Like other branches of the cause heretofore noticed, it had a very small beginning. In 1868 Prof. G. H. Bell opened a school in the old office building, on the northeast corner of Kalamazoo and Washington Streets, Battle Creek. In addition to this, in the spring of 1871, at the close of the General Conference, a four weeks' ministers' lecture course was held, designed to aid those engaged in ministerial and church work.

Call for a Denominational School

There appeared in the *Review* of April 16, 1872, an article entitled, " Shall We Have a Denominational School? " in which were clearly stated the necessities for such a school. In the *Review* of July 16 it was announced that the school opened with twelve scholars, which number, after two weeks, had increased to twenty-five, and an evening grammar class of fifty had been started. The second term of the school opened Sept. 16, 1872, with forty pupils. By December 16 the school

[1] Prov. 4: 5 - 7.

had become so large that it was moved to the meeting-house, where folding-desks were attached to the backs of the church-pews. A primary department of sixty-three scholars was also conducted in the gallery of the church.

Money Raised for a College

The General Conference in March, 1873, spent considerable time in considering the propriety of raising means for the erection of suitable buildings for conducting a denominational school, in which workers should be prepared for entering the various fields. The matter being decided favorably, a committee was appointed to take in hand the raising of the necessary funds. During the season able and important articles appeared from time to time in the *Review* upon this subject, from Elders Butler, White, and others, and by the efforts of Elders Butler and Haskell in the various camp-meetings a large sum of money was raised for the proposed school.

Another session of the Conference was held Nov. 16, 1873, when it was reported that $52,000 had already been pledged for the Seventh-day Adventist educational fund, to be used in securing grounds and erecting suitable buildings the next season. By vote, at the same session, a committee of seven was chosen to form an educational society and procure a site for the buildings.

At the conference just mentioned, Geo. I. Butler was elected President of the General Conference, and Sidney Brownsberger, Secretary. The committee elected by the General Conference were, Geo. I. Butler, S. N. Haskell, and Harmon Lindsay. The names of James White, Ira Abbey, J. N. Andrews, and Uriah Smith were added, to act with the General Conference Committee as the Committee of Seven, who incorporated as "The Educational Society of the Seventh-day Adventists." From this time Professor Brownsberger was connected with the Battle Creek College until he was called to take charge of a college then to be opened in Healdsburg, Cal.

Twelve Acres Bought for the College

December 31, 1873, this committee bought twelve acres of ground in the west part of Battle Creek, seven acres of which formed the campus of Battle Creek College.

The Battle Creek denominational school opened its winter term in the rooms of the third office building on Dec. 15, 1873, with one hundred and ten pupils enrolled.

Need of Denominational Schools

Respecting our need, as a denomination, of proper schools of education, Mrs. White wrote in 1873 as follows: —

" All the powers of the mind should be called into use and developed, in order for men and women to have well-balanced minds. The world is full of one-sided men and women, who have become such because one set of their faculties was cultivated while others were dwarfed from inaction. The education of most youth is a failure. They over-study while they neglect that which pertains to practical business life. . . .

A Symmetrical Education Needed

" The constant application to study, as the schools are now conducted, is unfitting youth for practical life. The human mind will have action. If it is not active in the right direction, it will be active in the wrong. In order to preserve the balance of the mind, labor and study should be united in the schools.

" Provision should have been made in past generations for education upon a larger scale. In connection with the schools should have been agricultural and manufacturing establishments. There should have been teachers of household labor, and a portion of the time each day should have been devoted to labor, that the physical and mental powers might be equally exercised. If schools had been established upon the plan we have mentioned, there would not now be so many unbalanced minds." [2]

Battle Creek College

During the summer and fall of 1874 the Battle Creek College building was erected. It was a brick structure, three stories above the basement, 75 x 75 feet, in the form of a Greek cross. It was completed and dedicated with appropriate exercises Jan. 4, 1875. The school opened in this building with over one hundred students and seven competent teachers for the different departments. With the opening of the college in the school year of 1877 it was reported that two hundred students were in attendance. The report of the Educational Society, made at the General Conference in October, 1880, showed that there had been 1400 students enrolled in Battle Creek College from 1873 to December, 1880.

Two More Schools Opened

At the General Conference, December, 1882, it was reported that two denominational schools had been opened under the auspices of the conference during the year, one being the Healdsburg College, located at Healdsburg, Cal., which was opened April 11; the other, South Lancaster Academy, located at South Lancaster, Mass., opened April 19.

Healdsburg College

In the *Review* of Jan. 15, 1884, appeared the following interesting statement respecting the Pacific Coast denominational school : —

" In September, 1881, the California Conference decided to open a denominational school, and appointed a committee to carry the enterprise into effect. By April, 1882, ample grounds, with a suitable building of ten rooms, had been purchased, two instructors had been employed, and a school of thirty-three students begun. During the college year (begin-

[2] " Testimony for the Church," No. 22, in Vol. III, pages 152, 153.

ning July 29, 1882), the school was regularly chartered as a college, an additional plot of five acres bought, a commodious hall [for a students' home] erected, a faculty of six teachers secured, and 152 students enrolled. Since its opening nearly $27,000 had been subscribed for the enterprise, much of which has been paid by the people of California."

South Lancaster Academy

The people of New England began their school in the house of worship at South Lancaster, Mass. Through the untiring efforts of Elder S. N. Haskell and the sacrifices of our people in New England, a suite of school buildings was ready for dedication in the autumn of 1884. The buildings owned by the South Lancaster Academy Association were then five in number, two being entirely new. The academy building was 60 x 65 feet, and the other newly erected building, the students' home, 36 x 88 feet. These were dedicated Oct. 19, 1884.

This institution, after twenty-one years of efficient service, is still prospering, and has sent out earnest laborers in the Master's cause to various parts of the world. The principal of the academy now is Frederick Griggs, who also serves as secretary for the Educational Department of the General Conference.

London (England) Training School

As the work in London, England, continued to advance and grow in strength, it was deemed advisable during the summer of 1887 to open a training school for Bible workers, with which active Bible work was to be connected. From this school workers have been sent to labor in other parts of the United Kingdom and the Colonies. A flourishing school is at the present time conducted at Duncombe Hall, North London, with Prof. H. R. Salisbury in charge, who received his early education in the college at Battle Creek, Mich.

Battle Creek College Enlarged

The demand for more room at Battle Creek College was such that in the summer of 1886 it became necessary to make an extensive addition to the college building, and the year following (1887), to erect a dormitory (known as the West Hall) for lady students. West Hall contains rooms for 150 students, and 225 can be accommodated in the dining hall; while the South Hall, erected in 1884, at the south of the college campus served as the gentlemen's dormitory. At the opening of the college for the winter term, 1886-87, there were 568 students in attendance.

In 1885 Prof. W. W. Prescott was placed at the head of Battle Creek College, and shortly afterward was appointed to the position of Educational Secretary for the denomination. This was demonstrated as a wise move. Not only was Battle Creek College benefited, but through the labors of such a secretary, with the blessing of God, there was brought about closer unity and greater efficiency in the work of all our denominational schools.

Emmanuel Missionary College

The Battle Creek College did efficient service up to the year 1901, when the ground and buildings were sold to the American Medical Missionary College Association, and the educational society was discontinued. A new college corporation was at once formed, called the Emmanuel Missionary College. A farm was secured near Berrien Springs, in southwestern Michigan, where buildings have been erected by the students, and a prosperous school is conducted. It is the fixed purpose of this school to give an " all-round education," in harmony with the instruction quoted in the former part of this chapter. To qualify laborers fully prepared for work in any part of the world where they may be called in the providence of God to labor, is the one great desire and aim of the teachers of the Emmanuel Missionary College.

Central Bible School, Chicago, Ill.

In a *Review* of March, 1887, a proposition was made by Elder Geo. I. Butler that a mission building be erected in Chicago, Ill., which should serve as a central Bible school for the instruction of Bible workers, and at the same time could be used as a chapel and mission house for our people in the city. In the fall and winter of 1888-89 the building was erected. The cost, including lots, house, furnishings, etc., was about $28,000. It was formally opened April 4, 1889, with a canvassers' institute. At the time of the dedication the statement was made that our people knew of at least one thousand persons who had already accepted the present truth in various parts of the country from the efforts of the Bible workers.

This school was ably conducted by Elder Geo. B. Starr until the spring of 1891. Then, with teachers appointed by the General Conference Committee, it continued its work until the year 1893, when it was found that the building was inadequate to meet the growing demand for Bible instruction. As arrangements were made to connect a Bible school with the Battle Creek College, the Chicago building was sold to the Medical Missionary and Benevolent Association. The building has been enlarged and equipped for a small sanitarium, and is now called the Chicago Branch of the Battle Creek Sanitarium.

Union College, Nebraska

The General Conference of 1889 had under advisement the proposition to construct a college at some point convenient for the following nine State conferences, namely, Iowa, Minnesota, Kansas, Missouri, Nebraska, Dakota, Texas, Colorado, and Arkansas. A committee was accordingly appointed by the conference whose duty it was to select a desirable location for the school. When the citizens of such places as Des Moines, Ia., Fremont and Lincoln, Neb., and other places learned what we were about to do, they vied with one another in offers of contributions to the enterprise, so desirous were those of each place of having the buildings located in their town. As Lincoln, Neb., made the most liberal offers, and as it was deemed the most feasible site, the school was located there.

The main building, Union College proper, is a structure 141 x 84 feet. The height from the ground to the top of the dome is 100 feet. Besides this building there are two dormitories, each 104 x 104 feet, three stories high. It was anticipated that the proceeds of land donated would meet at least one half of the expense of fitting up this central college of the denomination, in which workers were to be educated in separate departments in English, Scandinavian, and German by teachers in their native tongues.

The buildings were dedicated Sept. 24, 1891, and the school opened September 30. The enrollment for the first year was 301. In 1892 the school opened with an attendance of 222, and the enrollment for the year was 553. Of these seventy-one were in the German department, and eighty-five in the Scandinavian.

A farm is connected with the college, furnishing work for students who desire to labor in agricultural lines. The college has also a bakery, where health foods are manufactured to some extent. During the year 1903 an association was organized for the purpose of publishing papers and books in the German, Swedish, and Danish-Norwegian languages. This association owns its printing house and the whole American printing business of the denomination for these nationalities. The work is carried on principally by the students. Not only are they instructed in the printing business, but here they gain an experience by actually *doing* missionary work.

The medical work is also represented in connection with this college. By economizing room it was discovered that the school could dispense with one of its large dormitories, and thus, with a little expense, a sanitarium was put in operation, and is doing an excellent work.

Walla Walla College

This school is located near Walla Walla, State of Washington, and was dedicated Dec. 8, 1892. The school opened the day before with an attendance of 101 students. This number increased during the year to 185. A small farm and other industrial interests are connected with this school. It is in a prosperous condition, and is doing a good work. Prof. J. L. Kay is now at the head of the faculty.

Australian School

August 24, 1892, a school was opened in Melbourne, Australia, in a rented building, with a faculty of five teachers. L. J. Rousseau, from the College at Battle Creek, Mich., was the first principal of the school. In the year 1894 this school had an enrollment of 89 students.

Removal to Avondale

The promoters of the school being desirous to connect labor with study, a change in locality was deemed advisable, hence a removal from the large city of Melbourne to Avondale, Cooranbong, New South Wales, a rural district, where a farm was secured, and suitable buildings erected. The school is at the present time being successfully conducted on the industrial plan.

Prediction Concerning Avondale Fulfilled

In its founding and management it was the aim of the committee to have the school conducted as nearly as possible in harmony with the instructions given respecting industrial schools. This was to be a " model school," and assurance was given time and again that if properly managed it would be a success, not only as a school, but the land itself, which had been deemed worthless, would be productive. Time, with the blessing of the Lord, has demonstrated the truthfulness of the prediction. Notwithstanding the severe drouth for several years in succession, which brought disaster to agricultural pursuits and a failure of crops all around them, the Avondale farm was green and productive. This was a remarkable occurrence, so much so that the officials of the government came to inquire as to the methods used in farming to produce this wonderful success.

The report for the workings of the school for the year 1903, shows an increase of fifty per cent. in attendance. The finances were also in good condition — expenses all met, and a balance of $1,500 in the treasury to be used in the interest of the school. Prof. C. W. Irwin has been the manager and principal of the school for nearly four years.

Mt. Vernon Academy

The General Conference, in 1893, passed a resolution favoring the opening of an academy at Mt. Vernon, Ohio. This school has some industrial interests connected with it, and is reported as doing good work. Its enrollment for 1894 was 140. Prof. J. W. Loughhead had for several years served as principal of this school, until he was called to Washington, D. C. The address of the school is Academia, Ohio.

Keene Industrial School

The General Conference of 1893 approved the opening of an industrial school at Keene, Texas. A farm of over 130 acres was secured, buildings erected, and the school opened under Prof. C. B. Hughes and his assistants. It is carried on in harmony with the plan of combining labor with study. The enrollment in 1894 was 160 students. This school has also been a decided success.

Claremont Union College

This school is located at Kenilworth, near Cape Town, South Africa. Its faculty were mostly selected from the Battle Creek College. It opened in 1894, with an enrollment

of ninety students.   At the close of the first school year, the
number of pupils had so increased that it became necessary
to provide more room by enlarging the school building.   The
college is at this date under the supervision of Prof. C. H.
Hayton.

Seventh-day Adventists also conducted a village school
(primary) at Claremont with seventy students, and a church
school at Beaconsfield, which had, in 1894, an enrollment of
thirty pupils.

Summary of Educational Work, 1895

The following report was made by the educational secretary to the General Conference in February, 1895: —

" The educational facilities of the denomination may
be summarized as follows: There are five colleges located in the following places: at Battle Creek, Mich.;
College View, Neb.; Healdsburg, Cal.; College Place, Wash.;
and Kenilworth, South Africa.   There are four academies, or schools doing the work of the academic grades in
this country, at South Lancaster, Mass.; Mt. Vernon, Ohio;
Keene, Texas; and Graysville, Tenn. . . . Besides these there
is the Australian Bible School; a school in Mexico in connection with the medical mission; school for the native children
on Pitcairn Island; on Raiatea, of the Society group; in the
South Pacific Ocean; on Bonacca of the Bay Islands in the Caribbean Sea; about fifteen church schools in this country and
abroad; two General Conference Bible schools; and quite a
number of canvassers' and local conference schools not regularly organized."

In giving a summary of the attendance at the regular
colleges and schools of the denomination the secretary says:
"At safe estimate there are over 3,000 pupils of all ages
enrolled in Seventh-day Adventist schools at the present
time."

26

Summary of Educational Institutions, 1903

The educational work and institutions among Seventh-day Adventists have grown in proportion to other branches of the message. As shown from the General Conference Year Book for 1904, there are at this date nine colleges and academies in America, and five in other countries. Those of other countries are located as follows: At Avondale, New South Wales; Kenilworth, Claremont, near Cape Town, South Africa; Holloway, London, North, England; Nyhyttan, Järnboas, Sweden; Friedensau, near Magdeburg, Germany.

There are in America, intermediate schools, fourteen; in other countries, five. The latter are located at Copenhagen, Denmark; Honolulu, Hawaiian Territory; Diamante, Entre Rios, Argentine Republic, South America; Curityba, Brazil, South America; Brusque, Brazil, South America.

In addition to the above-mentioned educational institutions, there are 357 local church schools conducted by the denomination. Of these 317 are in the United States, and forty in other countries. Had we accurate statistics to date, these figures would be largely increased. Many schools have been opened since the close of 1902. For instance, the Nebraska Conference reported having ten church schools. Feb. 1, 1904, their report shows "twenty-four church schools," an increase of fourteen in one conference.

Truly the Lord's guiding hand has wonderfully directed and opened the way for the educational work among this people. May he give wisdom to those who are called to manage this branch of his cause, that the various schools may be conducted in harmony with the plan he has outlined. Then will there be multitudes of efficient, well-developed workers for the Master, and not men and women "one-sided" in education and character. "The Lord gave the word," says the psalmist, and "great was the company [army, margin] that published it."

CHAPTER XXVI

OUR FOREIGN MISSIONS

I T is written, To whom he was not spoken of, they shall see: and they that have not heard shall understand." [1]

Our first mission to a field outside of the United States was opened in 1874, when Elder J. N. Andrews was sent to Switzerland, and there began work.

THE CENTRAL EUROPEAN FIELD

Eight nations were at that time included in this mission; namely, Switzerland, France, Italy, Turkey, Belgium, Spain, Portugal, and Greece, a territory containing 140,000,000 people.

It may be of interest to mention, at this point, the circumstances that led our people to enter upon a mission so vast in territory, at a time when the denomination was numerically weak.

Elder Czehowski

In the year 1865, Elder M. B. Czehowski, a converted Polish Catholic priest, who had accepted present truth, desired our people to send him as a missionary to Central Europe. As this was impracticable at the time, he presented his case to the First-day Adventists of Boston, Mass., who, perhaps, considered him entirely disconnected from our people. Be that as it may, they secured the means required, and sent him to his desired mission.

[1] Rom. 15: 21.

Sabbath-keepers in Switzerland

In 1866, he taught the Sabbath truth and the third angel's message in Tramelan, Switzerland, which effort resulted in bringing out a company of Sabbath-keepers. Soon after, he left them to teach the message in Hungary. He said nothing to the company in Tramelan of our work in America, but Albert Vuilleumier, one of the number, could read English. He, by chance, saw a copy of the *Advent Review.* Through this means a correspondence between the two countries was begun.

Elder Erzenberger Sent to America

In 1869 James Erzenberger, of Tramelan, was sent to America for the purpose of learning the English language and becoming more fully acquainted with the doctrines and usages of the Seventh-day Adventists. He arrived in Battle Creek June 18, and remained in America one and one-half years. He left New York, on his return trip, Sept. 9, 1870. In June of the same year, Ademar Vuilleumier visited this country, where he remained about four years. On his return to the homeland, he was accompanied by Elder Andrews. They arrived in Neuchatel Oct. 16, 1874.

In 1875, Elder D. T. Bourdeau and his family left America for France, where they were appointed, by the committee, to labor.

A French Paper Started

In the following year, in July, 1876, there was begun at Basel, Switzerland, the publication of a paper in the French language, entitled *Les Signes des Temps (The Signs of the Times)*. May 13, 1882, six years later, Elder Haskell sailed from New York City for Europe. While on this missionary tour, he spent more or less time in Switzerland.

Elder Whitney Goes to Basel — Death of Elder Andrews

July 26, 1883, Elder B. L. Whitney and his family arrived in Basel, he being appointed by the General Conference Committee to take the management of that mission, to the relief of Elder Andrews, whose health was rapidly declining. A few months later, in October of that year, he passed away.

Elder Andrews did not in early life enjoy the advantages of the higher schools and colleges, yet he was well educated, being what the world calls a self-educated or self-made man. By his application to study he mastered Latin, Greek, and Hebrew, and in later years the French language. The French language he acquired for its aid in opening and prosecuting the work in the Central European Mission, where he labored for the last six years of his life, writing for and publishing the French *Signs of the Times,* as well as preaching in that language. It was while thus laboring that he fell under the hand of death.

Dr. Kellogg in Europe

In the spring of 1883, Dr. J. H. Kellogg visited Europe in the interest of medical research. He spent a few days at each of our missions, and his visits were a source of much encouragement to the workers, especially was his advice in regard to the work at Basel greatly appreciated by Elder Andrews.

Elder Butler Visits Europe

At the General Conference held in October, 1883, it was recommended to begin, as soon as possible, the publication of a paper in England. As the result of another vote passed at this conference, Elders Geo. I. Butler, M. C. Wilcox, and A. C. Bourdeau went over to assist in the work in Europe and England. Elder Butler landed at Glasgow, Scotland, Feb. 27, 1884. One object of Elder Butler's visit to the foreign missions was to learn by personal observation the difficulties in the prosecution of the work in foreign countries, and how to overcome them. He, too, spent more or less time in Basel, and in the Central European field. A. C. Bourdeau labored among the French people in the valleys of the Alps, among the Waldenses; while M. C. Wilcox connected with the printing and editorial work in England, remaining until the close of 1886.

Publishing House Erected in Basel

In 1884, the publishing house, Imprimere Polyglotte (the name signifying, *printing in many languages*), was erected in Basel. In March, 1885, H. W. Kellogg was authorized by the General Conference Committee to visit Basel, and purchase the necessary machinery for the printing house. This he did, and thus was a well-equipped printing plant, owned by Seventh-day Adventists, established in the ancient city of Basel.

During the time of Elder Butler's visit in Europe, a German paper called the *Herold der Wahrheit* was printed at the Basel office. The same year a Roumanian journal, *Avariulu Present (Present Truth)*, was also published at this office. And still another in Italian, called *L' Ultimo Messagio (The Last Messages)*. Both of the last-named journals were sixteen-page quarterlies. At the Swiss Conference, in October, 1884, it was stated that during the year there had been printed and circulated of these four journals 146,000 copies. Up to 1895, the time the printing office (in consequence of persecution in Basel) was removed from that city to Hamburg, Germany, there were published books and tracts in eleven different languages; viz., French, German, Italian, Roumanian, Spanish, Bohemian, Russian, Dutch, Hungarian, Armenian, Turkish, and Turkish-Greek. So it was, as its name signified, an institution " printing in many languages."

Mrs. White Visits Europe

Sept. 3, 1885, Mrs. White, her son, W. C. White, and family arrived in Basel. One and one-half years were they in the old countries, visiting the missions located in the Central European field, where invaluable service was rendered to the various missions.

The Swiss Conference Organized

Sept. 10, 1885, the Swiss Conference was organized. In a report given at that time it was stated that the conference was composed of one ordained minister, seven licentiates, ten churches, and 224 members. These paid a tithe the previous year of $1,645.11. Besides this donations had been made to the work of $2,041.22.

Elder Waggoner in Europe

Mrs. White, with W. C. White and family, returned to America in 1886. The same year Elder J. H. Waggoner was invited to connect with the Central European Mission. He spent over two years in this field, making his home, during this time, at Basel. It was in this city that his death occurred, April 20, 1889, as previously stated.

The failing health of Elder Whitney, and his subsequent death (April 9, 1889), was another grievous stroke to this mission.

Elder Robinson in Europe

Elder D. A. Robinson, who was laboring in England, was chosen as the successor of Elder Whitney. He labored efficiently in this district for about six years, when, by invitation of the General Conference, he left for India in the year 1895. His removal necessitated the appointment of another superintendent.

Elder Holser Superintendent of the Field

Elder H. P. Holser was the man selected for the position, and in addition to this office he was chosen as the manager of the whole Central European Mission. Here he labored untiringly and efficiently until 1901, when he, too, was obliged to succumb to the ravages of disease. He died in Canyon City, Colorado, Sept. 11, 1901.

Notwithstanding these adverse circumstances, the mission grew and the work advanced, as shown by a report made to the General Conference in 1895, which states that the Central European Conference is composed of nineteen churches with 484 members, who paid a tithe the previous year of $4,378.18. They had at that date four ordained ministers and five licentiates.

THE GERMAN-RUSSIAN MISSION

In 1870, J. H. Linderman, pastor of a church near Elberfeld, Prussia, and forty of its members, began the observance of the seventh-day Sabbath from the study of the Bible, not knowing of another company of Christians in the world who were keeping that day as the Sabbath. A knowledge of this company was conveyed to our people in a peculiar manner. A beggar called at the mission home in Basel on the Sabbath. The family were studying the Sabbath-school lesson with Bibles open before them. The scene impressed the man, and led him to ask questions.

The Elberfeld Company

On learning that they were not Jews, but Christians, observing the seventh-day Sabbath, he spoke of this company at Elberfeld. Elder Andrews thought it wise to investigate the statement; therefore, in company with Elder Erzenberger, he went to Prussia in the early part of 1875, where they found the company as represented. Elder Erzenberger remained for some time laboring in that part of Germany, and on Jan. 8, 1876, eight persons were baptized at Elberfeld, being the first baptism by Seventh-day Adventists in Germany.

The truth had gained a foothold in Russia as early as 1882, through reading matter sent by German brethren in America to their friends in the German colonies of Russia.

Elder Conradi in Europe

In 1885 Elder L. R. Conradi left America for the Central European field, to labor among the Germans. On June 28, 1886, he left Basel for the Crimea, Russia. Here, in company with Elder Perk, he journeyed to Berdebulat, where two sisters were baptized and a church of nineteen members was organized, this being the first Seventh-day Adventist church in Russia.

Elders Conradi and Perk Imprisoned

Immediately after this Elders Conradi and Perk were arrested for teaching contrary to the orthodox faith, and were imprisoned for five weeks in Perekop. After his release (by the intervention of the United States minister) Elder Conradi visited Eastern Russia, and then returned to Switzerland.

Work on the Volga, Russia

It was during this same year that Elder Laubhan began to labor in Russia, near his home, located on the River Volga. In the year 1880, Elder Klein, of Kansas, entered upon work in German Russia, and thus have laborers been raised up for this hard and difficult field, and though the believers have been subjected to banishment and imprisonment, the Lord has remarkably blessed the work.

Success of Canvassers in Germany

In the year 1880, colporteurs began work in Rheinish-Prussia, Würtemberg, Baden, and Alsace. So successful were the eight or ten energetic, faithful workers that in one year the following number of books were sold: "Life of Christ," 3,000; "From Eden to Eden," 2,000; and 12,000 pamphlets. As a result of this labor, in nearly every place the books were sold and read, some, one or more, embraced the truth.

Mission Opened in Hamburg

In May, 1889, the mission work was opened up in Hamburg, Germany, by Elder Conradi, and in a very short time a training-school for workers was instituted The following October a Sabbath-school of twenty-eight members was organized. It was during this year that Elder Haskell visited the mission and a church of twenty members was organized, and a book depository established.

Elder J. T. Boettcher was at this time engaged in the German work at Barmen. A report was given, in 1890, to the General Conference, stating that in the German-Russian mission there were nine organized churches, with an aggregate membership of 422, besides seventy-five Sabbath-keepers not yet organized. On April 7, the same year, twelve more were baptized, and united with the Hamburg church. In December the membership of this church had increased to forty. The amount received on book sales from the depository in Hamburg, Holland, Russia, and various parts of Germany, was $5,000.

Success in Europe

Slowly but surely the work advanced in the Central European Mission, as indicated in a report given at the General Conference in 1891. There were at that time five churches in Germany, with a membership of one hundred and forty, sixty-four of whom were members of the Hamburg church. The tithe paid was $1,000. The books sold on the ships, by the ship missionary in Hamburg, amounted to $500, while the sales of the canvassers for the year, in the entire field, were $6,000.   One hundred and fifty had accepteu the truth in Austria, and there were thirteen churches, with a membership of four hundred in Russia.

Five Russian Sabbath-keepers Banished

About this time (1891), five of the members of a Russian church, including the leader, had been arrested for teaching doctrines contrary to the established church, and condemned to five years' banishment to the Trans-Caucasus.   They were to be chained together, and were required to walk five hundred miles.   In this trial their faith sustained them, and they were happy in the Lord.   During the year a pamphlet had been prepared in the form of Bible readings in the Russian language, on the sufferings of Christ, sleep of the dead, which day and why, and can we know?

At the time of the General Conference in 1895, the membership in Germany had increased to 368, and the tithe the previous year was $2,327.43.

More Sabbath-keepers in Russia

In Russia, notwithstanding very many had emigrated to other countries, the membership had increased to 467, who paid a tithe of $841.60.

From the statement made by the foreign mission secretary in the week of prayer reading for 1896, we learn that " in the German-Russian field during the previous year their numerical strength had been nearly doubled; their number being augmented by an addition of over four hundred. In Berlin, Germany, sixty were attending the regular Sabbath services.   The erection of the mission chapel in Hamburg had strengthened the work there.   In Munich, in Bavaria, a number were awaiting baptism.   There were believers in Leipsic, Konigsberg, Magdeberg, Posen, Stüttgart, and other leading towns in Germany.   There were also a company in Rotterdam, Holland.

"In Russia, colporteurs had obtained permits from the government. Translations of literature had been made in the Lettish and Esthonian languages. The German paper had been moved from Basel to Hamburg, and at that office they were printing the truth in fourteen languages."

Baptism in Hungary

During the year the first baptism had occurred in Hungary, and the first ordinance meeting in Bohemia. A ship mission had been established at Galatz, in Roumania, for the Danube and the Black Sea.

Canvassing in Germany

In the *Home Missionary* for December, 1895, Elder Spies said of the canvassing work in the German field, " Those in charge of the canvassing work, when it was begun in this field, did not cease to *push* it, although assured by some of the leading publishers and book men in Leipsic that ' selling books by subscription would prove a failure.'

"In August of 1887 the first edition of ' Life of Christ ' was gotten out in the German language. About the time the book named was ready for circulation, a canvassers' institute was held in Basel; this marked the beginning of the canvassing work, not only in Germany, but in all Europe. The seventh edition of this book has now come from the press in the German language.

"Since Jan. 1, 1895, twelve new canvassers have entered the field. In June, 1895, the report showed fifty per cent. increase in sales. At present a special effort is being made with *Harold der Wahrheit,* our German paper. Some, not very large churches, take from fifty to two hundred copies, which they sell. And they have very pleasant experiences with the purchasers. In the *Review* of Feb. 18, 1896, Elder Conradi said, ' We close 1895 with fifteen hundred Sabbath-keepers in the German-Russian field.' "

THE SCANDINAVIAN MISSION

The mission to the Scandinavian people was opened by Elder John Matteson in the year 1887. On the 6th day of June he arrived in Vejle, in Jyeland, Denmark. When he went to that country there were a few who had begun the observance of the Sabbath through the reading of papers and tracts sent to them by friends in America.

In tracing the rise of this work, we learn that in 1850, four persons who had moved to America from Norway, began to keep the Sabbath of the Lord. They resided in Oakland, Wisconsin. Two of this number were the father and mother of Elder O. A. Olsen. In 1863 Elder John Matteson began the observance of the seventh-day Sabbath. He lived in Poysippi, Wisconsin. In the next six months, through his labors, about forty Danish-Norwegians embraced the doctrines of Seventh-day Adventists. The first active preacher who united with him in the ministry was Elder J. F. Hanson of Minnesota.

The First Book Published in Danish-Norwegian

In the year 1866, Elder John Matteson applied to the managers of the Review and Herald office to ascertain if they would print, for the use of the Scandinavians, pamphlets and tracts in their language. He was informed that a lack of funds at the office forbade their doing so; but there were persons of his nationality in Wisconsin and Minnesota who were so anxious to have the truth printed in their mother tongue that, although they were in moderate circumstances, and numbered less than fifty, they raised $1,000 in cash, and placed it in his hands for that purpose. With this money and a quantity of neatly prepared manuscript, Elder Matteson came to Battle Creek, and again made application for printed books. As he was prepared to meet the objections previously made, his desires were granted, and March 18, 1867, he began the reading of his manuscript, prepared for his book, "Liv og Dog," (Life and Death) to Elder J. N. Andrews and myself, who were then members of the committee on publication. In other words, he told us in English what his manuscript said in Danish-Norwegian.

Elder Matteson Becomes a Printer

At that time there was no printer who could be spared to set the type for him, and so he begged the privilege of learning to set it himself. He continued at this work until he had about one thousand pages of pamphlets and tracts printed in his own language.

With this new means for disseminating the truth among his people, he went forth with renewed courage, holding meetings in various States. From that date the work advanced quite rapidly among the Scandinavians.

The First Foreign Periodical

The work among the Danish-Norwegians had assumed such proportions that a demand was made for a monthly paper in which persons of that nationality could receive instruction and encouragement in their own language. Therefore, on Jan. 1, 1872, there was issued at the Review and Herald office, a Danish monthly, a twenty-four page journal in magazine form, bearing the name, *Advent Tidende* (Advent Tidings). The following year the size of this journal was increased to thirty-two pages. It was the first periodical issued by Seventh-day Adventists in a foreign language.

In 1874 the interest was such among the Swedish-speaking believers that a sixteen-page monthly was started in that language, called *Svensk Herold*.

At the time Elder Matteson entered upon the mission to the Scandinavian people (June, 1877) in the old country, 266 copies of the *Tidende* were being sent from America monthly to Denmark, and 60 to Norway. Through reading these journals a number of persons were already keeping the Sabbath in Scandinavia. As a result of his labors for one year in Denmark, companies of believers were raised up in several different places.

A Printing Office in Norway

After this Elder Matteson went to Norway, where, June 7, 1879, he organized a church of thirty-eight members, as the result of his labors in Christiana. Elder J. P. Jasperson, from America, joined him in the ministry about this time. In that year also a publishing association was formed in Norway, and property purchased in Christiana for a printing office, meeting-room for church services, and living rooms, at a cost of $14,580. For a time a small edition of a paper, *Tidernes Tegn,* was issued weekly from the Christiana office.

In the early autumn of 1880, Elder Matteson came to America to obtain help to enlarge the Scandinavian work. He attended the General Conference of that year, and returned to Europe in April, 1881, greatly encouraged. Soon after his return, a cylinder press was purchased and placed in the Christiana office.

Health Journals in Danish and Swedish

They at once began the publication of a health journal in Danish, called *Sundheds Bladet.* In 1883 he issued a similar journal in Swedish, and a religious journal, called *Sanningens Härold.* In 1884 they possessed an office outfit valued at $2,563. During this year there had been printed and circulated 115,000 papers in all, besides many thousands of tracts, and some books.

Elder Haskell in Scandinavia

The work in the Scandinavian countries received much help from the visit of Elder Haskell in 1882, and in 1884 they were materially aided by the labors of Elders Geo. I. Butler, B. L. Whitney, A. B. Oyen, and E. G. Olsen.

Mrs. White Greatly Aids Scandinavia

In 1885, Mrs. E. G. White, and her son, W. C. White, made a visit to Scandinavia, which was of inestimable value to the work in that field. Some had gotten the idea that tithes could not be paid by the poor in that country, and that it was useless to try to canvass for books. The testimony borne by Mrs. White was timely, and well received by the people, as was evinced by the response given in these words, "All that the Lord hath said will we do, and be obedient." During this visit an entire change was effected in the Scandinavian field, produced principally by the untiring labors of Mrs. White.

New Office Building Erected in Norway

In 1886 Elders O. A. Olsen and N. Clausen visited the Scandinavian countries, the latter remaining there quite a length of time. In 1885 a new office building was erected in Christiana, and for the year ending Sept. 1, 1886, the office realized from the sale of books and tracts alone, the sum of $5,386.68, while the amount received on subscriptions to periodicals was $3,146.03.

Twenty-Five Churches in Scandinavia

A report given to the General Conference in 1889 stated that in the Scandinavian field there were twenty-five churches, with 926 members, who paid a tithe of $2,548.75; it also had six ministers, four licentiates, and fifty-two canvassers. The book sales for Norway and Sweden in one quarter were $2,161.26.

School in Christiana

A school at this time was in operation at Christiana, with fifty students. In 1891 a Bible institute was conducted at Christiana, by Elders O. A. Olsen and E. J. Waggoner, with one hundred pupils in attendance. At this institute thorough instruction in the canvassing work was given.

Forty Churches in Scandinavia in 1895

Six years later, 1895, we notice a report given by Elder D. A. Robinson, then the district superintendent of the foreign field, which shows so clearly a marked growth in the work during this period of that time that we quote as follows: " Scandinavia has forty churches, and 1,458 members. The year's tithe was $5,585.55. There are fifteen ordained ministers, eleven licentiates, and the book sales for the year amount to $40,000. This large amount is principally due to the efforts of the canvassers, and that, too, in a country where, in 1885, booksellers, and even ministers of our faith, affirmed that selling books by canvassing could not be done.

Three Scandinavian Conferences

In the Scandinavian field there are at the present time three conferences, the dates of organization being as follows: Denmark, May 30, 1880; Sweden, March 12, 1882; Norway, June 10, 1887. Elder John Matteson, who first opened the Scandinavian Mission and pioneered the work so successfully, and who labored so earnestly and sacrificingly for the prosperity of that people, was stricken with that fatal disease, consumption, and died in El Monte, Cal., March 30, 1896, aged sixty-one years.

THE BRITISH MISSION

William Ings, a native of Hampshire, England, but an American in spirit and education, having lived in the United States from boyhood, reached Southampton, from Basel, Switzerland, May 23, 1878. At this time his stay was brief, being only two weeks, when he returned to the Continent for a short time. Soon afterward, however, he again went to Southampton, where, after four months of house-to-house labor

27

distributing tracts and doing such missionary work as presented itself, he reported ten keeping the Sabbath. December 30 of that year, myself and my wife arrived at Southampton, where our labors were united with those of Elder Ings, in holding meetings during the winter in Shirley Hall, and in our own hired house. In the summer of 1879, we held tent-meetings at Southampton. At this time and place Miss Maud Sisley (now Mrs. Boyd) connected with the work, giving Bible readings and doing house-to-house labor. As a result of this effort, several embraced the truth. In the following winter we held meetings in a hall in Ravenswood Villa, the building in which we lived and had our depository.

Tent-Meeting in England

In the summer of 1880, Elder Andrews, though feeble in health, came from Switzerland to assist in a tent-meeting at Romsey, where other persons embraced the message.

Jan. 11, 1880, a tract society was organized. In this work the members were much interested, and much literature was distributed.

Feb. 8, 1880, our first baptism occurred and was administered to six candidates. Up to July 2, 1881, twenty-nine candidates had been immersed at Southampton.

Laborers Increased in England

By vote of the General Conference held in the autumn of 1881, Elder A. A. John and his wife, Geo. R. Drew, and Miss Jennie Thayer went to England, and connected with the work in that mission field. During the year 1882, Elder Haskell visited the European field, and spent a number of days with the workers in the English mission, rendering valuable help by way of counsel and advice.

In March, 1882, a two-page British supplement to the *Signs of the Times* began to be printed, and was attached to one thousand copies of the *Signs* which were sent from

America. These were used in the missionary work in Great Britain. A report of the work, Oct. 1, 1883, shows that there were at that date one hundred Sabbath-keepers. The tithes paid from the opening of the mission, were $2,078.71.

Ship Missionary Work

Through the courtesy of the ship keepers, Elder Ings was permitted to send packages of tracts and papers *free* to eighty of the principal ports of the "Peninsular and Oriental Steam Ship Company," in South Africa, East and West Indies, Central America, and the Bay Islands. It was through the influence of the reading matter thus sent, that the interest was first awakened in the island of Demarara. This information we received through letters from the island.

"History of the Sabbath" Placed in English Libraries

A copy of Elder Andrews's "History of the Sabbath" had also been placed in sixty of the public libraries and free reading-rooms throughout Great Britain, and there the books are still, telling the story to those willing to read.

In 1884 Elder Butler visited England, accompanied by other laborers for this field. Elders S. H. Lane and Robert Andrews sailed from Boston to join the mission in Great Britain May 9, 1885. The visit of Mrs. White to England was a source of strength and encouragement to the workers. Mrs. White and her son spent a few weeks there before their return to America from the European field.

"Present Truth" Started

In the early part of 1884, soon after Elder Butler's arrival in England, it was decided to begin at Grimsby, with M. C. Wilcox as editor, an eight-page semi-monthly paper, called the *Present Truth*. The same is now being published as a sixteen-page weekly at London, England, with a weekly issue of some 18,000 copies.

In 1889, Elder Holser reported the British Mission as consisting of eight churches, with two hundred Sabbath-keepers, of whom sixty-five were in London. The tithe for the previous year was $1,244.58. There were two ordained ministers, two licentiates, two ship missionaries, and seven Bible workers. It was about this time that Elders Wm. Hutchinson and Francis Hope entered the English mission.

The Pacific Press in London

During the year 1890 the Pacific Press Publishing Company, of Oakland, California, established a branch office at 48 Paternoster Row, London, and a printing office at 451 Holloway Road, London, N. The book sales from the office for the first year, at wholesale prices, were $9,556.89.

In February, 1895, Elder Robinson rendered the following report: " In Great Britain there are eleven churches, 363 members, five ministers, and one licentiate. The tithe for the past year was $5,077.20, or an average of $13.98 per member. The property of the publishing office is now owned and managed by the International Tract Society, Limited, an English corporation."

In December, 1895, the Foreign Mission Secretary reported for Great Britain a membership of 560. The tithes had increased during the year $1,000. At that date, eight companies were meeting on the Sabbath at different places in London.

Thus the work in this mission field advanced, at times almost imperceptibly. Seeds do not spring up in some kinds of soil as quickly as in others. Their germination is slower, but their growth is surer and hardier. So with the truth of the third message in this kingdom. Its seed has been sown, taken root, and grown slowly till now it has reached comparatively large proportions.

THE AUSTRALASIAN MISSION

May 10, 1885, Elders S. N. Haskell, J. O. Corliss and his family, M. C. Israel and his family, Wm. E. Arnold, and Henry Scott sailed from San Francisco to open a mission in the Australian field. Eleven years before this time, in 1874, at a meeting held in Battle Creek, Mrs. White said that many nations would yet receive the truth, and that she had seen printing presses running, and books and papers being printed in various countries. When asked to specify what countries were referred to, the reply was that Australia was the only name she could remember.

"The Bible Echo"

Under the earnest and successful labors of Elder Haskell and company, the message was so rapidly advanced that the printing of a paper in Australia was deemed necessary. Accordingly, arrangements were made for publishing, and on Jan. 1, 1886, a sixteen-page monthly was issued at Melbourne, called the *Bible Echo and Signs of the Times.* Of the first number an edition of six thousand was printed, while the regular issue was only three thousand.

First Church Organized in Australia

Sunday, April 10, 1886, the first Seventh-day Adventist church in Australia was organized. There were eighteen present who had signed the covenant, and seven others applied for admission by baptism. These were baptized the following Sabbath, and each Sabbath for a number of weeks members were added, until the church numbered fifty-five. Up to May, 1886, the entire number enrolled was ninety. Besides these, there were about thirty-five in other places who were keeping the Sabbath.

In the printing office were two good presses and an engine, all paid for and owned by Seventh-day Adventists in that far-distant land — about seven thousand miles from our large office located in Oakland, Cal.

During 1886 the message extended to New Zealand. A report from the Australian field states that there were fifty Sabbath-keepers in New Zealand. The amount received from book sales at the office was $700. Besides this the canvassers had sold four hundred copies of " Great Controversy " in New Zealand, and one thousand copies of " Thoughts on Daniel " in Australia.

Australian Office Building

From a report rendered July 19, 1889, we glean the following facts: A building for a printing office in Melbourne has been completed, containing a chapel for church services.

Tasmania Entered

A conference has been organized both in Australia and in New Zealand, and the work extended, by Elders Israel and Steed, to Tasmania. In the latter place three churches have already been organized, with an aggregate membership of one hundred and thirty-six. Besides these there are other scattered Sabbath-keepers not yet organized.

The tithes for the year in the Australian field were $9,371. There were fifteen canvassers in the field, whose book sales amounted to $19,500.

In Elder Haskell's second trip around the world, he again visited Australia, attended their conference held in August, 1889, and in many ways rendered efficient aid, which was much appreciated by that newly organized company. Different workers from America have from time to time visited Australia in the interest of the one great cause — the upbuilding and strengthening of the work of God.

Mrs. White in Australia

In the fall of 1891, Mrs. E. G. White, her son, W. C. White, Elder Geo. B. Starr, and others left California for

Australia, arriving there in December — mid-summer in that continent. The testimony of Mrs. White, notwithstanding the bodily infirmity under which she labored during the nine years of her sojourn in that land, aided greatly in placing the work in a proper relation to the spirit and tenor of the third angel's message. During the time they were in Australia Elder J. O. Corliss again connected with the work here, and W. A. Colcord and others entered the field as ministers, teachers, etc.

Elder Olsen in Australia

During Elder O. A. Olsen's administration as president of the General Conference, he visited all of our leading institutions throughout the length and breadth of the land. This required extensive travel — a trip around the world. This he took the better to acquaint himself with their needs and the condition of the various missions, that thus he might be prepared to serve them impartially. It was on this journey, in 1893, that he spent several weeks in Australia.

Australasian Union Conference

During this time the Australasian Union Conference was organized, being composed of the Australian and New Zealand conferences and the Australian mission fields. This conference meets once in two years, and is conducted on the plan of the union conferences in other countries. During the year 1893 the few canvassers who were in this field sold an edition of 5,000 " Steps to Christ," and a second edition of the same number was printed. In the summer of 1894 - 95, they took 4,000 orders for subscription books in four months.

Elder Prescott in Australia

In 1895 Elder W. W. Prescott, the Educational Secretary of the denomination, spent a number of months in this conference, devoting much time and thought to this branch of the work. In the mean time he conducted an educational institute which was to them of great benefit.

The report made to the General Conference of the work for the year was rendered by Elder W. C. White and is as follows: " The Australian Union Conference is composed of seventeen churches with 1074 members, who paid a tithe the previous year of $9,810.10. This conference has twelve ordained ministers, two licentiates, three Bible workers, and fifty canvassers, who sold during the year $28,731.11 worth of books. During the year the colony of New South Wales, with six churches, and 321 members, was separated from the Australian Conference, and named the New South Wales Conference."

SOUTH AFRICAN MISSION

At the General Conference held in Battle Creek in 1886, the question was considered of opening a mission in South Africa. As action was taken favoring the undertaking, with the opening summer of 1887 an effort was made to establish the work in that distant land, where a few, who had already begun to observe the Sabbath, were calling for laborers.

Elders Boyd and Robinson in South Africa

For this purpose, on May 11, Elder C. L. Boyd and his family, Elder D. A. Robinson and his wife, with other workers, sailed from New York City, *en route* to Africa, by way of Liverpool and London. Three years later, at the General Conference, Mr. P. W. B. Wessels stated that when these laborers arrived in Africa there were about forty persons who were already observing the Sabbath of the fourth commandment as the result of reading publications on the subject and from the study of the Scriptures.

Elders Robinson and Boyd began the mission work in Cape Town, and from there it extended northeast nearly eight hundred miles to Kimberley, in the diamond fields.

Up to the year 1889, there were only two ministers, one licentiate, four churches, and eighty members; these paid a tithe of $2,798.36. During this year Elder Ira J. Hankins, of America, labored in Cape Town with good results, and Mr. and Mrs. Druillard came from Nebraska to connect with the work at this place, and share in the labors and privations that fall upon those called to pioneer the work in a new field. Mrs. Druillard's labors were confined principally to the book depository, where the business of this department was left to her management; while Mr. Druillard was occupied in the general missionary cause. During the year, on ships calling at this port, he sold books amounting to $750.

Elder Haskell in Africa

It was in August of this same year that Elder Haskell arrived in Cape Town. Five months were well spent in visiting and laboring with the different companies in South Africa. By this visit the cause was strengthened and built up, and his own heart encouraged in that he saw fruit of his labor. An interest in the educational work was aroused, insomuch that twelve students from Africa came to America to attend our denominational schools.

In the meantime the canvassing work received due consideration. An institute in the interest of this work was held in Cape Town, conducted by Mr. E. M. Morrison, which gave new life and energy to this important branch of the message. Immediately following the instruction given at this institute, thirteen canvassers, in six months, sold and delivered books to the amount of $5,621.28. In fact, so numerous were the orders that they completely " swamped " the London office, as books could not be prepared fast enough to meet the demand.

In the year 1892, Elder A. T. Robinson connected with the work in South Africa. At that time the work had grown to that extent that a new depository was required to take the place of the old. Hence a new building was erected sufficiently large to furnish room for meetings of the church.

College Building in Africa

Thus the work has continued to advance step by step, until at Claremont, a suburb of Cape Town, a college building was erected costing $35,000. The only help desired of the American brethren was to send a force of teachers qualified to teach a college course, and they themselves would meet the expense. This request being complied with, the school opened Feb. 1, 1893.

The South African Conference

The South African Conference was organized in 1892. At the General Conference in 1893 it was voted into the General Conference. It then had five churches, one hundred and thirty-eight members, who paid a tithe the previous year of $34,077.32. At this conference the South African Conference was represented by Peter Wessels, who generously donated to the General Conference $16,000, this being more than the General Conference had expended in opening up the work in South Africa. In addition to this gift, he and one of his brothers donated $40,000 to begin the free dispensary work in the city of Chicago.

At the General Conference in 1895 the Foreign Mission Secretary said of the African field: " The conference in South Africa has been organized but two years, but in that time the General Conference has sent into that field twelve workers. Two of these have gone into the interior as self-supporting missionaries, while the others have entered the work in various departments. That conference has a flourishing school, an orphans' home, and a sanitarium in process of erection. The statistics show their membership as 184.

Papers Published in South Africa

The subject of religious liberty in South Africa has aroused our people in the last few months to publish two papers, one in the Holland language, called *De Wachter;* the other in English, called *The South African Sentinel and Gospel Echo*. The latter has a circulation of 4,000.

South African Union Conference

In January, 1903, the South African Union Conference was organized, consisting of the Cape Colony and Natal-Transvaal conferences, and Basutoland and Matabeleland missions under the control of the Union Conference. In the conference there are fifteen organized churches with 595 members, nine unorganized companies of ninety members, and thirty isolated Sabbath-keepers, — a total of 715, who paid a tithe of $7,850. There were thirty-nine laborers, of whom twenty-one were on the pay-roll of the various conferences.

THE POLYNESIAN FIELD

In the year 1876, Elder James White and the writer sent a volume of the *Signs of the Times* and some tracts, accompanied by a letter, to Pitcairn Island. These documents were placed on a ship going around Cape Horn to New York. We were assured that the ship would stop at Pitcairn, and there the parcel would. be delivered. We knew not a person on the island, and knew nothing of the island itself, save its reputation as having for its inhabitants a devoted, godly people. The papers were sent at a venture.

Visit to Pitcairn

We heard nothing from the people or our literature until Mr. John I. Tay made his visit to the island, in the year 1886, ten years later, when we learned that as the result of reading the volume of the *Signs* and the tracts, the whole island, at one time, almost decided to change their day of worship from the first day of the week to the seventh day, and keep the Lord's Sabbath. This they did not do, however, until the time of Mr. Tay's visit. He had been for a long time deeply impressed to visit the island, but knew nothing of the people personally, nor of their interest already kindled in the truth.

After his return to America, he plead most earnestly for a ship to be constructed with which missionaries could be transported from island to island in the Pacific Ocean. He attended the General Conference held in the year 1889, with this thought uppermost in mind, and there he plead the cause of the Polynesian Islands. The conference, seeing the utility of the undertaking, voted to raise, by donations, the sum of $12,000 with which to build or buy a ship to work among the islands of the Pacific Ocean.

The " Pitcairn " Built

In harmony with this action the ship *Pitcairn* was built, in the summer of 1890, near Benicia, about thirty miles from Oakland, Cal., at a cost of $12,035.22. In three fourths of a year this sum of money was raised, and donated by the Sabbath-schools for this purpose alone, and never was a gift more cheerfully and enthusiastically made. The ship was dedicated at Oakland, Cal., Sept. 25, 1890. About fifteen hundred people assembled on the ship and wharf to witness the ceremony.

The " Pitcairn's " First Cruise

The vessel sailed on its first cruise from San Francisco for its distant field of labor, October 20. On board as missionaries were Elder E. H. Gates and his wife, Elder A. J. Read and his wife, John I. Tay and his wife, with a missionary crew under Captain Marsh. This vessel went first to Pitcairn Island, four thousand miles south of San Francisco, where it arrived November 25. When the ship left the island, December 17, eighty-two adults had received baptism, and had been organized into a Seventh-day Adventist church. The vessel then made its way to the Society, Hervey, Samoan, Friendly, and Fiji groups, leaving religious books and health and temperance tracts with the English-speaking people. During eight months, to September, 1891, the missionaries sold books to the amount of $1,900 besides distributing a large amount of reading matter *free.*

The missionaries were stationed as follows: Elder Read at Tahiti; Elder Gates remained at Pitcairn to finish the work already begun there; while Mr. Tay chose to labor on the island of Fiji. In the *Review* of April 14, 1904, Elder Fulton says of the work in Fiji: " There are now more than one hundred and fifty Sabbath-keepers in this mission field." From Fiji, the vessel sailed to Aukland, New Zealand, for necessary repairs and needed improvements, and also for a supply of books.

Death of Missionaries

After an absence of one year, eleven months, and eighteen days, the *Pitcairn* returned to San Francisco, where it arrived Oct. 9, 1892. During this time Captain Marsh had passed away, and been buried in the island of New Zealand. Mr. Tay was stricken with pneumonia, from which he never recovered. He, too, passed peacefully away, and was laid to rest in the distant land of Fiji; and thus were two precious lives given so soon to the Polynesian Mission.

The missionaries located on the island of Tahiti, at Papaete, were led to rejoice in seeing, almost immediately, fruits of their labor. They were enabled to send to the homeland, at this date, the cheering report of forty persons converted and organized into a Seventh-day Adventist church.

The " Pitcairn's " Second Trip

The vessel set sail from San Francisco on its second voyage, Jan. 17, 1893, with the following missionaries: B. J. Cady and his wife, J. M. Cole and his wife, E. C. Chapman and his wife, and M. G. Kellogg, M. D. Miss Hattie Andre, of Ohio, accompanied them as teacher for Pitcairn Island. In the fall of 1893, Mr. Cady opened a school at Raiatea, of the Society group, with sixty scholars. At the close of the first term the number had increased to one hundred and five. **At** the opening of the second term there were one hundred **and** twenty pupils in attendance.

The "Pitcairn's" Third Trip

The third cruise of the ship was taken in 1893 - 94. The missionaries for this voyage were G. O. Wellman and his wife and Lillian White, all of Michigan, who were booked for Raiatea, where they were to assist Elder Cady in his work. Mr. Stringer and his wife went as self-supporting missionaries. They stopped at Rurutu. At Raratonga (where the people kept Saturday for Sunday), Dr. Caldwell and his wife were stationed; while Elder Buckner and his wife, of California, were left at Pitcairn. During his sojourn with this people, many new industries were introduced, which have in many ways proved beneficial to the inhabitants. First of all, a windmill for grinding the corn which is now raised on the island was built, and from the same wind-power, light machinery is carried, which has led to other industries heretofore unknown to the islanders.

The "Pitcairn's" Fourth Trip

December 15, 1895, the Foreign Mission Secretary said: —

" The *Pitcairn* is now in port from its fourth cruise. . . . The work has been planted in nine different groups, and the following laborers are employed in the same: —

" In Pitcairn Island, *teachers,* E. S. Butz and wife, and Hattie Andre. Norfolk Island, some self-supporting missionaries are engaged in the work here, who came from Australia. Society Islands, *minister,* B. J. Cady; *medical missionaries,* Mr. and Mrs. R. A. Prickett. Raratonga, *medical missionaries,* Dr. J. E. Caldwell and wife, Misses Lillian White and Maude Young; *teachers,* G. O. Wellman and wife, Elder J. D. Rice and wife. Fiji, Elder J. M. Cole and wife. Friendly Islands, Elder E. Hilliard and wife. Rurutu, Mr. and Mrs. Stringer, self-supporting missionaries. Hawaii,

Elder E. H. Gates and wife; *teachers,* H. H. Brand and wife. Samoa, Dr. F. E. Braucht and wife. Elder D. A. Owen and son and daughter, self-supporting missionaries.

" The *Pitcairn* has sold and given away large quantities of literature during its four voyages. In consequence, Sabbath-keepers have sprung up in many places. Churches have been organized at Pitcairn Island, Norfolk, and Tahiti."

The "Pitcairn" Sold

As there are now facilities for reaching the Polynesian field which did not exist when the ship was constructed, the vessel has been sold, and other means employed for carrying on the work. Elder E. H. Gates is now superintendent of the Polynesian field, and reports progress in the various groups.

THE WEST INDIES

In the winter of 1889, Mr. Wm. Arnold, of America, began colporteur work in the West Indies. While thus engaged he was successful in obtaining the names and addresses of twelve hundred persons, which were sent to the International Tract Society for its use in missionary work. By correspondence and the sending of reading matter to these addresses, an interest was awakened in the truth, and thus was the way opened for the promulgation of the gospel through the preaching of the Word.

In response to the call made for ministerial labor, Elder D. A. Ball, in November, 1890, went to the Barbadoes and to other points, to labor. Several persons accepted the truth as the result of his efforts. In 1892, Mr. Patterson, from California, canvassed the islands for " Bible Readings " with good success. In 1893, B. B. Newman went from Florida to Jamaica to take the superintendency of the canvassing work during the absence of Mr. Arnold. Mr. Evans and Mr. Hackett also went to the Indies the same year, to engage in this branch of the work. In the month of May, Elder Haysmer and his wife entered this field to labor as the way might open.   Soon after this Mr. Arnold returned, this time to canvass for books treating upon the subject of health.   Up to July, 1895, books of this character had been sold in Jamaica alone to the amount of $8,200, while the sale of religious books amounted to $7,654, or a total of $15,854.   The distribution of so large an amount of literature aided much in establishing at Kingston a well-organized church of seventy-five members, and opening avenues for ministerial labor in other parts of the island.

Trinidad

The work here was introduced in a manner similar to that of Jamaica.   In the year 1889, Mr. F. B. Grant and his wife were invited to visit the island for the purpose of introducing our denominational literature, and by invitation Elder Flowers and his wife soon followed them to labor as the way opened. They met with good success, until Elder Flowers was stricken with fever, which caused his death, June 29, 1894.   Elder E. W. Webster was chosen as his successor, and he sailed from New York in August, 1895.

In 1896 the laborers in the West Indies were as follows: In Jamaica, Elder A. J. Haysmer and W. W. Eastman, and a number of canvassers were in the Bahama Islands.   In the Lesser Antilles, where Elder E. Van Deusen and his wife, with C. F. Parmlee and his wife as Bible workers, Mr. Bean and Mr. Hackett as canvassers.   In Trinidad, Elder E. W. Webster and his wife, with Miss Stella Colvin as medical missionary.   The results,— one hundred and ten Sabbath-keepers in Jamaica, and fifty Sabbath-keepers in Trinidad, centered around Couva ; one church in Barbadoes, and one company in Antigua, Lesser Antilles.

CENTRAL AMERICA

Elder F. J. Hutchins and his wife left the United States for the Bay Islands, Nov. 16, 1891.   At this time there were, principally in Ruatan, about twenty persons who were observing the Sabbath of the fourth commandment according to the decalogue, their attention being first called to this truth by reading matter sent them by post. Three years later, in 1894, W. A. Miller and his wife left California for Bonaca, where they connected with the educational work as teachers in a school which was opened July 4, 1894, in a school-building erected by Seventh-day Adventists. The attendance during the first term was an average of thirty-four. In 1895 the school was pronounced self-sustaining, as the number of pupils had increased to forty-five.

At the General Conference held in 1895, Elder Hutchins reported one hundred persons on the islands who were obeying the message, and he also stated that there had been two meeting-houses erected and were owned by Seventh-day Adventists. On account of a scarcity of land, and therefore very valuable for cultivation, one of these houses of worship was built over the water. These two buildings and the schoolhouse were deeded to the General Conference Association. The value of the Conference property on the island was estimated to be $1,789.60. The amount of books sold up to 1895 was $2,243.

Small Ship for Central America

The attention of the Conference being directed to the convenience and advantages of having a small ship by which missionaries could be conveyed from one island to another, it was voted that such a boat be constructed for the work among the Bay Islands at a cost not to exceed $3,000.

In 1896, there were only four laborers in Central America: Elder F. J. Hutchins and his wife, and Elder J. A. Morrow and his wife in Spanish Honduras. At Belize, the capital of British Honduras, was a company of believers who were keeping the seventh day according to the fourth commandment The greater part of the labor in this field has been performed

28

in the islands of the Caribbean Sea. Here several thousand dollars' worth of books had been sold, and sixty persons were rejoicing in the truth of the third angel's message.

Elder Hutchins' Death

About twelve years did Elder F. J. Hutchins labor most faithfully and earnestly in .the Central American field. At last his endurance failed, and he succumbed to disease. He now rests in sleep, awaiting the call from the Master — the call that shall awake the faithful.

SOUTH AMERICA

It was through the printed page that the views of Seventh-day Adventists were first introduced into South America. In October, 1891, Messrs. Snyder, Stauffer, and Nowlin began their work as canvassers in Argentine. In 1893, by vote of the General Conference, Elder F. H. Westphal, of Illinois, a German minister, connected with the work in this mission field, and in 1894, Frank Kelley, of California, went to the United States of Colombia as a self-supporting missionary. A few months later, these were followed by other laborers, and thus a beginning was made in this new mission. In 1896 the following report was given concerning the work in this field: Chile has one minister, Elder G. H. Baber, who arrived Oct. 19, 1895; and two canvassers, F. W. Richards and F. H. Davis. Argentine has also two ministers, F. H. Westphal and Jean Vuilleumier; and two canvassers, O. Oppegard and C. A. Nowlin. Besides these there are four Bible workers, Lucy Post, Mr. and Mrs. Snyder, and John McCarthy. Brazil has two ministers, Elder H. W. Thurston and F. H. Graff; and three canvassers, A. B. Stauffer, J. F. and J. A. Berger. British Guiana has two ministers, Elder W. G. Kneeland and Elder P. Giddings; and two medical missionaries, Dr. B. J. Fercoit and his wife.

In 1896, there had been one thousand dollars' worth of books sold in Chile, and thirty Sabbath-keepers had accepted the Sabbath and kindred truths by reading the literature purchased of the canvassers. In Brazil and Argentine books had been sold to the amount of ten thousand dollars; and what was still better, there were one hundred observing the Sabbath. One church and five Sabbath-schools had been organized. In Argentine there were three organized churches, at Buenos Ayres, Crespo, and San Cristobal, respectively. There was also one organized church in British Guiana, and fifty Sabbath-keepers, making a total of one hundred and fifty Seventh-day Adventists in South America.

THE SOUTHERN MISSIONARY SOCIETY

Strictly speaking, this society cannot be called foreign, notwithstanding it is doing a work in evangelizing a foreign people (Africans) in our home land. Much credit is due to the persevering efforts of Elder J. E. White, under the blessing of God, for the results already attained.

In the winter of 1893, when I was serving as president of the Illinois Conference, Elder White came to me heavily burdened for the colored people in the Southern States. As he was spending a few weeks in Chicago, he requested the privilege of laboring for the colored people living in the city. Most gladly was the request granted, and there really began his work for this unfortunate people.

Elder White's Missionary Steamer

From that time he was praying and planning for the Southern field. As he studied, his plans matured, culminating in the construction of a steamer near Lake Michigan, called the *Morning Star*. Provided with this floating " Bethel," he went to Chicago, thence down the Illinois and Mississippi Rivers, reaching Vicksburg, Miss., Jan. 10, 1895. Here, with a few associates he began his labors on virgin soil.

Work of the Southern Missionary Society

We quote from a report made by Elder White at the General Conference, April 9, 1903, which gives the results of labor, and shows the condition of the Southern missionary work at that date:—

" Our Society has built up and is now operating five schools in Mississippi. . . . These schools are located at Vicksburg, Yazoo City, Columbus, and Jackson. . . . Our laborers have also carried forward efforts in Nashville, Memphis, and Edgefield Junction, in Tennessee, and in Louisville and Bowling Green, in Kentucky.

Workers in the South

"At the present time there are twenty-seven workers in different departments of the Society. Five ordained ministers have been developed in the work of the Southern Missionary Society. . . . Thirteen school-teachers have in different ways been fitted for their work. . . . One young man is being educated by the Society as a physician, at the Meharry Medical College, of Nashville, and another is being assisted in his course at the same school. . . . Some good Bible workers have been developed. Some of the teachers are also becoming proficient workers in this department.

The Steamer " Morning Star "

" The *Morning Star* is my personal property, built with my own money. Further than this, the running expenses of this boat have all been paid from my own income. I will also say that the living expenses on the boat were always met by myself. Often the company numbered from ten to eighteen hands. . . . Even the salaries of all the workers employed by the Society for years were not taken from donations, but from my own personal income.

How Money Came for the Southern Mission

" The question may be raised, ' Where did you get this money?' The Lord gave it to us. Some little books were brought out. First the ' Gospel Primer,' the original design of which was for use in teaching the colored people. The sale of a few thousand copies was expected, but to our astonishment it has reached nearly a million copies.

" Mother [Mrs. E. G. White] helped us with the book ' Christ our Saviour,' which had a sale of three or four hundred thousand. Two or three hundred thousand copies of ' Best Stories ' have been sold. It is estimated that a sufficient number of ' Coming King ' have been circulated to make a column four miles high. With the royalties from these books, besides carrying many other enterprises and lines of work, we built the *Morning Star*."

IN MANY LANDS

Mexico

Our work in this country began in the year 1894, in the establishment of a medical mission at Guadalajara. In 1896 the force of laborers was reported as follows: Elder D. T. Jones and his wife, who had charge of the mission. The teachers were Ora A. Osborne, Mrs. A. Cooper, Kate Ross, and a native helper. The medical missionaries were Dr. J. A. Neal, A. Cooper, Mrs. A. J. Rice, Mrs. Bartlett, and Mrs. Rachel Flowers. Forty patients per day were patronizing the mission, and forty students attended the mission school. A new sanitarium was being constructed at this date, at a cost of $12,000.

Central Africa

In 1893 the cause of the third angel's message had so advanced that the General Conference Committee felt justified in recommending that a mission be established in Central Africa. It was therefore voted, " That as soon as practicable a mission be opened in Matabeleland." In harmony with this action a party of Seventh-day Adventists, in 1894, entered that country and selected a farm of 12,000 acres. At the conference in 1895, Elder C. B. Tripp and his wife, W. H. Anderson and his wife, and Dr. A. S. Carmichael were chosen as the missionaries for this distant field. They at once began preparations for the long journey, and after a prosperous voyage reached their destination July 26, 1895.

The Gold Coast

For a number of years the Macedonian cry for help had come to Seventh-day Adventists from the West Coast of Africa. An interest had been awakened in the truth by reading Adventist publications, but not until the year 1894 or thereabout was help sent. Then Elder Sanford and Mr. Rudolph were invited by the General Conference Committee to take up the work that had been so long waiting. They entered the field with zeal and courage. Not long afterward, however, Elder Sanford was smitten with the fever, so prevalent there that the country is called " the white man's grave." He had three attacks, and then, in order to live, he was compelled to return to America. Others were sent to the West Coast, among whom were Elder D. U. Hale, Geo. F. Kerr and his wife, and G. P. Riggs. The latter, however, was so weakened by disease that his life was despaired of, and he fled to England in the hope of being benefited by a change of climate; in this he and his friends were disappointed, for he gradually failed, and finally died, and there he was buried. He, too, awaits the coming of the Lifegiver.

India

Jan. 12, 1890, Elder Haskell sailed from Port Durban, southeast coast of Africa, for Calcutta, India, China, and Japan. Previous to this date, Percy T. Magan, his secretary, had joined him. The purpose of this journey to India was in the line of " prospecting " to gain information that would enable them to give counsel and advice when active missionary operations should begin by Seventh-day Adventists in that field. With the thought in mind of establishing a mission in India, the General Conference, in 1893, recommended that Wm. Lenker go to that country as colporteur. In compliance with this recommendation, he went to India and introduced the literature of Seventh-day Adventists. At a later date Mr. Lenker reported that he and four other persons had, up to 1896, canvassed in various parts of India, and had sold $10,000 worth of publications. To show the interest created by the books sold, he further stated that while canvassing in the vicinity of Madras, on the west coast of India, " a native preacher walked sixty miles to purchase a copy of ' Thoughts on Daniel and the Revelation.' "

Georgia Burrus in India

In 1895 Miss Georgia Burrus left California for India. On arriving there she at once began the study of the Bengali language, and soon entered upon the mission work. Up to 1896 several persons had begun the observance of the Lord's Sabbath through association with our workers.

The laborers in the field in 1896 were Elder D. A. Robinson and his wife. Miss May Taylor and Miss Georgia Burrus were Bible workers. Mr. Lenker and Mr. Masters were canvassers. A suitable building had been secured for the mission home, and calls for physicians, nurses, and further help to meet the demands that were pressing upon them had been made to the home land. To this call Elder Brown, with others, responded. Both he and Elder D. A. Robinson died at Karmatar, Bengal, India, the last of December, 1899.

Hawaii, Sandwich Islands

In the year 1884, Mr. La Rue and Henry Scott, at their own expense, went as missionaries to Hawaii. They began their labor by doing personal missionary work and selling books.

This awakened such an interest on the island that the General Conference, in November, 1885, voted that Elder Wm. Healy go the next season to Hawaii to labor, and that the California Conference be requested to loan a tent for this purpose. Thus equipped Elder Healy and those already on the island conducted a tent-meeting during the summer of 1886. As the result of this effort a number of persons accepted the message. Mr. La Rue remained in Honolulu till the year 1889, when he set sail for Hong Kong, China.

Chinese Work in Hawaii

But little ministerial labor was furnished the island until the General Conference convened in the month of March, 1895, at which time a vote was taken that " Elder Gates and his wife, with Mr. and Mrs. Brand as teachers for the Chinese, go to Honolulu to engage in missionary labor." The work of teaching began at once, and Elder Gates, although in feeble health, did what he could in pushing the work. A physician and nurses soon followed the missionaries, and the work in that line of the message was well begun.

Summary of Missions, Jan. 1, 1903

The report of the Foreign Missionary Secretary, rendered Dec. 31, 1902, presents the work of the message as carried on outside the United States as follows: —

The Australian Union Conference, made up of the conferences of Victoria, New South Wales, New Zealand, Queensland, South Australia, Tasmania, and West Australia.

The European General Conference, composed of the German Union Conference, West German, East German, South German, Holland and Flemish Belgium, Austro-Hungary, and Balkan States, German Swiss, South Russian, North Russian, and Middle Russian.

The Scandinavian Union Conference, consisting of Denmark, Norway, Sweden, Finland, and Iceland.

The British Union Conference, embracing North England, South England, Ireland, Scotland, and Wales.

The French Latin Union Conference, comprising the French-Swiss, France, and Italy.

The Oriental Mission, comprising Egypt, Syria, and Turkey.

The South African Union Conference, comprising Cape Colony, Natal-Transvaal, Basutoland, and Matabeleland.

Miscellaneous: Bermuda, Brazil, British and Dutch Guiana, Central America (South), China, Fiji, India, Jamaica, Japan, Lesser Antilles, Mexico, Nyassaland, Pitcairn, Porto Rico, River Plate, Raratonga, Samoa, Society Islands, Sumatra, Tonga, Trinidad, West Coast (South America), and West Coast (Africa).

The number of active workers in these different fields, including ministers, licentiates, Bible workers, colporteurs, and canvassers, is 754.

Strategic Points Established

From these brief statements in regard to our missions we can say, as did the Foreign Mission Secretary in the year 1896: " With these strategic positions now occupied by the message in almost every part of the world, God, by his infinite power, *can* accomplish a great and powerful work in a very *short* time. He *will* cut short his work in righteousness."

CHAPTER XXVII

OTHER TESTIMONIES CONFIRMED

EHOSHAPHAT stood and said, Hear me, O Judah, and ye inhabitants of Jerusalem; believe in the Lord your God, so shall ye be established; believe his prophets, so shall ye prosper." [1]

Years ago a testimony was given through the gift of prophecy that before the end the printed pages of this truth would be "scattered like the autumn leaves." How this could be accomplished unless the people believing the truth were in some way organized or marshaled to do the work, was the question that arose in the minds of many. In God's providence great results are frequently achieved from most humble beginnings; so it was in the development of a system of working that arose among us.

The Tract and Missionary Society

About the year 1870 the idea of a tract and missionary society was first suggested by the course of a few devoted sisters at South Lancaster, Mass. These sisters tried, for a time, the plan of mailing our denominational papers and tracts to different persons outside of our faith, afterward writing them letters. This resulted in several individuals accepting the truth, which brought to the mind of Elder S. N. Haskell the question, "Why may not all our people engage in doing what a few sisters have done?" During the year 1871, espe-

[1] 2 Chron. 20: 20.

cially, this subject was agitated more or less through the columns of the *Review*. At the special session of the General Conference held Dec. 29, 1871, Elder Haskell being present and setting forth the practical utility of the movement, a resolution was passed recommending the formation of tract societies. Elders S. N. Haskell, W. H. Littlejohn, J. N. Andrews, J. H. Waggoner, and I. D. Van Horn were appointed as a committee to perfect plans for the formation of such societies.

This movement introduced a new era in the prosecution of the work of the message. Hitherto the teaching of the truth had been confined almost exclusively to efforts put forth by the living preacher. For several years Elder Haskell labored very assiduously in studying up and introducing plans for making the tract and missionary society a success. It is only doing justice to him to state that he was really the pioneer in that line. This is not only true in the matter of the State tract and missionary societies, but it was he who, in 1878, introduced to the General Conference assembled in Battle Creek the plan for a general (since called International) Tract Society, whose field of labor is the territory outside of our conferences, not only in America, but also in foreign countries.

Efficient Secretaries — Maria Huntley

The Lord in his providence raised up efficient secretaries, who were a great assistance to Elder Haskell in this movement. Sister Maria Huntley was one who labored unflinchingly, even under (in after years) great affliction of body, and fell at her post about fourteen years ago. Through her efforts many of the present openings in foreign fields were first found. Other secretaries have joined in the same work, and as the field of labor has been enlarged a necessity has arisen for secretaries in different languages.

The Effect on Local Churches

But the most important result of the establishment of the tract society work among us has been the influence which it has exerted in the direction of creating and increasing a missionary spirit among the local church organizations. It has given every one an opportunity to do something by correspondence and the distribution of reading matter, and to feel the inspiration of direct labor for the salvation of souls.

Testimony Relating to Tract Work

To show the nature of the instruction given, through the spirit of prophecy, on the subject of the tract and missionary work, we quote from Testimonies Nos. 29 and 30: —

"If there is one work more important than another, it is that of getting our publications before the public, thus leading them to search the Scriptures. Missionary work — introducing our publications into families, conversing, and praying with and for them — is a good work, and one which will educate men and women to do pastoral labor.

"Not every one is fitted for this work. Those of the best talent and ability, who will take hold of the work understandingly and systematically, and carry it forward with persevering energy, are the ones who should be selected. There should be a most thoroughly ·organized plan; and this should be faithfully carried out. Churches in every place should feel the deepest interest in the tract and missionary work."

"The tract and missionary work is a good work. It is God's work. It should be in no way belittled; but there is continual danger of perverting it from its true object. Canvassers are wanted to labor in the missionary field. Persons of uncouth manners are not fitted for this work. Men and women who possess tact, good address, keen foresight, and discriminating minds and who feel the value of souls, are the ones who can be successful."

The disposal of over $8,000,000 worth of books, pamphlets, and tracts, during twelve years, by our churches and canvassers, goes far as proof of the practical value of the work of the Tract and Missionary Society.

Prophecy versus Worldly Wisdom

There was a word of prophecy given in connection with the work in the European field, which is being so literally fulfilled that it merits notice at this point. It was affirmed by laborers and people that the work could not be carried on there, especially in Scandinavia, as it is in America. Mrs. White, to their surprise, said it not only *could* be carried on successfully, but could be sustained in the same way it was in America, and that the Lord had shown her that if they took hold to pay their tithe, even of the small earnings they received, God would prosper them far beyond their anticipations. ·She also told them that canvassers could sell books by subscription in Scandinavia, and it would be a success. Managers of publishing houses in those countries said, " It cannot be done ; " they " never sold books in that way." The sequel has shown that what the angel of the Lord presented to her in this matter was far superior to the wisdom of the worldly booksellers and publishers. Success has attended the canvassing work there from its very beginning. Some of those who moved out to pay to the cause a tenth of their scanty income have become canvassers, and not only sustain themselves, but earn more means than ever before, and consequently are enabled to pay a much greater tithe.

More than $40,000 worth of books were sold by the canvassers in the year 1895 of works printed in our publishing house in Christiana, Norway. Mark this as another prophecy fulfilled, and that, too, in the face of protestations on every hand, both in the church and out of it, that it could not be done.

In reference to the work of the tract societies which were instituted in 1871 and onward, it is safe to say that almost as

many persons have been brought to the truth by the efforts
of such workers as through the personal efforts of the ministry. Through this agency the message is being published to
all nations and tongues of the earth.

Jewelry and the Tract Work

An interesting item was reported by the Tract and Missionary Society in California in April, 1873. It was that the
jewelry which had been donated to the society by those who
had accepted the truth in that State, up to that date, had
been melted, assayed, and sold at its actual gold and silver
value for the sum of $200; that this means had all been in-
vested in tracts, pamphlets, and periodicals, which had been
distributed, and that the society already had definite knowledge
of twenty who had been brought to the acceptance of the
truth by means of literature purchased with the proceeds of
the jewelry. Among those brought to the knowledge of the
truth by reading was John I. Tay, of Oakland, Cal.

San Francisco a Missionary Point

In 1875 an important testimony was given to the San
Francisco church, to which attention is now called because
of its being so strikingly fulfilled. This church from the
first had been under the necessity of renting halls for services,
and that, too, at considerable expense and some inconvenience,
as no series of meetings could be held in them because much
of the time they were required for other purposes.

On the evenings of April 14 and 20, 1875, the leading
members of the San Francisco church were called together at
the house of Mrs. J. L. James, Fifth Street, near Market
Street, and Mrs. White there related to us what had been
shown her in vision concerning the situation, which was that
San Francisco would ever be a missionary point, where the
work could be carried on; and that souls would, if the matter
was managed judiciously, continue to accept the truth. If

a house of worship was erected where the people could be invited, and where labor could be put forth, souls would be added to their number, who, in their turn, would help to meet the expense and lift the debt which must be incurred in preparing a meeting-house.

Mrs. White continued by saying that she had seen that when she should urge upon the San Francisco church the importance of erecting a house of worship, it would look to that poor church like a move in the dark; but she was bidden to say that as they moved out they would see the providence of God opening the way before them, step by step, and that friends would be raised up all the way along, until finally the debt would be entirely taken up.

Being one of the few who met in the meetings already referred to, I can say that the idea of that company, who were, nearly every one of them, of the poor of this world, taking hold to erect a meeting-house 35 x 80 feet, and that, too, in a city where the least expense for a lot seemed to demand an outlay of at least $6,000, looked indeed like " a move in the dark." They were induced to make the move only by the full confidence they had that the testimony borne to them by Mrs. White was from the Lord, and would surely be accomplished.

Having been connected with the enterprise more or less from its inception until the present, I wish here to state that the above testimony has been fulfilled in every particular. When we started out in quest of lots, we succeeded in obtaining a $6,000 lot for $4,000. One sister said she would give $1,000 if she could sel' her place. She immediately put the property in the hands of a real estate agent, who told her the price was too low. Within two weeks her place was sold for $1,000 more than she at first valued it, and her pledge was paid. Another, a poor brother who did not see how the church could be built, but said, " If the Lord says it must be done, he will open the way somehow," found, to his astonishment, the estate of one of his relatives settled up, and that he was the possessor thereby of $20,000. He gave $1,000 toward the building, and bought one third of the church lot on which to place a residence for himself, thus in two ways bringing relief to the society.

A Significant Favor to San Francisco

Thus we might mention many donations and favors which the committee met as they went on with the erection of the building. Suffice it to say that the church edifice was put up at an expense, with lot, of about $14,000, over one half of which was met by donations before the house was finished. Laguna Street, on which the building was erected, being a section of the city where there was a lack of buildings for school purposes, the school board came to rent the lower rooms in which to hold a school before the roof was on the house. Seventy-five dollars rent per month, received for nearly two years, met the interest and the running expenses, leaving the society to apply what it could raise toward the remaining debt.

A Hydriatic Dispensary

At the present time a small part of the debt then incurred remains, and in the basement of the church a full-equipped hydriatic dispensary is found, all free from pecuniary embarrassment, of much greater value than the remaining debt, which will soon be a matter of the past.

The part of the testimony concerning souls accepting the truth has been most wonderfully fulfilled. Not simply scores, but hundreds, have received the light of the truth in that city, and are now scattered abroad in various parts of the earth. From time to time as I visit San Francisco, I see anywhere from two to ten persons who have accepted the truth since last I met with them; and the end is not yet.

Elder White's Death

About the year 1880 Mrs. White was instructed through the spirit of prophecy to say to her husband, Elder James White, that he should lay off many of the cares and responsibilities he had borne, and let them pass into other and younger hands, while he should " prepare for his last change "— meaning that his earthly race was soon to close. This instruction he began to heed, and none too soon, for in the year 1881 his labors ceased, and he fell asleep in Jesus. July 31 he was attacked with malarial fever. August 3 he was removed from his home to the Battle Creek Sanitarium, where he received every care and attention which it was possible to give, but to no avail. He continued to grow worse. From the first of his illness he had a premonition that his " last change " had come.

Elder Smith's Statement

In speaking of this event, Elder Uriah Smith says : " The circumstances of his death could hardly have been more favorable. So long as he was conscious during the last three days of his illness he testified that he suffered no pain. A large company of sincere and tearful friends stood in and about the building while on that pleasant Sabbath afternoon his life ebbed slowly away. Like falling into a quiet sleep, so he went down in death ; and when all was over, a sweet peace seemed to sit embalmed on every feature. It was as if this prayer had been answered : —

> "' Spare me this hour to sleep,
>   Before thy sleepless bliss is given ;
>   Give me a day of rest on earth,
>   Before the work of heaven.' "

At the time of his death he was sixty years and two days old. The esteem in which he was held in Battle Creek was evinced in the fact that at least twenty-five hundred people

29

were present at his funeral, August 13, and he was followed to his last resting place in Oak Hill Cemetery by a procession of ninety-five carriages and a multitude of people on foot.

From the many testimonials given after his death, and published in the *Review,* we quote the following from the pen of Elder S. N. Haskell : —

" When I consider his sound judgment in almost every emergency, his tenderness of heart and nobility of soul manifested toward the erring, and even toward those who had abused him, whenever he saw evidences of their repentance, and his love for what he believed to be right, I can truly say, *A father in Israel has fallen.* And while he rests, the cause, as well as many individuals, will realize the want of his foresight and fatherly care."

When he died, our enemies claimed that the message must now stop. Not so; those institutions which, under the divine hand, had been established by him, were destined to grow to still greater magnitude, to be as " trees of the Lord's planting," from which should spread forth numerous and fruitful branches.

Religious Legislation Predicted

Fifty-eight years have passed since those giving the third angel's message said the time would come, according to the prophecy of Revelation 13, when people would be persecuted, in the United States and elsewhere, for keeping the commandments of God. In a book written by Mrs. White, entitled, " Early Writings," we read the following concerning this teaching : —

" Said the angel,' ' Look ye! ' My attention was turned to the wicked, or unbelievers. They were all astir. The zeal and power with the people of God had aroused and enraged them. Confusion, confusion was on every side. I saw measures taken against the company who had the light and power of God. Darkness thickened around them, yet they stood firm, approved of God and trusting in him. I saw them perplexed; next I heard them crying unto God earnestly. Through the day and night their cry ceased not: 'Thy will, O God, be done! If it can glorify thy name, make a way of escape for thy people! Deliver us from the heathen round about us. They have appointed us unto death; but thine arm can bring salvation.' [2]

" Then I saw the leading men of the earth consulting together, and Satan and his angels busy around them. I saw a writing, copies of which were scattered in different parts of the land, giving orders that unless the saints should yield their peculiar faith, give up the Sabbath, and observe the first· day of the week, the people were at liberty, after a certain time, to put them to death." [3]

Persecution in America

Our opponents have said persecution can never come in this country, because the Constitution of the United States declares that " Congress shall make no law respecting an establishment of religion, or prohibiting the free exercise thereof." And, in addition to this, the " Bill of Rights " of most of the States forbids religious legislation. In the face of these protestations our people have continued to proclaim the message of warning and the needful preparation to meet the conflict.

In 1863 an organization was formed having for its object the change of the Constitution of the United States and the laws of the land, so as to make it effective for the enforcement of religion. So rapidly have these ideas obtained adherents, and the principle of compelling men to do right, especially in regard to Sunday-keeping, gained ground, that persecution in good earnest has already begun in many States, even those whose Sunday laws make provision for those who conscientiously observe another day, and persons have been imprisoned for not keeping Sunday.

[2] " Early Writings, Spiritual Gifts," page 133.
[3] *Idem.*, page 143.

One Hundred and Sixteen Arrests

Before me is a list of one hundred and sixteen arrests of Seventh-day Adventists in America, from the year 1878 to March, 1896. Of these, one hundred and nine were convicted. Many of these have been imprisoned from twenty to sixty days, and about a dozen of them were compelled to work in the " chain gang " with murderers, thieves, and the worst sort of criminals. In every case they were admitted, by those imposing sentence upon them, to be the best of citizens.

The Religious Liberty Association

On July 21, 1889, there was organized in Battle Creek, Mich., an association called the National Religious Liberty Association, the object of which was to oppose religious legislation, to disseminate information to the masses on the true relation of religion and civil government, and to render aid to those who are persecuted for conscience' sake. This association did a vast amount of work in the dissemination of literature, and in enlightening the people as to the duties and dangers of the times in our own nation. In fact, it did a great work in extending the notes of warning contained in the message of Rev. 14: 9 - 12.

The Help of Secular Journals

The persecutions that were then raging against Seventh-day Adventists were taken up in the editorial columns of such papers as the New York *Sun,* the New York *World,* the Chicago *Inter Ocean,* etc. Articles appeared, speaking out freely concerning the unjust course taker against a citizen of the United States for obeying his own conscience, and for keeping the very day designated in the commandment. By means of newspaper articles of that character, this subject was brought before millions of readers. Within one month the central truth of the third angel's message was brought to the attention of more people than we had been able to reach in more than twenty years.

The Wrath of Man Made to Praise the Lord

Thus it is seen that the efforts of men to stay the work of God, and to obtain laws for the support of a rival Sabbath to the one enjoined in the fourth commandment, have served to open the way for the more rapid advancement of the truth.

In meditating upon what has been accomplished in a few months by these means, two scriptures are forcibly brought to mind. One reads, " We can do nothing against the truth, but for the truth; " [4] and the other, " Surely the wrath of man shall praise thee: the remainder of wrath shalt thou restrain." [5]

Prediction Concerning Sunday Laws

In Testimony No. 32, printed in 1885, is a statement as to *how* Sunday laws would be passed in the United States. It reads: " To secure popularity and patronage legislators will yield to the *demand* for a Sunday law." [6] We will for a moment consider how this has already been accomplished.

World's Fair Legislation

In 1892 a *demand* was made of Congress to prohibit the opening of the World's Fair which was to be held in Chicago, Illinois, from May to October of that year, from opening on Sunday. Such a law was passed July 19, 1892, under just such a pressure as above predicted. And be it remembered that this is the *first* time that the Congress of the United States of North America ever legislated on the Sabbath question.

The churches sent in immense lists of names, and petitions, and telegrams, not only petitioning Congress, but kindly (?) informing the congressmen " that we do hereby pledge ourselves and each other, that we will, from this time

[4] 2 Cor. 13: 8.   [5] Ps. 76: 10.   [6] Testimony No. 32, page 207.

henceforth, refuse to vote for or support for any office or position of trust, any member of Congress, either senator or representative, who shall vote for any further aid of any kind for the World's Fair except on conditions named in these resolutions." The conditions were that the Fair should be closed on Sunday.

Talks in Congress, 1892

As a sample of the talk on the floors of Congress, when the bill was passed, read the following: " I should like to see the disclaimer put in white and black, and proposed by the Congress of the United States. Write it. How would you write it? . . . Word it, if you dare; advocate it, if you dare; *how many who voted for it would ever come back here again?* None, I hope. You endanger yourselves by opposing it."

Boast Made by the Church

That those who have *demanded* and secured of Congress the passage of this bill considered it an important victory in their scheme of religious legislation, is clear from the fact that one of these prominent ministers, in a sermon at Pittsburg, Penn., just after it, said:—

" That the church has weight with great political or governing bodies has been demonstrated most effectually in the late World's Fair matter, when the United States Senate, the highest body in the country, listened to the voice of religion, and passed the World's Fair $5,000,000 appropriation bill with the church-instituted proviso that the gates of the great exposition should not be opened on Sunday. That grand good fact suggests to the Christian's mind that if this may be done, so may other equally needful measures The church is gaining power continually, and its voice will be heard in the future much oftener than in the past." Thus we see how that testimony given in 1885 has been and is being fulfilled.

Catholic and Protestant Unity

In this connection we will refer to another prediction made in 1885, and found also in Testimony No. 32:—

"When Protestantism shall stretch her hand across the gulf to grasp the hand of the Roman power; when she shall reach over the abyss to clasp hands with Spiritualism; when, under the influence of this threefold union, our country shall repudiate every principle of its Constitution as a Protestant and republican government, and shall make provisions for the propagation of papal falsehoods and delusions, then we may know that the time has come for the marvelous working of Satan, and that the end is near." [7]

To show how the first part of this prediction is already fulfilling, we need only to call attention to what is transpiring around us. See Protestants, both ministers and people, courting the favor of the Catholics, inviting them to attend their associations, etc. Be it remembered that hardly a vestige of what is now seen in this line was apparent in 1885, when the above testimony was given.

To illustrate how the Protestants are reaching for the hand and help of papists, I quote from the Kansas City (Mo.) *Star* of March 18, 1896.

Methodists and St. Patrick's Day

A speech was delivered in Coate's Opera House, Kansas City, Mo., on St. Patrick's Day, March 17, 1896, by Dr. Mitchell, pastor of the leading Methodist church of Kansas City. The *Star* speaks of a portion of the speech as a "dramatic little scene." Dr. Mitchell was loudly applauded when he said this:—

"Bigotry is the child of ignorance. We are bigoted because we do not know our neighbors well enough. We Protestants have been taught to believe unutterable things of Catholics. Catholics have been taught to believe unutterable things of Protestants. Now we discover our mistaken notions

[7] Testimony No. 32, page 207.

of each other when we get close enough to look into each other's eyes and clasp each other's hands; if we only knew each other more we would love each other better. We have stood apart and criticised. Shame upon the followers of the blessed Christ. All Christians have been redeemed by the same precious blood; we are sustained by the same divine grace, and expect to reach the same heaven. Say, brothers, we had better be getting acquainted with each other down here."

The *Star* continues :—

"Dr. Mitchell then turned to Father Dalton [Catholic priest] who sat just behind him, and, reaching out his hand, said, 'Here, Brother Dalton, is my hand.' Father Dalton arose and clasped the extended hand, and as Dr. Mitchell shook it, he said, 'It would be an awful shame if, after having lived so long in the same city on earth, we should have to get an angel to introduce us to each other in heaven. Let us get acquainted here on earth.' The audience applauded, and after Father Dalton sat down, Dr. Mitchell continued his speech."

Something Great and Decisive

We quote from another communication, dated Melbourne, Australia, Feb. 18, 1892: "All heaven is represented to me as watching the unfolding of events. A crisis is to be revealed in the great and prolonged controversy in the government of God on earth. Something great and decisive is to take place, and that right early."

Judge Brewer's "Christian Nation"

Eleven days after this document was written, and before it reached the United States, an event occurred which both Protestants and Catholics refer to as *decisive* in this nation's destiny. I refer to the decision of the Supreme Court of the United States, that " This is a Christian nation," rendered on the 29th of February, by Chief Justice Brewer. As already shown, on the 19th of July of the same year the Sunday Closing Bill for the World's Fair was passed. The ministers who plead so strongly for its passage, made earnest pleas on the ground that as the Supreme Court had declared this to be a Christian nation, as a matter of course the Christian Sabbath should be protected from desecration. And so the National Reform party reasoned. As this is a Christian nation, it should recognize God and his laws as the basis of the government, etc. Truly something *great* and *decisive* in this closing controversy did take place, " and that right early."

Ancient Prophets

Of the visions given to God's servants, the prophets, there seemed to be two kinds — one called " open visions," or those given where the individual could be seen while in the vision ; and the other called " night visions." Reference is made to the former visions in 1. Sam. 3 : 1. where is found the experience of the child Samuel in these words : " The word of the Lord was precious in those days; there was no open vision."

Open Visions

It was a vision of this character (an open vision) in which the hand of the Lord was upon the prophet Ezekiel. As the elders of Judah sat before him, they beheld him in open vision. [8] On another occasion the prophet Daniel was taken off in vision in the midst of the Chaldean rulers. Had they remained, they might have seen him in vision, but, instead, " a great quaking fell upon them, so that they fled to hide themselves." [9]

Night Visions of Mrs. White

The earlier visions of Mrs. White were all open visions. Since 1884, the character of the visions has changed in this

[8] Eze. 8: 1.   [9] Dan. 10: 7.

respect, as they are now what are called in the Scriptures "night visions," not simply dreams, but the same bright angel appears, giving her instruction, as in former years in the open visions. Many instances of " night visions " are recorded in the Bible, as is readily seen by reading Gen. 46 : 2 ; Dan. 2 : 19 ; 7 : 13 ; Acts 16 : 9 ; 18 : 9 ; 23 : 11 ; 27 : 23 - 25.

In these night visions of Mrs. White many important predictions have been made, which have been most accurately fulfilled, as previously noted. Some of the views of a later date I will now notice.

The Removal to Washington

In 1893, Mrs. White said : " Too many interests are now being piled up in Battle Creek. Were those interests divided and located in other cities, where the light and knowledge might bless other localities, it would be in God's order. The Lord does not want a second Jerusalem in Battle Creek. There will have to be strong reformations and transformations and transferring of facilities and institutions if the will of God is done."

At the General Conference in Oakland, Cal., in March, 1903, she said : " For years the warning has been given to our people, Get out of Battle Creek. But because of the many interests established there, it was convenient to remain, and men could not see why they should move."

" In reply to the question that has been asked in regard to settling somewhere else, I answer, Yes Let the General Conference offices and the publishing work be removed from Battle Creek. I know not where the place will be, whether on the Atlantic Coast or elsewhere. But this I will say, Never lay a stone or a brick in Battle Creek to rebuild the Review office there. God has a better place for it."

After hearing this instruction, the conference of believers voted " that the General Conference offices be removed from Battle Creek, Mich., to some place on the Atlantic Coast."

In the General Conference council held in Battle Creek, following the session of the General Conference, it was voted "that we favor locating the headquarters of the General Conference office in the vicinity of New York City." A large committee was accordingly selected to search for a feasible location. The committee communicated their plan to Mrs. White, and asked if she had further light for them. In reply she said:—

"May the Lord help us to move understandingly and prayerfully. I am sure that he is willing that we should know, and that right early, where we should locate our publishing house. I am satisfied that our only safe course is to be ready to move just when the cloud moves. Let us pray that he will direct us. He has signified by his providence that he would have us leave Battle Creek. . . .

"New York needs to be worked, but whether our publishing house should be established there I cannot say. I should not regard the light I have received as definite enough to favor the movement."

After spending nearly two weeks hunting about New York City and surrounding towns, the committee failed to find a suitable place for the publishing house. At this point a letter came, dated May 30, in which Mrs. White said:—

"As our brethren search for a location for the Review and Herald publishing house, they are earnestly to seek the Lord. They are to move with great caution, watchfulness, and prayer, and with a constant sense of their own weakness. We must not depend upon human judgment. We must seek for the wisdom that God gives. . . .

"In regard to establishing the institution in New York, I must say, Be guarded. I am not in favor of its being near New York. I cannot now give all my reasons, but I am sure that any place within thirty miles of that city would be too near. Study the surroundings of other places. I am sure that the advantages of Washington, D. C., should be closely investigated.

"We should not establish this institution in a city nor in the suburbs of a city. It should be established in a rural district, where it can be surrounded by land."

Prediction of Favorable Offer

With this information the committee began prayerfully to look about Washington, when a third letter came containing this instruction: "We have been praying for light regarding the location of our work in the East, and light has come to us in a very decided way. Positive light has been given me that there will be offered to us for sale places upon which much money has been expended by men who had money to use freely. The owners of these palaces die, or their attention is called to some other object, and the property is offered for sale at a very low price. . . .

"From the light given me, I know that, for the present, the headquarters of the Review and Herald should be near Washington."

The Predicted Location Found

With this communication in hand, the committee began prospecting in the District of Columbia for a site, but no land could be found for less than one thousand dollars per acre. Finally their attention was called to Takoma Park. The following is the report of the committee: —

"We found a tract of about fifty acres just outside the District, but within the city limits of Takoma Park, that we could purchase for six thousand dollars, or at the rate of one hundred and twenty dollars an acre. We gave this place thorough examination. We found that some years ago it was selected by a Boston physician for a sanitarium site. He is said to have expended about sixty thousand dollars in the purchase price and in clearing it of all the underbrush, logs, and rubbish. Financial difficulties prevented him from carrying out his plans, and the tract passed into the hands of a gentleman who held a mortgage on it, at a cost to him of fifteen thousand dollars.

"The citizens of Takoma Park, as represented by the mayor and some of the leading men, gave us a very hearty welcome to the place, and assurances of friendly co-operation in carrying out our plans.

"In all our travels and searching, we found no other spot that filled so fully the specifications of the testimonies as this one. We believe the providence of God has led us to the place he would have us occupy."

In view of the many fulfilments of testimonies presented in this and former chapters, let us "believe in the Lord our God, and so be established; and believe his prophet, and so prosper," that we may be prepared for the events yet in the future, and not be taken by them unawares.

CHAPTER XXVIII

A DOOR THAT NO MAN CAN SHUT

"I HAVE set before thee an open door, and no man can shut it; for thou hast a little strength, and hast kept my word, and hast not denied my name." [1]

Such is the language addressed to those in the Philadelphia state of the gospel church. This church was the one which had been developed by the proclamation of the near advent of Christ, or those who had held fast to what they had heard upon that subject; for he says of the Sardis church (the one immediately preceding the Philadelphia), "Remember therefore how thou hast received and heard, and hold fast, and repent. If therefore thou shalt not watch, I will come on thee as a thief, and thou shalt not know what hour I will come upon thee." [2]

The Sardis church, then, heard the doctrine of the Lord's soon coming. Those who held fast to what they had heard moved on in the truth as the "candlestick" was removed, and constituted the Philadelphia church, to whom he said, "Because thou hast kept the word of my patience, I also will keep thee from the hour of temptation, which shall come upon all the world, to try them that dwell upon the earth. Behold, I come quickly: hold that fast which thou hast, that no man take thy crown." [3] It is to this Philadelphia church, then, that he says, "I have set before thee an open door, and no man can shut it."

Here, then, is the emphatic declaration of Holy Writ that those who, in God's providence, are moved out to warn the

[1] Rev. 3: 8.   [2] Rev. 3: 3.   [3] Rev. 3: 10, 11.

world of the Lord's coming, and to entreat the people to prepare to meet God, have the special favor of God in their work.
Men may try to hinder, to defeat their movements, to close the
" door of utterance," but still the voice of God sounds out
above all clamor, " *I* have set before thee an open door."

Seventy-four Years' Progress

In the foregoing pages of this book we have gone briefly
over the space of seventy-four years, from 1831 to 1905,
tracing the rise and progress of the advent messages, and
especially the third angel's message. We have shown how,
from obscurity and poverty, this message has advanced with
accelerated force and power from year to year, until it has
missions encircling the earth. It surely is not because the message is one that is pleasing to carnal hearts, that it has thus
prospered; for it carries in its forefront the Sabbath of the
Lord, the observance of which brings a heavy cross, requiring
a separation from business with the world on the busiest secu-
lar day of the week. Neither has it advanced because of no
opposition; for this it has encountered from the first, and that
of the fiercest kind from without, as well as perplexities caused
by unconsecrated persons who for a time have found their
way into the ranks. As to the situation occasioned by the
designs and efforts of outside foes, we may well say in the
words of David the Psalmist, " If it had not been the Lord
who was on our side, now may Israel say : if it had not been the
Lord who was on our side, when men rose up against us : then
they had swallowed us up quick, when their wrath was kindled
against us : then the waters had overwhelmed us, the stream
had gone over our soul : then the proud waters had gone over
our soul. Blessed be the Lord, who hath not given us as a
prey to their teeth. Our soul is escaped as a bird out of the
snare of the fowlers : the snare is broken, and we are escaped.
Our help is in the name of the Lord, who made heaven and
earth." [4]

[4] Ps. 124: 1 - 8.

Help in the Lord

The Lord declares that he has set before his people "an open door, and no man can shut it." No marvel, then, that the message has gone steadily forward. It is God's message to the people, and it must succeed. In Rev. 7:2 the work of preparing a people to stand when the great day of God's wrath shall come is symbolized by an angel "ascending from the east," or, as some translate, "like the rising of the sun." Behold the dawning of the day — first appear the rays of light in the east; these blend into greater clearness until the sun's broad, distinct disk is seen. As the "King of Day" ascends to the zenith, its light, heat, and power become more and more vivid.

Such indeed has been the progress of the third angel's message since 1848, when its component truths were brought into distinct form, and from which point we have shown a marked and steady growth that is wonderful. This we can explain upon no other ground than that the Lord is verifying his word to those who in this time, when his salvation is about to come, [5] "keep the Sabbath from polluting it," and turn away their foot from doing their own pleasure on God's holy day, thus, through the "faith of Jesus," as declared in the third angel's message of Revelation 14, keeping all "the commandments of God." Of such the Lord said by the prophet Isaiah, "Then shall thy light break forth as the morning, and thine health shall spring forth speedily: and thy righteousness ["the Lord our righteousness." Jer. 23:6] shall go before thee; and the glory of the Lord shall be thy rereward." [6] With such assurances how could we expect aught else but that the work would be a success? "If God be for us, who can be against us?"

How Can These Prosper?

Looking at the situation when, in 1846, Elder Joseph Bates began to write that first book, the first ever issued on the

[5] Isa. 56: 1, 2.   [6] Isa. 58: 8, 13.

Sabbath question by Seventh-day Adventists, with twelve and one-half cents as the only available means he had in the world, and being called upon to spend that before his first day of writing had expired; and looking again at Elder James White printing his first little sheet, *Present Truth,* with money earned by mowing in the hay field, and sending out the paper *free* to all who would read, and talking of that as a message that was to go to the ends of the earth,— looking at these small beginnings, one might, in the language of the people in the days of Amos, inquire, " By whom shall Jacob arise? For he is small." [7] Contrasting that with the situation in 1905, when the publication of the truths of the message is being accomplished in twenty publishing houses, located in various parts of the world, often pressed to their utmost capacity to supply the demand for reading matter, we can indeed say, Behold, " an open door " that no man as yet has shut.

Of those in earlier times who supposed the work could never succeed, we may say, in the words with which the prophet Zechariah reproved those who thought to hinder the work of God in the rebuilding of Jerusalem, " Who hath despised the day of small things? " [8] Of things which appeared like mountains of difficulties in their way, the Lord said by the prophet,—

The Mountain Made a Plain

" Who art thou, O great mountain? before Zerubbabel thou shalt become a plain; and he shall bring forth the headstone thereof with shoutings, crying, Grace, grace unto it." [9] So it has been in the work of the third angel's message, and so it will be until " the headstone " is brought, or in other words, until the work is completed.

Look at the few in 1846, poor in means, poor in every sense excepting faith in God and in the store of truth, and see to what proportions their work has grown. Think of the facilities now in hand, books all prepared, translated, and

[7] Amos 7: 2. [8] Zech. 4: 10. [9] Zech. 4: 7.

30

printed in the various languages of the earth, and the hundreds of canvassers putting these books into the homes of the people at the rate of $400,000 worth annually. With a continuance of God's blessing upon the work, we can look forward to *success*. With these facilities and agencies which are being increased from month to month, with trust in Christ, we need expect nothing else but that which Solomon sang of the church of God as she came forth from her wilderness state, " leaning on the arm of her Beloved," when he represents her as looking forth, " fair as the moon, clear as the sun, and terrible as an army with banners." [10]

Aided by the Gift of Prophecy

Not only have we seen that the Lord's providence has opened the way for the spread of the truth, and his signal blessing has attended the efforts made to move in the ways of his providence, but in the rise and progress of the third angel's message he has communicated with his people through the gift of prophecy. This has not been in the form of a new revelation to take the place of the Bible, nor in a manner to pervert the Scripture teachings, but to show where, in this age, there is danger of departing from the simplicity of the gospel of Christ, where the people are in danger of falling under the tendency of the age, being satisfied with a *form* of godliness without the power.

Looking at this subject from the example [11] of the ancient prophets, which the Lord has given us as one of the rules by which such manifestations are to be tested, the same reasons are found why such manifestations are needed now as then; namely, the liability in each age of being swayed from the line of truth by the prevailing and peculiar doctrines and practices of the age. The apostle Paul, in speaking of the manifestation of the gifts which the Lord has placed in the church, says they are " for the perfecting of the saints, for the work of the ministry, for the edifying of the body

[10] Solomon's Song 6: 10.   [11] James 5: 10.

of Christ; till we all come in the unity of the faith, and of the knowledge of the Son of God, unto a perfect man, unto the measure of the stature of the fulness of Christ; that we henceforth be no more children, tossed to and fro, and carried about with every wind of doctrine, by the sleight of men, and cunning craftiness, whereby they lie in wait to deceive; but speaking the truth in love, may grow up into him in all things, which is the head, even Christ: from whom the whole body fitly joined together and compacted by that which every joint supplieth, according to the effectual working in the measure of every part, maketh increase of the body unto the edifying of itself in love." [12]

The same objections that are raised against manifestations of the gift of prophecy at the present time, might have been urged with the same force in ancient times; i. e., we have the Scriptures, and therefore have no need of such gifts. These same Scriptures tell us, however, that Christ has placed these gifts in the church to do their work until " that which is perfect [the perfect state] is come," and that the church is to " come behind in *no gift,* waiting for the coming of our Lord Jesus Christ." [13]

What Need Have We of Prophets?

The people anciently might have reasoned that they had the moral law of God as written by his own finger on tables of stone; that they had statutes, judgments, and instructions which had been spoken to Moses from the mouth of God, and which had been carefully written out; and what more was needed? But notwithstanding all those excellent truths which they had in their possession, God was pleased to speak to them " at sundry times and in divers manners by his holy prophets."

We find that the testimonies borne by the various prophets, as Isaiah, Jeremiah, Ezekiel, Daniel, Hosea, and others, in each case taught the same great principle respecting obedience to

[12] Eph. 4: 12 - 16.   [13] 1 Cor. 1: 6, 7.

God; yet each prophet had his peculiar reproofs for the people of his time, for their tendency toward being drawn from the sacred and holy principles of right by the prevailing customs of the age in which the prophecy was given.

Need of Gifts

While it may be argued that we have not only the excellent instruction of the Old Testament Scriptures, but in addition, the words of our Saviour himself, and of the apostles, what need have we of further light? The fact remains that these same holy apostles have pointed forward to the last days, when "*perilous* times shall come," and when men shall "have a *form* of godliness, but deny the power thereof," telling us also that "some shall depart from the faith, giving heed to seducing spirits and doctrines of devils."

In view of all this, that people of whom Paul speaks in writing to the Thessalonians, who will not be in darkness, that the day of Christ should overtake them as a thief, but who will be children of the light, are exhorted to "prove all things" in the way of "prophesyings," and to "hold fast that which is good." [14] This is equivalent to telling them that the people who will be looking for the coming of the Lord Jesus Christ, and who will at last be found in readiness for that day, will have "good," true manifestations of the gift of prophecy among them.

Tokens of the End

We are in the time when the tokens are abundant on every side that the day of the Lord is near at hand. We are in the very period of time when a people were to arise who would keep all the commandments, and who would also "have the *testimony* of Jesus" [15] — the "spirit of prophecy." [16] What do we find? That during the last sixty years such a people have arisen, bearing just such a message, among whom the gift of prophecy has been manifested. Testing the gift as mani-

[14] 1 Thess. 5: 5, 20, 21.   [15] Rev. 12: 17.   [16] Rev. 19: 10.

fested through Mrs. E. G. White by the Bible rules, we have
seen that it stands the test in every particular. There has not
been found, from first to last, in all the writings of Mrs. White,
a single line that gives the slightest license to sin, or that
tolerates in the least degree any departure from the word of
God. These writings have never placed themselves above the
Bible, but they do constantly exhort to the most careful study
of the word of God, pointing to it as the great standard by
which our cases will be examined in the final judgment. In
her writings Christ is exalted before us as the only pattern
for us to follow. He is in the most vivid manner declared to
be our only hope of victory here, our only refuge from the
wrath to come, the only name and means through whom we
can be saved.

A Personal Tribute

In regard to Mrs. White and the nature of her work, the
following is given, having been penned in 1877 by one who had
known her and who had studied her work for many years; and
after about fifty-three years' test, years of careful observation,
I give my unqualified indorsement to every sentiment therein
expressed: —

"As to the Christian character of Sister White, I beg
leave to say that I think I know something about it. I have
been acquainted with her for eighteen years, — more than half
the history of our people. I have been in their family time and
again, sometimes weeks at a time. They have been in our
house and family many times. I have traveled with them
almost everywhere; have been with them in private and in
public, in meeting and out of meeting, and have the very best
chances to know something of the life, character, and spirit
of Brother and Sister White. As a minister I have had to
deal with all kinds of persons, and all kinds of character, till
I think I can judge something of what a person is, at least
after years of intimate acquaintance.

"I know Sister White to be an unassuming, modest, kind-hearted, noble woman. These traits in her character are not simply put on and cultivated, but they spring gracefully and easily from her natural disposition. She is not self-conceited, self-righteous, and self-important, as fanatics always are. I have frequently come in contact with fanatical persons, and I have always found them to be full of pretensions, full of pride, ready to give their opinion, boastful of their holiness, etc., but I have ever found Sister White the reverse of all this.

A Friend of the Poor

"Any one, the poorest and the humblest, can go to her freely for advice and comfort without being repulsed. She is ever looking after the needy, the destitute, and the suffering, providing for them, and pleading their cause.

"I have never formed an acquaintance with any person who so constantly has the fear of God before him. Nothing is undertaken without earnest prayer to God. She studies God's word carefully and constantly. I have heard Sister White speak hundreds of times, have read all her testimonies through and through, most of them many times, and I have never been able to find one immoral sentence in the whole of them, or anything that is not strictly pure and Christian; nothing that leads away from the Bible and from Christ; but there I find the most earnest appeals to obey God, to love Jesus, to believe the Scriptures, and to search them constantly. I have received great spiritual benefit, times without number, from the testimonies. Indeed, I have never read them without feeling reproved for my lack of faith in God, lack of devotion, and lack of earnestness in saving souls. If I have any judgment, any spiritual discernment, I pronounce the testimonies to be of the same spirit and of the same tenor as the Scriptures.

"For thirty years [we may now say sixty years] these testimonies have been believed and read among our people.

How has it affected them? Has it led them away from the law of God? Has it led them to give up faith in Christ? Has it led them to throw aside the Bible? Has it led them to be a corrupt, immoral people? I know that they will compare favorably with any other Christian denomination.

"One thing I have remarked, and that is, that the most bitter opponents of the visions of Sister White admit that she is a Christian. How they can make this admission is more than I know. They try to fix it up by saying that she is deceived. They are not able to put their finger upon a single stain in all her life, nor an immoral sentence in all her writings. They have to admit that much of her writings are excellent, and that whoever would live out all she says would be a good Christian, sure of heaven. This is passing strange, if she is a tool of the devil, inspired by Satan, or if her writings are immoral or the vagaries of her own mind."

Strangers Testify of the Writings

As our periodicals containing Mrs. White's writings are sent out, they are sought by the most humble, God-fearing, and devoted. Reporting on what they read, they say, "We are especially interested in Mrs. White's writings. They are so practical, so full of instruction calculated to lead one nearer to the Lord, and make him more humble, God-fearing, and devoted. These writings are so much in the strain of Scripture that it seems as we read that Mrs. White must be *inspired* to write in the manner she does." Such is the testimony in scores of cases of those who are in correspondence with our missionary workers, those, too, who have not the slightest intimation that Mrs. White's ideas are received in holy vision.

Source of Opposition

Having before us the impression made by this gift, the question arises, *Whence* and *why* has opposition arisen to the manifestation of this gift? and what has been the outcome of those opposing? Having watched this matter carefully since 1852, I have found that for the most part the opposition to this manifestation has arisen from those who have been reproved for defects in character, for wrong habits, or for some wrong course in their manner of life. Many of the reproved would protest that they were not as bad as the testimony represented them, and they would show that they could hold on to the truth even though they should go contrary to the reproof given them. Time has shown the great majority of such renouncing their faith and leaving the ranks entirely. Some have seen their error, and have grasped the truth more firmly. The query arises, If those opposing this gift are led by the Lord, why should they lose their spirituality, and backslide from God? Our Saviour's rule is that a tree should be known by its fruit. He most emphatically asserts that " a corrupt tree cannot bring forth good fruit."

Failure of the Opposition

We recall instances where organized opposition has been raised against the testimonies of Mrs. White, with the declaration that great success was going to attend their work as soon as they should get rid of the testimonies. There has been, however, an utter failure in realizing the accomplishment of their hopes. After years of battling they have given no more evidence of spreading the Sabbath truth before the world than those of their kind did forty-nine years ago. If theirs was the special work of the Lord, why has no more prosperity attended their message?

Where is the Success?

On the other hand, as we look at that message by which the commandments of God and the faith of Jesus are being proclaimed to the world,— a message with which is connected this manifestation of the gift of prophecy, with its counsels, instructions, and reproofs,— we see it has made sure and steady advance from its very beginning to the present time. Heeding the Lord's counsels through that gift, moving forward in the Lord's strength, the message, as we have shown, has encircled the earth, and is fast making its way to "every nation, and kindred, and tongue, and people."

Of its progress in the past we can say, God's word has been verified in that he said, "No weapon formed against thee shall prosper." Truly, the hand of God has been manifest in the success attending the rise and progress of this great advent movement thus far, and for the future we rely upon the certain fulfilment of his word, "I have set before thee an open door, and no man can shut it." In this confidence we may sing with all assurance: —

> "For he has been with us,
> And he still is with us,
> And he's promised to be with us
> To the end."

INDEX

Religion in America
Series II

An Arno Press Collection

Adler, Felix. **Creed and Deed:** A Series of Discourses. New York, 1877.

Alexander, Archibald. **Evidences of the Authenticity, Inspiration, and Canonical Authority of the Holy Scriptures.** Philadelphia, 1836.

Allen, Joseph Henry. **Our Liberal Movement in Theology:** Chiefly as Shown in Recollections of the History of Unitarianism in New England. 3rd edition. Boston, 1892.

American Temperance Society. **Permanent Temperance Documents of the American Temperance Society.** Boston, 1835.

American Tract Society. **The American Tract Society Documents,** 1824-1925. New York, 1972.

Bacon, Leonard. **The Genesis of the New England Churches.** New York, 1874.

Bartlett, S[amuel] C. **Historical Sketches of the Missions of the American Board.** New York, 1972.

Beecher, Lyman. **Lyman Beecher and the Reform of Society:** Four Sermons, 1804-1828. New York, 1972.

[Bishop, Isabella Lucy Bird.] **The Aspects of Religion in the United States of America.** London, 1859.

Bowden, James. **The History of the Society of Friends in America.** London, 1850, 1854. Two volumes in one.

Briggs, Charles Augustus. **Inaugural Address and Defense,** 1891-1893. New York, 1972.

Colwell, Stephen. **The Position of Christianity in the United States,** in Its Relations with Our Political Institutions, and Specially with Reference to Religious Instruction in the Public Schools. Philadelphia, 1854.

Dalcho, Frederick. **An Historical Account of the Protestant Episcopal Church, in South-Carolina,** from the First Settlement of the Province, to the War of the Revolution. Charleston, 1820.

Elliott, Walter. **The Life of Father Hecker.** New York, 1891.

Gibbons, James Cardinal. **A Retrospect of Fifty Years.** Baltimore, 1916. Two volumes in one.

Hammond, L[ily] H[ardy]. **Race and the South:** Two Studies, 1914-1922. New York, 1972.

Hayden, A[mos] S. **Early History of the Disciples in the Western Reserve, Ohio;** With Biographical Sketches of the Principal Agents in their Religious Movement. Cincinnati, 1875.

Hinke, William J., editor. **Life and Letters of the Rev. John Philip Boehm:** Founder of the Reformed Church in Pennsylvania, 1683-1749. Philadelphia, 1916.

Hopkins, Samuel. **A Treatise on the Millennium.** Boston, 1793.

Kallen, Horace M. **Judaism at Bay:** Essays Toward the Adjustment of Judaism to Modernity. New York, 1932.

Kreider, Harry Julius. **Lutheranism in Colonial New York.** New York, 1942.

Loughborough, J. N. **The Great Second Advent Movement:** Its Rise and Progress. Washington, 1905.

M'Clure, David and Elijah Parish. **Memoirs of the Rev. Eleazar Wheelock, D.D.** Newburyport, 1811.

McKinney, Richard I. **Religion in Higher Education Among Negroes.** New Haven, 1945.

Mayhew, Jonathan. **Observations on the Charter and Conduct of the Society for the Propagation of the Gospel in Foreign Parts;** Designed to Shew Their Non-conformity to Each Other. Boston, 1763.

Mott, John R. **The Evangelization of the World in this Generation.** New York, 1900.

Payne, Bishop Daniel A. **Sermons and Addresses,** 1853-1891. New York, 1972.

Phillips, C[harles] H. **The History of the Colored Methodist Episcopal Church in America:** Comprising Its Organization, Subsequent Development, and Present Status. Jackson, Tenn., 1898.

Reverend Elhanan Winchester: Biography and Letters. New York, 1972.

Riggs, Stephen R. **Tah-Koo Wah-Kan; Or, the Gospel Among the Dakotas.** Boston, 1869.

Rogers, Elder John. **The Biography of Eld. Barton Warren Stone, Written by Himself:** With Additions and Reflections. Cincinnati, 1847.

Booth-Tucker, Frederick. **The Salvation Army in America:** Selected Reports, 1899-1903. New York, 1972.

Satolli, Francis Archbishop. **Loyalty to Church and State.** Baltimore, 1895.

Schaff, Philip. **Church and State in the United States** or the American Idea of Religious Liberty and its Practical Effects with Official Documents. New York and London, 1888. (Reprinted from *Papers of the American Historical Association,* Vol. II, No. 4.)

Smith, Horace Wemyss. **Life and Correspondence of the Rev. William Smith, D.D.** Philadelphia, 1879, 1880. Two volumes in one.

Spalding, M[artin] J. **Sketches of the Early Catholic Missions of Kentucky;** From Their Commencement in 1787 to the Jubilee of 1826-7. Louisville, 1844.

Steiner, Bernard C., editor. **Rev. Thomas Bray:** His Life and Selected Works Relating to Maryland. Baltimore, 1901. (Reprinted from *Maryland Historical Society Fund Publication,* No. 37.)

To Win the West: Missionary Viewpoints, 1814-1815. New York, 1972.

Wayland, Francis and H. L. Wayland. **A Memoir of the Life and Labors of Francis Wayland, D.D., LL.D.** New York, 1867. Two volumes in one.

Willard, Frances E. **Woman and Temperance:** Or, the Work and Workers of the Woman's Christian Temperance Union. Hartford, 1883.